Vive le Québec libre

Vive le Québec libre

Dale C. Thomson

DENEAU
1988

Deneau Publishers
760 Bathurst Street
Toronto, Canada
M5S 2R6

Copyright 1988

Book Design: M.J. Hale Graphics

Printed and bound in Canada

Canadian Cataloguing in Publication Data

Thomson, Dale C., 1923–
Vive le Québec libre

Bibliography: p.
Includes index.
ISBN 0-88879-151-8

1. Gaulle, Charles de, 1890–1970 – Views on Quebec
(Province). 2. Gaulle, Charles de, 1890–1970 –
Views on Canada. 3. Canada – Foreign relations –
France. 4. France – Foreign relations – Canada.
5. Quebec (Province) – History – 1960–1976.*
I. Title

FC248.G38T48 1988   971.4'04   C88-094665-2
F1029.5.F8T48 1988

"I am a man for the stormy seas,
not for the quiet streams."

Charles de Gaulle

Contents

This book is dedicated in loving memory to my wife Mena, who shared so much in its preparation, and to her three children, Wayne, Michele and John Peter, who also carry on under her abiding inspiration.

Preface

Montreal, July 24, 1967. On a state visit to Expo '67, General de Gaulle, French president and eminent world statesman, hurled the words "*Vive le Québec libre*" from the balcony of City Hall. The rallying cry of a Quebec separatist party, it not only sent a seismic-like tremor throughout Canada, but reverberated around the world. The Canadian government declared the intervention in the country's domestic affairs "unacceptable;" de Gaulle cancelled his visit to Ottawa and returned home.

Two decades later, uncertainty persists concerning his intentions in making the dramatic utterance. Was it a deliberate gesture of support for the independence of the Province of Quebec? Or was he carried away by the warm welcome he had received from the crowds that lined his route from Quebec City throughout that day? Was he giving vent to his anti-Anglo-Saxon feelings and cocking a snook at English Canadians and Americans? Or was he merely reacting to the separatists in the crowd below who were daring him to add the words to the string of vivats—"*Vive le Canada*," "*Vive la France*," "*Vive le Québec*," etc.— with which he had been ending his speeches? After all, he was not a man to avoid a challenge, or to allow his courage to be cast in doubt.

The central purpose of this book is to clarify, if not solve, that issue. In view of de Gaulle's complex personality, his secretive nature and his strategy of deliberate ambiguity, it is a considerable challenge. At the same time, it is a rewarding undertaking since it provides the opportunity to examine one of the great careers of modern times, and its impact on relations between the Canadian and Quebec governments during a critical period in the country's history. The book places the incident in the context of the triangular relationship between France, Canada and Quebec that developed in the 1960s under the impact of the Quiet Revolution in that province. In that sense, it is a sequel to my previous book, *Jean Lesage and the Quiet Revolution*, published in 1984.*

Conducting this research was often as captivating as unravelling a murder mystery. While pursuing innumerable leads and establishing various linkages, I incurred once again considerable debts of gratitude for cooperation received. In each of the three capitals I was granted interviews and given access to information without which this book would never have materialized. I was particularly touched by the consideration shown to me by the officers and personnel of the Institut Charles de Gaulle in Paris, and by the more than fifty former prime ministers, ministers, officials and close observers of General de Gaulle who took the time to answer my many questions and to help me attain a balanced view of my subject. On the grounds that shared truths increase not only understanding but amity, I hope that this book will contribute in some small measure to harmonious relations between Canada, my country, Quebec, my adopted province, and France, my second home and source of inspiration for a major part of my life.

I wish to acknowledge a research grant from the Social Sciences and Humanities Research Council to carry out this project. I also wish to express my deep appreciation to two exceptionally fine, hard-working and competent persons who contributed so much to bringing it to a successful conclusion. Thérèse Belisle typed the various drafts, mastered the McGill University computer system in order to put the manuscript on the mainframe, checked a myriad of details, and played her usual valuable role as an exacting critic. Elizabeth Richards, for her part, applied her vast and profound knowledge of the English language once more to bring my prose up to acceptable standards. I thank them both with sincere feelings of admiration and affection.

---

* English version: (Toronto: Macmillan of Canada); French version: (St. Laurent: Editions du Trécarré).

General de Gaulle speaking to the crowd in front of the Canadian Parliament Buildings, Ottawa, July 12, 1944. In foreground: Governor General Earl Athlone and Prime Minister Mackenzie King. (Courtesy Institut Charles de Gaulle)

Prime Minister William Lyon Mackenzie King greeting General de Gaulle on his arrival in Ottawa on July 14, 1944, on his first visit to Canada. (Courtesy Institut Charles de Gaulle)

De Gaulle addressing the crowd from the balcony of the Windsor Hotel, Montreal, 1945, on his first visit to Montreal. (Courtesy of *La Presse*)

De Gaulle welcomed in Ottawa by Governor General Georges Vanier and Prime Minister John Diefenbaker, April 1960. (Courtesy of Canadian Press)

De Gaulle and Prime Minister Diefenbaker in front of the Parliament Buildings, Ottawa, April 1960. Canadian Minister of External Affairs Howard Green directly behind de Gaulle, and to Green's right, French Foreign Minister Maurice Couve de Murville. (Courtesy of Canadian Press)

De Gaulle at dinner table with Madame Vanier at the French embassy, Ottawa, April 1960. (Courtesy of Canadian Press)

De Gaulle with Premier Daniel Johnson in his office in the Elysée Palace, Paris, May 1967. Their first meeting. (Courtesy of *The Gazette*)

French warship, *Le Colbert*, on which de Gaulle arrived at Quebec City, July 1967. (Courtesy of *La Presse*)

De Gaulle stepping onto Canadian soil from *Le Colbert* gangplank to begin his visit to Canada, July 1967. Advancing to meet him: Governor General Roland Michener, accompanied by Mrs. Michener. Premier Johnson at edge of photo. (Courtesy of *The Gazette*)

Fleurs de lys painted on the ''king's road'' between Quebec City and Montreal by the Quebec Department of Public Works to mark de Gaulle's route. (Courtesy of *La Presse*)

De Gaulle addressing a crowd between Quebec City and Montreal, July 1967. Placard bearing words "*Québec libre*" in background. (Nogues, France)

De Gaulle entering Montreal, July 25, 1967. Premier Johnson accompanying him, straightening his tie in anticipation. (Courtesy of *The Gazette*)

De Gaulle in victory posture after shouting *"Vive le Québec libre"* from the Montreal Hôtel de Ville balcony. (Courtesy of Canadian Press)

De Gaulle leaving Montreal Hôtel de Ville after *"Vive le Québec libre"* incident. (Archives, Hôtel de Ville)

De Gaulle listening to Mayor Jean Drapeau at luncheon before taking plane back to France, July 1967. (Courtesy of *The Gazette*)

De Gaulle and Madame de Gaulle boarding airplane to return to France, July 1967. (Courtesy of *La Presse*)

Vive le Québec libre

Chapter 1

The Persona General de Gaulle

The period in which our subject is situated, roughly the 1960s, was one of rapid change, frequent tension and even conflict in Quebec, Canada and France. In July 1960, the Liberal government of Premier Jean Lesage took office in Quebec; its primary objective was the rapid and comprehensive modernization of the province after several decades of conservative rule. A related objective was to strengthen Quebec as the home of over eighty per cent of French-speaking Canadians. That process, which became known as the Quiet Revolution, was marked by challenges to many traditional aspects of life in Quebec and also to relations with the rest of Canada within the federal system. The Lesage government was defeated in 1966, in large part because it had forced the pace of change too hard, and was succeeded by the rejuvenated *Union Nationale* under Premier Daniel Johnson. The essential thrust of the Quiet Revolution was maintained. Canada-wide, a Progressive Conservative government led by Prime Minister John Diefenbaker had been elected in 1957. Innovative in some respects, it showed little understanding of Quebec, and perceived the Quiet Revolution primarily as a threat to national unity. Relations between Ottawa and Quebec City deteriorated seriously during its tenure. In 1963, it was replaced by a Liberal government under Prime Minister Lester B. Pearson which contained several ministers from Quebec who were closely attuned to current developments there. Pearson, himself, an exceptionally open-minded person whose talent for conciliation and compromise had earned him a Nobel Peace Prize in the previous decade, saw Quebec's new dynamism as a positive development for all of Canada. However, he was concerned that the autonomist, and even separatist, currents that were part of the new set of forces there would, if not defused by actions that would reconcile national and provincial goals, endanger the very future of the country.

Across the Atlantic, in France, Charles de Gaulle had been recalled from political retirement in 1958 specifically to resolve the Algerian crisis, but, more generally, to extricate the country from a political impasse. By the end of 1962, he had created the Fifth Republic, had himself chosen as its first president, and had granted independence to Algeria and the African colonies. He had also resolved a wide range of domestic problems, and was ready to focus on his principal interest, the restoration of France's international influence. In 1960, just a few weeks after Jean Lesage became premier of Quebec, one of his ministers turned up in Paris and appealed for help to preserve and assert French Canadians' place in North America. In particular, he had in mind the establishment of a Quebec office in Paris so that direct contacts could be made between the French and Quebec governments without always having to go through the Government of Canada. De Gaulle looked on the request with favour, and a delegation general was established the following year. Thus was put in place the triangular relationship between Paris, Ottawa and Quebec which set the stage for the French president's dramatic intervention in July 1967.

In order to understand the events as they unfolded, some background information about General de Gaulle's personality and career is essential. Hundreds of books have been written about him, and their number continues to grow annually. The most ambitious is the three-volume study by French journalist Jean Lacouture.[1] In addition to being highly readable, it is the most complete compilation of knowledge to date about the famous French figure. De Gaulle himself wrote several revealing books as a military officer before World War Two, and two sets of memoirs, one covering his career as leader of the Free French Forces and as prime minister immediately after the war, the second dealing with his tenure in office beginning in 1958. Unfortunately, he did not live long enough to complete the latter, and it does not include the Quebec incident. While that gap is regrettable, it is not irremediable since he made his views on the subject known on several occasions. And at any rate, in presenting his version of events, he displayed what Lacouture has termed "a gift for embellishment," designed to leave to future generations his particular interpretation of the history which he helped shape. A further useful source of information is the series of his letters and written notes edited by his son, Admiral Philippe de Gaulle.[2] A man of letters, he preferred written to oral communication and his day to day handwritten texts provide valuable insights into his thinking and his activities.

Charles de Gaulle was in his seventy-seventh year when he visited Quebec in 1967. Since childhood, he had trained himself single-mindedly to be a great leader of men; now he was at the apex of his career, but acutely conscious that time was running out (few male members of his family had exceeded the age of eighty). Consequently, he was forcing the pace in a number of issue areas to maximize his impact.

Above all else, de Gaulle was a French patriot, a type of personality he himself once described as combining a love of country with a will to act, proud confidence and personal disinterestedness. He began to demonstrate those qualities at an early age. His father, Henri, was a highly traditionalist Frenchman who had hoped for a military career but, after being wounded in the Franco-Prussian War of 1870 in which France had gone down to disastrous defeat, he had settled for that of a secondary school history teacher. As for his mother, de Gaulle once described her as having for her country "an uncompromising passion equal to her religious piety."[3] He and his three brothers and one sister learned at home of France's glorious past and also of their own ancestors' roles in it. Their very name recalled ancient Gaul from which France had evolved; and one of their forebears had fought the English at Agincourt in 1415. In fact, he was believed to have been one of the six men who accompanied Joan of Arc to meet the Dauphin at Chinon when she offered to drive out the enemy. The children also learned that they had Irish and Scottish ancestors, and thus they identified with the Irish struggle against the English. In fact, their maternal grandmother had written a biography of Daniel O'Connell, liberator of Ireland. Henri de Gaulle took the children frequently to the Invalides near their home; for Charles, as he wrote later, it symbolized "all the glories of France." They also went on regular excursions with him to Versailles and other historic sites, and he showed them the spot just north of Paris where he had been wounded. Memories of that experience rekindled his revanchist sentiments towards Germany, but his abiding hatred was directed against France's historic enemy, "perfidious Albion."* In fact, when, in 1898, a British expeditionary force obliged a French one to withdraw from the Upper Nile region of Africa, Henri de Gaulle was so irate that he resolved not to teach his sons English. Describing himself as a "nostalgic monarchist," he railed endlessly against the institutions and functioning of the Third Republic, and denounced the political party strife that divided and weakened the country. His feelings were so strong that he refused to either teach or enrol his children in a public school. Charles attended the Jesuit *lycée* where his father taught, and, after the expulsion of the Jesuit order from France, he was sent to Belgium to complete his secondary education.

Charles de Gaulle was strongly influenced by his father's political views but keenly sensitive to the tensions between those views and the reality around him. He was a wilful child, given to petulant outbursts

---

* A pejorative name for England made famous by Victor Hugo.

when thwarted, and though only a middle child, he sought to establish his ascendancy over the others. He enjoyed playing with lead soldiers but insisted that he himself assume the role of king of France. At an early age, he decided on a military career. When he was fifteen, he wrote a description of a battle, situated in 1930 (when he would be forty), in which "General de Gaulle," commanding two hundred thousand men, developed a brilliant strategy which enabled him to crush the enemy before it could consolidate its position.[4] At about that age, he began to grow at an inordinate rate, apparently because of some hormonal imbalance, and soon towered over the other children. His ungainly appearance—a spindly body topped by an undersized head, a prominent nose that overshadowed a low forehead and receding chin—earned him the nickname of "asparagus." He was not traumatized by this development but, rather, turned it into an advantage. He learned to control his emotions, and would withdraw into an aloofness marked by long periods of imperious silence; the stratagem was designed to create an aura of mystery and authority. His sister remarked later about the radical change in personality that he appeared to have fallen into an icebox. It heralded the distinction, so important in understanding his actions in later years, between the private individual, Charles, and the persona, General de Gaulle. The maintenance of this dichotomy required exceptional willpower, a quality he already possessed in abundance.

The pursuit of his high ambition required de Gaulle to reassess his attitude towards school. Previously an unexceptional pupil, he now decided to enter the *Académie Saint-Cyr*, the most prestigious officers' training school in France, and the competition to be admitted was very keen. He was particularly interested in French history, but read very selectively, preferring the more glorious to the more sombre episodes and thereby buttressing his idealized image of his country. In order to resolve the dissonance between his father's monarchist sentiments and the republican régime under which he had to make his career, he espoused the position that French history was a long and continuous process with the different forms of government representing various stages. Within that perspective, France had existed since the dawn of history; the *Ancien Régime* had united it and created a solid state, while the republican régime had introduced popular sovereignty and human rights. Charles de Gaulle's vision of his country had a large emotional component as well. He espoused historian Jules Michelet's description of France as "a woman and an exemplary mother stimulat- ing admiration, love and devotion."[5] A mystical, even religious, element was also evident. De Gaulle referred to France frequently as "*Notre Dame la France*," a mother figure with eternal life. His own self-appointed mission was, simply and grandly, to serve her as great men such as Cardinal Richelieu had done. She was only herself when she was one of the world powers: his primary objective was to ensure her of that rank and prestige. He inclined towards a monarchical system, but if, for reasons of historical reality, that meant functioning within a republic, then so be it.

Fortified by his strong sense of mission, Charles de Gaulle passed the entrance exams to Saint-Cyr, and although far from popular with his instructors and classmates because of his haughty attitude, he graduated with an excellent standing in 1912. To the general surprise, he opted to serve in the infantry, not the most distinguished branch of the armed forces. There was a simple reason: the chances of advancement were greatest there. His first commanding officer was Colonel Philippe Pétain, a man of strong will and independent mind, but whose criticisms of established military doctrine had delayed his promotions. De Gaulle chose him as his mentor. He greeted the outbreak of the Great War with elation. Not only, he felt, would the defeat of 1870 be annulled, but the French, prone to internecine quarrels in time of peace, would be united in a great cause. "It is only necessary for France to show the sword for every fervour to merge in union," he wrote. "Everything which can contribute to such an upsurge—patriotism, religious faith, hope, hatred of the enemy—is at once strengthened by mass approbation."[6] In battle, de Gaulle was awe-inspiring in his self-control, leading his troops in repeated attacks. He was wounded three times and, the last time, was left for dead as the survivors withdrew. Pétain had him awarded a posthumous Legion of Honour. In fact, he had been picked up by the Germans, treated, and made a prisoner of war. Indomitable, he tried (with little success) to impose his leadership on the others in his camp; he made several attempts to escape, learned German, and even conducted a study of German organizational procedures which was later published.[7] "Know thine enemy" was also a rule he followed.

The period between the two world wars was a frustrating time for de Gaulle. He served for two years in Poland as a member of an advisory group helping to defend that newly reconstituted country against the Soviet forces. On his return, by then a captain, he taught one year at Saint-Cyr, married, and then was admitted to the *Ecole Supérieure de Guerre*, the top military training school. His inter-personal relations marred his stay there. One of his superior officers evaluated him as intelligent and talented with a strong personality, but added that he cancelled out his obvious qualities "by his excessive self-assurance, his severity with regard to the opinions of others, and his attitude of a king in exile."[8] He alienated members of the military establishment by criticizing the strategic doctrine of fighting from fixed defensive positions rather than employing more flexible and offensive tactics.

During a military exercise, a fellow officer found himself alone with him and commented, "I am going to tell you something that will certainly make you smile. I have this curious feeling that you have a great destiny."[9] De Gaulle answered after a pensive silence, "*Oui, moi aussi.*" The immediate prospects were less promising. He received the final grade of "*assez bien,*" or just acceptable. Not a man to accept the evaluations of others at the best of times, he was outraged and complained to Pétain, now the celebrated hero of Verdun, a field marshal and deputy chairman of the *Conseil Général de la Guerre.* Pétain summoned the director of army training to his office and insisted that the grade be revised in order not to prejudice the career of such a promising officer; it was raised to "*bien,*" or average. De Gaulle, who had hoped to teach there one day, swore not to set foot in the "dump" again except as commanding officer.[10]

The old man went further: he appointed him to his personal staff and set him to work on a manuscript he wished to publish on the history of the French soldier. And in 1927 he forced the commander of the *Ecole Supérieure de Guerre* to invite his protégé to deliver a series of three lectures, a coveted sign of recognition for a junior officer. Published later under the title *Le Fil de l'épée*, the sword's edge, they included a description of the ideal "man of character" which some saw as a flattering portrait of the field marshal, and others as the author's personal model.* One of the most striking revelations in the book, particularly in view of the strong tradition of Cartesian logic in France, is the importance de Gaulle accorded to intuition or instinct. Intelligence was necessary to a leader, he stated, but instinct gave him direct contact with reality and enabled him to identify with "the obscure harmony of the universe."[11] That achieved, the function of intelligence was to adapt the reality to meet the leader's plan. Another quality that he rated highly was the ability to take decisions, to seize opportunities and to adjust to novel situations. Ruses were a legitimate part of the leader's strategies, as were audacity and a deliberate aura of mystery. Lesser persons were critical of him, but in an hour of crisis, a popular "ground swell" propelled him to the fore, and he was praised, heeded and trusted.

Above all, the "man of character" had to bear the mark of "grandeur."[12] Ordinary men were so ridden with frailties, and their lives were so filled with trivia, that they responded positively to a collective action that associated them with something great. Authority could not be exercised without activating that lever. In the words of Chateaubriand, nations can only be led by dreams. De Gaulle added

* The following quotations are translations from the 1944 edition published by Berger-Levrault, Paris.

his own harsher judgment, "Crowds cannot be moved except by basic feelings, violent images and brutal invocations."[13] To fill such a role, de Gaulle recognized, implied efforts that discouraged most people. It implied a constant internal struggle that cut into one's soul "like the hairshirt of a penitent tears away at his body at every step."[14] Morever, "the sweetness of abandon, familiarity and friendship" had to be sacrificed to solitude, once described aptly as "the misery of human beings." Domination, and what was conventionally called happiness were mutually exclusive phenomena. But nothing was accomplished without great men, and they were great because they wanted to be.

The series of lectures showed de Gaulle to be a highly reflective and widely-read person, as well as a considerable craftsman of the French language. He had read the works of German philosopher Friedrich Nietzsche, and possibly Oswald Spengler, but the principal influences on him were clearly the French thinkers Maurice Barrès, Charles Péguy and Henri Bergson. His interpretation of French history was also revealing. The seventeenth century was clearly his favorite: it marked the destruction of "feudal diversity" and the establishment of a strong state that imposed order and coherence on the nation. The hitherto disparate elements were united by a "common passion" to serve the king, and thus great things were accomplished. The eighteenth century, in contrast, saw the weakening of this powerful entity under the impact of divisive new ideas and sentiments. Prussia, in turn, became united under the leadership of a great king, Frederick II, and imposed its military superiority during the Seven Years' War. (While de Gaulle did not raise the point, New France was founded in the seventeenth and abandoned in the eighteenth century.) The French Revolution had thrown the country into confusion, but gradually a sense of patriotism had returned. Napoleon had built on it, and a widespread feeling of grandeur, to restore France to its pre-eminent position. (De Gaulle later expressed criticism of Napoleon for his excessiveness, which led to his downfall.)

With his high ambitions, de Gaulle preferred to remain near the fount of power, but his superiors were of an opposite view. He was posted to the Rhineland, still an occupied part of Germany, and subsequently to Lebanon, a French protectorate. Only in late 1931 did he succeed in getting an assignment in Paris, and once again thanks to Marshal Pétain. He was attached to the secretariat of the *Conseil supérieur de la Défense nationale*. During those years he continued to develop his thinking on military and political subjects, and to write. Based on his reading of British military strategist Sir Basil Liddell-Hart, German Hans Guderian, and others, he became a proponent of mechanized warfare. In a book published in 1934, *Vers l'Armée de métier*,[15] de Gaulle advocated a highly mobile professional army equipped with tanks to supplement the fixed defenses of the Maginot Line. It could be in place, he argued, in six years. The book had little success, selling only seven hundred copies. It did serve as an entrée to certain centres of power; for instance, he identified Paul Reynaud as a rising star and got a copy to him. Reynaud was impressed. "I saw him," de Gaulle wrote later, "convinced him, and worked with him."[16] He became part of that group of French officers who combined military service and politics. For his lobbying activities, he became known as "*monsieur moteur.*" During his six years in the National Defence secretariat, de Gaulle was able to observe the political scene at first hand. He was not impressed. The experience of serving under fourteen governments demonstrated to him the frailty of the state, the essential instrument of French cohesion and power. He placed the blame primarily on the political parties, which he described as centrifugal forces comparable to the old feudal fiefdoms, pursuing their own interests and those of various groups at the expense of the nation. In that sense, the National Assembly was not representative of the true France, the population as a whole.

In 1933, de Gaulle returned to military field duty as commander of a tank regiment in Alsace. His new superior, General Henri Giraud, warned him caustically, "*Mon petit de Gaulle*, you will not impose your theories here in my lifetime."[17] He misjudged his man: de Gaulle's adversaries might determine his strategies, but they could not alter his goals. Even Marshal Pétain was not allowed to stand in his way. The old man, now in his eighties, had never completed the history of the French soldier on which de Gaulle had worked in the previous decade; he decided to expurgate it of everything that he had not written, and to publish it under his own name. He only informed Pétain when the manuscript was ready to go to press. They had a sharp altercation in which the marshal demanded that his contribution to several chapters be recognized in the preface. De Gaulle conceded the bare minimum: a formal dedication and a tribute to Pétain's personal qualities in the chapter on the Great War.[18] Their long relationship came to an abrupt end.

De Gaulle pressed on. He purchased a house, La Boisserie, at Colombey-les-Deux-Eglises, a village halfway between Paris and the German border, and installed his family there. It provided him with the solitude to think and write, and enabled him to commute in either direction. Sometimes even his great will power was tested. War clouds were again looming on the horizon and the country was totally unprepared. France, he wrote to his wife, following the signature of the Munich agreement, had "ceased to be a great nation."[19] His persona, de Gaulle assuming the grandeur of France, seemed futile; Charles, the much lesser individual, reasserted himself. A quote from Nietzsche recurred in his conversations. "Nothing is of any worth. Nothing happens, and yet everything happens. But it doesn't matter." In the end, another dictum, this one his own, always carried the day, "[One must] raise oneself above oneself in order to dominate the others and thus, events."[20]

De Gaulle was also a master strategist, and a realist. Chaos was a disaster for some people, but an opportunity for those who knew how to take advantage of it. When war broke out in September 1939, he made his case yet again for mechanized warfare in a memorandum and distributed it to eighty high-ranking political and military persons. It had no noticeable effect. In January 1940, he submitted a proposal to Paul Reynaud, then minister of finance, for a new government department to conduct the war; it ended with the suggestion, "Colonel de Gaulle [he had been promoted to the rank of lieutenant colonel at the beginning of the war] could be secretary general."[21] Once again, nothing happened. When, in March, Reynaud became prime minister —de Gaulle wrote his nomination speech—he tried to follow up on the suggestion, but it was vetoed by the previous prime minister, now minister of war, Edouard Daladier, because of his antipathy for the brash officer. De Gaulle returned to the front as commander of a new mechanized division and waited, in his own words, "without impatience" for the call he knew must come.[22]

The Germans launched their offensive on May 10. Still organizing his new command, de Gaulle led his troops into battle with his usual coolness and authority, and scored some notable successes against overwhelming odds. On May 28, the Cabinet appointed him brigadier general "*à titre temporaire*", a minimal promotion. By then, the British and French forces were in full retreat. De Gaulle was operating out of a château north of Paris when he learned that he was to be appointed to the most junior portfolio in the Cabinet, secretary general of war and national defence. He rushed to Paris with one major condition: that the government was prepared to carry on the war, from Africa if necessary. The prime minister gave him that assurance, and he was sworn in on June 6. He was given two tasks: liaison with the British authorities, and preparing to move the government to Africa. In view of his anti-Anglo-Saxon bias, the first was a curious assignment, but Reynaud was pleased to have a spokesman in dealing with the new British prime minister, Winston Churchill, who was equally determined to carry on the fight.

Churchill and de Gaulle met for the first time at 10 Downing Street in London on June 10. It was the beginning of a tempestuous relationship that has been described vividly by François Kersaudy in *Churchill and de Gaulle*.[23] The British leader was known in his own country as a "fanatic francophile."[24] He had made two trips to Paris in the previous two weeks to counter the defeatist attitude prevalent there. Should Britain be overrun, he would carry on the fight from Canada, he told the Reynaud government and urged it to prepare to do the same from Africa. At the same time, he advised Canadian Prime Minister Mackenzie King on June 6 that he did not know if it would be possible "to keep France in the war."[25] Complying with Reynaud's instructions, de Gaulle flew to London and assured Churchill of France's determination to pursue the war, from North Africa if necessary. In exchange, he asked for military reinforcements, particularly air support. The British prime minister argued that the twenty-nine remaining Royal Air Force squadrons were better kept at home to meet the expected onslaught on Britain by the German Luftwaffe. On the other hand, he offered to send the Canadian division, the only one that had not yet been committed on the continent. While he was impressed by Churchill himself, de Gaulle was disappointed by the response to his request, and saw it as proof of the widespread French view that the Anglo-Saxons always put their own interests first.

The two men met three more times in the next week, twice south of Paris as the French government retreated towards Bordeaux, and again in London. By then it was evident that France was lost. The Canadian troops were landed in the Cherbourg peninsula, but by then the military situation was hopeless and they were withdrawn before seeing battle. The purpose of de Gaulle's second trip to London was to ask for help in evacuating the government and as many military units as possible to Algeria. However, time had run out: when he caught up with the French government in Bordeaux that night, he learned that it had decided to resign and that Marshal Pétain had been asked to form a new one and sue for an armistice. The British airplane that had brought de Gaulle back was due to return to London early the next morning; he decided to go along. The only person who agreed to accompany him was his aide-de-camp. De Gaulle was not Churchill's first choice to carry on in France's name in such an eventuality; he would have preferred a more experienced politician. But he had been impressed by his strong personality and determination, and welcomed him. His country's "independence and grandeur," he assured the indomitable Frenchman, would be restored.[26]

On June 18, the day after his return to Britain, de Gaulle announced his decision to the French people in a BBC broadcast. "As my irretrievable words flew out [into space]," he recalled later, "I felt one life ending...at forty-nine. I was entering on an adventure like a man that fate was casting in a very special role."[27] In fact, it was the role of France's most loyal servant for which he had prepared himself since childhood.

There was no turning back. The Pétain government, installed in

Vichy, condemned de Gaulle to death in absentia. Churchill made him his personal protégé, ensuring that he received the necessary support to build military units from the French personnel who had been evacuated to Britain through Dunkirk and other French ports. He also invited him frequently to spend weekends at Chequers, the prime minister's country residence, for planning sessions. While they got on well, a fundamental disagreement on de Gaulle's role was soon to impair their relationship. For Churchill, de Gaulle was a military leader operating under British authority; for himself, he incarnated France in every respect, and, despite the current adversity, it was still a great power. Many of their difficulties in the coming months and years stemmed from the fact that he was not consulted or even forewarned of actions concerning France. There was a reason: the British authorities did not trust the Free French with military secrets; and indeed, there were grounds for their attitude. For instance, a naval expedition was sent to French West Africa in September 1940 to take Dakar and establish de Gaulle's headquarters there. He himself was on board. The Vichy government learned of the plan and was able to rush naval reinforcements from the Mediterranean. When the expedition arrived, the pro-Vichy governor was ready. The operation was called off when it became evident that heavy losses would be suffered on both sides.

De Gaulle's imperious attitude also caused serious problems. Many French officers refused to serve under him, and the British senior military staff generally resented him. While he appeared as unperturbed as ever in public, he was occasionally discouraged. On one occasion he told a senior British liaison officer, Major-General Edward Spears, that he would have to consider whether he could continue to work with the British, or whether he would retire to Canada as a private citizen.[28] Why he fixed on Canada is not clear; at any rate, he decided to carry on. Following the Dakar débâcle, he once remarked, he had even contemplated suicide. However, the British naval force had taken him on to Cameroon, where the governor rallied to his side. The reception he received buoyed his spirit again. Through that first contact with the Empire, he recalled later, "I discovered that there was a person named de Gaulle who existed in the minds of others and who was a completely different person from me."[29] Discovered? Confirmed —confirmation of his childhood plan—is a more accurate word. From Cameroon he went still further south to establish his headquarters in Brazzaville, capital of the French Congo.

De Gaulle's immediate objective was to rally as many colonies as possible to the Free French Forces, but he had a broader one: by asserting French authority overseas, to re-establish the country's place as a significant power. That goal led him into a continuous pattern of conflicts with his British mentors, and later with the

Americans as well. One serious clash occurred over Syria and Lebanon, French protectorates in a part of the world where the French and British had been vying for influence for many years. When the British signed a commercial treaty with the resident high commissioner of the Pétain government, de Gaulle interpreted the move as a step to supplant France there at the end of the war. He persuaded Churchill to undertake a joint Free French-British invasion of Syria and Lebanon from Egypt. It was successful, and the high commissioner asked for armistice negotiations, but he insisted that de Gaulle be excluded from them. The British agreed. He was furious at the concession and told an American journalist that they were exploiting the Vichy régime just like Germany; allowing it to exist as long as they could engage in "a mutually profitable exchange" with it.[30] It was Churchill's turn to be furious; he summoned the Free French leader back to London, then kept him waiting ten days before receiving him. After a stormy exchange, they made up. It was one of the rare occasions when de Gaulle expressed regrets. In May 1942, British units invaded Madagascar without even informing de Gaulle in advance, although he had submitted a detailed plan for a Free French operation three months earlier. Another stormy scene followed, with de Gaulle refusing to accept Churchill's explanation that he wanted to avoid French soldiers doing battle against one another. On June 6, de Gaulle called on the Soviet embassy in London to examine the possibilities of transferring his base of operations to Moscow.[31]

De Gaulle's difficulties with the United States began over St. Pierre and Miquelon. The islands, like Martinique and Guadeloupe, had remained under Vichy's control, and the American government, which had recognized the Pétain régime, was anxious not to disturb that situation in order to keep the war from spreading to the Western hemisphere. In December 1941, just a few days after the Americans entered the war, the Free French seized the islands in a unilateral, secret operation.* The American secretary of state, Cordell Hull, was very upset and wanted the *status quo ante* restored. While Churchill was annoyed, particularly since close relations with President Roosevelt were his highest priority at that moment, he succeeded in smoothing over the situation and the *fait accompli* was accepted. However, de Gaulle was to pay dearly for his independent-mindedness.

In November 1942, the Americans invaded Algeria and Tunisia as the first stage of the Allied counter-attack. Once again, de Gaulle was not informed. On receiving the news, he reacted, "I hope the Vichy people throw them back into the sea. One doesn't enter France like a

* Because Canada was involved in this matter, it is dealt with in detail in Chapter 4.

burglar."[32] In a few days, he recovered his equipoise sufficiently to explain in a broadcast to France that the area was being used as a base from which to liberate France. "*Voilà*," he concluded, "the war won thanks to France."[33] Although Churchill often felt aggrieved by de Gaulle's behaviour, the war effort was his primary concern. It was vitally important for both of them, he advised the Free French leader, to get along with the Americans. "See how I do," he said with regard to his relations with President Roosevelt, "I bend and then I rise up again."[34] De Gaulle retorted, "Because you are seated on a solid state, a united nation, a great army. Me, I'm too poor to allow myself to bend."

He was soon to demonstrate that he, too, was an adroit strategist. The Americans had fixed on General Henri Giraud, de Gaulle's previous commander who had recently escaped from a German prison camp, as commander-in-chief of the French forces in liberated North Africa. They even appointed Admiral François Darlan, a powerful figure in the Vichy régime who happened to be in Algiers on a private visit when they landed, as high commissioner for North Africa. That move was intended to wean the Pétain régime away from subservience to Germany. Darlan was assassinated a few weeks later. Churchill argued that the only feasible solution was a bicephalous authority under de Gaulle and Giraud. After several months of trying negotiations, the two men agreed, and the *Comité français pour la libération nationale* was formed under their joint presidency. As de Gaulle left London to take up his new responsibilities, British Foreign Minister Anthony Eden, one of his strongest supporters, remarked, "Do you know that you have caused us more difficulties than all our other European allies?"[35] "I don't doubt it," de Gaulle rejoined, "France is a great power." To make a very long, complex and bitter story short, in the next twelve months, he succeeded in evicting Giraud from the joint presidency and became sole leader of a new body, the provisional government of the French Republic. An equally impressive feat, he brought the National Resistance Council on the French mainland under his authority.

By June 1944, de Gaulle's prestige was so great that one would think he could no longer have been ignored. Not so: he was excluded from the preparations for the Allied invasion of France, and only brought to Britain to be informed of the plan at the last possible moment. Although he had another violent exchange with Churchill, he demonstrated that he had learned a few lessons in political manoeuvering. He was authorized to visit the Normandy beachhead eight days after the first landing, but forbidden to hold any public meetings. When he appeared in the little town of Bayeux, a few kilometers inland, he was given a tremendous welcome and responded in kind. "It was necessary," he remarked, "to face the Allies with a *fait accompli*. You'll see that they won't say anything."[36] He was right. Indeed, President Roosevelt invited him to Washington, D.C. the following month. The visit was an unquestioned success: in private they were both conciliatory, in public they declared each other to be friends. New York gave him a hero's welcome. He returned to Europe via Canada.*

On August 24, by pre-arrangement with the Allies, the Leclerc division of the Free French Forces took Paris. The next day, General de Gaulle arrived, went straight to the office he had occupied briefly as a minister four years earlier, and declared, "France has returned home."[37] At the Hôtel de Ville he proclaimed, "Paris liberated. Liberated by its people with the help of the French armies, with the support of all France...eternal France."[38] The Allied contribution was ignored. The next day, he led a parade down the Champs-Elysées to the acclaim of over a million Parisians. He felt fulfilled. "Each one of them," he wrote later, "had chosen, in his heart, Charles de Gaulle as a recourse against his suffering and as the symbol of his hopes...and at the sight of him, national unity shone forth."[39] To him, it was one of "those miracles of national consciousness" that marked the history of France. In the midst of the explosion of emotions, he felt that he was "performing a function far beyond his own personality, to serve as an instrument of fate."

Through his contact with the common people, de Gaulle drew the strength to pursue his vocation. While the problems he faced were enormous, his resolve was at least commensurate, and the four years of leadership experience had honed his persona and sharpened his talent. His distrust of political parties and politicians was as intense as ever. He told the nuclear scientist Frédéric Joliot-Curie that autumn, "I have confidence in very few men."[40] His greatest concern was that France would once again fall victim to the fractionalized politics of the pre-war period. Frenchmen had a proclivity for divisions dating back to the early Gauls, he once commented.[41] And he added, "It's not possible without an effort to unite a country with two hundred and sixty-five special cheeses."† He had to make that effort; it was essential to France and to himself. "Only vast undertakings can compensate the ferment of dispersion in the French people," he wrote in his wartime memoirs. "In short, France cannot be France without greatness."[42]

De Gaulle's strategy was to remain above the mêlée, or in his own words, never to submit to the rules of conduct of ordinary mortals.[43] He referred to himself in the third person as "de Gaulle" or "General de

* See Chapter 5.
† De Gaulle himself was as austere in this regard as in others; his three favorite cheeses were among the most innocuous on the market.

Gaulle," and excluded human warmth from his official relations. Olivier Guichard, who worked with him for over twenty years and who loved him as a second father, wrote that de Gaulle had close personal relations with no one "except perhaps with his family."[44] Very occasionally, he allowed his feelings to show. He once wrote in a note to Gaston Palewski, another of his long-time aides, "You know the sentiments I have for you, under the armour."[45] His cutting remarks and his black humour were notorious. As an example of the latter, Guichard recounts that during a visit to Marseilles, a man in a crowd yelled at him and at the dignitaries with him, "Death to all fools."[46] De Gaulle muttered in response, "A big job." He seems to have recognized the contradiction between his need to inspire loyalty and support, and his offensive demeanour. "There are two ways of saying things," he once admitted, "a pleasant and a repellent one; I can't help it, I always take the second."[47] Evidently, his self control was not as complete as it appeared.

When he assumed power in France in August 1944, de Gaulle's primary objective of returning the country to great power rank was beyond the imagination of most people. Large parts of it were devastated, it was completely dependent on the Anglo-Saxons, and the population was deeply divided, first between Pétainists and Gaullists, and second between Communists and anti-Communists. His first priority was to re-establish the authority and strength of the French state. Notwithstanding the hopes and plans of some people for a supra-national authority, for him the basic reality in the world was still a constellation of independent countries negotiating the conditions of their co-existence. In that situation, France needed to regain its independence of others, or in his words, its "*mains libres.*"[48]

To that end, de Gaulle used both his military and political experience with remarkable skill. To most other leaders he was like a rogue elephant, charging through the countryside and wreaking destruction out of pure wilfulness. A few were able to recognize the superb tactician behind the apparent heavy-handedness. One astute British observer qualified the analogy: elephant-like, yes, Sir Gladwyn Jebb has commented, but when he came up against an immovable obstacle, he simply went around it. "Come on," de Gaulle once commented to politician Antoine Pinay, "you know very well that, in politics, when you lack strength, ruse is the best instrument."[49] Another asset that de Gaulle had developed during the war years was his oratorical talent. He had an exceptional command of the French language and used it efficiently as an instrument of power, appealing to ordinary people to rise above their daily concerns and to dare to dream of great things, particularly of the greatness of France. He knew full well that France could not be everything he wanted it to be, Olivier Guichard has explained, but he coaxed and cajoled his audiences in that direction by making his personal goals seem desirable and even natural to them.[50] He was also a master of ambiguity. His words were carefully chosen to create a specific effect without committing himself more than he wished. Inversely, he also turned silence to advantage. "Nothing increases authority better than silence," he had written in *Le Fil de l'épée*. When he wanted to impose his will on someone, he would fall silent and stare at him with piercing eyes until the person lost his composure. Similarly, in a disagreement with other authorities, for instance, the Allies, he would withdraw and remain incommunicado for long periods of time. He usually won the war of nerves to see who would re-establish contact first. Finally, he had become adept at using crises to advantage. Often he even created them. From time to time it was necessary to upset the flower pot, he once remarked, in order to get something one desired.[51]

In August 1944, de Gaulle needed all the talent and devices he could muster. One of his most pressing problems was to get the Communists under control. They had played a major role in the Resistance and were determined to do the same in shaping France's future. Another major problem was how to return the country to constitutional democracy without allowing it to fall prey once again to political in-fighting; furthermore, how he could lead it without becoming, himself, just another politician. One writer has described de Gaulle's political concepts as those of a "republican king."[52]

De Gaulle was convinced of the necessity for a presidential system of government, with the president elected by popular suffrage and endowed with strong executive powers, and a parliament empowered to debate issues and pass laws but not able to destabilize the system by causing frequent changes of government. In the first post-war elections in October 1945, the French population voted—as de Gaulle requested—in favour of a constituent assembly; however, they also elected a majority of Communists and Socialists to that body. Four days later, de Gaulle was chosen by the assembly as prime minister, even though he had not been a candidate for a seat. He formed a government in which the major parties were represented. Very quickly, the parties returned to their old divisive ways, and a consensus emerged in the assembly in favour of a constitution not significantly different from the pre-war one. His threats and appeals to public opinion proving to no avail, de Gaulle resigned on January 20, 1946, and withdrew to a château not far from Paris. "In less than eight days, they [the politicians] will come in a delegation to ask me to return,"[53] he predicted to a staff member, "and I'll pose my conditions again." They never came. Nor did the population demand that they do so. War-weary and still basking in the atmosphere of liberation, many

Frenchmen were pleased to be rid of such a difficult taskmaster. After a few months he returned to Colombey-les-deux-Eglises to wait for the call he felt must come.

He had committed a tactical mistake. A year later, he committed another. In February 1947, de Gaulle confided to a visitor that, "suffering profoundly" to see France in such a bad situation, he had decided to form a "*rassemblement*," a mass organization, to make a come-back.[54] "It's the only hope," he added, not specifying whether for de Gaulle or for the country. But then, for him, they were synonymous. The *Rassemblement du Peuple Français* was launched at Strasbourg before a crowd of some fifty thousand. He felt exhilarated, and again on course. "I had the impression," he recalled later, "that something was happening as important as the beginning of the Resistance after the collapse of 1940."[55] Back in action, he flailed away in speeches across the country at the political régime and the politicians, particularly the Communists, whom he acccused of "separatism." (An allusion to their ties with the Soviet Union and international Communism.) National unity, he stormed, required that this "horrible wound" be healed.[56] He enjoyed an initial success: candidates supported by the RPF won some forty per cent of the vote in municipal elections in October 1947. However, he had to wait four years for the next National Assembly elections. By then, de Gaulle was perceived by many Frenchmen as a politician, even though he still refused to be a candidate. In 1951, the RPF won about 120 (some affiliations were rather tenuous) out of 600 seats, and ran second to the Communists. Subsequently, a number of RPF deputies voted to support a government led by Antoine Pinay. The movement began to disintegrate. The municipal elections of 1953 proved disastrous for it. For de Gaulle, the loss of popular support was a greater blow than the political defections. The French masses, he wrote to his son Philippe, "have never been so spineless, so indifferent, so egotistical."[57]

The persona, General de Gaulle, seemed to have run its course. The private person, Charles, reasserted itself. He withdrew to Colombey-les-deux-Eglises in 1954 and began work on his wartime memoirs. Visitors found him bitter and pessimistic. "I was submerged [in 1946] by a wave of national decadence," he wrote to one correspondent, "however, that is the fate of the world."[58] Still, he never quite gave up hope. He kept an office in Paris and was available there every week or so to talk to supporters. He also made occasional speeches, and even visited the French colonies under government auspices. One trip to the Pacific took him around the world. He insisted on not setting foot on foreign soil, even though that entailed one long sea journey, and he remained on board the aircraft during fueling stops in Brazil and Australia.

In 1954, France lost Indochina; in 1956, it suffered a humiliating reversal over the Suez Canal. The decolonization movement was sweeping Africa: Morocco and Tunisia became independent in 1956. Most of the French armed forces became bogged down in an anti-guerrilla war in Algeria. Governments were again falling in rapid succession and being reconstituted, largely with the same personnel. De Gaulle observed the events with concern and disgust, but also with the realization that, because of his advancing years, his day might not come again. In December 1956, he conceded to New York *Times* correspondent Cyrus Sulzberger that he did not totally exclude a return to power, but added, "First, a certain chaos has to exist."[59] That condition was met in the spring of 1958. Divisions over the Algerian war increased; reports of a military coup were widespread. Thoughts again turned to de Gaulle as the nation's saviour. On May 15, he issued a brief statement which concluded, "I am prepared to assume the powers of the Republic."[60] On May 29, the call came from President Coty himself. A majority of politicians were prepared to accept him on his own terms, which included a new constitution.

De Gaulle was sixty-seven years old in May 1958; his "exile" had lasted twelve years. It was very late to set about realizing his great ambitions for his country. "Don't think that I am going to give you the spectacle of my decrepitude," he told veteran Gaullist Jacques Chaban-Delmas when they met again.[61] He had grown heavier, more imposing. His views had not changed, but he was an even better strategist, more suave when the occasion called for it, seemingly, at least, more detached. Back in the only role in which he could find fulfillment, he acted with a vigour that belied his years. The National Assembly approved his appointment as prime minister, granted him exceptional powers and began a long recess.

Almost immediately, de Gaulle flew to Algiers, where he addressed a huge crowd of French military personnel and civilians who greeted him with cries of "*Vive l'Algérie française!*" the slogan of the opponents of Algerian independence. He approached the microphone and responded, "*Je vous ai compris*"—I have understood you. There followed a brief moment of stunned silence, then an eruption of joy. The crowd thought that he had endorsed their cause. Not at all. While "apparently spontaneous," he recounted later, the four words were "carefully calculated" and designed "to stir up enthusiasm without committing me any further than I was determined to go."[62] His objective had been "to make contact with the souls" in front of him in order to get his message across. In fact, he had concluded by then that the independence of Algeria was unavoidable, and his primary concern was to concede it under the best possible conditions for France. Two days later, after an exhausting schedule, he concluded his Algerian visit with a speech to a largely Moslem crowd in Mostaganem. Many of them were shouting "*Vive l'Algérie française*" and waving placards bearing that slogan. He concluded his speech, "*Vive Mostaganem, Vive l'Algérie française! Vive la France!*" Once again, the audience was caught by surprise. For two days, the anti-separatists had waited in vain to hear the words, and he had tenaciously avoided them. Had he finally been convinced that the territory could be saved for France? There was some evidence that he was at least leaning in that direction. At the airport, he confided to General Jouhaud, "Anyway, we aren't going to leave here."[63] The next day, however, he remarked privately that, while he regretted it, it was not possible to keep Algeria French.[64] After sifting all the evidence, Jean Lacouture concludes that, tired from his heavy schedule, and carried away by the emotional reception he had received, de Gaulle had "cracked" a little and had said involuntarily what he had in his mind.

In September 1958, the French electorate approved a new constitution in a referendum that, reflecting de Gaulle's requirements, greatly strengthened the power of the executive branch of government. In November, a new Gaullist party, the *Union pour la nouvelle république*, won nearly half the seats in the National Assembly, and a comfortable majority in alliance with the Independents. De Gaulle was installed—without election—for a seven-year term as the first president of the Fifth Republic.

In his element once again, he acted with impressive vigour. He succeeded in resolving the Algerian question—in favour of independence —but it took him four years, and in the process he had to deal with a military revolt that nearly cost him his life in an ambush. In keeping with one of his favorite dicta, "Nothing prevails against the spirit of the times," he concluded that nationalist movements, if supported by the whole population, were irresistible, and that France must adapt to the new situation. In a speech in Solferino, Italy, in 1959, he declared that the organization of the world could have no other basis "than the right of a people to decide its own future, providing it has the will and the capacity." He granted independence to the remaining African colonies, while maintaining strong French influence in all but Guinea. Then, having taken his distance from the colonial past, he presented France as the champion of the emerging countries. "Cooperation [in international development]," he announced in 1960, was "henceforth the great ambition of France."

In East-West relations, de Gaulle informed the United States that he was dissatisfied with the place given to France within the North Atlantic Treaty Alliance. He also ordered an acceleration in the programme that he had authorized in 1945 to develop France's own nuclear weapons and which had been maintained by successive governments. He also sought to carve out a position for France as an independent, albeit Western, power in relations between the two blocs. In Europe, he blocked the first proposal for British entry into the Common Market, and, through establishing a personal rapport with Chancellor Adenauer of West Germany, he paved the way for a partnership between the two countries that would make them the predominant force on the continent under French leadership. If he did not succeed in restoring France to its full grandeur in world affairs, he certainly gave it more influence than it had enjoyed since World War One. On the domestic plane, the country enjoyed, thanks in considerable measure to the economic and social programmes of his government, a decade of prosperity and progress.

De Gaulle's second tenure of political office provides a rare example of a single man's ability to impose his imprint on his country's evolution, and even to affect the course of history. It can be divided into three periods: the first four years in which he liquidated old accounts and laid the groundwork for future enterprises; five years in which he attempted, through bold ventures, to set France on new and irreversible courses; and finally, the last two years marked by a decreasing ability to direct events and a decline that led to his resignation. Whether incidentally or because of its significance, de Gaulle's visit to Quebec in July 1967 marked the beginning of the third period. For that reason, its importance goes beyond the intriguing question of his motives in shouting "*Vive le Québec libre!*"

Chapter 2

Quebec before de Gaulle

Relations between France and the descendants of the original settlers of New France had been tenuous ever since the government of Louis XV ceded it to Great Britain in 1763. In the course of the Seven Years' War, a British naval force had taken Quebec City. The inhabitants of the colony waited for a fleet to appear in the St. Lawrence River to liberate them. However, the French forces had overextended themselves in a thrust into Germany and had been obliged to retreat to the Rhine. Their primary concern became the defense of their own soil. The Treaty of Paris reflected that priority in that it stabilized the situation in Europe, at least for a time. One day the *"Canadiens,"* as they were becoming known, learned that the mother country had abandoned them, but, adding insult to injury, had kept other overseas possessions such as the islands of Martinique and Guadeloupe in the Caribbean Sea and the port town of Pondicherry in India, which had more commercial value. The cruel decision seemed to reflect Voltaire's description of New France in *Candide*, first published in 1759, as "a few acres of snow" not worth the money being spent in fighting over it. After more than a century of harsh existence, but also frontier-type liberty, the settlers had become restless under the autocratic and highly centralized rule of the French government, and the first signs of resistance had appeared. Historian Michel Brunet has argued that French-Canadian nationalism first appeared under the French régime. Resentment at being deserted added to the feeling of alienation, a sentiment that persisted throughout the years.

The Treaty of Paris gave the residents of the colony the right to return to France if they so desired. Nearly all of the élite did so, taking with them most of the books, paintings, fine furniture and other artifacts of civilization. The *"habitants,"* who lived off the land, had no choice but to stay on. With the tenaciousness of their French peasant origins, they resisted any attempts of their new political masters to change their way of life. Local leaders, particularly native-born parish priests, developed the existing rudimentary forms of local government, including a code of justice, to preserve the population's autonomy, the Catholic religion and the French language. Education proved a major problem: the French authorities had forbidden the establishment of a printing press in the colony, so practically no books were available. At one time, there was only one grammar book in the whole colony. Illiteracy, already widespread, increased.

The British authorities, for their part, made no serious effort to assimilate their new subjects. Initiating a colonial policy that they were to practise throughout the British Empire, they sought to rule indirectly, that is, through spokesmen for the population. The Quebec Act, passed by the Imperial Parliament in 1774, confirmed the "*habitants*'" right to their religion, language, local laws and customs. At the insistence of recent British immigrants, the Constitutional Act of 1791 went further and established a parliamentary system patterned on the one in Westminster, but with more power remaining in the hands of the local governor and his executive council. It also re-named the colony Canada, in conformity with its unofficial designation. In order to reduce friction already becoming manifest between the French and English, it split the colony into Upper and Lower Canada, each with its own appointed Legislative Council and elected Legislative Assembly. That step marked the beginning of both democracy and federalism in Canada. Participating in their own language and with an assured majority of members in the Legislative Assembly of Lower Canada, French Canadians soon came to recognize the value of the new institutions for the preservation of their way of life. As a result, they resisted the inducements of Americans, such as Alexander Hamilton, who tried to persuade them to join the United States. At the same time, the horrors and anticlericalism of the French Revolution further alienated them from their mother country and encouraged them to make the best of life under British rule.

During the Napoleonic wars, communications with France were almost non-existent, but, subsequently, they were re-established, and books and newspapers arrived regularly. The French Revolution of 1830 was followed with keen interest by a small group of French-Canadian leaders, chafing under the restrictions placed on majoritarian democracy by the governor and a largely English coterie around him. Led by Louis-Joseph Papineau, a former Speaker of the Legislative Assembly, they undertook an armed uprising in 1837. However, having learned over the centuries to survive by keeping their heads down, the "*habitants*" gave them little active support. Papineau fled to the United States and then to France. A parallel action in Upper

Canada, led by a Scottish immigrant, William Lyon Mackenzie, and motivated by the same resentment against oligarchical rule, ended in the same manner. As de Gaulle would have said, the situation was not yet "ripe." The incidents led to an investigation by a British liberal peer, the earl of Durham, who recommended full "responsible government," that is, popular control of the administration through an elected assembly. A second recommendation was more controversial: judging that the French Canadians had no chance of survival as an ethnic group in North America, he proposed that they be absorbed into the English-speaking population, by then a majority in Canada, through abolishing the linguistic and other rights that perpetuated their distinctiveness. He underestimated the French Canadians' capacity for survival: that recommendation remained largely a dead letter.

In 1839, a new constitution, the Act of Union, was approved in London. The two parts of Canada were reunited with a single parliament, but remained separate for administrative purposes, which meant duplicating the ministerial posts. Each part was also to have the same number of parliamentary seats. The result was a dual political system in which governments had to have two leaders, one from each part, or in practical terms, one French- and one English-Canadian. It was a formula for political instability. Coalition building became the order of the day, and governments were formed and fell in increasingly rapid succession.

Finally, when, in 1864, no more combinations seemed possible, it was agreed to try for a new constitution. The result was the British North America Act, 1867, which divided Canada into two provinces, Quebec and Ontario, added two more on the Atlantic coast and made provision for still others in order to create a federation, or Confederation as it was called, extending from sea to sea. English Canadians accepted the arrangement, in part as a means of escape from what they considered to be the tyranny of the French-Canadian minority. (Through heavy immigration, English Canadians had become the larger group.) French-Canadian leaders, strongly supported by the Roman Catholic hierarchy, welcomed it as a means of guaranteeing French-Canadian distinctive institutions and values in Quebec while still sharing in the promise of the much heralded great new nation. Once again, French Canadians proved adept at making the system work to their best advantage. Because of their numbers in Quebec, they had control of the government there; they also had a near veto on the federal level since it was difficult for a party to win a parliamentary majority without them. In 1896, Wilfrid Laurier became the first French-Canadian prime minister. Between then and 1984, French

Canadians held the post of prime minister for forty out of eighty-eight years.*

Because of the conservative nature of Quebec society, the government of Quebec remained modest in size. The Roman Catholic Church remained primarily responsible for education and social affairs, while private enterprise dominated the economic and financial sectors. Even within the general public, the provincial government was viewed with distrust, it being perceived as an unfriendly external force, first in the hands of the Imperial French, then of the British, and finally of a combined French-English élite. As a political body, it was also felt to be corrupt by nature; and, indeed, favoritism and nepotism were usually rife. In that situation, many ambitious young men preferred to enter federal politics where there was not only greater scope but where the British model was applied more equitably. That pattern was only broken in 1960, although it had been gradually undermined through changing economic and social conditions. The industrialization of the province, begun around the turn of the century and accelerated rapidly during the two world wars, broke down the isolation of French-Canadian society. The years of prosperity during and after World War Two enabled French Canadians to move beyond their traditional preoccupation with survival and to improve their material circumstances. The advent of television extended their horizons. A new élite began to emerge, better educated, more cosmopolitan and forward-looking. The Liberal party, the official opposition in Quebec since 1944, was able to identify with this modernizing current and ride it to power in 1960. The "quiet revolution" that it launched overflowed onto the international scene and led to a renewal of relations with France.

The first official contacts between France and its former colony can be traced to the period of the Second Empire. In 1855, French Canadians participated in the Universal Exhibition of Paris, displaying their products and rediscovering the mother country. The process was reciprocal: the attention of the French press was drawn to them and it referred in glowing terms to Canada, whose population, it noted incredulously, had not only survived but had grown since the Treaty of Paris, less than a century earlier, from sixty-five thousand to some eight hundred thousand. In August of that year, the Imperial government of Napoleon III despatched a small warship, *La Capricieuse*, to Quebec City to symbolize the re-establishment of relations and, more to the point, to explore the possibilities of trade. The

---

* Excluding the present prime minister, Brian Mulroney, who is of Irish-Canadian origin on his father's side, French-Canadian on his mother's side. A lifelong resident of Quebec, he is thoroughly bilingual and relates well to both language groups.

commander, Paul-Henri de Belvèze, was instructed to be very circumspect. He had no cause for concern: the British government had signed a treaty with France the previous year; it also had a free trade policy. The Canadian authorities and population welcomed the visit. As the vessel sailed up the St. Lawrence, bonfires were lit along the shores. During Belvèze's three-week stay, he was feted regally at a full schedule of banquets, and triumphal arches were erected to mark his passage through the principal towns. Ten thousand people gathered in Montreal's Champ de Mars, next to the Hôtel de Ville, to hear him deliver his message of French friendship. On his return home, the French government agreed to lower its customs duties on some Canadian products, and in 1859, at Canada's request, it opened a consulate general in Quebec City.

Their interest renewed, educated French Canadians followed news of France through the still-new wireless services, printed material, and a trickle of pilgrimages to their ancestral home. The Franco-Prussian War of 1870 stirred considerable enthusiasm among them initially, but that sentiment turned to disappointment when the French forces collapsed and Napoleon III was taken prisoner. France's prestige suffered another blow when it withdrew its forces from Rome where they had been protecting the Vatican against the Italian nationalists led by Giuseppe Garibaldi, considered by Quebec leaders as an enemy of the Roman Catholic Church. While France's attempts to recruit soldiers in Canada for its own purposes had failed, some three hundred volunteers enrolled in the pontifical guards to defend the Pope. French Canadians were still attached to "*la vieille France*" as their mother country and the cradle of their language and culture, but clearly they no longer identified with it as their homeland. Louis-Joseph Papineau himself had been happy to return home after a few years of exile there and, again taking the oath of allegiance to the British Crown, to resume his place as a legislator.

Before Confederation, Canada had maintained offices in Great Britain and on the European continent to encourage trade, investment and immigration. A year after its inauguration, the Canadian government called a meeting with the provinces at which it was decided to operate a dual system with both federal and provincial offices abroad, the latter being "duly accredited by the general [i.e., federal] government."[1] (The overall responsibility for foreign policy remained with the Imperial government.) Accordingly, the federal government appointed a representative in London, (later to become a high commissioner), and Quebec opened an agency there in 1871. In 1881, the premier of Quebec, Adolphe Chapleau, spent six months in France, where he was received elegantly and with the emotional declarations of joy at the fraternal reunion that were to become the pattern on such occasions. On his return, he appointed Hector Fabre, a senator in the Canadian Parliament, as agent general in Paris. Shortly afterward, Fabre was also appointed commissioner general for Canada. There was no suggestion of conflict between his two roles.

Although he served for thirty years, Fabre met with only modest success in his triple mission to encourage immigration, trade and cultural exchanges. The French had difficulty in comprehending his position as the representative of a British Dominion, and at the same time of a largely French-speaking province within it. In the area of immigration, the French birthrate was stagnant while that of Germany, the past and future enemy, was highly positive. Accordingly, the French government was opposed to able-bodied citizens being lured away; and in any case, the French themselves were not inclined to emigrate. Fabre was more successful in the commercial and financial field, but his accomplishments were modest compared to those of his counterpart in London. Even culturally, the results of his efforts were disappointing. In 1891, Premier Honoré Mercier, a strong Quebec nationalist, visited France with the primary goal of raising ten million dollars. He was entertained with impressive pomp and splendour by President Sadi Carnot and other dignitaries and given the Legion of Honour, but returned home with only four of the ten millions he had sought. In 1897, Canadian Prime Minister Wilfrid Laurier received similarly lavish treatment. When Hector Fabre died in Paris in 1912, he was succeeded by another senator, Philippe Roy. Two years later, the Quebec post was abolished, presumably for reasons of economy, but Roy remained in Paris as the Canadian representative. At the same time, the Quebec office in London was upgraded to agency general, and in 1915, an agency was also opened in Brussels. Both Premiers Lomer Gouin (1905–1920) and Alexandre Taschereau (1920–1936) made the journey to France, again with few tangible results.

Gradually, and partly under the impetus of French Canadians desiring greater independence from Great Britain, the Canadian government asserted its presence on the international scene. In 1907, the federal minister of fisheries, Ernest Lapointe, negotiated a fisheries treaty with France; in conformity with the legal situation, it was signed subsequently by the British ambassador in Paris. Canada signed the principal treaties that put a formal end to World War One, albeit as a member of the British Empire, and became a member of the League of Nations. In 1931, the Statute of Westminster, passed by the Imperial Parliament, recognized Canada's independence and transferred the treaty-making power to the Canadian government. That action bore the seeds of future difficulties since, while it recognized the authority of the federal government to conclude treaties, it restricted the authority to implement them, pending agreement with the provinces, to subjects falling under federal jurisdiction. In the words of the Judicial Committee of the Imperial Privy Council, the provinces remained "sovereign" in their areas of competence. While the Canadian government began to open diplomatic posts abroad, exchanging legations with France in January 1927, the Quebec authorities showed little interest in external relations. On the contrary, they closed the offices in Belgium in 1925 and in London in 1935. In 1936, the newly elected *Union Nationale* premier, Maurice Duplessis, had legislation passed abolishing all agencies abroad. In office under the leadership of Adélard Godbout from 1939 to 1944, the Liberals rescinded that legislation but specified that agencies should concern themselves principally with tourism, trade and industrial promotion. In 1943, one was opened in New York. When Duplessis returned to power, he let it continue but restricted its budget so severely that it could do little more than stay open.

Back in office from 1944 until his death in 1959, Premier Duplessis went to New York regularly to watch his favourite baseball team, the New York Yankees; his only other trip abroad was to visit Scotland, one of his ancestral countries, and to attend the Highland Games. He had no desire to visit France and, in the words of his biographer, "didn't especially like the French."[2] French Canadians, he liked to remark, were "improved Frenchmen." A perhaps apocryphal story of his encounter with President Vincent Auriol during the French president's visit to Canada in 1951 reflects that attitude as well as his acerbic wit.

"Are you really sure, Mr. President," he asked after they had chatted for a few minutes, "that your government hasn't been defeated by now?" Auriol retorted, "Perhaps, Mr. Premier, but I am told that the opposite problem exists here: governments do not change often enough."[3] As indicated by that rejoinder, Auriol's attitude was equally negative. He had been warned that "ninety per cent of the electorate" was "very hostile," particularly because of his socialist, and thus presumably anticlerical, political orientation. "They don't like *la belle France*," he noted in his diary.[4] The president was informed that a mass in the chapel of the University of Montreal had been scheduled for the Sunday he was to spend there. "I saw through the little plot," he recorded later, and requested that the service be held in the Cathedral and in memory of the Frenchmen and Canadians who had died for France. The change was made and everyone, out of respect, remained standing during the ceremony; thus the need to genuflect was avoided! He then went to the university where he made a speech in the traditional vein which, in his words, "was such a success that everyone was weeping and tears were flowing down the Archbishop's cheeks."

The president was also to speak at Stanislas College. Not sure of what to say, he took along a quotation from Jean Jaurès, the nineteenth century socialist leader, on the subject of courage, and read it without attribution. It having made a strong impact, he revealed the name of the author with impish delight. He was told later by one of his advisers that the real act of courage was to read Jaurès there. Auriol's encounter with the mayor of Montreal also turned out more pleasantly than he had anticipated. Camillien Houde, he had been warned, was a former Fascist. (He had been interned during the Second World War for advising French Canadians to resist conscription.) He turned out to be a lovable and very colourful character who made sure Montrealers gave their guest a warm welcome. The president ended his visit to Canada with a state visit to Ottawa, where he addressed a joint session of the House of Commons and the Senate. He noted in his diary that Canada and France were "in complete agreement" on international affairs. Domestic affairs do not appear to have been raised.

Another practice was developing of Canadian prime ministers visiting France at least once during their term of office, usually as an extension of a trip to London. Similarly, French prime ministers visited Canada on the way to or from the United States. They were largely symbolic occasions. Prime Minister Louis St. Laurent made a two-day stay in Paris in 1951, where he was received at a state dinner at the Elysée Palace by President Auriol, placed the customary wreath under the Arc de Triomphe, and exchanged the usual messages. In turn, he received Prime Ministers Pierre Mendès France and Guy Mollet. Mendès France evoked considerable interest in Ottawa because of his personal competence and his efforts to disengage France from Indochina, a step that the Canadian government heartily endorsed. He was touched by the helpful attitude of Lester B. Pearson, the Canadian secretary of state for external affairs, who urged his American counterpart, John Foster Dulles, to support the French premier's policy.

Notwithstanding Duplessis' isolationist stance, interest in France increased among French Canadians during the post-war years. Modern communications played a role in that regard; economic prosperity made it possible. The subject of some inter-governmental link between Quebec and France was raised sporadically. In late 1957, the retiring Canadian ambassador to France, Jean Désy, approached the premier and offered to look after Quebec's interests in Europe. To avoid the expense involved, he suggested that "some large industrial or financial company" might appoint him as its representative.[5] In March 1958, a close confidant of the premier, Legislative Councillor Gérald Martineau, called on Désy in Paris and they discussed, among other things, the designation of a "delegate general for Europe," a title which, unlike "agent" or "commissioner," they felt would avoid any suggestion of subordination to the federal government.[6] Carried away perhaps by his enthusiasm, Désy wrote that if the plan were carried out, he and his wife "would have the feeling of ending our career by devoting ourselves to a cause of our own, without having to struggle continually against contrary and often hostile influences on the part of our so-called anglophone brothers."[7] Unfortunately for his continuing diplomatic aspirations, another Quebec Cabinet minister, Attorney General Antoine Rivard, visited Paris during that same period to open a French-Canadian commercial exhibition at the Magasins du Louvre. Such events did more for Quebec, he advised the premier, than the appointment of a delegate general.[8]

Still, in the pre-dawn of the Quiet Revolution, the subject would not go away. In September 1958, the French consul general in Quebec City, René Chabon, suggested at a luncheon of the Comité France-Amérique du Québec that an "office" should be re-established in Paris.[9] One newspaper, *La Tribune* in Sherbrooke, took up the cause, arguing in favour of Quebec representation abroad, particularly to attract investment capital. Duplessis even received a letter from a friend at Christmas 1958 saying that the new Canadian ambassador to France, Pierre Dupuy, was "very friendly" to him and favoured Quebec representation in Paris; the premier himself would also be well received, he was assured, if he visited France.[10] In declining health and increasingly reticent to make changes, Duplessis did allow fifty thousand dollars to be included for that purpose in the 1959–60 estimates of the Department of Industry and Commerce, but complained—prophetically—that an office in Paris would cost a million dollars a year within five years.[11] And in March 1959, he sent six thousand dollars to Désy as a sort of consolation prize and expressed his regret that it was necessary "to adjourn until later the achievement of the ambitions which we cherish on this subject."[12] Désy had to resign himself to living out his remaining years on a federal pension.

Chapter 3

The Free French and Canada

Like the vast majority of Frenchmen, Charles de Gaulle had little knowledge of Canada and Canadians when he arrived in London in June 1940. Relatives on his mother's side of the family had emigrated to western Canada when he was young, but he had no direct contact with them. In 1937, his son Philippe won a school prize for an essay on the former French colony which reflected the popular image of a branch of the French people cut off from the homeland by historical circumstances, surviving tremendous adversity, but still attached to the mother country and maintaining the French way of life. Other Canadians were, at best, of little interest to the boy, and, at worst, a negative element. Where had he gained that perspective, he was asked later? Among other sources, he had heard his father and others discussing the subject.[1]

Probably the first Canadians that de Gaulle met on arriving in London in June 1940 were Colonel and Mme Georges Vanier. A World War One hero who had lost a leg in the Allied offensive of August 1918, Vanier had been appointed minister to France in January 1939.* Seventeen months later, on the day that the Franco-German armistice was signed, he flew to London in the British ambassador's airplane. The new foreign minister, Paul Baudouin, whom he called on before leaving, expressed surprise at his departure; with a break with Great Britain almost inevitable, he hoped that Canada might serve as a contact between the two countries. In London, Vanier was attached to the high commission pending clarification of the situation. Officially, he remained minister to France. At the same time, he and his wife, Pauline, admired General de Gaulle's heroic decision to carry on the war and were anxious to meet him, which they had not done in Paris.

* The rank of ambassador had not yet been introduced into the fledgling diplomatic service.

The opportunity arose soon after their arrival in the British capital through a dinner given by friends. Pauline Vanier was seated beside de Gaulle at table. Undaunted by his lofty demeanour, she told him with characteristic enthusiasm that she had enlisted in the Red Cross and was helping to care for wounded French soldiers who had been evacuated through Dunkirk. Impassively, he commented that he assumed she was also convincing them to join him. She couldn't do that, she replied naively, her husband was a diplomat and had to remain politically neutral. He snapped back, "I thought you were a friend of France." She burst into tears.[2] Georges Vanier comforted her later by explaining that the importance of the cause that de Gaulle had taken up outweighed any trivial incident.

In the days following his broadcast, de Gaulle received a number of telegrams from Canada expressing encouragement and offering to organize support on his behalf. However, he did not know a single person whom he could put in charge of such an operation. Nor did he know the political and other circumstances under which it would be carried out.

Canadians generally had been stunned by the collapse of France, but their subsequent reaction varied. English-Canadian opinion leaders were inclined to find hope in de Gaulle's determination to carry on the war from Britain; French Canadians, on the other hand, were reassured by Marshal Pétain's assumption of power and his vow to restore the old virtues of France, including the Catholic faith. The two viewpoints were reflected respectively in editorials in the Toronto *Globe & Mail* and the Montreal *Le Devoir* at the end of June. General de Gaulle, the former declared, had "emerged from the débâcle and humiliation of Bordeaux to proclaim anew the spirit and virility of the real France,...[and] to carry on the battle at the side of Britain in defence of freedom and civilization."[3] *Le Devoir*, for its part, told its readers that, out of the badly shaken edifice of France, the tall figure of an old patriot, that of Marshal Pétain, had appeared and assumed the superhuman task of uniting and restoring the country.[4] The notable exception to this line of thought in French Canada was *Le Jour*, a small liberal newspaper published by Jean-Charles Harvey. It threw its support behind de Gaulle and denounced Pétain as, among other things, "the senile smoke screen of Valhalla." However, Harvey's endorsement was hardly an asset; he frequently espoused unpopular causes, for instance, secular education and greater use of English, so his advocacy was more likely to stir a negative reaction.

Underlying the division of opinion over the French leadership was a serious domestic issue, the level of Canada's contribution to the war. Most French Canadians had viewed World War One as just another European power struggle which was none of their concern; on the other hand, the Canadian government, dominated by English Canadians, had committed the Dominion completely to the Allied cause. The result was one of the most serious crises in Canadian history. When World War Two erupted, Prime Minister William Lyon Mackenzie King, who had opposed conscription in 1917, and his Quebec lieutenant, Justice Minister Ernest Lapointe, realized that they had to do their utmost to avoid another French-English confrontation. Mackenzie King's personal views were, if not pro-de Gaulle, then at least anti-Pétain. The new French government, he wrote in his diary, was "a Fascist group" and he accused them of "a complete sell-out" of French interests.[5] Publicly, however, he carefully refrained from any criticisms of the marshal or of recent events in France. Lapointe, for his part, felt closer to Pétain, whom he had met and admired, and he was still more sensitive to French-Canadian opinion.

For both men, the worst possible scenario was for Canada to be allied with the British Empire in a war in which France was on the other side. That became a real possibility in early July 1940 when France broke off diplomatic relations with Great Britain following the British attempt to destroy the French fleet at Mers-el-Kébir on the North African coast. Accordingly, Mackenzie King welcomed the messages arriving from Vichy, the new seat of the Pétain government in unoccupied France, urging that relations between the two countries be maintained. He also kept in close touch with the French minister to Canada, René Ristelhueber, to monitor the situation. The first test of this Canadian balancing act came as early as June 19 when a French naval vessel, the *Emile Bertin*, arrived in Halifax with three hundred million dollars worth of gold that the Bank of France had sent for safekeeping in the Bank of Canada. The Pétain government ordered the ship to proceed to Martinique. Consulted by Canada, the British government, recognizing that it would be a tidy sum to help finance the war, and possibly de Gaulle's forces, asked that it be prevented from leaving for the moment at least. Mackenzie King intervened personally to allow it to sail. Called on to make a statement on the Mers-el-Kébir battle, he defended the British attack as a tragic necessity, but also praised the French admiral and sailors for their courage in resisting it. In no country, he declared, had "the calamity of France received more understanding sympathy than in Canada."[6]

That was the situation when, in mid-July, de Gaulle made his first request of Canada. He asked it to complete the training of 150 student pilots who had escaped from France and whom he saw as the nucleus of the future *Forces Aériennes Libres Françaises*. With the Battle of Britain underway, and airports, aircraft and instructors at a premium, they were merely marking time. In addition, they knew little or no English; de Gaulle assumed that, in Canada, they would be trained in

French. The Canadian response was hardly encouraging. The Commonwealth Air Training Plan, essentially a British operation, was just beginning and Canada itself had few training facilities functioning in English, let alone in French. In its initial response, Ottawa suggested, in effect, that de Gaulle address his request to the British government. Arrangements were eventually made to train French pilots in Canada, but by then the situation was no longer as urgent.

Casting about for a link with Canada, de Gaulle discovered that a possible intermediary existed in his own London headquarters. Elisabeth de Miribel, a dynamic and resourceful young Frenchwoman, was working at the French economic mission in London when he arrived. She immediately offered her services to him and was put to work typing the various drafts of his famous radio address of June 18. Anxious to make better use of her considerable talent and training, she volunteered for the Canadian assignment. She had relatives in Quebec, she pointed out to him, and she had met Pauline Vanier at the hospital where they were both working as Red Cross volunteers. The Vaniers had offered her a wide range of contacts, extending into the highest levels of the Canadian government. De Gaulle gave her the assignment and she sailed at the end of July.

On August 1, the Free French leader made his first broadcast to Canada.[7] It was addressed specifically to the "French Canadians" whom he described as "a branch of the old French trunk that has become a magnificent tree." The soul of France was reaching out to them, he said, because it recognized "their role and importance within the British Empire" which was defending almost alone the cause of those who wished to be liberated. Canada was indispensable as "the link between the old and the new worlds" and freedom could not triumph without the help of the American continent. The text, and particularly the implicit assumption of French-Canadian sympathy, confirmed that de Gaulle was venturing into unfamiliar terrain. Lapointe described the broadcast as a blunder and expressed satisfaction that the Quebec press paid little attention to it. "Nothing could be more dangerous," he told his Cabinet colleagues later, "than to start a controversy in Quebec as between Pétain and de Gaulle."[8]

One of the likely subjects of such a controversy was the degree of recognition to be accorded by Canada to the Free French and to the Vichy régime. With regard to the former, the situation was relatively simple, at least for the moment. The United Kingdom had recognized de Gaulle as "leader of all Free Frenchmen, wherever they may be, who rally to him in support of [the] Allied cause."[9] Those words did not mean, it explained to the Canadian government, that he had been recognized as "head or organizer of an alternative government."[10] That would depend on the support he received from Frenchmen themselves.

With regard to Vichy, the situation was more complex. In mid-July, the Pétain régime sent a message to Ottawa, urging that Vanier return to France and resume his diplomatic functions as soon as possible. Consulted by the Canadians, the British agreed and the Vaniers began preparations to move to Vichy. Once again, Mackenzie King was circumspect, this time out of concern for the English-Canadian reaction. In the end, the matter was resolved when the minister of defence asked that Vanier be brought back to Canada as district commander of the Quebec Military District, but essentially to encourage voluntary enlistment of French Canadians. The prime minister agreed, but to protect his other flank, decided that Vanier should retain his title of minister to France and only be recalled "for consultation."[11] To sever the link to Vichy at the moment, he told the British, would be "disastrous" for Canada. Pierre Dupuy, the former first secretary in Paris, became acting chargé d'affaires to France but remained in London.

Elisabeth de Miribel arrived in Quebec City in early August and spent the next few weeks assessing the situation in various parts of the province. Her findings came as a severe shock to her. Most of the people she met, including her relatives, were ardent Pétainists. They did not like England, she reported to London, and distrusted an anticlerical France.[12] While they "esteemed and venerated" Marshal Pétain, and hoped that he would succeed in wiping out the last vestiges of the French Revolution, they reproached de Gaulle with being a tool of the English. Some even described the Free French as "mercenaries of England." The French consul in Quebec City encouraged such attitudes, for instance, by referring to the Free French as "judeo-communist Gaullists." Montreal was the most hostile area of all.

The young woman was almost overwhelmed by the task that she had undertaken, but her reporting officer in London, Geoffroy de Courcel (the aide-de-camp who had accompanied de Gaulle to London), urged her to persevere. Public opinion would change, she was assured, when the situation became clearer. She found a room in Montreal, a part-time job as a translator at McGill University to meet her basic material needs, and set out determinedly to develop the contacts that the Vaniers had given her. She was soon to have a pleasant surprise: the Vaniers arrived and became, in her words, her "adopted parents." De Gaulle received another first-hand assessment of the situation in Canada. Through a supporter in New York, he arranged for a French professor, Meyer May, to visit Quebec and advise him on how to approach its population. The French Canadians had achieved a real "*tour de force*" in conserving their culture, May reported after his trip, but the result was a certain "aggressiveness" and an egocentrism that led them to view history from their particular viewpoint. That made it difficult for them to understand the larger international issues.[13] They also subordinated a part of their judgment to what they believed to be in keeping with the interests of the Catholic Church. As a result, they considered the war to be "England's War" and liked Marshal Pétain because they thought he represented old France and was both Catholic and anti-British. The Canadian government was obliged to handle them with great care, and for that reason, it was not prepared to take the risks involved in accepting the extension of the Gaullist movement into Canada. Any attempt to recruit French Canadians or raise funds would also be unwelcome. Still, the situation was not hopeless. A number of Frenchmen living there were well disposed, and Mademoiselle de Miribel was demonstrating that it was indeed possible to influence the thinking of French Canadians. The best strategy was to form a non-political organization emphasizing the French culture and also their common interests with English Canadians. That approach would assist the Canadian government in its difficult task; after all, its policies were in the best interests of the *Forces Françaises de Libération.*

A further problem for de Gaulle was the choice of an official representative in Canada with sufficient prestige to lead such an organization. As de Miribel reported, the French community was divided not only between Gaullists and Pétainists, but the Gaullists were divided among themselves. Small groups were appearing as far afield as western Canada, but were usually built around a few individuals, and not coordinated with one another. Acting on what scanty advice was available, he finally settled on Dr. Henri Vignal of Montreal, who, while allegedly a difficult person, seemed to have the necessary qualities of leadership and integrity. It turned out to be a poor choice; bickering and vying for position among the FFL supporters continued. Elisabeth de Miribel recommended that a special emissary of General de Gaulle be sent from London to resolve the situation and also to follow up on the contacts she had been making.

The Canadian government continued its balancing act during the last months of 1940. It resisted strong pressures from the British to turn over to them two further consignments of gold from the Bank of France that had already reached the Bank of Canada before France collapsed. Churchill intervened personally to argue that Britain's reserves were becoming dangerously low. Mackenzie King asked that a check be made to see what its holdings were in the United States. In the end, the gold remained in Canadian hands until the end of the war. The prime minister was equally prudent with regard to the Dakar expedition. Canada was not consulted on the plan to take the West African colonial capital and to establish de Gaulle there, but the British Admiralty sent a message a few days beforehand, warning that, as a result of impending operations, Vichy might declare war. Mackenzie King sent an urgent telegram to London, warning of the seriousness of such a break; he also asked to be advised in advance of any operations that could possibly have such an outcome and to provide justification for them. That cry of alarm did produce a response from Churchill, which reached Ottawa the day before the operation was to take place and outlined the plan. Afterward, the Canadian prime minister was pleased that Canada had been ignored in the whole matter.[14] "Apparently," he remarked to his colleagues, "too much credence had been given to reports of General de Gaulle.... The status accorded his Free French Movement had been greater than circumstances had warranted."[15]

On another matter, the Canadian government was more cooperative. In mid-October 1940, a Frenchman named Louis Rougier appeared in London, travelling with a diplomatic visa issued by the Vichy régime and, he stated, with the knowledge and assent of Pétain and Baudouin. His message: while there were still defeatists in Vichy, many people there had been profoundly impressed by the British resistance to the Germans, and some had come to believe that a British victory was the only hope for France.[16] General Weygand belonged to the latter group and had gone to North Africa to organize the colonial army "against aggression from any quarter." Rougier intimated that these forces might soon swing to the Allied side. However, for that to happen the Free French had to abstain from attacking them for at least six months.* The message intrigued Churchill and the few other individuals who were privy to it. Whether by chance or because he was one of that select group, the Canadian high commissioner in London, Vincent Massey, suggested to the British secretary of state, Lord Halifax, that Dupuy, as chargé d'affaires, might be a useful communication channel with Vichy. The British government picked up the suggestion and requested that he visit Vichy discreetly on some plausible grounds. Mackenzie King was quite willing to be helpful to the British, but concerned about any possible publicity. In the end, he gave the plan his blessing.

Dupuy arrived in Vichy on November 22, 1940, via Spain and Portugal. Four weeks earlier, Pétain had met Hitler in Montoire and agreed, it was learned later, that the Axis powers and France had "a common interest in bringing about the defeat of England with the least possible delay."[17] Furthermore, the marshal committed his government to supporting "within the bounds of possibility, the means taken to this end by the Axis powers." Three days later, he replaced Baudouin as foreign minister by Pierre Laval, probably the most pro-

* Rougier had other conditions which need not concern us here—author.

German of the Vichy politicians. He in turn was removed a few days later, because of disagreements with other ministers, and was replaced by Admiral Darlan. Pierre Dupuy spent ten days in the French capital, trying to make sense of the often contradictory information circulating there. On his return to London, he reported immediately to Prime Minister Churchill, then prepared a summary for his own government. He had been received by Pétain, Admiral Darlan, the powerful commander of naval forces, and an impressive number of other officials, it stated. In general, his findings were optimistic. The marshal was "still alert and hoping for a British victory."[18] (Curiously, the Canadian minister of defence, J. L. Ralston, who attended the meeting with Churchill, recorded that Dupuy had found Pétain tired and that he had almost fallen asleep three times.)[19] However, he felt that "the present atmosphere of tension between France and Britain should be maintained as [a] smoke screen" to possible cooperation between France and the Commonwealth. The Vichy government was organizing the defence of the Colonies and would "apply for our support in material and men at a later stage." There was no danger of the French fleet's falling into German or Italian hands, since many ships were out of reach in North Africa and others could leave Toulon on short notice or be scuttled. Nor would the fleet ever be used to try to reconquer the colonies now in Free French hands. At the same time, de Gaulle's efforts would be better deployed in fighting the Italians in North Africa than in trying to occupy more colonies. Dupuy saw the expulsion of Laval from the Cabinet after such a short interim as proof of the government's readiness to resist "as far as possible" any German interference in its policies.

The British prime minister was delighted with the results of the mission and Dupuy's role as what he termed "my little window on the Allier [river]." The only element he objected to was the suggestion of the Vichy régime that de Gaulle should use his resources against the Italians rather than in extending his control over the French empire. He had no intention, Churchill stated, of manacling his friends and making enemies of them in the hope that his enemies would one day become his friends.[20] He sent a telegram to Mackenzie King, expressing his appreciation for Dupuy's "magnificent work" and for granting him access to the "Canadian channel." Mackenzie King, too, was gratified at the success of the mission, but his pleasure was dampened considerably when he read the essentials of the report in the Toronto *Star* even before he received his own copy. He would have been even more upset if the press had gotten hold of a further report from Dupuy, addressed to him personally.[21] Before leaving London, the chargé d'affaires recounted, he had been very suspicious of Vichy, but his opinion had "changed altogether" when he saw what the people there

were doing to protect what remained of "their country and people."
Pétain himself had treated him "like a son." There was no doubt that
they were doing their best from every point of view, playing for time
and strengthening their two means of resistance, the fleet and the
colonies. In the circumstances, it was imperative not to give the
Germans any pretext to intervene and upset the strategy. On the
matter of the press leak, Dupuy identified two possible culprits: the
Foreign Office, which had circulated a report of his conversation with
the British ambassador in Madrid on his return journey, and the Free
French, which circulated a note in their headquarters on his conversation with Lord Halifax. If he ever had any secret information he wished
to have distributed, Dupuy commented, he would only have to whisper
it in General de Gaulle's entourage. In fact, de Gaulle, who had not
been informed of the mission, had learned of it through sources in
Madrid and, always quick to take offense, had seen it as Canadian
complicity in a British double game.

Above such minor annoyances, Winston Churchill was intrigued by
the prospects of a joint British-Vichy French operation to keep
Morocco, Algiers and Tunisia out of German hands. Through contacts
established by Dupuy in Vichy, he sent a message to Pétain, offering to
send "a strong and well equipped expeditionary force" to the area for
that purpose.[22] The proposal was conditional, he made clear, on the
French government's either deciding to move to North Africa or to
resume the war there against Italy and Germany. Churchill sent
Mackenzie King a copy of the message with a request that Dupuy be
allowed to return to Vichy via Algiers, where General Weygand was
based, in order to assess the possibilities of putting the plan into effect.
Once again, the Canadian government gave its approval.

Dupuy was unable to get permission to visit North Africa, apparently because of concerns that the Germans would hear of his movements,
so he went directly to Vichy from the Iberian peninsula. In his second
report, he told Mackenzie King that the marshal was "in perfect
health" and "more determined than ever not to go beyond armistice
terms."[23] At the same time, he was finding himself in an increasingly
difficult situation with the Germans intensifying the pressure on him,
the food situation worsening, and the power struggle within the
government continuing. Even though he distrusted him, Pétain had
appointed Darlan as foreign minister because he felt he could control
him. Dupuy also reported that the French military leaders were
becoming "more and more favourably disposed towards us."[24] As a
proof of Allied good faith, he recommended that the naval blockade of
the continent be relaxed to allow food shipments into occupied France.
Whether Dupuy discussed with the marshal Churchill's proposal for
joint action in Africa is not clear. Back in London, he became embroiled

in a disagreement over the significance of a visit to Casablanca by members of a German control commission. The Free French were warning that the port city, and Morocco in general, was in danger of falling into German hands; Dupuy reiterated assurances he had received from Pétain that no such likelihood existed. The Free French were prepared to intervene themselves, he informed Mackenzie King, but they would probably have "the same success as in Dakar."[25]

Pierre Dupuy made his third and last trip to Vichy in July and August of 1941. That time, he was not even able to see Pétain, he reported afterward, because of a "veto imposed by Admiral Darlan."[26] However, through a private contact, the marshal "reaffirmed his policy of gaining time without serious collaboration with Germany." Clearly, the old man was losing control of the government. Nonetheless, Dupuy remained optimistic about the possibilities of the Allies and Vichy joining forces against the Axis powers. Opposition to collaboration with Germany was increasing, he noted, as the Germans encountered growing difficulties in their Russian campaign and in Syria. Once again, he was critical of the Free French: even people favourable to the movement blamed de Gaulle for pitting Frenchmen against one another, and considered him and other Gaullists "too interested in politics and not enough in fighting."

Obviously relishing his peripatetic role, Dupuy planned to return to the continent again soon. However, the situation had evolved significantly since Churchill had first felt the need for a Canadian "window on the Allier." The Allies were growing steadily stronger, Britain was secure from an invasion, and the Vichy régime was falling increasingly under German control. The British prime minister was turning more towards de Gaulle as, in his own words, "much the best Frenchman now in the arena."[27] Furthermore, both in Ottawa and London, reservations and even resentment were being expressed about the usefulness of the exercise and about Dupuy's lone star attitude. "He wants to be a negotiator," complained Sir Alexander Cadogan, permanent under secretary at the Foreign Office, "I want him to be a postman."[28] One of Churchill's closest advisers dismissed Dupuy's reports as useless and even inaccurate, a reference probably to what was interpreted as a pro-Vichy bias.[29] Within the Canadian Department of External Affairs, the feeling grew that he was forgetting that his primary responsibility was to it, and not to the British. His plans for further trips were postponed and eventually the enterprise lapsed without having had any significant impact on the course of the war.

On February 18, 1941, de Gaulle called on Vincent Massey at the Canadian high commission in London to ask permission for a personal envoy to visit Canada; his mission would be to meet with supporters of the Free French and other persons, and to off-set the "propaganda pouring from Vichy."[30] He assured the Canadian diplomat that the envoy would not make "public speeches or...engage in propaganda which might be embarrassing to the Canadian authorities."[31] The person he had chosen for the assignment was Commander Georges Thierry d'Argenlieu, who had served as a naval officer in World War One and subsequently joined the Carmelite Order of which he had become the provincial, or head, in Paris. Recalled to military service in 1939, he had been captured, but escaped to Britain. With his strong personality and religious credentials, he seemed an ideal representative to deal with the French Canadians. He was to be accompanied by a young naval ensign, Alain Savary. Accepting de Gaulle's assurances of discretion, Ottawa approved the visit.

That decision was probably facilitated by an important change that had taken place within the Department of External Affairs a few weeks earlier. At the end of January, the long-time under secretary of state for external affairs, Dr. O. D. Skelton, had died of a heart attack. He had enjoyed the complete trust of the prime minister, whose natural inclination to use caution and avoid commitments he encouraged. Skelton was succeeded by Norman Robertson, a generation younger, more innovative, and, as Elisabeth de Miribel had already discovered, more favourable towards the Free French. He was supported by other young officials of similar bent, notably Hugh Keenleyside, Thomas O. Stone, who had served in the Canadian legation in Paris and who was a committed Gaullist, and, Lester B. Pearson, a senior member of the high commission staff in London. In the Prime Minister's Office, the eloquent Leonard Brockington, who was doing his wartime service as Mackenzie King's speechwriter, shared their views.

D'Argenlieu and Savary arrived in Quebec City in late March and were met not only by de Miribel but by General Vanier, who guided and counselled them throughout their stay. A Canadian diplomat, Jean Désy, was assigned to help with their schedule. They paid courtesy visits on Mackenzie King and Lapointe and made a very favourable impression on both.[32] In a significant breakthrough, the prime minister and justice minister agreed that a Canadian official should be appointed to act as liaison with the Free French and that French supporters of de Gaulle could carry Free French identity cards. D'Argenlieu and Savary met Robertson and a wide range of other officials; Stone even invited them to stay in his home. In Quebec City, they met Premier Adélard Godbout, who had defeated Maurice Duplessis in provincial elections in late 1939 and who was much more favourable to the war effort, although he had to be somewhat

circumspect in expressing his views because of public opinion and
Duplessis' constant attacks on the war effort. They also met Cardinal
Rodrigue Villeneuve who was in a similarly delicate situation: his
sympathies, too, were with the Allies but most of his clergy, particularly at the parish level, were Pétainists or, at best, neutral. D'Argenlieu
made a strong impression on the cardinal, who made the significant
gesture of attending a public reception in his honour. Gradually, the
ice was broken and, with Vanier's approval, the two emissaries
transgressed the agreement with Massey and made several speeches.
Savary, still only twenty-two years old, spoke to six hundred students
at Laval University; on the other hand, he drew only five students at
the University of Montreal. The metropolis was still, in Elisabeth de
Miribel's words, the "*point noir*" of the country. With the Quebec
nationalists still solidly behind Pétain, and the French divided and
subdivided among themselves, the reaction to the visitors was sometimes cruel and vindictive. Rumours spread that the commander was
an unfrocked priest, and that de Miribel was his mistress.[33]

On the whole, the results of d'Argenlieu's mission were highly
positive. Lapointe confided to him that the Canadian government was
shifting away from Pétain and towards de Gaulle, but had a serious
problem in dealing with public opinion in Quebec. In Quebec City, a
member of Premier Godbout's staff, Willie Chevallier, agreed to serve
on a coordinating committee to encourage support for the Free French.
More important still, the federal government agreed to the appointment of a Free French delegate in Ottawa. For that position,
d'Argenlieu chose Colonel Martin Prevel, a French citizen working in
the Department of Munitions and Supply under the *nom de guerre* of
Philippe H. Pierrené. His appointment eliminated the position held by
Dr. Vignal.

Elisabeth de Miribel was instructed to transfer her base of activities
to Ottawa and develop a Free French Information Office there under
Pierrené's authority. During d'Argenlieu's visit, she discovered a
kindred spirit in the person of Gladys Arnold, a Canadian Press
correspondent in Ottawa.[34] Gladys Arnold had gone to Europe in 1936
to learn French and had stayed on out of love for French life and
culture, paying her way by writing for Canadian newspapers. She, too,
had escaped from Paris at the last minute and had made her way to
London. There she succeeded in interviewing de Gaulle for the
Canadian Press, and filed some of the first copy to appear on him in
Canada. She also offered her services to his cause, but he told her it was
more important for her to return home and to explain what he was
trying to accomplish. She took the advice and had herself transferred
to the Parliamentary Press Gallery in Ottawa. There she met
Elisabeth de Miribel. They became fast friends, and she soon joined the

valorous Frenchwoman in establishing and operating the new Information Office.

On his return to London in May, d'Argenlieu telegraphed to de Gaulle, then in Brazzaville, "Canadian mission happily completed. Perfect relations established with the highest personalities Government Ottawa and Province and Cardinal Villeneuve. According to reliable witnesses, French Canadian opinion strongly shaken and leaning towards us."[35] His confident assessment was at the least premature. Canada continued to have formal diplomatic relations with the Vichy régime, and Norman Robertson made a public statement that Colonel Pierrené was merely "General de Gaulle's confidential and personal representative in Canada;" he had no diplomatic status and was "in no sense accredited to the Government." Furthermore, when the French minister complained that de Miribel had been given temporary desk space in the Office of Public Information by sympathetic friends, Mackenzie King ordered her to be moved out at once.[36] As for public opinion, it had not been noticeably "shaken" by the visit. On the other hand, perhaps the over-optimistic message served a valuable purpose in encouraging the man who, against terrible odds and in the face of constant difficulties and frustrations, was gradually emerging as the true voice of France.

Chapter 4
St. Pierre and Miquelon

The crisis over St. Pierre and Miquelon at the end of 1941 sorely tested
Canada's policy of avoiding a choice between Vichy France and the
Free French and almost led to an open confrontation with de Gaulle.
Two windswept islands some eighteen kilometers off the south-west
coast of Newfoundland, they were already being used by French and
other fishermen when Jacques Cartier "discovered" the area in 1535
and claimed them as part of New France. They were annexed to
Newfoundland by the Treaty of Utrecht in 1713, but restored to France
as a fishing facility by the Treaty of Paris in 1763, when Canada was
ceded to Britain. They changed hands several times through force of
arms during the next half-century before French ownership was
confirmed after the Napoleonic Wars. In the twentieth century, they
became notorious as a smugglers' haven; alcohol was brought from
France and the Caribbean islands of Martinique and Guadeloupe,
trans-shipped onto fishing boats and shipped illicitly into the lucrative
North American market. For the generally impoverished population
of several thousand, that activity brought a record era of prosperity,
and the French government resisted Canadian pressure to curb it.
When they were particularly exercised over the situation, Canadian
leaders sometimes argued that the French title to the islands was a
historical anomaly that should be corrected. However, any Canadian
move to take them over was certain to meet with the determined
opposition of Newfoundland (still not part of Canada), which invoked a
prior claim on geographical and historical grounds.

When General de Gaulle set out to create the Free French Forces and
to rally as many as possible of the colonies, St. Pierre and Miquelon
were naturally discussed. Vice-Admiral Emile-Henri Muselier, who
became commander-in-chief of the *Forces Navales Françaises Libres*,
recounted in his memoirs that, following the Mers-el-Kébir incident,
he and de Gaulle considered asking the British fleet to transport them

to some part of the French Empire, and that de Gaulle had thought of Pondicherry in the Indian Ocean or St. Pierre and Miquelon[1] (and not Canada as de Gaulle himself once stated). The vision of the Free French leader striding across the barren rocks on his daily walks while history was being played out elsewhere is highly incongruous. During the summer of 1940, messages of support arrived in London from the islands, and in particular, from members of the War Veterans' Association. De Gaulle responded in a handwritten letter to the association that was read at a public meeting, and a motion was passed in his support. On his way to Dakar in September, he sent a telegram to Muselier in London, asking him to prepare "a spontaneous change of administration" in St. Pierre and Miquelon and Guyana, as had been done in some African colonies.[2]

The British were favourable in principle to such an operation, but they recognized the more immediate interest of Canada and of the United States. Once again, the Canadian government was concerned over the impact on domestic public opinion and preferred to leave the current governor, Count Gilbert de Bournat, a strong Pétainist married to a German, in place for the moment at least. As for the Americans, they had convened a meeting of members of the Pan-American Union* in Havana in July and had a resolution passed to prevent the war from spreading to the Western hemisphere. If any non-American state attempted to replace another in "the sovereignty or control which it exercised over any territory located in the Americas," it declared, that territory would be placed under the provisional administration of one or more American states.[3] Not being a member of the Pan-American Union, Canada was not invited to the meeting and was therefore not a party to the agreement, but the terms appeared to encompass its sphere of legitimate interest. In November 1940, the United States concluded a parallel agreement with Admiral Jean Robert, French high commissioner in the West Indies.

Governor de Bournat visited Washington and accepted the *status quo* ordinance. He also had discussions in Ottawa and promised to inform the Canadian government of any unusual developments in the area. As proof of his good faith, he agreed to send the only armed vessel under his authority, the *Ville d'Ys*, to Martinique. For its part, the Canadian government undertook to maintain shipping services and to authorize the continued purchase of food and non-military supplies. The American and Canadian governments committed themselves to consulting each other on possible forms of cooperation if the *modus vivendi* was threatened. With such arrangements in place, Ottawa reacted negatively to a British suggestion made in September 1940

---

* The predecessor the present Organization of American States.

that "an internal loyal movement without external assistance" be organized to swing St. Pierre and Miquelon into the Free French camp.[4] Canada's role was to be limited to economic pressure. The Canadian government answered that it could see no reason for the change "whether in the name of General de Gaulle or otherwise."[5] At any rate, it insisted, no such step would be considered without prior consultation with the United States.

Suspicious by nature, de Gaulle saw in the policy a plan to take over the French islands, or to have the Canadians do so. His concern was not totally misplaced. On one occasion, President Roosevelt did enquire of the Canadian minister to the United States whether his government had given thought to the future of St. Pierre and Miquelon after the war.[6] They were of no interest to the United States, he remarked, but he wondered if Britain or Canada had considered acquiring them. He seemed to assume that they would not remain French. While the Canadian authorities replied non-committally that the matter could not usefully be discussed at that time, a current of Canadian opinion in favour of such a move did exist.

When he learned of the Havana agreement, de Gaulle sent a message to the American government from Brazzaville, stating that any unilateral occupation of Martinique, Guadeloupe, Guyana or St. Pierre and Miquelon would cause all Frenchmen "a profound affliction," particularly in such a moment of "distress and humiliation."[7] He now had sufficient ground, naval and air power, he declared, to ensure their protection "in cooperation with the American fleet." The message went unanswered, lending credence to his misgivings. During the fall of 1940, Muselier developed his naval command, mainly composed of half a dozen corvettes transferred from the Royal Navy, and in November he submitted a plan to the British Admiralty to take St. Pierre and Miquelon in the name of Free France. The British were still sympathetic, but counselled patience.

The matter remained dormant throughout the winter, but was revived in the spring of 1941 as the Battle of the Atlantic intensified and Allied convoys were attacked by submarines just a few hundred miles off St. John's. The Canadian and American press, the Newfoundland authorities, and the St. Pierrais living in Canada began agitating for some action against the Pétainist administration. Rumours spread that Canada was about to intervene; they were taken seriously enough for the American minister to Canada to remind Robertson that the two governments had agreed to consult before making any move to change the *status quo*. He was assured that there would be no unilateral action.

In late May, the Canadian government sent an RCMP officer to St. Pierre, ostensibly to deal with the smuggling problem, but in reality to check on the whole situation there. In addition to reporting that the population was overwhelmingly Gaullist, he brought back the alarming information that a new and powerful shortwave station was in constant communication with Bordeaux and Fort-de-France, capital of Martinique. That meant that it had the capacity to transmit information such as weather conditions and Allied ship movements to the enemy, including to submarines operating in the area. The news confirmed the feeling among Canadian military leaders that the time had come to act. At the end of June, the minister of defence for naval services reported to the prime minister that there existed a real danger of the islands being used "as a refuelling, victualling and rest base for submarines or aircraft, and as a centre for the collection and transmission of enemy intelligence."[8] Accordingly, plans had been prepared, in the eventuality of a break with the Vichy government, for "the immediate occupation of these islands, if necessary by force." "Fully detailed operational plans" were being worked out by the three armed services. Such action would be of vital importance for two reasons: the actual threat arising from enemy use of the islands; and "the clear indication" that if the Canadian government failed to act quickly and vigorously, the United States government was "almost certain to do so." Even the prime minister was not told that the Canadian army was launching Operation "Q", the training of an élite corps of some two hundred soldiers, to seize the islands.[9]

Across the Atlantic, de Gaulle followed the public debate with growing concern. In a further message to Washington, he referred to statements by prominent Americans about "preventive occupation" of St. Pierre and Miquelon and other French possessions, and reiterated his strong "anxiety" to keep them within the Empire.[10] He suggested the establishment of provisional (Free French) régimes which would serve the dual purpose of protecting them from German aggression and preserving French sovereignty. Admiral Muselier, for his part, intensified his lobbying of the British Admiralty, who gave him his operational orders, for authorization to proceed. His fleet of six corvettes had been assigned to convoy escort duty in the Atlantic, and three were to be based in Canadian or Newfoundland ports; when they arrived there, he suggested, one of them should simply put in at St. Pierre and rally the islands.[11]

Once again, the British were sympathetic, and checked with the Canadians and Americans. By that time, the view was gaining credence in Ottawa that a Free French action would best solve the problem; at the same time, it was felt to be vitally important that the United States should be in agreement. Accordingly, the Department of External Affairs, too, sounded out Washington. The reaction there was negative. The arrangements that had been made with Admiral Robert had been fully respected, Under Secretary of State Sumner Welles responded, and it would be unfortunate if the matter were re-opened, as it would even if Canada decided to take over the islands.[12] If the Canadians were primarily concerned about the radio transmitter, an *ad hoc* arrangement might be made to dismantle it without stirring up broader questions.

Eager to carry out the operation, the Canadian military leaders made a formal recommendation to Cabinet to that effect, but the War Committee rejected it on the grounds that such an action might be used as a pretext by the Germans to take parallel action in North Africa.[13] In order to monitor the situation, it was decided, instead, to station a Canadian official in St. Pierre, and in September, a young diplomat, Christopher Eberts, took up his duties as acting consul. (The United States already had a consul there.) He reported, in early October, that the man in charge of the radio-telegraph facilities was "quite definitely pro-Vichy and...anti-British," and that he was attempting to build a still more powerful sending and receiving set, using imported American equipment.[14] He would be "a willing tool" in using it to the detriment of the Allied war effort. This disquieting information was followed shortly by an equally alarming message from the British government.[15] Four transatlantic cables ran through St. Pierre and there was evidence that one was being tapped and information on convoy movements was being passed to Vichy. Fishing vessels operating out of the islands were also suspected of reporting on vessels leaving Halifax. In the circumstances, the British chiefs of staff considered "the removal of Vichy influence" to be "very desirable, preferably by an operation by Free French Forces, but if necessary by the Canadian government." Canadian concurrence was requested for a Free French operation, and, if granted, the matter would be taken up with the United States.

By the time the British proposal reached Ottawa, officials there were developing their own plan. It called for a team of four Canadian wireless operators to be sent to the islands to check all outward bound messages and to prevent the use of cyphers that the Allies could not read.[16] The radio equipment of fishing boats would also be inspected to ensure that it was not capable of long distance transmission. The proposal was designed to meet both the Canadian desire for a meaningful role in the area and the American requirement that the political *status quo* be maintained. Not that there was any serious opposition to a Free French take over; on the contrary, most people in Ottawa were in favour of it, but, to accommodate the Americans, they preferred a popular uprising or some other way of bringing it about to a military operation.

The principal hold-out was the prime minister; *de facto* seizure of a

Vichy possession by Canada, he warned, was "all that was needed to give Darlan an excuse to turn over the [French] fleet to Germany."[17] He finally agreed that the plan be submitted to London and Washington for comment. Once again, he proved adroit at getting his way. The American Department of State responded that even that modest step was too "drastic" until other means such as economic pressures had been tried to ensure the compliance of the administrator of the islands with the neutrality proviso. After all, the Canadians were reminded, he did depend very largely on French funds held in Canada and the United States. The British, on the other hand, rejected the plan as inadequate. Replying on December 15, a week after the Japanese attack on Pearl Harbour, Churchill argued that the islands would remain a threat as long as they were in Vichy hands and that the Free French should be authorized to take them over.[18] The matter had reached an impasse, and Mackenzie King had won his case that nothing should be done.

The Canadian and American strategists reckoned without one man: General de Gaulle. Two months earlier, he had decided that the moment for action had arrived. During the previous summer, he had been thwarted by the British in an attempt to gain control of the French protectorates of Lebanon and Syria. The Vichy forces there had been defeated by Free French and British units, but, in the end, the Vichy authorities had been allowed to repatriate four thousand soldiers instead of their being given an opportunity to join the Free French; and the British had taken control of the area. Simultaneously, the British were negotiating with the Vichy governor in Djibouti with a view to at least neutralizing that colony. De Gaulle denounced them publicly for making deals with the Pétain régime, and he suggested that they were playing the same game in the Western hemisphere in complicity with the Americans.[19] The outburst had led to one of the stormiest confrontations between him and Churchill in a relationship that was marked by many such incidents. From de Gaulle's viewpoint, the incident may have had a positive fall out: perhaps anxious to disprove the charge of collusion with Vichy, the British prime minister supported him as strongly as he could with regard to St. Pierre and Miquelon.

On October 13, de Gaulle wrote to Anthony Eden to sound him out on a possible expedition to rally the islands. The British foreign minister was a strong supporter of the Free French, but he felt obliged to point out that "the express agreement" of Canada and the United States would be required.[20] The Free French leader was not prepared to invite an almost certain rebuff. He issued instructions to Muselier in early November to inspect the three corvettes and the only submarine under his command, the *Surcouf* (the world's largest submarine at the time), which were on the other side of the Atlantic. He also gave him a secret order: to detour to St. Pierre and Miquelon, if the circumstances were right, and take them over in the name of Free France. "I provoked it [the crisis that ensued] to stir things up," he wrote later, "as one throws a stone into a pond."[21]

Full of enthusiasm, Muselier sailed from Scotland on November 24. With him aboard the corvette were Commander Héron de Villefosse as his chief of staff and Lieutenant Alain Savary, who had earlier accompanied d'Argenlieu to Canada. Among their provisions was a supply of rifles and machine guns that they spirited aboard past the British security inspectors. They were between Iceland and St. John's, Newfoundland, fighting heavy seas, when they learned that the Japanese had attacked Pearl Harbour. The admiral reacted, "For St. Pierre, that changes everything."[22] With the Americans' entry into the war, he reasoned, their diplomatic relations with Vichy would become untenable and the Free French would be recognized as their true allies. In the circumstances, it was not advisable to indulge in covert operations against their will. Arriving in St. John's on December 9, where the Free French corvettes were waiting, Muselier met with the governor and members of the Cabinet and told them of his plan. They expressed their approval. The Canadian naval commander for the area also seemed favourable but told him he needed the proper authority to proceed. The ships he was to inspect were in Halifax. Before leaving for the Canadian port, Muselier sent a telegram to de Gaulle, informing him that he was ready to carry out the operation around December 14, but in view of the "new general situation," he was first going to Ottawa to obtain the agreement of the Canadian and American authorities. He asked the general to do the same with the British and to communicate the result to him.[23]

De Gaulle's reaction to the attack on Pearl Harbour had been characteristically peremptory, "Well, then, this war is over."[24] Then he added more somberly, "From now on, the British will do nothing without Roosevelt's agreement." When Muselier's telegram arrived, de Gaulle realized that the admiral had placed the secret mission in jeopardy by deciding to consult the Americans. Nothing had happened to justify his decision not to proceed, he declared angrily. Certainly American agreement was desirable, but it was not essential; the operation was an internal French affair.[25] Still, since the plan was being revealed, he concluded reluctantly that the British should be brought into the picture, if only to avoid recriminations later. He sent a letter to Churchill informing him that the admiral was at sea between St. John's and Halifax and planned to "proceed immediately to rally St. Pierre and Miquelon;" he himself completely approved and he wanted to know at once if Her Majesty's government had any objection to the "little helping hand." Consulted, the Foreign Office reacted positively. In fact, far from objecting to the operation, it preferred that outcome. The chiefs of staff were even more enthusiastic: they were strongly in favour of Admiral Muselier's being authorized to rally St. Pierre and Miquelon to Free France "without saying anything about it until it had been done."[26]

Based on that advice, Churchill responded to de Gaulle on December 15—the same day that he told Mackenzie King that it was not enough merely to supervise the radio station—indicating agreement but asking the Free French leader to delay issuing a formal order for thirty-six hours to give him time to ascertain whether the action would be considered in any way embarrassing by the United States government.[27] In his message to Washington, the British prime minister put the case as strongly as possible, emphasizing the threat to the convoys and stating that only outright seizure of the islands would offer complete security.[28] The Free French had made preparations to do that, he informed the Americans, and Admiral Muselier was already on the western side of the Atlantic. Free French headquarters were being informed that the British saw no difficulty in their going ahead.

On this occasion at least, de Gaulle's assessment of the American reaction proved more accurate. On December 13, Roosevelt had sent a message to Pétain, assuring him that even though the United States was now at war with Germany and Japan, it intended to abide by the Havana Convention guaranteeing the *status quo* in the Western hemisphere. An American admiral was being despatched to Martinique to confirm the arrangements with Admiral Robert. In the circumstances, London was advised that the president was "strongly opposed to the suggested action."[29] At the same time, Roosevelt himself told Sumner Welles that he "favoured Canadian action," and that information was relayed to Ottawa. The American reply reached London on December 17, and Churchill recognized immediately that Anglo-American unity was more important than the fate of the islands. The text was communicated to the Free French commissioner for foreign affairs, Maurice Dejean, with the advice that it was "vital that any order that might have been given for the operation should be cancelled."[30] The matter was referred to General de Gaulle, and the British were assured, according to a Foreign Office memorandum, that "no orders would be issued for this operation."[31]

In the meantime, Muselier arrived in Halifax with his little fleet, inspected the submarine *Surcouf* which was in dock there, and, together with de Villefosse and Savary, took the train to Ottawa. Before leaving, the admiral received a "secret and personal" telegram from de Gaulle, dated December 13, in response to his announcement of the change in plans.[32] He had requested British agreement to the operation, de Gaulle told him, but was not counting on a positive response since they considered the United States and Canada to be "the principal interested parties." At any rate, time was too short for negotiations. As he had said before the admiral's departure, he left to him the matter of "the result to be obtained if possible by your own means," and would "cover any initiative" he considered feasible.

Confident that he had *carte blanche* to deal with the matter, Muselier and his travelling companions reached Ottawa on December 15. Having informed the Canadian government through Colonel Pierrené of their arrival, they were met in Montreal by the senior Quebec minister, P.J.A. Cardin (Ernest Lapointe having died in late November), who accompanied them to the capital. There they met immediately with the minister of national defence for naval services, Angus Macdonald, and the chief of the naval staff. The naval leaders were clearly favourable to the Free French seizure of the islands; German submarines had been very active in the waters around Newfoundland in recent weeks and one had been sighted less than a hundred miles from St. Pierre and Miquelon. The chief of the naval staff even agreed to send a telegram to the British Admiralty requesting permission for Muselier to keep the three corvettes and the submarine for a few more days in order to carry out the operation. T.O. Stone, who took them to meet Norman Robertson, was openly enthusiastic, and even Robertson himself seemed—and indeed was— well disposed. The Canadians had been considering an operation themselves, Muselier quoted the under secretary later as saying, but had abandoned the plan, and, in any event, he himself preferred the Free French one. But—the eternal qualification—the agreement of the United States would have to be obtained.

The admiral's interpretation of the Canadian government's position was unduly optimistic. Some elements, particularly within the army, still favoured a Canadian action, even the modest one that the United States had approved. More important, the prime minister himself was still unconvinced of the advisability of either option and found Stone's eagerness, and even Robertson's carefully reasoned support of the Free French, worrisome. Brimming with confidence, Muselier obtained an immediate appointment with the American minister, Pierrepont Moffat, and rushed over to convince him. In addition to arguing the case for rallying St. Pierre and Miquelon, he insisted on the necessity for the Free French to participate in any operation concerning Martinique and Guadeloupe, and offered, as a personal friend of Admiral Robert, to go there as a mediator. On a third matter, the recent American requisition of the French luxury liner, *Le Normandie*, and several merchant ships, Muselier proposed that de Villefosse go to Washington immediately to work out a mutually satisfactory arrangement. Moffat listened with apparent personal sympathy and explained that he would have to ask Washington for instructions.[33] Once again, the admiral left the meeting under the impression that everything was working out satisfactorily. Accordingly, he was shocked when the American minister informed him the next day that the United States considered that, at the moment, the proposed Free French action was "inopportune."[34] It still preferred the plan for Canadian control of the communications system. As for Martinique and Guadeloupe, no change was envisaged; and the matter of the requisitioned ships would be settled with the Free French delegation in Washington.

Indignant, Muselier responded forcefully to Moffat, first orally and then in writing.[35] The desire of Free France had always been to do nothing that would hamper the policy of the United States government, he stated, and that was now more true than ever. It was for that reason that he had insisted on obtaining its agreement before acting. That having been said, he had to draw attention to the consequences of the position adopted in Washington. A population of five thousand would remain oppressed and foreign controls would be placed on a French territory. That would be seen by Frenchmen as a breach of sovereignty and would be exploited by pro-Nazi propagandists to argue that the Allies' objective was to grab hold of French colonies. It could also serve as a pretext for similar actions by Germany. The conclusion of the admiral's letter was somewhat ambiguous; he did not acquiesce in the American decision, but he indicated that he would not proceed with the operation. In his telegram to de Gaulle on December 17, he stated, "I consider the operation to be only deferred and am keeping available the four ships."[36]

Within the Canadian government, opinions remained divided. At a meeting of the Cabinet War Committee on December 17, the minister of national defence for naval services proposed that the Free French action be approved. Other ministers were prepared to proceed with the U.S.-supported Canadian plan. In the end, the committee came to the conclusion that, if any action was necessary, it "should be taken by Canada."[37] Mackenzie King was still unhappy with the prospect of Canadian involvement without the agreement of Britain and the United States, and, two days later, a message from London gave him the opportunity to change that decision: he was told that de Gaulle had agreed not to proceed "now" with the Free French operation.[38] The British also had serious reservations about the Canadian plan, and recommended that nothing at all be done "for the time being." That position suited the Canadian prime minister perfectly; he had it endorsed by the War Committee.[39]

Even before he learned of the American position, de Gaulle was becoming increasingly upset over the way matters were going. He had

had serious clashes with Muselier in the past over challenges to his authority and saw the admiral's decision to go to Ottawa as another sign of insubordination. His concern grew when a journalist reported that he was going on to Washington. On December 16, de Gaulle sent him a blunt telegram, telling him that such a trip was "completely contrary" to his intentions and those of the French National Committee,* and asking him to return to London as soon as his "mission of inspecting the North Atlantic Naval Forces" was completed.[40] Muselier decided to follow instructions and had requested three seats on a military aircraft from St. John's when another telegram from de Gaulle arrived on December 18: "Our negotiations have shown that we can do nothing concerning St. Pierre and Miquelon if we wait for the permission of those who claim to have an interest. It was foreseeable. Solution is an action on our own initiative. I repeat that I am covering you completely in that matter."[41] He realized that some reaction in Washington was "inevitable," de Gaulle wrote later, but calculated that, at the worst, it would be confined to "a little ill humour in the office of the State Department."[42]

The following day, the British Foreign Office told de Gaulle that Canadian forces, acting with American consent, would soon land in the islands and neutralize the transmitter.[43] De Gaulle was enraged: he saw his restraint in agreeing to postpone Muselier's action as being repaid with contempt, and a flagrant violation of French sovereignty. He was being forbidden to occupy French territory, he wrote later, yet foreigners were being encouraged to do so. In the circumstances, "there could no longer be any hesitation."[44] On December 18, he sent new instructions to the admiral, "We have, as you asked, consulted the British and American governments. We know, from a source beyond doubt, that the Canadians intend to carry out the destruction of the St. Pierre radio station themselves. In these conditions, I order you to proceed to rally St. Pierre and Miquelon by your own means and without saying anything to the foreigners. I take full responsibility for this operation, which has become indispensable in order to keep these French possessions for France."[45]

Muselier and his travelling companions were on the point of leaving Ottawa for Montreal on their return journey when they received the order. Their first reaction was one of consternation. They had received another cable from a member of the Free French naval staff in London shortly before, informing them that the American president "formally opposed" the operation.[46] Moreover, they had received no intimation that the Canadians were preparing any such action. Finally, they had given their assurances that they wished to do nothing to embarrass the

* The official governing body of the Free French in London.

United States. On the other hand, as a veteran officer, he knew he could not disobey a formal order. Putting aside his serious misgivings, he resolved to go ahead with the operation, but to disassociate himself on his return to London from any more of the general's decisions by resigning as a member of the National Committee.[47]

The decision once taken, Muselier acted with his usual vigour and determination. He left for Montreal on schedule, picked up two Gaullist St. Pierrais residing there to serve as guides, and took the train to Halifax. From there he sent a telegram to de Gaulle, informing him that his order would be carried out as soon as possible, but was being delayed by a violent winter storm.[48] He also filed with the senior Canadian naval officer a bogus order to the commanders of the other corvettes to report for naval exercises to be carried out between the mainland and Newfoundland. In view of the submarine activity in the area, he urged absolute secrecy concerning his movements. The Canadian officer concurred. Once again, the Free French reputation for leaky security almost placed the operation in jeopardy. On December 17, and again on December 23, the French minister, René Ristelhueber, called on the Department of External Affairs to express his concern about reports he had received that it was imminent. He was assured that they were without substance.[49] On the early morning of December 22, a New York *Times* correspondent, Ira Wolfert, appeared in Muselier's hotel in Halifax and announced that he had come to cover the operation. The admiral had already agreed to take along a correspondent from the pro-Gaullist Montreal newspaper *Le Jour*. After denying the plan for a while, Muselier decided that the only secure course of action was to lock the American up in one of the ships and take him along.

By the morning of December 23, the bad weather had abated sufficiently for the ice and snow to be cleared off the ships' armament and they were able to sail. For most of the day, they went through the practice manoeuvres while gradually moving northward. In the evening, the admiral issued the real orders, to head for the islands. They arrived before dawn on December 24. "Don't stand beside me," the admiral told de Villefosse as they eased up to the dock in St. Pierre, "the person who does is always killed."[50] But there was no resistance; the single policeman on duty had left his post earlier to fetch some coal and had then decided to spend the rest of the night in his own bed. Finally, someone appeared, sleepy and heavily clothed, to take the moorings; he had no idea who the strangers were. Gradually, a crowd assembled. Muselier explained what was happening. Pro-Gaullist cheers erupted, but no opposition. A detachment of ratings led by Savary went ashore, arrested the administrator, and brought him aboard the flagship. The radio station and other key buildings were occupied. The whole operation was carried out peacefully in less than half an hour. Later that morning, a cryptic message arrived in Ottawa from Eberts, "Three corvettes and one submarine under Admiral Muselier occupied Archipelago at 8 a.m. this morning without incident."[51]

Ira Wolfert got his scoop; the news spread rapidly by radio on both sides of the Atlantic to people preparing to spend their third Christmas at war. The general public reaction on the Allied side was positive; the New York *Times* commented approvingly that the operation was carried out "with a display of style and manners in the best tradition of Alexandre Dumas."[52] In official circles in London and Ottawa, there was discreet pleasure as well. Thomas Stone reflected a widespread Canadian viewpoint when he told Moffat that it was a good thing that the blister had been broken, even if in an irregular fashion.[53] The prime minister was more concerned about the consequences for the triadic London-Washington-Ottawa relationship. In his diary, he described himself as "terribly annoyed as well as distressed."[54] He sent Robertson to assure Ristelhueber that Canada had not been involved in any way and that he himself was very annoyed. His attitude towards the Free French was summed up in a brief telegram to High Commissioner Vincent Massey in London: "In view of circumstances of Free French occupation of St. Pierre today, do not send Christmas message to General de Gaulle."[55]

Mackenzie King's reaction was mild compared to that in Washington. Churchill had arrived there on December 22 for his first meeting with Roosevelt after Pearl Harbour. Mackenzie King was to join them on Boxing Day. On their agenda, as a relatively minor item, was the resolution of their differences over St. Pierre and Miquelon. While the president was not unduly concerned at the news of the occupation, Secretary of State Cordell Hull saw it as a serious violation of the American strategy. Overworked and under severe stress, he issued a terse two-sentence statement at noon on Christmas Day, declaring that "the action taken by three so-called Free French ships at St. Pierre-Miquelon was an arbitrary action contrary to the agreement of all parties concerned and certainly without the prior knowledge or consent in any sense of the United States government."[56] The latter had inquired of the Canadian government "as to the steps that that government is prepared to take to restore the status quo of these islands."

Suddenly Canada, which Mackenzie King had tried to keep out of any controversy, was being thrust into the middle of the crisis, and, even worse, being charged implicitly with collusion in causing it. In Ottawa, Pierrepont Moffat called on Robertson, and in what was described in a subsequent report as "an extremely condemnatory line," demanded that Canada reverse the situation.[57] Any course other than restoration of the Vichy administration, with Canadian supervision of the wireless facilities, he told L.B. Pearson (who had just returned to Canada as assistant under secretary of external affairs), would be "one hundred ninety degrees removed from United States policy."[58] He even made, in Pearson's words, "certain obscure observations on the unfortunate results that would ensue if Canada adopted a separate policy in this matter." Pearson was annoyed at the implication of Canadian bad faith and pointed out to the prime minister "the fallacy of this view...in no uncertain terms." The United States had made an agreement with the Vichy authorities in Martinique without the knowledge of the Canadian government "purporting to cover all the French territory in the Western hemisphere," he reminded him, and Hull had just issued a public statement "of the most damaging and embarrassing kind to Canada," and in both instances without any consultation.

The Americans were not alone in imputing some responsibility to Canada. Ristelhueber appeared in the Department of External Affairs on December 26 and reminded Hugh Keenleyside of his warning that Muselier was preparing the "*coup de main.*"[59] Robertson had assured him that the Canadian government had dissuaded the admiral from such an adventure, and he had informed Vichy accordingly. Furthermore, in insisting that the *Ville d'Ys* leave the islands, and in "acting cooperatively" with the de Bournat administration, Canada had incurred a moral obligation to maintain the *status quo*. There was also the fact that Muselier had sailed from a Canadian port. In the circumstances, Ristelhueber added, he was convinced that the Canadian government would want to "formally disapprove the *coup de force*...and take steps to ensure that the authority of the legal Government of France, which it itself recognized, was restored."[60] General de Gaulle joined in impugning Canada's role in the affair. In a letter to the British secretary of state for foreign affairs, he protested strongly against American and Canadian approval of a plan for Canadian personnel to intervene in St. Pierre and Miquelon while they rejected steps by the Free French to bring the islands over to the Allied side.[61] He declared his strong opposition to any Canadian action to take over the wireless station.

When Mackenzie King arrived in Montreal, late Christmas night, en route to Washington, Pearson was able to brief the prime minister by telephone, and he, the three Canadian defence ministers and Robertson (also en route to Washington) held an emergency strategy session. They approved a statement declaring that Canada was "in no way responsible for the Free French occupation of St. Pierre and Miquelon."[62] The government had kept in close touch with both the

United Kingdom and the United States, it continued, and had "always been ready to cooperate in carrying out an agreed policy," but had declined to commit itself to any action without such a policy. In the circumstances, and pending discussions with Churchill and Roosevelt, Canada could not "take steps requested to expel the Free French and restore the status quo in the islands." In his diary that night, the prime minister congratulated himself on his tenacious refusal to allow any action at all to be taken in the previous weeks and months.[63]

His protests aside, de Gaulle was undoubtedly the happiest of the four Allied leaders. Muselier's telegraphic report, which reached London in the afternoon of December 24, was succinct: "Rally of St. Pierre carried out in the early morning without incident and to the cheers of the population. Rally of Miquelon under way. Details follow."[64] Later in the day, he sent another message confirming the "unanimous rally" of Miquelon, the appointment of Alain Savary as Free French administrator and the organization of a plebiscite for Christmas Day.[65] He also had cordial relations, he assured the Free French leader, with the Canadian and American consuls. De Gaulle's reaction was that of a man who had regained the initiative; "Friendly congratulations," he wired back, "I ask you to keep in St. Pierre and Miquelon adequate force to clearly establish the *fait accompli* until we have been able to clarify the inevitable reactions of our various allies."[66] He had precipitated the storm; he now advanced into it with evident satisfaction. On December 26, after learning of the first reaction of the Americans, he sent a highly optimistic message to Muselier.[67] The "tempest" raised by the State Department "need not disturb" him: its annoyance stemmed from the fact that it had concluded an arrangement with Admiral Robert separate from and unacceptable to the Free French. "We threw a stone into a frog pond." "Complete satisfaction" reigned on the British side. Vichy was "enraged."

The plebiscite was held in St. Pierre immediately after Christmas Mass. The choice on the ballots, while hardly unbiased, was clear: "rally to Free France," or "collaboration with the Axis powers."[68] The results: Free France 651; collaboration 11; blanks or spoiled ballots 140; abstentions 188. The message that went out to the world was that ninety-eight per cent of the valid votes were cast in favour of Free France. A few days later, a similar result was obtained in Miquelon. In the next few days, the admiral consolidated his position. De Bournat, who was proving recalcitrant, was confined to the adminstrator's residence. A few other committed Pétainists, including the local doctor, the bishop and the chief wireless operator, were placed under surveillance. Recruits were enrolled in the Free French Forces for both overseas and local service. Revelling in his achievement, Muselier assured de Gaulle that he could be counted on to defend French sovereignty "to the hilt."[69] The general encouraged his feeling of satisfaction. "We had proof that Canada was preparing to occupy St. Pierre and Miquelon," he telegraphed on December 27. "Your action came just in time."[70]

Muselier's enthusiasm did not blind him completely to certain uncomfortable realities, and his distrust of his leader persisted. On December 26, he called on Christopher Eberts and the American consul to explain the events leading up to the rallying of the islands and to express his embarrassement vis-à-vis Canada and the United States over the way it had been carried out.[71] He had been acting in good faith, he said, when he stated in Ottawa that he did not intend to take any action without the consent of the Canadians and Americans. On receiving the order from de Gaulle to proceed, his first reaction had been to resign; however, his sense of duty to his commander-in-chief and his concern for the consequences to the Free French movement of an open split between himself and de Gaulle had led him to conclude that he must obey. Subsequently, the plebiscite demonstrated the population's commitment to Free France, and he felt he had to defend the islands against all "possible attackers." He wanted the Canadian and American authorities to be aware of that fact. As the days passed and he analyzed the radio reports from Canadian and American sources, his uneasiness grew that his action had created discord among the Allies. On December 29, he reminded de Gaulle in a telegram that he felt it preferable to obtain agreement with the British, Americans and Canadians before undertaking the operation, and he still believed that he would have succeeded in bringing it about.[72] He was also convinced that no Canadian occupation had been imminent. Still, he had carried out orders and would now defend the population to the last man.

Mackenzie King's first meeting on arriving in Washington on December 26 was with Cordell Hull. His anger having subsided, the secretary of state was apologetic about his Christmas Day statement, saying that he had been under strong pressure and had not thought about the political effects in Canada.[73] That morning, he had tried in a press conference to place the matter in better perspective and had "urged the press to soft-pedal the situation in St. Pierre." A compromise solution had already been discussed by the president and Prime Minister Churchill, Hull reported. It included Canadian or joint Canadian-United States control of the wireless station. To prepare the terrain, Churchill had sent a message to de Gaulle, telling him that his action had been helpful in eliminating a source of potential danger and in bringing about a change in the administration of the islands. Pleased at the more conciliatory attitude, Mackenzie King remarked that de Bournat could not be restored to his post as he was unreliable and had a German wife. He, himself, had always been opposed to the use of force to resolve the matter, at least without agreement among the governments concerned.

With that preliminary discussion, the two men went over to the White House for tea with Roosevelt and Churchill. Probably alluding to the expression "so-called Free French ships" that Hull had inserted in his Christmas Day press statement, the president asked where Muselier had got the corvettes and the submarine. Mackenzie King assured him that they were "his own."* Roosevelt suggested a commission of Vichy, Free French and Canadian representatives to supervise wireless transmissions, the restoration in office of the administrator, and the withdrawal of the Free French. Churchill urged a compromise settlement. He had agreed at one stage to the Free French action, he acknowledged, but had reversed his position when he found that the United States was opposed. Now he was prepared "to take de Gaulle by the scruff of the neck and tell him that he had gone too far and bring him back to his senses."† Attributing the plan to Hull, Mackenzie King proposed that de Gaulle be allowed to feel that, while he had been "precipitate," he had rendered a service in making it possible to have the radio transmissions properly supervised. The secretary of state, beginning to feel caught between his categorical position and a favourable press and public reaction to the Free French, declared that he and the Canadian prime minister were "98 per cent agreed on what should be done." They were assigned the task of working out a possible arrangement.

By the time Mackenzie King and Hull met the next morning, the latter had reverted to a harder line and was worried about the reaction in Vichy to the consensus that had seemed to be emerging in the White House. He decided to send for the French ambassador, Gaston Henry-Haye, and to outline to him a solution consisting of control, possibly by Canadian and American experts, of the wireless station, and return of authority to the Vichy régime. He still leaned towards re-imposing de Bournat, but Mackenzie King said he thought that would be impossible. At that point, the Canadian position was to send some technical experts, operating with appropriate protection, to supervise the transmissions, and to devise a face-saving formula for de Gaulle, "telling him that he had helped out in a difficult situation re transmission of wireless, but now to get out and save the situation from

* This version of the meeting is drawn from J.W. Pickersgill, *The Mackenzie Record*, vol I, 1939–1941 (Toronto: UTP (SP) 1960), 321–3. No other is available.
† The threat was reminiscent of another by Hitler who vowed that he would "wring England's neck like a chicken." Churchill had responded "some chicken, some neck."

becoming critical."[74] The vital flaw in that approach was the misappreciation it revealed of de Gaulle; any assumption that he could be induced to abandon the territory was an illusion. If the general were asked to back down too far, the Free French representative in Washington, P.A. Tixier, warned, he would resign and wreck the Free French movement.[75] Hull continued to press for a solution that would include some form of restoration of Vichy's authority. However, his position was becoming weaker. Public opinion in the United States, Britain and Canada was strongly favourable to the Free French, and he was coming under personal attack from noted newspaper columnists such as Walter Lippmann and Dorothy Thompson. On the evening of December 27, Robertson reported to Pearson that there was no longer any suggestion that "Canada should eject the Free French."[76] Nor would there be a restoration of the Vichy administration.

At that juncture, Churchill interrupted his stay in Washington to visit Ottawa. In an address to the Canadian Parliament on December 30, he surprised even Canadian officials by his forceful denunciation of the Vichy régime and his eloquent praise of the Free French.[77] He described the former as lying "prostrate at the foot of the conqueror," while other Frenchmen "would not bow their knees and...have continued to fight on the side of the Allies" under General de Gaulle. If the Canadians were pleased, de Gaulle himself was even more so. The British leader's words had "touched the whole French nation," he telegraphed. "In the depths of its misfortune, old France places its hope first of all in old England."[78] Churchill's response was both a message of encouragement and an admonition. He had pleaded the Free French case strongly in the United States, he told de Gaulle, but "your having broken away from agreement about St. Pierre and Miquelon raised a storm which might have been serious had I not been on the spot."[79] The general's activities had made matters more difficult with the United States and "prevented some favourable development from occurring." That "development" could only have been greater American acceptance of the Free French.

By the beginning of 1942, the Canadian government had fallen back to a more passive position, to wit, that the ball was now in the Department of State's court, and that Canada would go along with whatever the United States and Great Britain agreed upon. Hull continued to be caught in the cross pressures as he tried to provide minimal satisfaction to Vichy while recognizing the *fait accompli*. Churchill returned to Washington after his visit to Ottawa, and the St. Pierre and Miquelon matter continued to occupy the attention of the two Allied leaders. Both were anxious to resolve it and get on to other more important subjects. On January 1, Roosevelt told the British leader that he "thought it inadvisable to resuscitate this question."[80]

Muselier had "declined to leave St. Pierre" and the United States could not "afford an expedition to bomb him out." Finally, they agreed on a public statement.[81] The islands, it declared, were French and would remain French. They were to be "neutralized and demilitarized" and "considered out of the war." All armed forces would be withdrawn. American and Canadian observers would supervise and control the wireless stations. The current administration would be withdrawn and the islands would be administered by a "Consultative Council."

Informed of the text, the Canadian Cabinet War Committee recognized quickly that public opinion would never endorse such a solution. The new minister of justice, Louis St. Laurent, remarked that feelings had changed dramatically in Quebec. With the exception of *Le Devoir* and *Le Droit*, the French-Canadian press had welcomed the Free French action. He was not prepared to face a public meeting in that province if the Free French were compelled to leave the islands against their will.[82] Mackenzie King sent an urgent message to Roosevelt and Churchill, telling them that Canada could not support any coercion and expressing the earnest hope that it could be avoided.

It fell to Anthony Eden to try to obtain de Gaulle's acquiescence. By then, he and some other ministers had decided that British public opinion, too, would reject the plan. More important, de Gaulle had decided that he had, in fact, won. "The matter is settled," he advised Adrien Tixier, his representative in Washington, on February 12. "The best is to maintain silence. Limit yourself to saying that the National Committee ignored the agreement between Canada and the United States when it indicated that the operation would be postponed. Add that the committee was never informed that the Canadian government had renounced its plan as it is supposed to have advised Washington on December 22. Nothing more."[83] In his wartime memoirs, de Gaulle has recounted his meeting with the British foreign minister.[84] Eden "put up a show of insisting," but he stood firm. Asked what he would do if the United States sent warships to dislodge the admiral, he replied with a confident smile that he had "confidence in the democracies." In fact, the two men did make real progress. De Gaulle indicated his willingness to agree to the terms in the text if three secret conditions were accepted, effectively cancelling out the public ones: the admiral would remain, but as part of the Consultative Council, which would be under the authority of the French National Committee. The Free French marines would remain on the island.[85] And a Canadian and an "English" wireless officer would be posted on St. Pierre, but with no direct control over the wireless facilities.[86]

Churchill and Roosevelt agreed to delay further action until the British prime minister returned to London and he had the opportunity to make good his "scruff of the neck" threat. What he later described in a message to the president as "a severe conversation" took place on January 24.[87] Two versions exist of what transpired, one by de Gaulle in a telegram to Muselier,[88] the other a note in the British Foreign Office files.[89] Churchill, seconded by Eden, insisted "with the greatest force," the general recalled, that he accept the public statement worked out in Washington. Churchill charged, according to the British version, that de Gaulle "had no right to take action in these unimportant territories without consideration of the Great Alliance without which France could not be restored." The general said that the proposed arrangement was contrary to the agreement the two had made in 1940 (with regard to the Free French role in the war). The prime minister replied that the agreement had been "based on the hope, which had since proved false, that de Gaulle would be able to rally an impressive number of Frenchmen." Once the two men had unburdened themselves of their pent up grievances, Eden was able to interject that, once the communiqué was issued, the matter would be forgotten. Whether the British foreign minister said so explicitly, de Gaulle interpreted the comment to mean that Savary could then carry on as *de facto* administrator, and local Free French recruits could act as a defence force. The men who had enlisted would also be able to join the Free French Forces. In short, he interpreted Eden as saying, the concessions would be concerned with appearances, the realities would be preserved. It was a question, he told Muselier, "of saving the face of Cordell Hull and the State Department." It was now the turn of the liberator of St. Pierre and Miquelon to be inflexible. Entrenched in his precarious bastion, his patriotism thoroughly aroused, Muselier was prepared to resist any challenge. Furthermore, the telegrams he had been receiving from his temporary replacement in London fuelled his basic antipathy for de Gaulle and convinced him that he was being betrayed. He asked that any decision concerning the islands be delayed until he returned to London. De Gaulle did not wait. He ordered the admiral to organize the Consultative Council with Savary at its head and to maintain the local defence forces.[90] That accomplished, he agreed to his return to London.

The Americans were not happy with the outcome, but they had more important matters to deal with. On February 2, Cordell Hull advised the president that "further negotiations or discussions of the matter be postponed for the period of the war."[91] Then he left the capital for an extended rest in Florida. The Vichy government, falling increasingly under German domination, accepted the *fait accompli* as well. The Canadian government was relieved. There were some things one could do no good by injecting oneself into, Mackenzie King told Ristelhueber when the French minister raised the subject, and this was one.[92] Once the Savary adminstration was installed, the Canadian and American consuls arranged for wireless operators to be attached to their respective offices, with a mandate to "consult" with the St. Pierrais on the operation of the stations. Harmonious working relations were established. However, de Gaulle remained distrustful. In May 1942, he warned Savary that the Americans still had designs on the French territories in the Western hemisphere and instructed him not to allow them or the Canadians to establish themselves on St. Pierre and Miquelon "under some strategic pretext."[93] No military unit from any foreign power was to be allowed access to the islands without the formal permission of the National Committee in London.

General de Gaulle won the St. Pierre and Miquelon incident. (So did Canada, and Britain, too, for that matter, since Free French occupation was their preferred option from the outset.) He defended French sovereignty, asserted his personal authority and became a heroic figure to millions of North Americans. A Hollywood studio planned a film on the heroic leader of the "Fighting French" and writer William Faulkner was commissioned to prepare a script, but the project was cancelled for reasons that remain obscure. The most likely explanation is that someone in Washington intervened. On the other hand, de Gaulle paid a high price for his victory. Cordell Hull harboured strong feelings of ill will towards him until he resigned as secretary of state in 1945 and was still bitter when he wrote his memoirs. A year after the incident, Roosevelt remarked to his son that he couldn't imagine a man he trusted less than de Gaulle. De Gaulle's relations with Churchill became still more difficult. He was not invited to plan and participate in the liberation of any other French territory. For instance, in May 1942, the British excluded the Free French from the invasion of Madagascar; in November, the Americans did the same with regard to North Africa. He was not even informed of the Normandy landings until a few hours before the event.

De Gaulle's relations with Canada, tenuous as they were, did not suffer. Norman Robertson confided to Elisabeth de Miribel his satisfaction with the outcome and, then, in a gentle slap on the wrist, expressed the wish that the Free French had kept him better informed of what they were up to. (In fact, she and other members of the Free French delegation in Ottawa had been kept as much in the dark as the Canadians.) De Gaulle's increasing popularity in Quebec at the expense of Pétain eased the position of the Canadian government and enabled Mackenzie King to look forward to the day when he would no longer have to perform a balancing act between the two French authorities. De Gaulle never abandoned his position that he had acted unilaterally because the Canadians, "in agreement with the United States if not at their instigation," were about to invade a French territory.[94] He was misinformed and that was the root of the crisis.

Chapter 5

De Gaulle's Discovery of Canada

De Gaulle's first encounter with Canada left him with the impression of a colony only just emerging from British tutelage but already falling under the strong influence of the United States. He was also kept informed by the Free French office in Ottawa of the continued support for Pétain, and consequently for the Vichy régime. In May 1942, Elisabeth de Miribel reported on a 'plebiscite'—referendum would have been a more accurate term—in which the Canadian government asked the population to relieve it of its commitment not to introduce military conscription for overseas service. The campaign polarized public opinion anew on the war effort, with Quebec voting overwhelmingly against, and the other provinces equally decisively for, the proposition. De Miribel pointed out that the entry of the Soviet Union into the war on the Allied side had added anti-Communist to anti-British sentiment among French Canadians, and reinforced isolationist sentiments among nationalist intellectuals and the clergy. These groups listened faithfully to the propaganda broadcasts from Paris, Vichy and Rome, and distributed the material to the population; they largely ignored de Gaulle.

An opinion survey conducted by three young diplomats, Marcel Cadieux, Saul Rae and Paul Tremblay, all three future distinguished diplomats, confirmed de Miribel's assessment.[1] While hardly scientific, it did cover most of Quebec. Only twenty per cent of those interviewed thought that the Allies were fighting for freedom and civilization; the others thought the war was a struggle for markets, financial interests and political domination. Sixty-six per cent were opposed to any Canadian contribution to what they considered to be the defence of the British Empire; eighty-five per cent did not think that Canada's security would be affected if Great Britain fell to the Germans. With regard to France, seventy-five per cent would not accept conscription to preserve its freedom. An equal proportion approved of Pétain and thought he had the support of the majority of Frenchmen. Accordingly, sixty per cent would not approve of a declaration of war against Pétain's France.

While the statistics, together with the outcome of the vote on conscription, illustrated clearly the need for Mackenzie King's cautious policy, there were signs of change. A small but growing number of French Canadians, led by the Vaniers, increasingly by Cardinal Villeneuve, and more recently, by the new minister of justice, Louis St. Laurent, were having some impact on public opinion; and the press, with the notable exception of *Le Devoir*, was becoming more outspoken in support of the Allies. The United States' entry into the conflict accelerated that trend.

In Ottawa, representatives of the Free French—or rather Fighting French, as they were now called—were treated increasingly as the true spokesmen of France. Mackenzie King continued to maintain close personal relations with Ristelhueber, who was more and more unhappy to be representing the Vichy régime, and even assured the French minister that he could stay on as a private citizen if he decided to resign. In April 1942, when Pierre Laval was appointed prime minister by Pétain, the United States recalled its ambassador; the Canadian government considered following suit by refusing to deal further with Ristelhueber, but both the British and the Americans asked it to make no change until the situation in Vichy became clearer.[2] Ottawa acceded to the request but did order the French consulate in Quebec closed. Vanier had already been relieved of his position as minister to France at his own request; the Pétain government had been "conceived in the sin of betrayal," he wrote to Mackenzie King, and he could not reconcile the appointment with "a sense of honour, decency, and of patriotism."[3] He expressed the hope that before long the Fighting French would be able to "establish a government in conformity with those glorious traditions that are a natural heritage of France."

Quite apart from the difficulties of running a diplomatic operation that had no official status with the government, one of the problems that plagued Colonel Pierrené was the continuing fractiousness of the Frenchmen in Canada. Well-meaning but politically inexperienced, he found himself out of his element. De Gaulle made a new appointment, but his choice was a recent defector from the French embassy in Washington, D.C., and a campaign of innuendo rendered him ineffective. The Canadian government requested that he be replaced. The next appointee was Commander Gabriel Bonneau, a professional diplomat who had been serving at the French embassy in Afghanistan when France collapsed; he had immediately offered his services to de Gaulle and been assigned to represent him in Cairo. He proved an excellent choice.

On August 19, 1942, Canadian troops played the major role in the first military operation against the French mainland. With the tide of the war swinging in favour of the Allies, pressure was building to go on the offensive. The German invasion of the Soviet Union, launched in the summer of 1941, had been halted but at tremendous cost, and Moscow was appealing for some action in the West to relieve the pressure. In Britain, highly trained Canadian troops, some there since late 1939, were spoiling for a fight. A plan was devised to send a force of several thousand across the English Channel to seize the port town of Dieppe. While it was recognized that it could not possibly be held for long, a moral victory would be achieved, and the German defences would be tested.

The expedition was a disaster.[4] Anticipating some kind of attack, the Germans had strengthened their forces along the Channel and put them on a high state of alert. Moreover, the Allied strategy was a colossal blunder. Naval and aerial cover was inadequate; most of the landing sites were directly in front of the town and in the full line of fire of German guns; no parachute units were used to attack from the rear. As a result, many of the troops were killed before they set foot on the beach; most of the heavy equipment never fired a shot. De Gaulle's son-in-law, Lieutenant Alain Boissieu, was on one of a small number of French escort vessels, the only Fighting French units to take part in the operation. Its exit doors jammed when it collided with another vessel, and the crew was unable to land its cargo of motorized vehicles. Nevertheless, a few enemy posts were taken before the retreat was sounded. In a period of nine hours, 3367 of some 6000 troops were killed, captured or wounded. Canadian losses were 3350 out of nearly 5000, of whom 906 were killed. Churchill defended the raid later as "an indispensable preliminary to full-size operations."[5] Lord Louis Mountbatten, head of the Combined Operations Organization and thus a leading architect of the plan, wrote later, "The Duke of Wellington said the battle of Waterloo was won on the playing fields of Eton. I say that the battle of Normandy was won on the beaches of Dieppe."[6] No record has been found of a statement by General de Gaulle, although Boissieu recalled later that he had enquired with some concern about the French Canadians who had taken part.[7] The Pétain government sent congratulations to the Germans on their victory and thanked them publicly for the "rapid cleansing" of the soil of France.[8] The message confirmed the Vichy régime's subservience to Germany and stirred pro-Gaullist newspapers in Canada to fresh demands to break off relations with it.

The landing of the American (officially the United Nations) force in North Africa on November 8, 1942, seemed to offer the Canadian government a way out of its increasingly embarrassing position. The same day, Mackenzie King issued a statement explaining that diplomatic relations with Vichy had been maintained thus far at the request of the United States and Britain, but, even if that situation changed, it did not mean that Canada was at war with "the real France."[9] The next day, he telephoned Roosevelt and suggested that, since the Vichy government had ordered resistance to the American forces, notwithstanding Roosevelt's statement that the operation was directed not against France but against Germany, it "could not be described as a legal or constitutional Government in any sense representing the French people....In other words, they had really committed suicide."[10] "In other words," the president replied jokingly, "they ain't." To the prime minister's delight, the Americans decided to break off diplomatic relations with the Pétain government, and since Britain had done so two years earlier, the way was clear for Canada to follow suit. On November 9, Canadians were informed that the Vichy régime "was only a German puppet government," and that, according-ly, diplomatic relations were terminated. That night, the prime minister recorded in his diary his rejoicing "over the manner in which we permitted Vichy to become separated from Canada without severing any relations ourselves with the French people."[11] Hitler's renunciation of the Franco-German armistice, and the German occupation of southern France, the following day lent credence to that statement. Canada had survived the dilemma of a divided France and could turn to de Gaulle as its true leader.

The deal made by the Americans with Darlan appointing him high commissioner for Africa* was greeted with surprise and skepticism in Ottawa. Darlan was a doubtful personality, Norman Robertson advised the prime minister, and the French generals in North Africa who were allegedly supporting him did not "represent the spirit of the real France nearly as faithfully as...the Free French."[12] He urged that no action be taken to recognize any provisional government under the admiral's name, but rather to wait and see how the situation developed. His advice was accepted. On November 19, again acting in concert with the United States, the Canadian government decided to formalize relations with the French National Committee in London by appointing a representative, to act in consultation with it "on all matters relating to the conduct of the war."[13] De Gaulle was asked whether he "would welcome the creation of this post and whether he would be agreeable to the appointment of Brigadier Vanier" to such a post. "No choice could be more agreeable," he responded.[14]

Most delighted of all with the appointment were the Vaniers themselves. For them, it meant not only a return to full-time

* See Chapter 1.

diplomacy and eventually to France, but also that Canada was at last adopting what they considered to be the honourable course of action. "Since my departure from France in 1940," Vanier wrote to de Gaulle, "your voice was always for me the voice of the French people....You incarnate the spirit of resistance, springing from the moral strength of France developed over a thousand years and which constitutes its greatest heritage."[15] Promoted to the rank of major-general, he left for London in February 1943. For de Gaulle, official recognition of the French National Committee was, in fact, already outdated, as was Vanier's mandate to consult it only on "matters pertaining to the war." In addition to endorsing Vanier's nomination, he had expressed the hope that his mandate would be broadened to include "the general interests of France in the war,"[16] or, more explicitly, political matters. Ottawa was still not prepared to go farther than the United States; and so it did not respond.

The Americans were still determined to play every possible card to keep those French forces still under Vichy's authority, and particularly the fleet in Toulon, out of German hands. "If Laval gives me Paris, I will deal with Laval," Roosevelt told two representatives of the French National Committee on November 23.[17] At the same time, the president was coming to recognize that de Gaulle was a force to be reckoned with. The possibility of a visit by the Fighting French leader to Washington was discussed with the two Frenchmen, and, according to Lacouture, Roosevelt actually extended an invitation.[18] In public, however, he restricted himself to the comment that, if de Gaulle came on his own initiative, he would "willingly receive him."[19] Formal invitation or none, de Gaulle decided to go, and a meeting was scheduled for December 10. The Canadian high commissioner in London was asked informally by the Fighting French office there if he would also be invited to Canada. Again, Ottawa was prudent. The word "invite" had not been used by Roosevelt, Robertson advised the prime minister, and there was "no strong reason why we should go further than the President."[20] At any rate, a suggestion that de Gaulle visit Montreal to see Fighting French supporters there was considered inadvisable in view of Pétainist support among the population there. Finally, Mackenzie King replied that if de Gaulle did go to the United States and also desired to visit Ottawa, he would be pleased to receive him.[21] In the end, the problem resolved itself when events in North Africa caused the trip to be postponed.

As it turned out, de Gaulle's rival, General Henri Giraud, visited Canada before he did. Following Darlan's assassination on Christmas Eve 1942, the Americans arranged for Giraud to become French high commissioner for Africa. From London, de Gaulle called for a meeting with him to establish "a provisional enlarged central power, based on

national union...until the nation has made its will known."[22] Giraud
was reluctant, but the British and Americans endorsed the idea. The
negotiations, which took place in Algiers, were long and arduous,
lasting nearly four months. Churchill and Roosevelt met in Casablanca in May and helped to bring about what the president described as "a
shotgun wedding."[23] In June 1943, the French Committee of National
Liberation (or FCNL) was formed under their joint chairmanship. The
Canadian government was anxious to recognize the committee officially, and Vanier urged from London that, since Canada had the
largest French-speaking community outside France, Canada should
be "among the first, if not the first" to do so.[24] However, the United
States delayed, to see if the new arrangement would work. Keeping to
its policy of coordinating its actions with those of its Allies, Ottawa
delayed as well.

American policy makers continued to be motivated by a deep
distrust of de Gaulle and openly demonstrated their preference for
Giraud by inviting him to the United States shortly after the FCNL
was formed. Canada followed suit. The only Canadian official who had
met Giraud previously was Pierre Dupuy. Giraud had invited the
Canadian diplomat to Algiers in May, presumably to win support in
his difficult negotiations with de Gaulle. The Canadian government
had agreed to a "private and unofficial visit" in order to receive first
hand information on the situation. Once again, Dupuy's sympathies
were with de Gaulle's adversaries. In his first report sent through
American channels, he described Giraud as "the ideal type of simple,
honest, patriotic and non-ambitious Frenchman," unprepared to play
any political role.[25]

Giraud made a strong impression during his brief stay in Canada. It
was agreed beforehand that he would be received as a distinguished
French general and that controversial political subjects would be
avoided in public. Indeed, any direct contact with the population would
be avoided. He respected this condition, and never so much as
mentioned de Gaulle in his speeches. He was received at official
dinners by the prime minister and the premier of Quebec in Montreal,
and given a reception by the mayor of Montreal. In his private
discussions with Mackenzie King, Giraud stressed that it was he who
had made most of the concessions in his negotiations with de Gaulle in
order to establish the FCNL, even conceding a majority of members on
the executive committee to the Fighting French, and giving de Gaulle
practical control over civilian affairs. Unfortunately, some Frenchmen, he commented pointedly, were "putting their own personal
interests ahead of their country's future."[26] Giraud himself considered
that the main concerns at the moment were military, and that every
patriotic Frenchman must do his duty "without selfishness." When the

country was liberated, "then, and then only" would the population decide on the political régime it wished to adopt. For the moment, he had received assurances of military aid from the United States and wished to have more from Canada. He also hoped for Canadian recognition of the FCNL, although he conceded that this was difficult as long as the United States demurred. As an interim solution, he suggested that Canada appoint a representative to the headquarters of General Eisenhower, the United Nations commander-in-chief in North Africa.

Mackenzie King was impressed with Giraud's apparent self-abnegation in contrast to what he had heard of de Gaulle, and he described Giraud in his diary as "a great patriot."[27] St. Laurent called him "an honest man speaking fearlessly and simply in regard to a great episode in history." The visit removed many of the Canadians' doubts about the advisability of recognizing the FCNL, and they joined the British in urging the Americans to take that step. Early recognition would strengthen Giraud's hand against de Gaulle, Washington was told; if the committee broke up, the latter might well emerge as the sole French leader.[28] Ottawa also warned that if joint action was not taken soon, Canada might be forced to act on its own.[29]

The matter was still undecided when Roosevelt and Churchill arrived in Quebec City in August 1943 for what became known as the first Quebec Conference. Mackenzie King was invited as host and, for some matters, as a participant. Before the president arrived, Churchill and Mackenzie King chaired a joint meeting of the British War Cabinet and the Canadian Cabinet War Committee, where the subject of recognition of the FCNL—"this tiresome business," in Churchill's words—was thoroughly examined.[30] Despite the difficulties with de Gaulle, Churchill stated, there was "no gainsaying his identification with the forces of French resistance," and so there was no point in delaying recognition.[31] In fact, he had thought of inviting de Gaulle to Quebec to facilitate matters. Would that be helpful from the Canadian point of view? he enquired. The Canadian reaction was negative: a visit to Quebec by General de Gaulle, at that time, might have "a disturbing effect." Notwithstanding their negative feelings about the Fighting French leader, the two leaders agreed to press the United States for immediate recognition.

The Americans resisted strongly, refusing to contemplate use of the word "recognition" in any joint statement.[32] Cordell Hull predicted that, far from uniting the French, the FCNL would destroy itself. Discussion of the subject took an inordinate amount of time on a heavy agenda. Finally, it became evident that complete agreement was impossible, and each government decided to make its own statement. Only the British and Canadians used the word "recognize." The

Canadian statement, still somewhat equivocal, recognized the FCNL "as administering the French overseas territories which acknowledge its authority and as the body qualified to ensure the conduct of the French effort in the war within the framework of inter-Allied cooperation."[33] It also noted "with sympathy" the desire of the committee "to be recognized as the body qualified to ensure the administration and defence of all French interests" and promised "to give effect to this request as far as possible while reserving the right to consider in consultation with the Committee the practical application of those principles in particular cases as they arise." The British text contained a similar wording.

On October 5, Vanier's name was submitted to Bonneau as representative of Canada to the French Committee of National Liberation. He was also given the personal rank of ambassador (Canada having decided to raise its legations to embassy status.) By that time, de Gaulle had succeeded in eliminating Giraud as co-chairman and in relegating him to the position of commander-in-chief of the French forces under the authority of a military committee chaired by himself. In November, he re-organized the committee and set its priority, "the return of a great power to its place of great power."[34] When the Vaniers arrived in Algiers in January 1944, they found him in full control.

The Canadian representatives took up their functions with enthusiasm. Elisabeth de Miribel, recently transferred from Ottawa to become information officer for the FCNL, recounts that they welcomed to their home so many new arrivals from the continent that they earned the affectionate title of "ambassadors of the Resistance."[35] Among their regular house guests was Pauline Vanier's cousin, General Leclerc, who was becoming famous for his successful campaigns in Africa. De Gaulle himself also came to dinner occasionally, and while he still terrified his hostess as a table partner, he was less abrasive and more appreciative of the Vaniers' efforts on France's behalf. Vanier's despatches to Ottawa had a significant impact in making de Gaulle's position as the pre-eminent French leader acceptable there. While the Canadian government continued to defer to Great Britain and the United States in broad policy questions relating to the war, and to make agreement between them a primary consideration in deciding Canada's positions, de Gaulle's legitimacy as spokesman for Free France was no longer questioned. In May 1944, the FCNL was transformed into the provisional government of the French Republic with de Gaulle as president; Ottawa accepted the designation as a more accurate description of the real situation, but made no public statement to that effect pending American recognition.

In Washington, hostility towards de Gaulle died hard. Roosevelt described him about that time as "a narrow-minded French zealot with too much ambition for his own good and some rather dubious views on democracy."[36] He predicted that, after the liberation of France, other parties would spring up there and that de Gaulle would become "a very little figure." When Churchill raised once more the possibility of a visit by de Gaulle to the United States, the president responded that he had "no objection," but still refused to issue an invitation. Although he was anxious to make the trip, de Gaulle stood his ground: he merely stated that he would be happy to receive an invitation. The Americans' insistence that he be kept completely in the dark concerning the invasion of Normandy did not facilitate matters, but his emotional reception in Bayeux a few days later demonstrated once more the increasingly anachronistic nature of that attitude. When Vanier called on the French leader in late July in Algiers, he urged him to go to Washington regardless of whether he was formally invited; once there, the ambassador argued, the subjects he wanted to raise, particularly the future administration of France, could not be avoided. Vanier also mentioned a possible visit to Canada, but could not go further since he was not authorized to issue an invitation until the American arrangements were completed. Finally, de Gaulle, having reached the same conclusion as Vanier, decided to make the trip in early July. Vanier was able to deliver the invitation to visit Canada just three days before the French leader left Algiers.

As it turned out, the meeting with the Americans was a distinct success. The president, Cordell Hull and others were very cordial and talked candidly about the current situation and future prospects. De Gaulle was on his best behaviour. Afterward, the colourful mayor of New York, Fiorello La Guardia, organized a hero's welcome for him, complete with a parade along Wall Street under a blizzard of ticker-tape and confetti. The event was a confirmation of his place, in the minds and hearts of the public at least, as the personification of France.

De Gaulle began his visit to Canada with a brief stop in Quebec City. In his war memoirs, he summed it up in a single sentence. "First of all, visiting the City of Quebec, I felt submerged in a wave of French pride, soon to be overlaid by one of inconsolable pain, both originating in distant history."[37] Vanier joined him there and they flew to Ottawa where Mackenzie King greeted him at the airport and accompanied him to the governor general's residence, Rideau Hall, where he was to stay as guest of the governor general, the earl of Athlone and his wife, Princess Alice, granddaughter of Queen Victoria. De Gaulle made his first public address to a large crowd in front of the Parliament Buildings. The Canadian people, he declared, had "not been opposed to ours at any point in history" and had "always opened their minds and hearts to ideas and feelings that rose from the French soul."[38] While he recognized that "in the veins of many," there flowed "blood that came from France," he addressed himself to all Canadians who had built "a united State with the consciousness of its own value and loyalty to the Commonwealth." As she resumed her place in world affairs, he was sure that France would find "beside her and in agreement with her," all countries that knew her well, and "in first place, Canada." The warm words set the tone for the visit. He and the prime minister chatted over lunch at Government House, then at greater length in the Parliament Buildings in the afternoon. St. Laurent acted as interpreter. De Gaulle remarked that he had "much enjoyed" his talks with Roosevelt who had "shown a very open mind."[39] He had also "liked" Cordell Hull! He and the Americans had agreed that the civil administration of the liberated areas of France should be carried on whenever possible by the French, but that Eisenhower should be the judge, as military leader, of when the territory should be turned over to them. On the subject of recognition of the provisional government, de Gaulle remarked that the subject was not a matter of urgency; when a government was formally established in France, the United States would have to have an ambassador there, and that would constitute recognition. He was more concerned with winning recognition for France in international affairs. Standing as she did for democratic ideals, she should be in the group that would have most to do with shaping the new world order. Mackenzie King, for his part, offered some insights into Canada's emerging foreign policy. It was prepared to have Britain, as the leading member of the Commonwealth, act as one of the great powers, he explained, but expected to be consulted on matters of direct relevance to it. Norman Robertson, who was present, explained the "functional" principle that the government had adopted to determine in which areas it should get involved. Smaller countries like Canada should not overextend themselves, he stated, but should have a role with regard to matters that interested them and that they had the capacity to do something about.

In late afternoon, de Gaulle held a press conference; Mackenzie King admired his "remarkably skilful replies."[40] That evening, the two men had what the Canadian prime minister described as "an exceedingly interesting chat," during a state dinner in de Gaulle's honour. Seated at the head table, they had no interpreter, but Mackenzie King found that de Gaulle spoke English "remarkably well." Taking advantage of the opportunity to hear the other side of a story that was familiar to him through the reports of Churchill and Roosevelt, he asked de Gaulle to explain his differences with the British leader, and the Americans' reluctance to recognize him as head of a provisional government. De Gaulle traced their relations beginning in June 1940. As France was collapsing, he recalled, Churchill had refused to send over the aircraft he still had available, preferring to keep them for the defence of Britain. "It was then that I had the impression that Britain would abandon France as soon as it felt threatened itself."[41] As for the Americans, President Roosevelt had instructed his ambassador not to follow the government from Paris to Bordeaux, nor, in other words, to identify with the Frenchmen who were prepared to fight on. When they found they would get no help from the United States, some ministers felt the situation was hopeless. De Gaulle had argued that they still had the French Empire, and that the British, with their Dominions, would help. Someone predicted that the British would be beaten in six days, and that, in those circumstances, the Dominions would not fight. Subsequently, the Americans found it difficult to recognize his role with regard to North Africa and in other matters. No doubt he himself had been "difficult" and said "sharp things at times," but he had "to maintain his position as representing what he believed to be France." The more the Americans attacked him and had dealings with Vichy, the more they rallied "true Frenchmen" to his side and helped him to be recognized as "head of the French nation." The French people came to look on him as "standing for the freedom of France." But all that was in the past. The main thing henceforth was "friendship for France," and he was "satisfied to allow everything to be subordinated to that."

Evidently impressed, Mackenzie King rose to an unusual level of eloquence in introducing his guest. Champlain had sailed up the Ottawa River, right past the present site of Parliament, he recalled, and had founded the colony of New France, thus enabling the tenets of Christianity to be spread. Later, the colony had become British North America, and finally "one country," Canada. Now de Gaulle had come "to express his appreciation of what Canada was doing towards the restoration of old France." It was the second time in a quarter of a century that it had performed that role. A deeply religious man, the prime minister concluded by saying that he hoped God would bless his guest and give him "strength and vision" for his great task, and that de Gaulle would live to see "the France he loved and served so well, and to which he had been so faithful, enshrined again not only in the hearts of all her own people, but enshrined in the hearts of the free nations of the world." When he sat down, de Gaulle turned to him and said, in one of the brief, succinct phrases he favoured in English, "Your words are deeply moving." Louis St. Laurent followed in French, assuring the French leader that "all Canada" was united in the defence of the Allied nations. In his response, de Gaulle appealed for "true international cooperation" and gave the assurance that France was ready "not to divide, but...to play its role in...assuring world peace."[42]

The following day, de Gaulle gave Mackenzie King a photograph of himself inscribed *"en témoignage d'amitié française."* The prime minister placed it beside that of his grandfather, who, in 1837, had led the uprising in Upper Canada (present-day Ontario) against autocratic rule. The two men, he reflected, had "played similar roles" and were "true patriots." He concluded that the visit was a "great inspiration" and would "do great good."

One unscheduled and unannounced meeting during de Gaulle's stay in Ottawa was highly significant for his future plans. Following a reception for members of the local French community, he was asked by Bonneau to grant a private interview to three scientists who were working on a highly secret British-Canadian-American research project.[43] It was the "Tube Alloys" project to develop an atomic bomb. The possibility of achieving nuclear fission, the basic step before a bomb could be built, had interested scientists before the war in several countries, including Germany, but Frédéric and Irène Joliot-Curie, in Paris, appear to have made most progress. When France collapsed, the Joliot-Curies decided to remain in Paris, but several of their colleagues made their way to England and eventually to Montreal where they joined the tripartite project. By mid-1944, the team of scientists was racing to develop the bomb before the Germans, who were known to be working in the same direction, could produce one. The Frenchmen were sworn to the utmost secrecy, but their sense of patriotism took precedence in their minds and they decided to tell de Gaulle of their activities and of the potentially enormous consequences for the world if the project was successful. One of them, Pierre Auger, who had met de Gaulle, was granted precisely three minutes to explain what it was they felt was so urgent for him to know. Auger did so in three points: the possession of the new weapon by the United States would give the United States a "very considerable advantage" during and after the war; French atomic research should be resumed as soon as possible; and there were probably important supplies of uranium, the essential raw material, in Madagascar, a French colony off the coast of Africa.[44] De Gaulle listened intensely, but made little comment. Afterward, he was introduced to the two other scientists, Bertrand Goldschmidt and Jules Guérin, along with some Free French representatives in Canada. When he shook Goldschmidt's hand, he said simply, *"Monsieur le Professeur*, thank you, I have understood very well."

From Ottawa, de Gaulle flew to Montreal, which the Canadian government had evidently decided was no longer dangerous for him to visit. Following a reception at City Hall, the mayor, Adhémar Raynault, presented him to a crowd from a balcony of the Windsor Hotel. "Nothing can convey the thunder of vivats that came from all hearts," he recorded later.[45] Presuming that his audience was French-speaking, he declared that his fellow countrymen would always remember what they owed "to the French Canadians who, during the dark days, made every effort to hold high the flame of French culture in the civilized world."[46] Clearly there was a large measure of exaggeration in both his speeches and his later memories of the event, but it does reflect his positive feelings at the time. Even Mackenzie King seems to have made a very favourable impression on him. Describing him as "a strong and worthy man in all his simplicity," he noted that Canada had followed him during the war in his commitment to freedom, something that was all the more meritorious since the country was made up of "two co-existing but not integrated peoples" and that the war was far off and Canada was not directly involved.[47] On leaving Canada, de Gaulle sent a message of thanks to Mackenzie King, referring to the "moving confirmation of fraternal friendship between France and Canada" that had been "consecrated again by the blood of Canadian and French soldiers flowing in a common battle."[48] Back in Algiers on July 18, de Gaulle called in Vanier to express his enthusiasm over the warm welcome he had received in Ottawa. He also encouraged Canada to insist on equal status, whenever it had a special interest, in the negotiations to determine the character of the post-war world. Whether he was simply endorsing the "functional" principle that Robertson had mentioned or advising the Canadians to be more assertive in international affairs, is not clear. Whichever the case, his attitude was evidently positive. On the Canadian side, Mackenzie King was persuaded by Robertson to raise with Churchill, in his report on de Gaulle's visit, the advisability of recognizing the French provisional government. The step, he suggested, could well have a "helpful psychological effect."[49] A response came back from London, warning that it was still dangerous to "go beyond the President's words."[50] Mackenzie King backed off and interpreted the incident as a "helpful lesson" to his officials not to get out of step with Canada's major allies.[51]

By then, the Americans were merely fighting a rear-guard action. On August 25, 1944, Paris was taken by the Fighting French troops and de Gaulle led a parade down the Champs Elysées to the cheers of a million Frenchmen. When the second Quebec Conference convened in September, Churchill and Eden were determined to overcome the Americans' resistance. The Soviet Union was also threatening to recognize the French provisional government unilaterally. The Canadian government was becoming concerned lest the major powers grant recognition without warning it in advance, so that it would appear to be merely following suit. At a private dinner attended by the governor general and Princess Alice, the Churchills, the Roosevelts and Mackenzie King, the latter was surprised to hear Roosevelt say that he and de Gaulle were now friends.[52] Emboldened, he, in his own words, "stood up" for de Gaulle, as did Princess Alice.[53] Even Mrs. Churchill was favourable to him. Churchill himself spent so much time grumbling about the French leader's conduct, that it sometimes was not clear where he stood. Roosevelt remarked that, within the year, de Gaulle would either be president of France or in the Bastille. British Foreign Secretary Eden worked hard throughout the conference, but in vain, to convince the Americans to accept the inevitable. At the end of the conference, the president reported to Cordell Hull that he and Churchill were both "very much opposed" to recognition of the French provisional government at the moment as it had "no direct authority from the people."

With de Gaulle consolidating his authority over vast stretches of liberated France, the situation was becoming ludicrous. In early September, Vanier flew from Algiers to London, and on September 10, he arrived in Paris in a Canadian plane and with a two-Spitfire escort. He was met at the airport by René Massigli, the commissioner for foreign affairs in the provisional government. He reported back to Ottawa that de Gaulle was "universally accepted...as the country's leader."[54] The following day, the Canadian government authorized Gabriel Bonneau to take possession of the French legation in Ottawa that had been vacant since relations with the Vichy régime had been terminated. It also decided to close the consulate in St. Pierre and Miquelon since Canadian security was no longer in danger there. Meanwhile, more and more countries were recognizing the provisional government, and the United States and Great Britain had already recognized the government of liberated Italy. Finally, the pressure of public opinion and the urging of the British became irresistible, and on October 22, the Americans gave in and notified the British that they would announce recognition the next day. The British, Soviets and Canadians rushed to act simultaneously. De Gaulle commented to the press, "The French government is satisfied to be called by its name." Undoubtedly one of the happiest and most relieved of men was Georges Vanier, who realized at last his cherished ambition of becoming Canada's first ambassador to France. At a meeting on October 10, de Gaulle assured him that he understood that the delay had not been Canada's wish, but rather the fault of the British and Americans.[55] Subsequently, he appointed Count Jean de Hautecloque as ambassador to Canada.

Charles de Gaulle made his second visit to Canada in August 1945, three months after the Allied victory in Europe. With that felicitous outcome of the six-year struggle, Mackenzie Kings's constant preoccupation with the possibility of an open split between French and English Canadians had disappeared. Shortly afterward, he and his fellow Liberals were returned to power in general elections. Nevertheless, the prime minister was not in the mood for another visit. The founding conference of the United Nations in San Francisco, followed by the election campaign, had sapped his already overtaxed resources. He was sleeping badly and finding it difficult to cope with his ordinary routine. On the other hand, it was almost impossible to avoid extending an invitation since de Gaulle was visiting Washington, and the pattern had developed of visiting both capitals. His reticence soon disappeared when he met de Gaulle at the airport again on August 28. The French leader, he recalled later, was "particularly friendly," and soon put him at ease.[56]

De Gaulle's primary objective in making the visit was to obtain Canadian assistance for the reconstruction of France. He had already appealed through Vanier for supplies of food and paper, and had received an initial loan from Canada for such purchases. He also asked for fuel, transportation and other equipment to get the economy functioning again. As on the previous occasion, the two men had a discussion of broader questions. Shortly before, both Roosevelt and Churchill had disappeared from the international scene, the former through death, the latter through defeat at the polls. According to Mackenzie King's version, as recorded in his diary, while de Gaulle seemed more friendly towards Great Britain, he still seemed to "have a little feeling against Roosevelt."[57] The prime minister tried to dispel that feeling, but to no avail. "There is something in the U.S. relations to France," he concluded, "that I do not comprehend." Mackenzie King repeated the view he had expressed the previous year that Canada should have a role in the post-war settlement proportionate to its "very great contribution" to victory. In fact, he stated, it merited a place on the Council of Foreign Ministers created at Potsdam, and to which France and China had been admitted, as a sort of directorate of post-war affairs. Just as France had wanted to be part of the Big Four, so Canada wanted to be part of the Big Five. De Gaulle appears to have limited his response to an inquiry whether Mackenzie King had made representations along those lines to Britain, and was told that a message had been sent, arguing that the wartime pattern of the smaller countries following the major Allies should not be continued.

In his memoirs, de Gaulle has recorded an exchange that appears to have impressed him.[58] Canada had a five thousand kilometer border with the United States, Mackenzie King told him, and that situation created an "often overwhelming proximity." It was also a member of the Commonwealth, and that, too, was "sometimes oppressive." Nevertheless, Canadians meant to act "with complete independence." Their ambition was to develop their enormous territory and resources. Accordingly, they had "no reason to clash with France in any of its areas of interest. On the contrary, everything made them want to support it within the limits of their interests and capability." De Gaulle responded in the same vein. The two world wars had demonstrated the value of their alliance, he said, and, in time of peace, the French would doubtless have the occasion to take advantage of Canada's friendship. "What you have just said proves to me conclusively that France was right a thousand times over to come and sow civilization here." In a press conference before leaving Ottawa, de Gaulle repeated that message. Nothing separated the interests of the two countries, he declared, and they were "at the beginning of a vast development" in their relations.[59]

In his conversations with Mackenzie King, de Gaulle also spoke of the constituent assembly elections that were scheduled to be held in France in October, and he expressed optimism that his plans would be approved for constitutional changes to strengthen the powers of the president and reduce, if not eliminate, the scourge of political instability. He was reflecting his aims rather than the reality. The new assembly was as deeply divided as in pre-war years, with the Communists the largest group, followed by the Socialists. Although he himself had not been a candidate, he was asked to form an interim government. The Communists demanded three major Cabinet posts: foreign policy, defence and interior; he refused. On November 19, the day before the assembly was to vote on the composition of the government, de Gaulle asked Vanier to come to his office.[60] He might not be able to form a government, he advised the ambassador, and in that case, he felt that he should leave France for a while. He would like to go to Canada for a period of rest. Apparently he planned to leave immediately in the event that the assembly vote went against him. He did not specify precisely where he wished to go in Canada, but he grumbled to Madame de Gaulle, "I'll catch fish and you will cook them."[61] The Canadian government responded immediately that, while it would greatly regret a situation that made him feel such a move to be necessary, it would facilitate any arrangements he might decide upon. As it turned out, his adversaries capitulated and he proceeded to form a government. He sent an urgent message to Vanier to forget the request, and not to mention it to anyone. A few days later, he called in the ambassador again to express his appreciation for the prompt and favourable response.

De Gaulle's withdrawal was merely postponed. In the assembly and within the Cabinet, the parties continued to assert their power, and chances faded of obtaining a new or revised constitution. In mid-January 1946, he went to southern France for a week of isolation, then returned and informed the Cabinet that he was retiring. "The exclusive régime of the parties has come back," he is quoted as saying. "I disapprove of it. But short of establishing a dictatorship by force, which

I don't want and which would probably turn out badly, I lack the means to prevent this experiment."[62] He did not again raise the possibility of going to Canada, probably because he thought he would soon be recalled and wanted to be near the scene of action. He was to wait twelve years for the call.

During those years of "exile," the Vaniers kept in touch with the de Gaulles and visited them at Colombey-les-Deux-Eglises several times. They retired to Canada at the end of 1953 and Jean Désy became Canadian ambassador to France. De Gaulle appears to have had few other contacts with Canada. He did have some distant relatives, the Jaspars, who had emigrated to western Canada in his youth. They had been in touch with him during his wartime visits and had exchanged letters with him. He commented with sadness how much their French had deteriorated. In the wartime memoirs that he completed in 1957, he had nothing but praise for Canada. But in his second memoirs, written shortly before his death, he explained that, in his visits in 1944 and 1945, his view had been obscured by the "war machinery."[63] Accordingly, he had only been able to get a glimpse of "the deeper realities that make the Canadian federation a state perpetually ill at ease, ambiguous and artificial." A judgment coloured by his later experience? Probably. It is also probable that he had become sensitive to the situation of the French Canadians, who were preoccupied with survival on a continent in which even the Canadian government felt obliged to follow the American lead.

Chapter 6

Renewing Contact with the French of Canada

Recalled to power in May 1958 to resolve the Algerian war, Charles de Gaulle had little opportunity in the next two years to concern himself with Canada and the situation of the French Canadians. Keenly aware that, at sixty-eight, his time was limited, he threw himself into his Herculean task with the extraordinary energy and decisiveness of a man in his element. He made his first trip to Algeria in early June to assess the situation. Through a referendum, he had a new constitution approved in September that embodied the concept of strong presidential government that had been rejected by the politicians in 1945. And by the end of the year, in a *volte face* reflecting his often harsh realism, he granted independence to France's African colonies—while preserving French interests in all but one of them.* Domestically, he moved to restore the strength and authority of the state, the essential instrument of French power, and assigned economist Jacques Rueff the responsibility for implementing a comprehensive plan to develop the economy.

During his absence, the programme that he had authorized to develop an atomic bomb had been continued; he ordered that it be accelerated. In July, he informed the American secretary of state, John Foster Dulles, that France was about to become a nuclear power, and that it could not accept a position subordinate to the United States within NATO.[1] Any nuclear arms on its soil would henceforth be under its control, and decisions as to their utilization would have to be a matter of French responsibility "with American participation." A few weeks later, he sent a memorandum to President Eisenhower and British Prime Minister Harold Macmillan, proposing a "tripartite directorate" to manage the North Atlantic Alliance. The Americans never gave a direct answer to the proposal, but suggested improve-

---

* Guinea, which opted for unabridged independence.

ments in consultation procedures. Simultaneously, de Gaulle moved to assert France's leadership in Europe by developing ties with the francophile chancellor of West Germany, Konrad Adenauer, and blocking British entry into the Common Market until conditions suitable to him were negotiated.

When de Gaulle resumed office, John Diefenbaker was prime minister of Canada and Maurice Duplessis premier of Quebec. General Vanier had retired to Montreal, but spent part of each year in Vézelay, an ancient cathedral town two hours' drive south of Paris. Diefenbaker sent de Gaulle a message of congratulations and good wishes and extended an invitation to visit Canada again. De Gaulle responded warmly, referring to "the friendship uniting our two countries and the spiritual heritage inspiring it."[2] "The noble Canadian nation," he was confident, wanted France to play its role fully in the world, just as it was carrying out "so successfully and efficiently" its own vocation at home. The Canadian prime minister was fascinated by world statesmen and thrilled at the contact with the last of the great wartime leaders still in office. He asked to call on de Gaulle during a world tour he was planning to undertake later in the year. The meeting was arranged for early November. When he arrived, de Gaulle had just won the referendum on the new constitution and was about to become the first president of the Fifth Republic. In view of his busy schedule and other higher priorities, he saw Diefenbaker's visit as just a courtesy call. He arranged a small private luncheon, preceded by a chat.

John Diefenbaker's French was notoriously bad, and de Gaulle had abandoned his own attempts to speak English; they conversed through an interpreter.[3] At the beginning, de Gaulle appeared disinterested. Neither man mentioned Franco-Canadian relations or internal Canadian matters, but Diefenbaker did voice his concerns about the repercussion on Canadian exports of eventual British membership in the Common Market. Then, keen to have a world statesman's views on current issues, he oriented the conversation towards broader questions. De Gaulle told him of the proposal he had made to the Americans and the British for a triumvirate to direct NATO affairs. The Canadian prime minister objected that this would diminish Canada's role in the organization. De Gaulle suddenly became alert, apparently struck by the manifestation of Canadian national feeling such as Mackenzie King had displayed at their last meeting in 1945. The exchange became livelier and more meaningful.

Lunch was a purely social event with Madame de Gaulle and Mrs. Diefenbaker, plus eight or ten other persons, in attendance. In contrast to the coldness and rigidity that marred his social relations during the war, for instance, at dinner with the Vaniers in 1940, de Gaulle proved a sophisticated host, making light conversation and putting his guests at ease. To the suprise of the Canadians, he suggested at the end of the meal that he and the prime minister return to his office and continue their discussion for a little while. The visit ended on a very cordial note; Diefenbaker thought back on it later as a great event in his career. (Reports circulated in Canada that Diefenbaker was insulted at the lack of protocol, but these cannot be substantiated.) The communiqué issued afterward was brief: it stated that the two leaders had discussed "the principal contemporary world problems...in the spirit of deep and abiding friendship" that united the two countries.[4]

A year later, General de Gaulle had another opportunity to assess the current Canadian leadership when the minister of external affairs, Howard Green, called on him during a visit to Paris to meet with Canadian diplomats serving in Europe and the Middle East. Green was a thoroughly nice man, but he was a novice in international affairs. He had not been overseas since his military service in France in World War One, and his guiding principle was unflinching loyalty to Great Britain. His French was non-existent. The conversation between de Gaulle and the Canadian minister was brief and inconsequential, being limited largely to their respective 1914–18 wartime experiences.[5] No communiqué was issued. On leaving the Elysée Palace, Green, obviously impressed, commented that the president was "a great man."[6]

In April 1960, de Gaulle paid his third visit to Canada while en route to the United States. Just previously, he had visited Great Britain as the guest of Queen Elizabeth. He was given a magnificent reception there, being invited to stay in Buckingham Palace, and to address the British Parliament (with the very aged Churchill in attendance). The public gave him a rousing welcome. It must have been a gratifying experience for him after his grating dependence on the British authorities during the war. In contrast, his three-day stay in Canada was in a minor key. The weather in Ottawa, where he landed first, was still cool and patches of snow lay on the ground. Prime Minister Diefenbaker had given instructions that he be received in a manner similar to his own reception in Paris, and civil servants were given time off work to greet him when he visited Parliament Hill. However, few appeared. (There was nothing exceptional in such behaviour in Ottawa; when Churchill passed through in 1955, the weather was excellent and he rode up Parliament Hill perched on the back seat of an open car; nevertheless, only a modest crowd gathered to see him.) But de Gaulle was warmly received by the new occupants of Rideau Hall, Governor General and Madame Vanier.

In keeping with his practice of preparing speeches carefully in advance, de Gaulle arrived with a set of very conventional texts. At Ottawa airport, he expressed his pleasure at the opportunity to meet

again with Vanier, for whom he had "deep and friendly esteem."[7] In
the current dangerous international context, he felt it was essential to
"make contact with the government and people of the dear, strong and
vigorous Canada." "*Vive le Canada*," he concluded, "*Vive la France!
Vivent les peuples libres!*" That evening, he was offered a state dinner,
and, the next morning, he had a private conversation with Prime
Minister Diefenbaker. A Canadian official acted as interpreter. De
Gaulle used English words occasionally to ensure that his statements
were well understood. As in Paris, he and Diefenbaker talked in
general terms, and, according to the notes taken by the official, the
place of French Canadians within the country was not raised.
Afterward, they met the Canadian Cabinet, but no serious exchange
occurred there either. Most of the ministers spoke no French, and the
French Canadians, few in number and low in political prestige, were
too awed by the famous statesman to engage in a dialogue with him.
The only possible impression that de Gaulle could have received was
that the Canadian capital was dominated by English Canadians, with
French Canadians in a subsidiary position.

  Whatever his thoughts on that score, the general stuck to his scripts.
"Who are you in our eyes?" he asked rhetorically at a luncheon given
in his honour by the prime minister. And he answered:

> Materially, a new country immense in size, with great
> resources, inhabited by a hard-working and enterprising
> people. Politically, a State that is able to unite two
> communities very different in origin, language and reli-
> gion, and that practises its independence while coming
> under the British Crown and being part of the Common-
> wealth; that is developing its national character even
> though it is a neighbour, over a stretch of five thousand
> kilometers, of a very powerful federation, a solid and stable
> state...; morally, finally, a people very sensitive on the one
> hand to order in society and on the other to the dignity of
> man.[8]

As for relations between France and Canada, he went on:

> the country, the State, the people you are arouses the
> highest interest, liking and confidence of France. Not only
> no dispute over claims or ambitions, or even basic differ-
> ences separate us; on the contrary, the French feel at one
> with the Canadians in their perception of and approach to
> the problems of our times.

Whether flattery or genuine praise, the statement indicated that Franco-Canadian relations were at least as good as on his previous visit fifteen years earlier. The programme in Ottawa concluded with a further discussion between the two leaders, this time accompanied by their foreign ministers and ambassadors, and a dinner hosted by de Gaulle at the French embassy.

The next day, the president flew to Quebec City, with only a brief stay in Montreal. In the historic capital of New France, which he had visited only briefly once before, he was received by Lieutenant-Governor Onésime Gagnon and Premier Antonio Barrette, both former ministers in Duplessis' Cabinet. Duplessis had died the previous September, and the party he had founded, the *Union Nationale*, while still in power, was rent with dissension, and the tide of popular opinion was running against it. Three days earlier, the Legislature had been dissolved and elections called for June 20. Premier Barrette was a moderate nationalist in Quebec and a strong supporter of John Diefenbaker at the federal level. He was also more open to the outside world, including France, than Duplessis. At a dinner given by the government of Quebec, he told de Gaulle that in the previous two centuries, French Canadians had "lived happily in a British colony, and in an independent Canada in the midst of the Commonwealth;" but France remained a country which after their own was "perhaps the dearest in the world" to them.[9] They shared its "griefs and sorrows," as well as its "joys and victories," as their own. For instance, they had "learned with consternation" of the fall of France in 1940, but that feeling had been alleviated on June 18 when a voice from London asserted that "nothing was lost...and that one day victory would come." Now they welcomed their guest as "the eternal France" and one of those great figures that Providence had always called forth in critical periods, such as Joan of Arc, Napoleon and Clemenceau. They assured him of their admiration along with that of "the English population," with which they, "the French of America," continued to have a "cordial understanding."

With his wartime background, de Gaulle was well able to recognize the words as unctuous oratory, but, as in Ottawa, he went along with the scenario. In his response, he thanked the successive generations of those "who were French" for their great success in building a country, and thus adding "a jewel...to the crown of that which belongs to all of us, the French fact."[10] In retrospect, it is evident that his message was somewhat ambiguous, suggesting that he was still testing the terrain. He made no reference to fresh links with French Canadians or joint efforts on behalf of their common heritage. At the official dinner, he met Jean Lesage, the Liberal leader, who was asking in the election campaign for a mandate to bring about sweeping changes in Quebec society; they had no opportunity to discuss such matters. While in Quebec City, de Gaulle also visited Laval University, then still located in the old city near the Basilica; and he travelled to Ste. Anne de Beaupré, some thirty kilometers further down the St. Lawrence River, to attend Mass at the famous shrine. He was also given the usual tour of the Plains of Abraham where the British had defeated the French in 1759. That could only have been a sad experience for him.

The visit to Canada ended in Toronto where de Gaulle was received by the lieutenant-governor of Ontario, Keiller Mackay, and by the premier, Leslie Frost. Except for the federal minister of finance, Donald Fleming, who accompanied him as representative of the federal government, none of his hosts knew French. When Mackay made a valiant attempt to speak a few words of French in introducing him at a banquet, de Gaulle remarked that he would follow His Excellency's example and speak French as well. That matter aside, his stay in Toronto appears to have gone off well. From there he flew to the United States where he was welcomed enthusiastically by both public officials and by the population in Washington, D.C., New York, San Francisco and New Orleans. Fitted in between the visits to Britain and the United States, the reception given him by the Canadians seemed colourless and their attitude almost indifferent.

Still, the visit to Canada had gone smoothly, and relations between the two countries, if somewhat tenuous, seemed to be problem-free. Nothing that transpired in public foretold the interpretation de Gaulle would put on the event in his second set of memoirs, written a decade later.[11] Although in 1944 and 1945 he had only glimpsed "the deeper realities that made the Canadian Federation and State perpetually ill at ease, ambiguous and artificial," he recalled, in 1960 he had been able to "discern clearly, although still under a filtered light," a very different situation than that which appeared on the surface. Even his friend, General Vanier, while carrying out his functions with "the greatest dignity and loyalty," and "deploying his great charm to give the impression that everything was right and normal," was not exempt from "the inherent contradictions in the Federation." He was functioning as a head of state in a "territory" claimed to be independent, yet he was appointed by the Queen of England. "Entirely French" in origin, spirit and taste, the Vaniers' "race" had only been able to maintain itself "by an unrelenting struggle against all forms of oppression or seduction applied by the conquerors to reduce and dissolve it." Canada, de Gaulle continued, was a country almost limitless in size but almost uninhabited, rich in resources but without capital, its security apparently guaranteed by its immensity but, in fact, bordered on the one hand by the Soviet Union and on the other by the United States, which was "bursting with men, money and power." Even the warm reception he was given and the "spectacle" of economic growth could not conceal from him "the impediments of its structure and situation." In Montreal, the mayor had shown him "numerous buildings...rising out of the earth under the suzerainty of American capital" and had deplored the fact that very few funds came to the "second French city in the world" from its country of origin. There as in Quebec City, he had received the impression of "a diffused anguish caused by the increasing control of Anglo-Saxon owners and managers of the factories and banks, and by the resulting economic, social and linguistic subordination of the French as a result of the actions of the federal administration which anglicizes the immigrants as a matter of course." Even in Toronto, he had sensed "the anxiety about becoming a branch plant of the United States, located just across the lake." The lieutenant-governor and the premier of Ontario themselves had expressed "a great deal of melancholy" about the situation.

De Gaulle had discussed with Diefenbaker "the duality of two peoples co-existing under his government," he also recorded, but the prime minister "affected" to see the situation as a matter of language that increasing bilingualism would resolve. In that regard, he tried to set an example by "expressing himself now and then and with great difficulty in French." De Gaulle had considered his host's intentions "certainly very praiseworthy" and had told him that France "was prepared to have much closer relations with his country." "In order for it to do so warm-heartedly," however, and "in order for Canada as a whole to have the necessary strength and weight," it needed to have "the desire and ability to solve the problem posed by the existence of its two peoples, one being the French people which, like any other, must be able to decide its own future." As he flew south to the United States at the end of his visit, de Gaulle had wondered if "the creation of a State of French stock, beside one of British stock,...preferably establishing some form of cooperation between the two independent units in order to safeguard them," was not the way for Canada to "wipe out the injustice that characterizes it and organize itself in conformity with its own reality, and thus be able to remain Canadian."

Several intriguing questions arise with regard to that assessment. On what information was it based? Did he receive a briefing, for instance from the French ambassador to Canada, François Lacoste, and his staff, that caused him to re-examine the viewpoint reflected in his prepared texts? At that time, the French representative had the best of relations with Ottawa officialdom and seemed uncritical of the prevailing situation. Did French Canadians tell de Gaulle of their difficult plight and appeal to him for help in alleviating it? Only his official hosts had access to him, and while they certainly referred to the long and often bitter struggle of the French Canadians to preserve their identity, they were far from being separatists; indeed, the new wave of Quebec separatism was barely existent. Was the text incorporated in his memoirs, written shortly before his death, as a *post hoc* rationalization to justify his intervention in 1967? Perhaps. At the same time, it does reflect his personal concepts of nation-state relations, and his interest in the fate of French Canada had already been demonstrated.

The testimony of an eye-witness, de Gaulle's aide-de-camp, Commander François Flohic, throws some light on the matter. While serving on a Free French corvette in World War Two, he had visited several Canadian ports and had become aware that "a real French-Canadian problem [existed] inside the Canadian federation."[12] On one occasion, he had noted that a French-Canadian non-commissioned officer had saluted him readily but had refused to salute an English-Canadian officer of still higher rank. The man explained, "I'm French-Canadian; I don't salute the English." Then, in 1960, while de Gaulle stopped briefly at the cenotaph commemorating the battle of the Plains of Abraham, a French-Canadian aide to Lieutenant-Governor Gagnon had muttered to Flohic, "That was when you bloody Frenchmen abandoned us." Upset by the remark, and "shocked" by "the psychological conditions imposed on the French of Canada in the land they discovered," he recounted the incidents to de Gaulle. Later Flohic himself became an ardent proponent of the independence of Quebec. He feels that he had a strong influence on de Gaulle's thinking in that regard.[13] The claim has some credibility in view of de Gaulle's sensitivity to the fate of the French Canadians.

Even more difficult to explain is de Gaulle's reference in his memoirs to a discussion with Diefenbaker over the "duality of two peoples." No record exists of such an exchange and the prime minister later denied discussing the subject. Diefenbaker would not have forgotten it given his strong commitment to one united Canada, nor would he have passed it off lightly. Not even Howard Green, his closest colleague, who as secretary of state for external affairs had a direct interest in being informed of any such exchange, ever heard anything of the matter.[14] Some of de Gaulle's longtime associates have suggested that he might have mentioned it obliquely to test the waters, a tactic he often employed, or merely to make a point, but that it made no impression on his host. As so often when one tries to explain de Gaulle's actions, no conclusive answer is possible.

The testimony of another first-hand witness suggests that, even in the top echelons of government, Frenchmen knew little about Canada. In his own memoirs, Maurice Couve de Murville, who accompanied de Gaulle as French foreign minister, has presented, a, to say the least, outdated image of French Canadians. "Modest peasants," they had been

> abandoned after the defeat by their *seigneurs* and the upper clergy, French and Catholic, with only the poor *curés* able to read, segregated in their rural areas. Without links with the dominating power from whom everything separated them—language, religion and feelings—playing neither a political nor an economic role, they lived in that way, preserving their identity, increasing their numbers to the extent that they competed with the inflow of foreign immigrants, determined to survive, maintain their identity and not merge with anyone at all.[15]

Indeed, in that spring of 1960, he concluded they were "still asleep."[16] As for Canada as a whole, it was not "a real country" with a national character.

Chapter 7
De Gaulle and Quebec's Quiet Revolution

Two months after de Gaulle's third visit to Canada, the Quebec Liberals, led by Jean Lesage, won power in Quebec with the slogan, "It's time for a change." During their first weeks in office, they took decisions so rapidly, and with such sweeping implications, that a journalist proclaimed that a "quiet revolution" was under way. The term caught on and came to express the rapid modernization process initiated by the Lesage government. The new premier himself was wary of using the slogan lest it stir fears of violence in the population. He had been a minister in the federal government of Louis St. Laurent (1948–1957), and his objective now was to develop a competent and honest provincial administration patterned on the model he had known in Ottawa. He intended to use this administration to act in areas of provincial constitutional jurisdiction, many of which his predecessors had allowed the federal government to occupy by default. By enabling Quebec to catch up to Ontario in economic development, he hoped to ensure that French Canadians living there would have comparable opportunities and living standards.

International relations were not even mentioned in the 1960 Liberal election programme, nor did they figure in Lesage's plans except as a means to attract further capital and industry to the province. Not so for his attorney general, Georges-Emile Lapalme. Lesage's predecessor as Liberal leader, Lapalme had suffered two electoral defeats at the hands of Maurice Duplessis, and wanted to leave politics after having helped to bring about the 1960 victory. But the new premier enticed him to stay on, at least for a while, with the promise that he could establish Quebec's first department of cultural affairs and then pass the attorney general's portfolio to another minister. Lapalme was in essence a man of letters and this project was very dear to him; indeed, it was he who had caused it to be included in the election programme. He could hardly refuse the opportunity to bring it about. He was also very aware that he would be emulating his ideal, André Malraux, whom President de Gaulle had appointed France's first minister of cultural affairs two years earlier.

During the election campaign, Premier Antonio Barrette had promised to open Quebec offices in Paris and London, presumably for commercial purposes, and while the Liberals did not match that promise, the press speculated during the summer of 1960 that the new government would carry out the commitment. In Paris, Charles Lussier, the director of the *Maison Canadienne*, a students' residence at the *Cité Universitaire*, and a part-time broadcaster on cultural affairs, read the speculation in the August 5 edition of the Montreal newspaper *Le Devoir*. He wrote to Gérard Pelletier, a prominent Montreal newspaperman whom he knew well, and asked him to pass on to the appropriate minister his offer to be of assistance. According to existing legislation, the responsibility for offices abroad lay with the minister of industry and commerce, André Rousseau; however, Pelletier, knowing of Lapalme's interests, sent it on to him. The message struck a responsive chord. Quite apart from his feelings of affinity with French culture, Lapalme, a highly sensitive man, had developed a resentment on his visits to the French capital against the staff of the Canadian embassy there. He felt they had abandoned their origins in favour of the more sophisticated European life-style, and, even worse, considered visitors like him to be an unnecessary intrusion in their pleasant existence. He viewed the establishment of a Quebec office in Paris as an opportunity to circumvent and even thumb his nose at them. Planning a holiday in Italy and Greece, he wrote to Lussier that he would see him on his way through Paris in September.

Charles Lussier was at Orly airport when Lapalme arrived with his friend, lawyer Maurice Riel, and their wives, and drove them to their hotel. After an hour's chat, Lapalme declared, "*Vous êtes mon homme!*" and told him that he would be appointed to establish the new office; economists and other personnel would be sent to support him. By hiring someone already on the spot and with good connections in Parisian cultural circles, he stated, he would save two years in making the operation effective. Taken by surprise by the turn of events, Lussier could only acquiesce.

That matter being settled, Lapalme and Riel met some of the latter's French business associates for lunch and, delighted with their coup, told them of the plan. Several of the historic provinces of France had "*maisons*" in Paris, someone pointed out, and there was no reason why Quebec, although not a province in the same sense, should not have one as well. The question arose how to raise the subject with the French government, preferably without going through the Canadian embassy. One of the Frenchmen remarked that a colleague had served in the Resistance with André Malraux and was still in touch with him; he offered to see if a meeting could be arranged. Lapalme was ecstatic at the prospect of meeting the famous figure. At nine o'clock the next morning, the telephone rang in his hotel room: the minister would receive them that afternoon at three in his Palais Royal office, across from the Louvre.

André Malraux had visited Quebec once, in 1937. A Communist then, his purpose had been to enlist support for the Republican forces in the Spanish Civil War. *Le Devoir* had denounced him as a "notorious Communist" and quoted at length François Mauriac's denunciations of him; he was shunned by most of the élite. Since then both men had rallied to General de Gaulle, who took pleasure in pointing to them as proof of his intellectual support. In 1959, Marc Drouin, Speaker of the Canadian Senate and another man of broad culture, had invited Malraux to tour the Canadian Arctic and see the Eskimo settlements where the soapstone carvings, becoming famous as examples of primitive art, were being produced. While the trip did not materialize, he did show interest. When General de Gaulle had returned from North America in the spring, he had mentioned "the enormous potential of Quebec" and had asked Malraux to take an interest in it. And the very day the Quebecers arrived, he had raised the matter again in Cabinet and said "Malraux, we have to do something about Quebec."[1] The request for an interview was a fortuitous coincidence.

Lapalme and Riel were ushered into the august presence, Riel recalled later, with fear and trembling.[2] In response to Malraux's question, "*Messieurs*, what can I do for you?" Lapalme plunged into his presentation, expressing, in Riel's words, "the ardent nostalgia of the Quebec soul for France." The French minister listened silently, then told them of de Gaulle's comment the previous day. Coming out from behind his huge desk, he sat down near them, placed an ashtray on the floor, and, chain-smoking, began one of his famous monologues on Western civilization, in which, to his guests' delight, he managed to incorporate the little white churches of New England, those of Quebec's Ile d'Orléans, and Quebec's wood sculptures and other forms of handicraft. When he had finished, he turned directly to the subject of the interview. He had a feeling of guilt towards French Canadians, Malraux avowed, for the way France had neglected them. Now, however, "a man of genius," General de Gaulle, had recognized the situation and seen its potential. "Let us start from there," he advised. "You are isolated in North America, next to one of the largest powers in the world." They were right to seek a "*rapprochement*" with France. Were the French government to take the initiative, its motives would be suspect, particularly after ignoring French Canadians for two hundred years. "Go ahead with your plan," he told them, "open that *maison du Québec*, establish yourselves in Paris, and we will meet you half way." Emboldened by the warm endorsement, Lapalme said that he would not only go ahead, but hoped that General de Gaulle would attend the opening of the *maison*, or delegate Malraux to do so. "If the General sends me," the minister responded, "I will be there. You can count on me."

"We left the office walking on air," Riel recalled later. Afterward, the two men had to pace up and down for an hour in the gardens of the Palais Royal to settle their emotions. Invited to lunch later by the Canadian ambassador, Pierre Dupuy, they took a mischievous pleasure in breaking the news to him. When they landed at Montreal's Dorval airport on their return home, Lapalme could not resist mentioning the news to journalists who met him. He even revealed the name of the future director. Premier Lesage and the other ministers were taken completely by surprise. Another very sensitive person, André Rousseau, did not appreciate the intervention in his area of responsibility. Lesage, too, was annoyed over the unauthorized initiative, but he needed Lapalme in the Cabinet, and realized that if a fuss were made over the matter, he might well resign.

Before the subject came before Cabinet on November 2, a compromise solution was devised. The project would go ahead, but it would fall under the responsibility of the minister of industry and commerce, an arrangement made necessary by the fact that he alone had the necessary credits; and, at any rate, the Department of Cultural Affairs did not yet even exist. Rousseau concurred, but grumbled that it was more important for economic and financial reasons to establish an office in London. That step, too, was already being prepared. The same newspaper report that had attracted Lussier's attention had also come to the attention of the Canadian high commissioner in London, George Drew. He had written enthusiastically to Lesage, a personal friend, pointing out that Quebec was the only province not represented there, and offering all possible cooperation in correcting the situation. The premier agreed, and a search was undertaken for a suitable appointee.

There were still several obstacles to be overcome before the delegation general—the title was suggested by officials in the Canadian Department of External Affairs—became a reality. Lapalme withdrew into a pained silence at having his project pre-empted; Rousseau procrastinated to manifest his displeasure at being faced with a *fait accompli*. Finally, Lussier's appointment was approved by Cabinet on January 13, 1961. However, he was given no specific mandate. He devised his own, "to strengthen relations with France," "develop economic relations,"and "encourage francophone immigration."[3] Cultural affairs were not mentioned specifically. Nor was Lussier given any instructions with regard to his relationship to the embassy. In Ottawa, the matter was put in the hands of Marcel Cadieux, the associate under secretary of state for external affairs and a specialist in international law and diplomatic practices. While Cadieux was generally favourable to the project, he was determined that constitutional lines of authority be respected. That meant, in general, that while a province like Quebec could have contacts with foreign governments in its fields of jurisdiction, the Canadian government had responsibility for foreign policy, including the treaty-making power. In short, Quebec had to operate within the framework set by Ottawa, and under its watchful eye. That was the clear implication of a statement by Ambassador Dupuy to Lussier: "You are under my control."[4] Still a neophyte in the field of diplomacy, the delegate general voiced no objection.

Once the official announcement was made, pressure became intense to start operations as soon as possible. Matters such as relations between the two levels of government, and even the legal status of the delegation general in France, were left until later. In March 1961, Lussier found a suitable building not far from the Invalides; it was purchased for a quarter of a million dollars. Again to expedite matters, the Royal Bank of Canada loaned him one of its officials as commercial counsellor. Lapalme selected Robert Elie, a well known literary figure in Quebec, as cultural counsellor. A less welcome addition to the small team was a Frenchman who had developed a thriving business by advising wine exporters how to operate the patronage, or kickback, system of the Duplessis government to obtain contracts with the Quebec Liquor Commission. During the 1960 election campaign, he had advised the exporters to make their financial contributions to the *Union Nationale* party as the most likely to win and to serve their interests, but shortly after the Liberal victory, he was able to assure his clients that he also had excellent contacts with the new government. As proof, he produced a letter signed by Premier Lesage, thanking him for his services to the province and appointing him "*Conseiller d'honneur.*" Armed with this document, whose origin remains a mystery, he appeared in Lussier's office and announced that he was available. The delegate general was, quite rightly, wary, all the more since he was being deluged with offers of assistance from both Frenchmen and French Canadians, most of which cloaked varying degrees of self-interest. The world of diplomacy was proving more delicate and complex than he had anticipated.

Not the least of Lussier's problems concerned his relations with his superiors in Quebec. Georges-Emile Lapalme had by no means abandoned his claim to the paternity of the project; he appeared in Paris in mid-1961 to inspect its progress and also to have another chat with André Malraux. He also gave instructions that Elie, whom he had made an official of the Department of Cultural Affairs (established in early 1961), was to report to him directly and not through Lussier. That arrangement was to become a continuing source of tension and caballing. Rousseau, too, continued to be difficult, taking umbrage at any direct contact between the delegation general and his Cabinet colleagues, and complaining that the funds would be better allocated to industrial promotion at home.

The official opening of the delegation general was set for October 5, 1961, and Jean Lesage agreed to lead a delegation to Paris for the occasion. General de Gaulle took a personal interest in the arrangements, and while protocol did not allow him to attend the ceremony, he delegated Malraux to represent him. French officials advised Lussier that, even if it could not be stated publicly, France wanted to receive the premier "as a head of state."[5] Accordingly, the president had decided to give a dinner at the Elysée Palace for the principal dignitaries, to be followed by a reception for several hundred people. He also intended to grant a private audience to the premier.

An aircraft was chartered to fly the Quebecers, including about half the Cabinet, to Paris. The *Union Nationale* party boycotted the event on the grounds of expense and accused Jean Lesage, who had adopted President de Gaulle's slogan, a policy of grandeur, of seeking to emulate him. The premier already knew Paris fairly well, having attended conferences there in the 1950s as parliamentary secretary to the then Canadian secretary of state for external affairs, Lester B. Pearson. Combining business and pleasure, he and his wife, Corinne, started their trip early, crossing the ocean by ship and spending a few days first in London with the Canadian high commissioner and another friend, the recent appointee as Quebec agent general in London, Hugues Lapointe, and their wives. The Lesages then flew to Rome, where they were received by Pope John XXIII, and to Milan where Lesage announced the appointment of a Quebec commercial representative there.

When they reached Paris on October 4 by a regularly scheduled Air France flight from Nice, some three hundred Quebecers had already assembled for the occasion. Limousines had been provided for the ministers, and information services for the others. The atmosphere was reminiscent, not of the return of the prodigal son, but of relatives returning home after a long absence. On setting foot on French soil, Lesage declared, with evident emotion, that he had the impression of having "previously lived here." Undoubtedly it was an atavism, he remarked, an "inheritance from his forefathers." Foreign Minister Couve de Murville received him and his ministers at noon; the president received him "in private audience" at four o'clock. It was their first meeting, except for the brief encounter in Quebec City the previous year, and provided de Gaulle with an opportunity to assess the man who was leading the process of change in Quebec to which he had drawn Malraux's attention. While no record of their conversation has emerged, it appears to have gone well and with Lesage making a strong impression. A handsome man of distinguished bearing and with an elegant diction—hardly the French stereotype of a French Canadian—the premier appeared at ease and obviously enjoyed the occasion. He was also an exceptionally hard worker and had prepared himself thoroughly for that and every other part of the programme. Both he and de Gaulle were engaged in renewing their respective societies and were looking for opportunities to work together in pursuing that objective. There appeared to exist all the ingredients for a fruitful relationship.

At five thirty p.m., the premier led a parade of limousines up the Champs Elysées to the Arc de Triomphe to place a wreath on the Tomb of the Unknown Soldier. Something was bound to go awry in such a lengthy schedule, and there it did. With so many details to attend to, no one had arranged for a wreath to be handed to him. Recognizing the embarrassing situation, the commander of the honour guard said reassuringly, "It will be a spiritual bouquet." Jean Lesage reacted with typical aplomb: he drew his rosary out of his pocket and deposited it instead. Those who knew French Canada as an overwhelmingly Roman Catholic society might have thought that the change in procedure had been pre-ordained. The day ended in a pleasant anticlimax with a reception offered by Ambassador Dupuy and a dinner by Charles Lussier.

Although Jean Lesage was prepared to play on the emotional aspects of the visit, he was also careful, in view of press speculation, to set clear limits on what he considered to be the proper direct links between France and Quebec. At a press conference at the luxurious Hotel Crillon, on Place de la Concorde, on the morning of October 5, he drew attention to an information kit distributed to journalists. The government of Quebec, it stated, was operating scrupulously within the framework of the Canadian constitution. Canada was "a federation of provincial States" in which "the central State" had jurisdiction over international treaties, but the "provincial States" enjoyed complete autonomy in their fields of jurisdiction, notably the right to legislate with regard to "industry, commerce, education and culture." In the circumstances, the delegation general would work "in collaboration with the Canadian embassy in economic and cultural matters." Quebec wanted to "draw closer to the United States of Europe in order to free itself from the embrace of the United States of America." In the economic sphere, the government was prepared to guarantee European investments "in new factories, mineral discovery and processing."

Culturally, the new Department of Cultural Affairs was seeking "to extend the French culture in North America and to draw closer to France and the other countries of French language and culture." In that regard, the role of the delegation general was "to assist the cultural services of the Embassy in their tasks, to present an accurate picture of French Canada, to increase exchanges between Quebec, France and other countries of French language and culture, and, on a basis of cooperation, to take joint steps to assist the newly independent countries of French language and culture."

Similarly, at the inauguration of the delegation general, Lesage was at pains to explain the government's perspective on Quebec's place within Canada. The expression recently coined, "the State of Quebec," he stressed, did not signify that Quebec had become a distinct country. Rather, it referred to the governmental organization as "the common base, the lever" to ensure French Canada's "presence in Canada and our survival in the American setting." It reflected the fact that "the French-Canadian people" had become "aware of itself and of its place in the world." Two centuries earlier, France was withdrawing from North America; now he and the others were there to bear witness to "the perpetuity of the French fact" there. Some had spoken of the miracle of their survival. That term could now be abandoned; "we live." But they continued to need the inspiration of France, just as others in North America needed Quebec's inspiration in order to remain French. Their purpose was not to transform Quebec into "a northern extension of France;" rather, it was to be better able to remain themselves without any "bonds of dependency." Since a nation did not live only from spiritual nourishment, Quebecers wanted to take their place in "the European economic universe," offering it, and France first of all, investment opportunities as well as cooperation in developing the province's resources and in the increased trade that would result. Once again he pointed out that the new international initiatives were not motivated by a desire to compete with Canada's embassies abroad, nor were they a duplication of efforts. As a federal country, Canada had a divided jurisdiction. Indeed, several Canadian embassies had requested Quebec representation at their side, and the new offices had received a very favourable reception. The natural diversity of Canada called for a variety of approaches.

On behalf of the French government, André Malraux welcomed the new Quebec presence in Paris. He placed his emphasis on cultural values, expressing the hope that Canada's artists might bring to Western culture what Europe had never known, the reflection of the vast northern reaches of North America. "If, in pursuing their great common enterprise [of Western civilization] Canada wanted the support of France," he declared, "it would consider it an honour to respond."

In his subsequent public statements, Jean Lesage combined tributes to France with reminders of Quebec's distinctiveness. French Canadians proclaimed "with pride" their debts towards the mother country, he declared at a luncheon offered by Prime Minister Michel Debré. "How can we not love her, since it is she who conceived us?" But, as with children, the only way to pay that debt was not to become a pale replica or to copy the parental model, however beautiful, but to make maximum use of the means and examples given to them to develop their own personality. "Scratch a French Canadian," he told a group of French parliamentarians later in the day, "and you will find a 'Gaulois'!"* Nevertheless, they felt perfectly at ease with British political institutions; in fact, they had "literally acclimatized them" and made them their own. Those institutions were among the reasons for their survival and had helped to produce "a new nation where tradition and progress are in harmony."

At a reception offered by the French Academy, the premier defended the distinctive traits of the French spoken in Quebec. Language was the verbal expression of a population's mentality and thought processes, he pointed out, and for that reason the government had to take an interest in its quality. The problem was that the French Canadian was "fiercely individualistic" and impossible to regiment. He adapted the French language to his needs just as a worker leaves his mark on his tools. It would be "grotesque" for him to imitate the European French accent and style slavishly; at any rate, the mode of expression of French Canadians who respected their language was perfectly legitimate.

After Lesage's remarks, he, Lapalme and the Quebec minister of youth, Paul Gérin-Lajoie, sat in on a session of the Academy preparing a new dictionary of the French language. The word "*chaud*," or hot, was up for discussion. Not one to be easily intimidated, Lesage explained to his illustrious hosts that, in Quebec, it also meant half-drunk. And the English term "hot dog" was translated as "*chien chaud.*" His attempts to add some colour to the solemn proceedings had little effect, but it was made more acceptable by his own impressive mastery of the language.

In a busy schedule of official events, the premier continued to develop his theme. At the Hôtel de Ville, he referred to the "danger of exceptional gravity" to French Canada from the "cultural invasion" of the United States. Indeed, all of Canada was in danger of becoming a "cultural satellite." Fortunately, in a "delicious paradox," the more enlightened English Canadians recognized in the French culture "the

* An inhabitant of historic pre-French Gaul, known for his rugged ways and bawdy humour.

only efficient antidote to excessive Americanization." The fact that English Canadians desired its survival as much as French Canadians was "the sweetest revenge that France could dream of since the loss of Canada in 1759." Putting their preoccupation with survival behind them, he continued in another forum, the *Institut France-Canada*; Quebecers were demanding "a new life-style" and "the integration of Quebec into Confederation." His government was being asked to do nothing less than to "bring Quebec into line with the modern world." After being accustomed for many years to consider that the province's cultural traits were its only wealth, he stated at a luncheon of the *Cercle de l'Opinion*, the Quebec people had come to realize the importance of developing its resources through an "economic reconquest" in order to assert itself as "a distinct ethnic group." Before still another audience, the members of the *Société du Louvre*, he invited Frenchmen to come with "their talent and capital" and join in developing the "land of the future."

General de Gaulle spoke only once in public during the Quebecers' visit. Proposing a toast to his guests at the dinner in the Elysée Palace, he declared that, since they had been "left there" two centuries earlier, the French had not ceased "to follow, to admire and to love the unbelievable effort of this branch of our stock" which, after overcoming so many obstacles and ordeals, now appeared as "a vigorous tree."[6] Quebec's watchword was *"Je me souviens."* France echoed that sentiment. Historical evolution had separated them, and now it had brought them together again; they had "many things to do together." France too was "deeply engaged in a process of renovation," and the French understood "better than anyone" Quebecers' concern to take control of their economic affairs. In asserting and developing their own personality, they were rendering a service to all Canada, which he saluted "with all our deep friendship." Further, "the general equilibrium of the world" could only benefit from "the presence and...the expansion, on the soil of the New Continent, of an entity of French stock, culture and activity."

Once again, de Gaulle's public statements did not concur entirely with his later memoirs, nor for that matter, with the intentions of Jean Lesage. The objective of the premier's visit, de Gaulle wrote later, was "to organize the direct assistance of France to the Canadian branch of its people, which had lost its sovereignty, but which, pressed on all sides on American soil by elements of other origins, seeks to remain faithful to its soul."[7] Accordingly, the two governments had arranged "between themselves and without any intermediary," the beginnings of the aid that France would provide henceforth to "the French of Canada." Quite apart from the fact that the expression "the French of Canada" was not one that French Canadians would apply to themselves, the statement went far beyond anything that Jean Lesage had in mind.

In addition to the premier's activities, the Quebec ministers met their French counterparts to discuss possible joint projects. Both the French and Canadian media gave the visit extensive coverage, the French press alone publishing some six hundred articles. Canadian journalists, both English- and French-speaking, were titillated whether Lesage had, indeed, been received with the honours due to a head of state, something which could be interpreted as a slight to Ottawa. Jacques-Yvan Morin, a professor of international law at the University of Montreal who was on hand for the occasion, declared that Lesage had indeed been so treated; *Le Devoir* correspondent Jean-Marc Léger asserted that the delegation general was in fact the embassy of Quebecers in Paris.[8] Later, Jean Lesage, who in addition to his positive qualities was not exempt from hubris, boasted occasionally of his reception by de Gaulle as a head of state, but those who knew him did not take the remark seriously. In fact, he had been careful to respect the prerogatives of the Canadian embassy, and Ambassador Dupuy had been present at all functions he would normally attend. Asked on television after his return to Quebec if he had given encouragement to the new separatist movement that was part of the effervescence associated with the Quiet Revolution, the premier replied, "On the contrary; they can see an encouragement if they want, but I am not giving them any." When the public discussion persisted, he issued a press release, "Monsieur Lesage's whole career proves the importance that he attaches to the place and role of French Canadians in Confederation. They have been historically at the *avant-garde* of Canadianism."[9] While de Gaulle's views on the subject were unknown, his foreign minister evidently shared Lesage's outlook. Meeting Charles Lussier not long afterwards, Couve de Murville warned him that if Quebec wanted to establish a base in Paris "to promote secession," it would not work. Assured by the delegate general that such was not the case, he said: "Alright then, carry on."[10]

The exchange of effusive declarations over, the next stage was to give form and substance to the good intentions that had been expressed. That was to be a much more difficult and time-consuming task. In early 1962, a new and exceptionally dynamic French ambassador to Canada, Raymond Bousquet, was appointed. While he made no reference to it in presenting his credentials to Governor General Vanier, he had specific instructions to give special attention to relations with Quebec. Cultural attachés were also appointed for the first time to the French consulates general in Quebec City and Montreal. In October 1962, a group of French businessmen, led by

Wilfrid Baumgartner, former minister of finance and economics, visited Canada to explore investment opportunities. The same month, two members of the National Assembly's Commission on Foreign Affairs, Charles Bosson and Edmond Thorailler, arrived "to study the totality of matters of common interest between the two countries."[12] They discovered, according to their subsequent report, a country which was not only "the reflection of eighteenth century France and Victorian England," but was also an extension of the United States. In fact, even French Canadians were "living on American time." Yet despite this "constant and deep impregnation," intellectual life, at least in French Canada, maintained its originality. The French language universities were throbbing with activity, and the University of Montreal had recently taken the initiative in creating the *Association d'Universités partiellement ou entièrement de langue française* (AUPELF). The arrival in power of Jean Lesage and his "young and dynamic team" determined to "breathe new life into the French people" gave the visiting parliamentarians the impression of witnessing the birth of "a new Age of Enlightenment." But while the premier wished to see Quebec, as "the national State of French Canadians," develop its personality as much as possible, he was not "yielding to the temptation of separatism." Yet, that temptation was real, and several groups had been formed. The largest, the *Rassemblement pour l'Indépendance Nationale* (RIN), had some five thousand supporters, largely from "a certain intellectual bourgeoisie." The clergy, although still powerful, appeared to be staying on the sidelines, but half of the students in the faculties of social sciences were separatists. As for the masses, they appeared to be too imprisoned in the amenities of "the American way of life" to support a course of action "the consequences of which would be, to say the least, economically hazardous." Still, the separatist movements were forcing the English Canadians and the federal authorities to recognize the necessity of giving French Canadians their proper place in the country.

The motto, "*Je me souviens,*" Bosson and Thorailler noted, until recently reflected a certain resentment and reserve towards the France of Louis XV and of 1789; now that French Canadians and the French, brothers in the same family, had found the path they would follow together, it could and would take on its full meaning. France should therefore increase its cultural and economic relations with Canada, and particularly with the state of Quebec; it was the duty of a sister nation; it was also a matter of national interest. Officially established less than a century ago, the Canadian nation had not yet found its personality, and now more than ever, was in danger of not doing so. With so many factors operating in favour of its integration into the United States, the two parliamentarians asked, was not

French Canada, combining tradition and a new spirit of renewal, best placed to support the "British" provinces by giving the country a distinctive personality and enabling it to carry out its liaison mission between America and Europe within the framework of the Atlantic Community?

The diagnosis of Bosson and Thorailler, while understandably European in perspective, was insightful and the French policy that they proposed was realistic. However, it did not address the more difficult problem of developing specific projects. Nor was the Baumgartner mission any more successful in that regard. While Canada was fourth among the world's trading nations and eighth as an industrial power, ranking close to France on both counts, it was indeed, "functioning on American time." The French, for their part, were still functioning on "European time," or looking to their former colonies for profitable ventures. Lending credence to that analysis of the situation, Jean Lesage, who doubled as minister of finance, followed up his voyage to Paris with one to New York in February 1962. In contrast to the euphoria that marked the former, and particularly after the evocations of the spectre of Americanization, his message was down-to-earth. The premier's principal speech was made to the Canadian Society of New York, made up largely of businessmen; he also met privately with members of the financial community and the press. The province was moving from an economy based primarily on agriculture and forestry, he told the Americans, to one based on mining and hydro-electric power, sectors of almost unlimited potential.[13] Foreign capital was needed and even welcome, providing it was used in such a way as to enable the population to participate in new developments, particularly through local processing of natural resources. The government had recently taken steps to ensure such participation through the establishment of a publicly-owned holding company, the General Finance Corporation, which could join the private sector in financing development projects. In that and other ways, it was hoped to ensure close cooperation with investors so that both their objectives and those of Quebecers as a whole could be met. In order to accelerate that cooperation, the commercial section of Quebec's agency general in New York was being expanded.

In May 1963, Lesage undertook his second mission to Europe. In the meantime, in November 1962, his government had won a fresh mandate from the electorate with a programme calling for the nationalization of the principal electric-power-producing companies, largely owned by English Canadians. The cost of the takeover was in excess of six hundred million dollars. With that and other expensive commitments, the limits to the province's borrowing capacity were being reached. Foreign capital was needed more urgently than ever.

The premier's first port of call was London, where he officiated at the opening of Quebec House, and met with British businessmen, including leading members of the powerful Rothschild group. Quebec was a "land of opportunity," he told members of the Canadian Chamber of Commerce; French Canadians were friendly and hospitable, and resources and manpower abundant. The welcome mat was out for investors. While it was true that Quebecers were asserting themselves, he stated, they were not motivated by narrow self-interest, but seeking to make "an even larger contribution to the national development of Canada as a whole."[14] From Britain, Lesage went on to Belgium for discussions with members of an engineering group that was carrying out a feasibility study for the General Finance Corporation of a comprehensive steel-producing factory, SIDBEC, to process the rich iron ore deposits in northern Quebec. His main concern was with the cost and he tried—in vain—to persuade the Belgians to undertake the whole project, including paying for it. Even in Paris, his final stop, he spent most of his time on financial and economic matters. A year after his previous visit, French investments in Quebec were still under one hundred and fifty million dollars and no significant new projects were under consideration. In meetings with representatives of both the private and public sectors, he argued strongly for some concrete action.

Once again, Lesage had a private audience with de Gaulle. Responding to the president's invitation to make Quebec's needs known, he put forward a series of tangible projects, including SIDBEC, in which he also hoped for French involvement. A second project, also developed by the General Finance Corporation, called for the establishment of a French automobile assembly plant. The reasoning behind it was that, because of the cultural affinity of Frenchmen and French Canadians, there was a natural market in Quebec for the vehicles. For French manufacturers, it was asserted, Quebec also offered not only a familiar environment, but, even more important, a springboard for the whole North American market. By the time Lesage arrived in Paris, the Citroën firm had already decided not to become involved, mainly because it was not prepared to meet North American standards of quality. Peugeot was also hesitant, and even the management of Renault, a state enterprise, was sceptical because of the limited sales potential in Quebec. Lesage asked de Gaulle if he could apply pressure, particularly on Renault, as a state-owned firm, to obtain a favourable decision. Another subject raised by the premier concerned the purchase, currently under consideration by the Canadian public airline, Trans Canada Airlines, of a new fleet of aircraft. One model under consideration was the French Caravelle. Lesage inquired whether its producers, another state enterprise, could be persuaded to have the machines built in whole or in part in Montreal. Such a commitment, he pointed out, would greatly strengthen the case for choosing the Caravelle over a competing American model.

Lesage's final request concerned the need for greater exchanges of information between France and Quebec. The Canadian Broadcasting Corporation, he pointed out, had a radio and television correspondent based permanently in Paris; could not the French equivalent do the same in Montreal? he asked. General de Gaulle took careful written notes of the requests and agreed to look into them. Most were to prove difficult even for him to meet. The exception was the request for a *Radio-Télévision Française* reporter: that was an organization over which the president had direct control.* Within a month, Pierre-Louis Mallen was chosen and despatched to Quebec; in a short time, he became an enthusiastic proponent of Quebec's independence. That was not at all the kind of reporting that Jean Lesage had had in mind.

Following the meeting, de Gaulle gave a luncheon in the premier's honour which was attended by Prime Minister Pompidou, Foreign Minister Couve de Murville, and some fifty other French and Canadian guests. Lesage also had meetings with Ambassador Dupuy and Delegate General Lussier, who assured him that relations between their organizations were harmonious. The principal problem that they had not been able to resolve, he was told, concerned the official status of the delegation general. On behalf of the Canadian government, Dupuy had suggested the model developed in London for the provincial agencies general. While the latter fell under the general authority of the Canadian high commission, they enjoyed most diplomatic privileges and easy access to British government officials. French protocol, however, did not recognize such an intermediate status: one was entitled to full diplomatic privileges or to none, and neither the legal advisers of the Ministry of Foreign Affairs, nor their counterparts in Ottawa, were in favour of the first option. And pending an agreement, the second option of no privileges applied. For Lussier, quite apart from having to pay full prices for vehicles, alcohol and other French items, that meant that he and his staff had to spend many hours clearing shipments of material from Quebec through French customs offices, and to pay duty on them. Briefed on the situation, Jean Lesage's first reaction was one of impatience: to shake the French bureaucrats out of their rigid attitude, the rule of reciprocity should apply, he declared; the French consulates on Quebec territory would henceforth receive the same privileges as those accorded to the delegation general. On reflection, he realized that too much was at stake for such strong measures, and said that he would raise the

* He once commented, "My opponents have the printed press; I have the RTF."

matter on his return to Canada with Paul Martin, the new secretary of state for external affairs and a personal friend and former colleague in the St. Laurent government.

The Diefenbaker government had been defeated during federal general elections in April, and the Liberals had been returned to power under the leadership of Lester B. Pearson, another of Lesage's friends. In fact, he had good personal relations with over half of the new ministers. The new government was much better disposed than its predecessor towards French Canada; indeed, some representatives of the new generation of reformers from Quebec were in the Cabinet and the prime minister himself, an exceptionally open-minded man, had committed himself to recognizing the special place of Quebec as the homeland of French Canadians, and to ensuring the equality of Canada's two "founding peoples." One of the first decisions of the Pearson government had been to establish a royal commission to recommend ways of achieving that equality. Lesage had been consulted on the terms of reference and had publicly endorsed the initiative. With those excellent contacts and compatible views, Lesage was confident that minor matters such as the status of the delegation general could be settled without difficulty, at least on the Canadian side; and he had the most powerful of allies, de Gaulle himself, in France.

Within the delegation general, other problems persisted. André Rousseau had been defeated in the Quebec elections of 1962, and Gérard-D. Lévesque had succeeded him as minister responsible for the offices abroad. On the other hand, Georges-Emile Lapalme, by then full-time minister of cultural affairs, was still sensitive at not having received authority over the *maison du Québec*, as the delegation general was generally known, and continued to ignore Lussier's authority over cultural matters. The delegation general was also being caught up in the mounting debate over the future of Quebec within Confederation. In Quebec, the *Rassemblement pour l'Indépendance nationale* was receiving publicity far in excess of its numerical strength. Its first president, Dr. Marcel Chaput, was reprimanded for engaging in political activities while a federal government employee; he resigned on principle and acquired something of a martyr status. His book, *Why I Am a Separatist*, became a best-seller.[15] By 1963, the independence movement was not only drawing on traditional nationalist sentiment, but it was linking up with the current worldwide decolonization process. That phenomenon, and particularly the Cuban and Algerian revolutions, was brought into Quebec homes via television and fueled the debate on the future of French Canadians.

Individuals found themselves forced to take sides on the issue. Pierre Trudeau, law professor at the University of Montreal, emerged as the intellectual leader of the opponents of Quebec independence; Jean-Marc Léger, *Le Devoir* journalist and secretary-general of the *Association des Universités entièrement ou partiellement de langue française*, became the most lucid advocate of the opposite position. In addition to being a fervent admirer of General de Gaulle, Léger had travelled widely in French-speaking Africa and had met such distinguished personalities as Senegal's President Leopold Senghor and Ivory Coast's President Felix Houphouët-Boigny. In a series of articles published in *Le Devoir* in July 1963 entitled *"Le Québec dans le monde francophone,"* Léger described Quebec as "prisoner of the Canadian pseudo-federation open only to the anglophone world" and declared that French Canada needed to establish as soon as possible "a vast network of relations with all the French language countries."[16] The federal government, he asserted, could never accomplish that; the only possibility was "the vigorous, imaginative and persistent action of the Government of Quebec." Such a development would follow naturally if Quebec were a sovereign state rather than a "subject, dominated, colonized nation."

In September 1962, Chaput broke with the RIN and formed the *Parti Républicain du Québec*. He was a candidate in the November elections, but made only a modest showing. The following March, the RIN too became a party under the leadership of an outstanding young orator, Pierre Bourgault. In April and May 1963, terrorist bombs exploded for the first time in Montreal against English-Canadian targets, causing one death; a clandestine organization, the *Front de Libération du Québec* (FLQ), claimed responsibility for the acts. Eighteen arrests were made a few weeks later. The lively debate over Quebec separatism stimulated by such actions spread to Paris and, inevitably, the delegation general became caught up in it. Some federalists viewed the delegation as a direct link between the Lesage and de Gaulle governments established for the purpose of promoting Quebec independence. At the other extreme, Lussier was criticized by pro-separatists for attempting to remain strictly neutral in the debate. A small group of Quebec students in Paris was using the library of the delegation general as a source of documentation to promote the independentist cause among the French population, but that appears to have been the only grounds for federal suspicions.

Within the French government, a small number of persons were sympathetic to the activities of the separatists. Most of these officials had been in the colonial service and had taken part in the decolonization process, the objective of which was not only to grant formal independence to the French colonies, but to maintain French influence through the appointment of French advisers to the new governments, various forms of aid or cooperation, and French leadership of the

French-speaking community. For these officials, an independent Quebec was a natural and desirable addition to that community. Several of these Quebec sympathizers had personal knowledge of Canada. Xavier Deniau, a Gaullist member of the National Assembly, had married a Canadian. Martial de la Fournière, employed in the office of the minister of defence, and Philippe Rossillon, in the *haut Commissariat de la Langue française* (which was attached to the Prime Minister's Office), had visited Quebec in the 1930s as delegates to student conferences. When, in the summer of 1963, a University of Montreal student, Pierre Gravel, went to Paris as spokesman for the *Parti Républicain du Québec*, he was given Rossillon's name as a key contact. A man who delighted in mystery and intrigue, Rossillon received him warmly, helped him find an apartment and even gave him financial support. In return, he asked him to write occasional pro-separatist analyses of Quebec politics which, he intimated, would reach the president's desk, and also that a network of supporters of Quebec independence had been established throughout the upper echelons of the French government, extending into the Elysée Palace.

General de Gaulle's own perception of Quebec and the prospects of Franco-Quebec relations at that particular time remain unclear. After his return to power in 1958, he had quickly reached the conclusion that, if a people desired to be independent, its will could not be thwarted, and the only realistic course of action was to accommodate to that situation. That reasoning had led him to grant independence to the colonies in Africa and also to Algeria. He certainly saw an analogy in Quebec, and this viewpoint was bolstered by his strong feelings for the "French of Canada." But was he, in fact, pro-separatist? Shortly after the first bombings in Montreal, he encountered Lussier in the receiving line at a reception in the Elysée Palace. "Well," he asked, "are you being tempted by separatism?" Lussier interpreted the question as an implicit criticism, and as the other guests stopped to listen to the exchange, assured him that the government he represented was not so inclined. It seems likely that de Gaulle was employing a tactic that his entourage called a 'provocation,' asking a 'trap question' of an interlocutor to probe his thinking without revealing one's own views. Clearly he was monitoring the situation, but, in another of his common expressions, he probably felt that the situation was not yet "ripe." When, on his second visit to Paris, Jean Lesage raised with him the possibility of his visiting Quebec, de Gaulle replied non-committally that two of his ministers, André Malraux and Finance Minister Valéry Giscard d'Estaing, would be making the trip soon. Later he asked the two ministers not to appear simultaneously "in order to avoid causing anxiety in Ottawa."[17]

The occasion for Malraux's visit was the French Economic Exhibition in Montreal in October 1963, but his main interest was in the place of French-Canadian culture in the broadest context of the "human condition" (the title of one of his most famous works). "I have not come here to tell you what France offers you," he said on his arrival and paraphrasing President John Kennedy, "but to tell you what France expects of you."[18] What France expected, he continued, was that, within ten years, French Canadians would express their unique setting through great music and poetry. He made no secret of the fact that separatism held no attraction for him; clearly, it clashed with his universalist approach to life. A Quebec dependent on France would be "ridiculous and dangerous," he declared at the end of his stay; the ties between them were "historic and artistic rather than political."[19] At a dinner that he gave in Malraux's honour, Jean Lesage picked up that theme and added that the best way to remain true to French Canada's origins was to remain in the Canadian Confederation, "the antidote against the americanization of our cultures."[20] Still, Malraux was obviously intrigued by political developments in Quebec. On one occasion, he drew an analogy between his experience in the French Resistance movement, during World War Two, and that of French Canadians who, "from the depths of their night," were able to develop the means for their own emancipation. And, shortly before returning home, he could not resist asking Lesage about the terrorist situation in the light of several recent arrests. The matter was "resolved, finished for ever," the premier responded categorically.[21] Obviously dubious, Malraux did not pursue the subject. Lesage supported the cultural projects that Malraux and Lapalme agreed upon during the visit, but his own priorities remained financial and economic. When Malraux outlined the projects to him, he asked, "All that will cost us how much?"[22] "Not a cent," he was assured.

The premier was increasingly impatient at the lack of progress on the projects he had discussed with General de Gaulle several months earlier. On his instructions, Gérard-D. Lévesque wrote to Pierre Dreyfus, head of the Renault firm, about the proposed automobile assembly plant; and he himself wrote to Prime Minister Pompidou to urge an early and favourable decision. Pompidou responded non-committally. The top executives of both Renault and Peugeot still had serious reservations about the viability of the project, feeling that the Quebec market was too small to be profitable, and that the population had a preference for American car models. They asked for financial participation and guarantees from the Canadian or Quebec government, or both, to reduce the risks. The government of Ontario had shown an interest in having the plant built in that province, which would have greatly enlarged the potential market and made the venture more attractive.

Alarmed at such a prospect, Lesage wrote directly to General de Gaulle.[23] The projects they had discussed were important economically, he told the president, but there were other considerations, particularly "the question of affinities between two peoples." The "logic of fate" made Quebec "an instinctive collaborator of France." While there were admittedly problems in establishing the assembly plant, they would be easier to resolve "between partners of the same language and...common ethnic background." Should "a province with an overwhelming English language majority" be chosen as the site, Quebec's "French pride would be seriously affected." The strong words reflected the urgency being felt in Quebec City. De Gaulle responded reassuringly but also prudently.[24] "You know well enough the interest I take personally in the development of French Canada, tied as it is to France not only by so many memories and affinities, but also by such great common hopes for all manner of developments, not to doubt my keen desire, too, to see that the projects you mention are carried out." The two automobile firms were continuing their studies, he reported, and he hoped that the results would be positive, "after the analysis of all the factors that enter into consideration in this kind of matter, and, among them, naturally, the profitability of the project." At any rate, Lesage could be assured that the French government would "make every effort to facilitate a decision in accordance with your wishes and which, as you say so rightly, are in keeping with the logic of current trends." There were evidently limits to even de Gaulle's ability to impose his will.

The matter of the delegation general's legal status continued to rankle as well. Following Lesage's visit to Paris in May, officials in the Quai d'Orsay finally suggested a subterfuge to circumvent the rigid rules of protocol: if the Canadian embassy were to address a letter to the Ministry of Foreign Affairs stating simply that "Monsieur Charles A. Lussier is a Canadian adviser," then he could receive the privileges of a duly accredited Canadian diplomat.[25] Lesage sent the suggestion along to Paul Martin. The minister of external affairs responded that a fictitious designation would be a distortion of the reality, since Lussier's functions were not determined by the embassy and he had no direct link with it; nor would it solve the real problem.[26] On an interim basis, Ottawa hoped that an informal "*entente*" could be reached with the French authorities to overcome the most bothersome difficulties and obtain, at the very least, a customs exemption for official mail. In Paris, Ambassador Dupuy took up the cause again, calling on the director of American affairs at the Quai d'Orsay and following up his visit with a formal letter. He was authorized to "insist," the letter read, that the customs formalities be removed, at least from official mail from the Quebec government to its delegate general. The French official countered with a suggestion that Lussier be allowed to use the Canadian diplomatic bag; Dupuy rejected this as impractical. All he achieved was a commitment that the subject would be raised with "the competent authorities." By the end of 1963, no resolution was in sight.

While few tangible results had yet been achieved from the renewal of direct links between France and Quebec, the increasing activity stirred the federal government into taking several new initiatives. The articles published by Jean-Marc Léger in July 1963, and particularly his assertion that the federal government was not interested in reflecting the aspirations of French Canadians abroad, also struck a sensitive nerve in Ottawa, particularly among French-Canadian diplomats. Foremost among these was Marcel Cadieux, acting under secretary of state for external affairs (replacing Norman Robertson who was seriously ill). These officials were motivated by a desire not only to improve the status of the French language within the Department of External Affairs, but also to defend federal prerogatives. The provinces had two alternatives, they advised Paul Martin, either the federal government could be allowed to act as their agent in international matters, or the provinces could develop the means to look after their own interests. Léger's articles raised the possibility that Quebec might adopt the second alternative. If that happened, the officials warned, the repercussions at home and abroad would be very serious.

Concurrently, the Canadian embassy in France began to urge new federal government initiatives to enable it to assert its presence there. One despatch argued that the growth of a more dynamic society in Quebec and of a more assertive French-Canadian personality presented both a great opportunity for reinforcing Canadian independence and a great danger to Canadian unity. At the same time, Canada's increasing dependence on the United States, particularly in economic and defence matters, and the relative strengthening of Western Europe, in which France was assuming a primary role, called for efforts to establish a better balance in Canada's relations with the two continents. Closer links with France could be a significant beginning in that direction. The most promising field was cultural and technical cooperation. French support would be useful in strengthening Canada's bicultural foundations, and France, for its part, would react well to the opportunity to expand its cultural influence. Activities in those sectors would stimulate interest, and then cooperation, in others.

As a result of this initial assessment of relations with France, a task force was set up within the Department of External Affairs in August 1963, to be followed by the establishment of an interdepartmental committee focussed on financial and economic relations with France.

Cabinet also approved a policy giving the French language the same status in foreign affairs that had just been recognized in principle by the Pearson government within Canada. A major effort was to be made as well to increase the proportion of French-speaking diplomats, and relations were to be developed with France and other French-speaking countries.

With the administrative structure already in place, there appeared to be no serious difficulties in intensifying relations with France; but contacts with its former colonies were still very tenuous. Canada had recognized Tunisia and Morocco on their accession to independence in 1956, but no resident ambassador had been named. Instead, the ambassador to Switzerland was accredited to Tunisia and the ambassador to Spain to Morocco. The Tunisian and Moroccan ambassadors to the United Nations were accredited to Canada. In 1960, Ambassador Dupuy, who had met several of the new African leaders in Paris, made a tour of French-speaking Africa. To avoid concern on the part of the French authorities that Canada was intervening in France's sphere of influence, his trip was announced as a merely "courtesy tour." He did submit a series of recommendations afterward, but the Canadian government found them too ambitious for the moment.

In April 1961, three hundred thousand dollars had been allocated as the first Canadian aid to francophone countries, but a large portion of it was never spent because of the difficulty of identifying suitable projects. Presidents Bourguiba of Tunisia and Diori of Niger got in direct touch with Prime Minister Diefenbaker in their search for development assistance, but to no avail. The fault did not lie entirely with Diefenbaker: the Canadian External Aid Office had no senior French-speaking personnel, and its efforts were concentrated in the Commonwealth countries. Cameroun became the first former French colony south of the Sahara to be recognized officially by Canada. The choice was made in a very unconventional manner: External Affairs Minister Green found himself seated beside his Camerounian counterpart in the United Nations General Assembly and developing a liking for him. He was also impressed by the fact that Cameroun was officially bilingual, having been created through the fusion of French and British colonies. The former Belgian Congo, whose first premier, Patrice Lumumba, visited Canada in 1960, was recognized about the same time. From that beginning, diplomatic relations were gradually extended, using the device of having each ambassador accredited to several African countries.

Soon after taking office, the Pearson government increased the allotment of aid to francophone countries to four million dollars. Once again, concern over Quebec's plans served as a spur. While in France with Premier Lesage to participate in the inauguration of the delegation general, the Quebec minister of youth, Paul Gérin-Lajoie, had made a speech in Montpellier in which he had called for the establishment of a "cultural community of the French-language peoples" along the lines of the Commonwealth. (Incidentally, the speech was made one year before the publication of President Leopold Senghor's article in *L'Esprit*, defining *la francophonie* for the first time as "an intellectual and spiritual community in which the official language, or language of work, is French."[27] The article is generally considered, erroneously, to have been the first public call for such a body.) While Gérin-Lajoie stated that Canada as a whole desired to support French culture in the world, he added that Quebec intended to play its own role through development assistance programmes and by opening its universities to African students. In evoking that prospect, Gérin-Lajoie was not speaking on behalf of the government so much as reflecting the views of a few individuals whom he consulted regularly, notably Jean-Marc Léger and André Patry. Patry was a professor of international law at Laval University with a long-standing interest in the countries bordering on the Mediterranean basin. Sharing the negative feelings of Lapalme and Léger about the Department of External Affairs, he took advantage of his personal acquaintance with Premier Lesage to urge the government to develop direct relations with countries in North Africa. On one occasion, he visited the area on his own initiative and also discussed the prospects with the Tunisian ambassador to the United Nations, the son of President Habib Bourguiba. He recommended to Lesage that Tunisia be selected as Quebec's first recipient of Quebec aid. He also explored the possibilities of cooperation with Morocco. While his initiatives bore little fruit, he did start a competition between Quebec City and Ottawa that was to accelerate Canadian involvement in Africa.

One of the comments in Léger's articles that was carefully noted in the federal government was his reference to the fact that Pearson, on becoming prime minister, had rushed to consult the British prime minister and then the American president, but had not called on the president of France. "Homages to France, moving speeches on the contribution of France to the world, a few research scholarships to French citizens, modest funds for francophone countries in Africa?" he asked sardonically. "Of course, but, as soon as it is a question of serious business, do not expect the slightest French influence."[28] In point of fact, the prime minister's main objective had been to meet as soon as possible with President Kennedy to correct the serious deterioration in relations with the United States during the last months of the Diefenbaker administration. However, he had felt obliged to go to London first to avoid criticism by pro-British elements in Canada that he was leaping into the Americans' arms. Except for Léger's comment, few people would have noticed that he had not gone to Paris. Certainly, the current level of development of Franco-Canadian relations did not warrant such a step.

Embarked on the new policy of bilingualism, Pearson decided that he had to correct the lapsus as soon as possible. Paul Martin discussed a possible prime-ministerial visit to Paris with Couve de Murville at the United Nations in New York in October. It was the first of many meetings between the two men over the next four years. They were in many respects a study in contrasts. Couve de Murville was highly sophisticated, cool-headed and often impenetrable; Martin was a voluble, ambitious politician who had risen to high office through sheer hard work and determination. At the same time, Martin had good credentials for his assignment as secretary of state for external affairs. He had an interest in international affairs dating back to his student years, and while minister of national health and welfare in the St. Laurent government, he had often replaced Pearson, then secretary of state for external affairs, at the United Nations and in other international forums. Half French-Canadian and bilingual—although his spoken French was somewhat rudimentary—he reflected the new image that the Pearson government wished to present of Canadian foreign policy. Some people questioned, however, whether he would be able to hold his own in negotiations with the French foreign minister. As developed by Marcel Cadieux, Martin's position on Franco-Canadian relations was clear: the Canadian government had to insist rigorously on respect for its prerogatives in international affairs; at the same time, it was anxious, both for internal political reasons and in order to strengthen Canadian foreign policy, to establish the best possible rapport with de Gaulle and his administration. In his memoirs, Paul Martin reports that he felt his first meeting with "Couve," as he called him, went well. "I found him understanding and anxious to help when I explained that Canada genuinely wished to improve its official contacts with his country."[29]

Prime Minister Pearson also had good credentials for a mission to France. He had served there as a pilot during World War One, had visited Paris frequently during his career as a professional diplomat and later as secretary of state for external affairs, and had won the Nobel Prize for Peace for his negotiating ability in settling the Suez Crisis in 1956. Always ready to listen to another person's view, he was, by temperament as well as by profession, the ultimate conciliator, convinced that almost any problem could be solved by a few more concessions on one side or the other, and ready to make some of his own. In that respect, his personality was diametrically opposed to de Gaulle's, but he had admired the president greatly since they had both been in London during World War Two. He did have two handicaps in dealing with de Gaulle: he was an English Canadian, and his spoken French, already weak, appeared even less adequate because of a lisp.

When Malraux was in Ottawa in the fall of 1963, he advised Pearson, as a recognized world statesman, to concentrate on international affairs during his discussions in Paris. That was the prime minister's preference, particularly in view of the higher profile that de Gaulle was giving to France on the world stage. But above all, he wanted to convince de Gaulle that his government empathized with French Canadians in their current aspirations and that the French government should work closely with it in helping to meet them. He was not aware that de Gaulle's thinking had already evolved markedly in the opposite direction. The president wrote on September 4, 1963, in a note only made public fourteen years later:

> We will receive Mr. Pearson. We can develop our relations
> with Canada as it still exists. But, above all, we must
> establish special forms of cooperation with French Canada,
> and not allow what we do for and with it to be submerged in
> an arrangement involving the totality of the two Canadas.
> At any rate, French Canada will necessarily become a
> State and it is necessarily in that persepective that we
> must orient our actions.[30]

By coincidence, Pearson's visit was scheduled at a turning point in de Gaulle's own course of action. Having resolved most of the outstanding problems he had inherited on returning to power, he was now in a position to pursue more vigorously his longer-term international objectives. Foremost among them was to maximize France's independence and, consequently, its impact on the international scene. In 1960, the first French atomic bomb had been exploded, and a nuclear *"force de frappe,"* or strike force, was being developed to reduce France's dependence on the United States. His demands for a stronger voice within NATO having fallen on deaf ears, he was also preparing to disengage from at least the military aspects of the Western alliance. That policy orientation, perfectly consistent with his wartime attitude, and indeed with his lifelong view of France's role in the world, was leading to charges of anti-Americanism. While Pearson, too, was uneasy about the dominance of the United States in the Western World, he considered it fortunate for the West to have a leader of such essentially democratic qualities to meet the Soviet threat. As for the North Atlantic Alliance, he, himself, had played an active role in bringing it about in 1949 and in making it a cornerstone of Canadian foreign policy. He saw it not merely as a military pact, but also as an instrument for Atlantic cooperation in other sectors, and as cold war tensions subsided, for the negotiation of gradual improvements in relations with the Soviet bloc. Characteristically, he also believed that more influence could be exercised on the Americans through quiet diplomacy, that is, through persuasion and negotiations out of public view, than through public displays of differences. As he prepared his visit to France, he was determined, he wrote later in his memoirs, to "disabuse" de Gaulle of the notion that Canada could not withstand American pressures, and even to convince him that the United States was "not only a great but a good country."[31] In view of the president's conception of world politics and of his wartime experience, it was, to say the least, a considerable undertaking.

Quite apart from Quebec's links with France, other issues beclouded the bilateral relationship. One was the possible sale of Canadian uranium to France. In a move to prevent the proliferation of nuclear weapons, Canada had unilaterally abstained from their production even though it had many of the prerequisites, including the uranium ore and the expertise. It had also signed an international agreement to limit sales of uranium to countries committing themselves to using it only for peaceful purposes. Since the United States and Great Britain had already developed the capacity to produce nuclear energy when the agreement was made, it did not apply to them. De Gaulle denounced the measure as an attempt to restrict nuclear weaponry to an Anglo-Saxon cartel. His indignation increased when, in 1962, British Prime Minister Harold Macmillan concluded an agreement with President Kennedy to acquire American Polaris missiles to carry British warheads, rather than join in a Franco-British arrangement. De Gaulle interpreted the step as further proof of British subservience to the United States, reminiscent of World War Two. He used the agreement to block the latest British attempt to enter the Common Market, declaring that it would lead to "a colossal Atlantic Community under American dependence and leadership."[32] Strengthened in his determination to have France build up its own nuclear arsenal, he rejected categorically the Canadian condition that its uranium be used only for peaceful purposes. Pearson was caught on the horns of a dilemma, since he was not only anxious to remove any differences with France, but the principal uranium mines were located in his own constituency and created a considerable amount of economic activity there. On the other hand, he was committed to the non-proliferation policy.

Another cloud over the relationship was a recent decision by Trans Canada Airlines to purchase a fleet of American aircraft in preference to the French Caravelle. Although publicly owned, the airline was completely autonomous in such matters, but French-Canadian nationalists and some Frenchmen portrayed the choice as a meaningful test case of Canada's seriousness about developing closer relations with France. The French ambassador to Canada, Raymond Bousquet, had mounted a vigorous lobby on behalf of the Caravelle, meeting with members of parliament from Quebec, and notably with Social Credit members who saw themselves first and foremost as spokesmen of French Canada. These parliamentarians warned that to make any other choice would be proof that the government and the rest of Canada harboured anti-Quebec sentiments. Prime Minister Pearson told the management of the airline that he hoped that, all other considerations such as technology being equal, a French or British model would be chosen. The public debate had reached a high pitch when Gordon McGregor, the president of Trans Canada Airlines, announced in November 1963 that the American DC-9 had been chosen. To add insult to injury, he commented that the Caravelle was more accident-prone, a difficult basis of comparison since the DC-9 was not yet even in production. The government tried to dissociate itself from the decision, but the French were unconvinced; comparable public bodies in France were used as instruments of government policy. On the Canadian side, there was strong resentment over Ambassador Bousquet's foray into partisan politics.

In Quebec City, Jean Lesage regarded the prime minister's trip as a normal occurrence, but others around him were concerned. A small group of officials and advisers led by Claude Morin, deputy minister of federal-provincial affairs, were working to put in place a series of Franco-Quebec programmes in a way that would establish the province's right to negotiate international agreements in its areas of jurisdiction independently of the federal government. They viewed the prime minister's trip, and not without reason, as part of a counter-offensive by their opposite numbers in Ottawa to assert federal authority over foreign policy, and to occupy the terrain themselves. As evidence of that strategy, they cited the arrangements, recently concluded, to send a small number of Quebec civil servants each year to the prestigious *Ecole nationale d'administration* where France's administrative élite was trained. In fact, it was not a very practical programme. In the first place, the French public service was very different from the Quebec one, which operated more on the North American model. Second, the ENA students, selected through a rigorous entrance examination from among graduates in law, political science and other disciplines, immediately became civil servants and spent much of their time attached to government offices to learn the complex and rigid French bureaucratic procedures. There was no flexibility in the training programme to meet the particular needs of foreigners. Still, at first glance, the possibility of offering a few of the most promising Quebec civil servants the opportunity to spend some time in the famous school was very attractive. Patrick Hyndman, the recently appointed economic counsellor at the delegation general and a graduate of the French *Institut d'études politiques*, negotiated the arrangement, but Canadian embassy officials were also involved. The Department of External Affairs posed one condition for its acquiescence: that of the ten positions allocated, one or two should go to federal civil servants, thus making it something more than a purely Franco-Quebec arrangement.

Even more upsetting for Morin and his colleagues was a letter from Martin to Lesage, informing him that Pearson intended to discuss with the French authorities a possible cultural "accord" to which the federal government would contribute initially $250,000 per year. The money would be used for scholarships and research grants to bring Frenchmen to Canada, and also to send theatrical troupes, orchestras, art exhibitions and other forms of Canadian culture to Europe. France would be asked to undertake a reciprocal programme. In fact, many of those activities already existed on an *ad hoc* basis; for instance, French professors lectured regularly at Quebec universities thanks to funds from the federal Canada Council for the Arts, Letters and Social Sciences, and for many years Canadians had studied in France with French scholarships and taken advantage of the minimal tuition fees there. It was not a Canadian practice to sign broad formal agreements with regard to such matters, but the Europeans regularly did so, and Department of External Affairs officials saw it as a useful way of staking out the federal authority.

Martin's letter to Lesage stated that the federal government had two objectives: to reinforce national unity and to strengthen its diplomatic relations with francophone countries. Once the agreement was concluded with France, he announced, similar ones would be negotiated with Belgium, Switzerland and others. Federal officials clearly wanted to give some *éclat* to Pearson's visit to Paris, Morin commented to Premier Lesage caustically, and get some publicity for the government's policy of biculturalism.[33] However, Martin seemed to be confusing culture and education, and the latter, which encompassed scholarships and research, was within a provincial field of jurisdiction. Once again, he argued, Ottawa was intervening in Quebec's domain without prior consultation, and merely asking for the province's cooperation in carrying out the terms of the agreement that had been prepared. Morin suggested to Lesage that he reply that "constitutionally and practically, Quebec was better able to carry out the proposed measures; the federal government need only transfer the necessary funds to it and they could be brought about." The premier did not have the time to act on the suggestion before the prime minister left for France.

Pearson, accompanied by Martin, Cadieux and other advisers, arrived at Le Bourget airport outside Paris on January 15, 1964, after a turbulent overnight trip, feeling, in his own words, "tired and somewhat apprehensive."[34] Prime Minister Pompidou was on hand to greet him and sought to create the best possible tone for the visit by declaring that Franco-Canadian relations were so good that they could not be improved upon; nevertheless, he expressed the hope that cultural and economic ties would be strengthened.[35] Since de Gaulle was not accustomed to revealing his thoughts on subjects he was still cogitating, even to his principal collaborator, it is not clear whether or not Pompidou was aware of the president's thinking, but his comments appear to have reflected his own desires. He saluted Canada as a great friend and ally whose soldiers had "fought and died on our soil" side by side with their French comrades in arms, and where there lived "five million who speak our language and guard our culture and in whose veins flows our blood." The Canadian prime minister responded by describing France as "one of the two motherlands of our nation," and as "the source, the inspiration and the defender of much that is fine in Western civilization." That first contact augured well for the visit. Pompidou spoke no English and Pearson had to strain hard to follow him in French, but a Canadian embassy official, Marc Beaudoin, served as interpreter as they drove into the city. Pearson took that first opportunity to assure his host that things were going well in Canada, and that sensational newspaper reports about conflict between Quebec and the rest of Canada were "greatly exaggerated."[36] He also made the point that he and his colleagues were anxious to strengthen ties with France within the Atlantic Alliance.

Pompidou appeared to be more interested in his guest's views on international affairs, and volunteered the information that France was about to recognize Communist China. It was a step to which Pearson had always been favourable in principle, and in 1950 he had almost persuaded the St. Laurent government to take it (following the example of Britain and India), but the outbreak of the Korean War had made it impossible at that time. Subsequently, the British experience had proved very disappointing; the Maoist régime was in a belligerent mood, and no effective relationship was possible. As a result, Canada had decided to wait and see how the situation evolved. Strong American opposition to recognition also made it difficult for Canada to act. Concerned about the isolation of China from the Western world, Pearson congratulated Pompidou for succeeding in obtaining agreement with Peking on a basis for diplomatic recognition.

General de Gaulle received Pearson for the first time at four o'clock the same afternoon. The two men were a study in contrasts, the president larger than life and self-groomed to greatness, the prime minister, with his boyish smile, looking as if he would be more at ease in a baseball uniform (a sport in which he had excelled) rather than in a morning coat and striped pants. Employing a familiar stratagem to impose his presence on others, de Gaulle greeted Pearson formally, then returned to sit absolutely silent behind his huge desk, staring at him. The tension added to his guest's feeling of discomfort—as was intended. To break the ice, Pearson launched into a statement on the importance of France in international affairs, seeking to convince the sphinx-like personage that, in his own words, he "really wanted to hear [his views]...and...had great respect for him and his career." De Gaulle gradually relaxed and delivered one of his eloquent exposés of the world situation.[37] "He speaks with great clarity and ease," Pearson recorded later,

> beautiful French, slowly expressed. So I had little difficulty understanding him. He is often philosophic and historical in his comments on developments and very certain of the logic and rightness of his own conclusions. But not arrogant or aggressive in expressing them, at least not to me.

Notwithstanding their very different approaches to international affairs—Pearson's internationalism constrasting sharply with de Gaulle's nationalism—they had a good discussion of the current issues. When they turned to relations between their two countries, Pearson was much less reticent, and de Gaulle—again in character— listened attentively. "I was anxious to remove any impression that he might have received that our country was breaking up," the prime minister wrote afterwards, "that Quebec alone was Canada and that the rest [was] merely a part of the USA and that we Anglo-Saxons didn't really care much about our relations with France." He explained that he would like to develop Canada's relations with France to the level of those with Great Britain and the United States. De Gaulle, probing, expressed pleasure that contacts were increasing, but felt it was difficult for Canada to extract itself from the "Anglo-Saxon" orbit. That was not his aim, Pearson rejoined; he was happy to be both an Anglo-Saxon and a North American, while strengthening other ties. It was hardly a remark designed to reassure de Gaulle about the country's future, or his guest. France had great affection for Canada, the president continued, and appreciated its position, character and role. It was important that "Canada remain Canada," and not become something else. The new dynamism of French Canada could help to ensure that. At any rate, France would not create any difficulties for Canada.

As the atmosphere became increasingly relaxed, Pearson managed to inject into the conversation his regrets that Trans Canada Airlines had not chosen the Caravelle, and assured de Gaulle that the government had not been able to influence the decision. When he made a move to leave after an hour, as he had been advised to do beforehand, the general asked him to stay to discuss the situation in the Far East and particularly the French decision to recognize China. Pearson felt he was pleased by Canada's "sympathetic understanding" of the proposed move, rather than following the hard line adopted in Washington. But the prime minister did warn of a strong American reaction. At one stage in their talk, Pearson noted that the president was to make a trip to Mexico shortly, and asked if he would consider returning via Canada. De Gaulle said that was not possible, but expressed the hope that he would be able to make a visit before long.[38] When the audience ended, the general escorted Pearson to the front door of the Elysée Palace and photographs were taken. For the prime minister, the friendly gesture was "a happy change" from the way their meeting began. Summing up the meeting afterward, he wrote that he had found de Gaulle "impressive and far more sympathetic" than he had expected, but

> very proud, very French, very sensitive about Anglo-Saxons, and unforgetting of the treatment he had received from them during the war. He really did not believe that we English-speaking Canadians had a chance to maintain our separateness against U.S. pressures.

Pearson was "determined to disabuse him on that score."

A couple of hours later, Pearson, together with Martin and their wives, returned to the Elysée Palace for a state dinner in his honour, which was followed by a reception for an extended list of guests. Imperial in its grandeur, the event awed the Canadians and, whether or not that was the intended effect, made them feel inferior. "They really laid it on," Pearson recalled later, "and I never felt...so out of my natural, informal element."[39] De Gaulle played his role of magnanimous host to perfection, and they felt he was doing his best to make them feel welcome and at home in the rarefied surroundings. The toast he proposed to the prime minister was, in Pearson's words, "short, eloquent, very friendly and even moving." He described the occasion as a "visit of friendship" reflecting "the bonds of sympathy developed between France and Canada over a long period and that we feel deeply."[40] Of course, he went on, everything that was happening "in the fields of the spirit, the heart, language and culture," and could happen in the economic and other fields, between the "French of France and those inhabitants of your vast territory who are our people living in Canada," did not fail to "move and interest us very especially and deeply." Nevertheless, there could be nothing in "that special and natural solidarity" that could impede "the happy relations of the French Republic with your federal State." He saw in Canada "a faithful and valiant ally" in two world wars and whose position on the Atlantic, Pacific and Arctic Oceans gave it "an essential role" in the defence of the free world. It was also "a considerable economic presence destined, thanks to its resources and human capacities, to achieve a level of economic expansion sufficient to assure its independence, the essential condition of our desire to develop our mutual relations." Finally, the president saluted in the Canadian personality a "set of human values" that were already enabling it to play "a fruitful and disinterested role" in the development of the civilized world. And he predicted that, as a result of the visit, there would result "a better understanding of our respective problems and a closer cooperation between Canada and France, to the advantage of all who wanted a balance of forces in the world, progress and peace."

Through the veil of compliments and subtle inferences, two messages were perceptible to those persons initiated into de Gaulle's manner of speech: he had a very special interest in French Canada and intended to pursue it directly, and Canada's credibility in his eyes depended on its demonstrating its ability to resist the forces of integration with the United States. When he rose to reply, Pearson was, in his own words, "as nervous as I have ever been."[41] Canada, he told his host in the best French he could muster, was, by her history and the language and tradition of many of her citizens, a part of France.[42] But France was also part of Canada, since one hundred thousand Canadian soldiers were "resting in peace in this sacred soil." Canada wished to strengthen its political, economic and cultural ties with France, and to see it play "a leading part" in resolving world problems. He also paid an eloquent tribute to de Gaulle himself. All Canadians, English- and French-speaking, he declared, had "feelings of great respect and admiration for him" and considered him to be "one of our greatest leaders during the war." His name was for them "synonymous with honour, loyalty and devotion" and they rejoiced in "the new prosperity and influence of France" under his guidance. The president seemed touched by the tribute. At the end of the evening, he accompanied the Pearsons and Martins to their limousine and waved as they drove out of the palace gates. Paul Martin, according to the prime minister, "was almost misty-eyed with pleasure and perhaps relief." The Canadians went to bed at the end of the long day "totally exhausted."

The rest of the visit also appeared to go well. On January 16, Pearson laid a wreath at the Arc de Triomphe, then visited the *maison du*

Québec. Ever the conciliator, he spent an hour with Charles Lussier and his staff, trying, in his words, "to make them feel that they—as well as the Embassy—were part of the Canadian visit to Paris."[43] In Ottawa, he had been advised that the delegate general had separatist leanings; he was pleased to find it was not true. He had a "good talk" with him which he hoped would be "helpful." Immediately afterwards, he sent a telegram to Jean Lesage, telling him that he had been impressed by everything he had seen and that Lussier "could not have been nicer." Next, Pearson met with Pompidou for a wide-ranging survey of bilateral and international topics. He also raised the still unresolved problem of the status of the Quebec delegation general and appealed to him to intervene directly with the French bureaucracy to bring about an early solution. They had lunch together, then Pearson returned to the Elysée Palace for another meeting with General de Gaulle, this time around the Cabinet table and accompanied by their foreign ministers and several leading officials. The atmosphere, the prime minister recalled later, was "much less formal, the ice had been broken."[44] Certainly the Canadians were more relaxed. As for de Gaulle, in view of his opaque personality it is impossible to do more than speculate, but he appears to have liked both Pearson and Martin, while finding them somewhat naive and idealistic. However, he had demonstrated many times in his lengthy career that personal feelings did not influence him in the pursuit of higher objectives, namely the interests of France. The fact that his guests did not recognize that fact bore out his assessment of them.

Pearson's schedule included a series of speaking engagements and meetings with small groups designed to give him the opportunity to spread his message beyond government circles. He made his principal statement at a luncheon of the diplomatic press corps.[45] Canadians, he remarked with his typical self-deprecating humour, aspired to create a society combining the best of the United States—"a bathroom for every bedroom, an electric tooth brush, etc.,"—with the best of European culture. Like almost all other countries in the current "confusing and volatile period of human history," Canada had problems of cohesion, he conceded, but the population tended increasingly to "forge a national soul." One thing he could guarantee: Canada would grow as a nation "thanks to the contributions of not one, but two, founding peoples and cultures, each respecting the traditions and language of the other." "The peoples from other countries" would continue to make their contribution as well. While relations between the two principal linguistic groups were not always easy, he conceded, Canadians had learned to get along together through a spirit of cooperation. Tolerance and moderation were of the essence of Canadian life. There were always some dissatisfied elements, and "a small minority of extremists" had sometimes manifested that dissatisfaction violently. Indeed, "tensions and constraints" were inherent in a federal system, particularly when constitutional divisions coincided with "racial and linguistic differences." But Canadians were resolving the difficulties and would go forward as a nation. He could "guarantee" that as well.

Pearson also addressed Canada's relationship with the United States. While it had maintained its transatlantic ties, particularly with its mother countries, he stated, it was also "irrevocably tied to the fate of the United States." Indeed, those ties were so "intimate" that some foreign observers saw them as a threat to Canada's identity. Some Canadians worried about them too, but they recognized "with gratitude" that the most powerful state in world history did not misuse its power; Canada's independence was proof that American policy was not aggressive and that Americans were not an imperialist people. Canada was "master of its destiny—as much as any country can be today." The French component of the population was of great import-ance in developing a distinctive North American state with its own values, loyalties, future "and, of course, its own problems." In a bow to Gaullist thought, he illustrated the need to reconcile nationalism and interdependence by referring to the European scene. France would never be "submerged," he declared; it was and would remain—and that was his personal wish—"at the head of a new assertive Europe."

While Pearson's statement reflected a high level of good will and even idealism in human affairs, it also contained a large element of self-justification and even self-reassurance. That was hardly surpris-ing in light of doubts being expressed by Canadians as well as others, whether the half-continent could, in fact, be moulded into a cohesive country. The strain put on the political system by the assertive forces of Quebec's Quiet Revolution had increased such questioning. Two months earlier, Premier Lesage, dissatisfied with the federal-provincial tax-sharing arrangements, had forced Ottawa and the other provinces to agree to a conference in Quebec City that was being described as "the last chance" for Confederation. While the gravity of the situation was exaggerated, Pearson took the threat very seriously, and the fervent tone of his speech was evidently intended as a counterweight to fears, including his own, about the future.

The prime minister repeated his message in a lengthy interview published in the newspaper *Le Monde* in which he explained the policy of "cooperative federalism," adopted by his government to deal with the current tensions. He also paid a visit to NATO headquarters. And he decided on the appointment of a new ambassador to France, Pierre Dupuy having been made Canadian commissioner to Expo '67, the international exhibition scheduled to be held in Montreal during the summer of 1967. A short time earlier, Lionel Chevrier, minister of justice in the Canadian Cabinet, had retired from political life to become high commissioner to London. To balance off the presence of a French Canadian there, consideration had been given to sending an English Canadian to Paris; however, Pearson did not want to lend credence to the argument of some Quebec nationalists that the federal government was an Anglo-Saxon power base and that Quebec City was the true French-Canadian capital. (Indeed de Gaulle later expressed his regret that the Canadian ambassador to Paris was not an English Canadian on the grounds that it would have been easier to deal with him as a representative of English Canada.) In the end, the appointment went to Jules Léger, the first French Canadian to have held the post of under secretary of state for external affairs, and in addition to being the brother of Cardinal Paul-Emile Léger, a man known for his personal integrity and moderation.

The Canadian visit ended on a friendly note. Prime Minister Pompidou escorted Pearson back to Orly airport, and the two men issued a strikingly positive communiqué. Franco-Canadian relations had been examined in "the spirit of cooperation" that guided the two governments, they stated, and there was a mutural desire to work together still more closely. The French government noted "with great interest" that the Canadian government intended to undertake a programme designed to develop cultural relations between the two countries, and promised to be helpful. The arrangement to admit Canadian candidates to the *Ecole nationale d'Administration* had been confirmed by an exchange of letters between the two foreign ministers. A further agreement concluded between the *Association pour l'organisation de stages en France* (ASTEF) on the one hand, and the province of Quebec and the University of Toronto on the other, would be of considerable importance for the training of engineers. Both governments were also interested in exchanges of academic personnel and practitioners of the performing arts. In the economic sector, the two prime ministers expressed the hope that commercial exchanges would be developed "to the fullest extent;" they "took note" of the interest in French business circles in new investment possibilities in Canada; and they "noted with satisfaction" that joint projects in the field of defence production were under study.

So much for official statements: what was the real balance sheet of the visit? According to Pierre Trottier, then cultural counsellor at the Canadian embassy and one of the rare persons who was able to grasp all three perspectives in the triangular relationship, General de Gaulle had been up to one of his favourite stratagems of testing his guest (as he had tested Diefenbaker in 1958). He had extended a lure to Pearson, offering him France's cooperation if he was ready to make a real commitment to ensuring the future of French Canada, and dis-entangling Canada as a whole from the American grasp. The prime minister had not grasped the message and had stuck to his prepared position. De Gaulle had found him likeable, but , particularly in the light of his ineffectiveness on the Trans Canada and uranium issues, was confirmed in his view that the Canadian government could not be relied upon to satify the needs and aspirations of the "French of Canada." That perspective was in marked contrast to Léger's as he prepared to take up his new assignment. "I want to assure you of my wholehearted cooperation," he wrote to Lesage with whom he was on friendly terms. "My role will be to maintain and develop the ties between our two countries, but Quebec will have a special place in that regard....We must establish a climate of warmth and understanding between Canadians and Frenchmen...in order to make the most of our cultural heritage. France has a lot to offer us, but we have a rich and unique contribution to make as well, and one that will only increase with time."[46] On his trips to Canada, he would see it as his duty to consult with Quebec City as well as with Ottawa.

Chapter 8

Developing the Franco-Quebec Connection

The web of direct relations between Paris and Quebec City continued to thicken. The ASTEF agreement, although it included the University of Toronto, was essentially between Quebec and France and was formalized through an exchange of letters signed by Quebec's youth minister, Paul Gérin-Lajoie, and the president of ASTEF, Gaston Demongue. The French were to provide an initial amount of Fr 1,500,000, the Quebecers $150,000, or roughly the equivalent. In May 1964, Gérard Filion, director general of the General Finance Corporation, signed a "*protocole de principe*" with the Peugeot automobile company to build the long-awaited assembly auto plant in Quebec; a similar document was signed shortly afterward with Renault. And Ambassador Bousquet appeared frequently in Quebec to put together a variety of cooperative arrangements including the construction of electric generators, the production of ammonium phosphate and insulation materials, and even of helicopters.

Since all these arrangements were concluded with French administrative agencies and not with the government *per se*, they did not constitute treaties, and thus did not require the legal sanction of the Canadian government. At any rate, that situation was not accepted universally in Quebec; and it was viewed as an anomaly by a number of Frenchmen accustomed to a unitary form of government. Historically, it had arisen out of the recognition of Canadian sovereignty by the Imperial Parliament through the Statute of Westminster in 1931. The statute transferred treaty-making power from the British to the Canadian Parliament; at the same time, the division of powers between the federal and the provincial legislatures remained intact. In the only related case to come before the Judicial Committee of the Privy Council in London (then the highest court of appeal in the Commonwealth), the Labour Conventions Case 1937, their Lordships did not address that matter directly; the Canadian government took the position that the Privy Council decision did not impair federal treaty-making powers, and that was still the attitude of the Pearson administration. Over the years, some lawyers in Quebec had challenged that position, arguing that the provinces had, or should have, the right to conclude treaties in their fields of jurisdiction. One person who held that view was Louis Bernard, senior legal officer in the Department of Federal-Provincial Affairs. He had recently completed a doctoral thesis at the University of London on the subject, and advised Premier Lesage that, since the matter had not been dealt with in the Labour Conventions Case, it could be asserted that Quebec possessed the treaty-making power, even if it had never made use of it. If the French government could be persuaded to sign an agreement directly with the Quebec government, he advised, a valuable precedent would be established to force Ottawa to recognize the provinces' right to enter into binding international agreements, whether they were called treaties or something else.[1] Quebec's case would even be strong enough to take to the Canadian Supreme Court (since 1949 the final court of appeal) and obtain a favourable decision. In that way, the Quebec government would not only be assured of "a vast sphere of activity," such as membership in international organizations, but "would deprive the separatists of one of their principal arguments."

Premier Lesage did not take much interest in the subject, but Gérin-Lajoie, who had prepared a thesis at Oxford University on constitutional amendment in Canada, followed it closely. A small team of scholars at the *Institut de recherche en droit public* at the University of Montreal undertook an extensive study of the international powers of Quebec and comparable cases in other federal states.[2] And in Quebec City, the creation of a precedent by signing an agreement with France became a primary objective for Claude Morin, Louis Bernard and a few other like-minded officials. In Paris, they found willing allies in what Philippe Rossillon called "the little francophone and pro-Quebec clan," or more simply, the "Quebec mafia."

One member of the group, Gaullist deputy Xavier Deniau, arrived in Quebec in the spring of 1964 as a member of the Committee of the National Assembly on Cultural, Family and Social Affairs that came to study developments in the province. Jean-Marc Léger summed up his attitude in *Le Devoir*: France was "following with very favourable attention the emancipation of Quebec" and was "disposed to contribute to it."[3] Deniau's main purpose for the trip was to bring about a cultural and educational agreement between France and Quebec, to be signed prior to, and thus short-circuiting, the one that Ottawa wished to negotiate with Paris. He and Bousquet delivered a draft text to Gérin-Lajoie at the latter's home in Dorion, on the outskirts of

Montreal. It included an ambitious programme of exchanges of university professors and researchers, and a sharp increase in the number of scholarships for young Quebecers to study in France. Titillated by the game of out-manoeuvering Ottawa, but, at the same time, respectful of existing proprieties, Gérin-Lajoie met with Paul Martin and obtained his acquiescence that the project be pursued on condition that the federal government's prerogatives in the field of international relations were respected. Presumably, that meant that the federal government would eventually have to sanction the agreement through a treaty, or an equivalent, with France. On July 2, the Quebec Cabinet authorized Gérin-Lajoie to start the negotiations.

Nor were the federal authorities idle. On May 7, 1964, Marcel Cadieux was confirmed as under secretary of state for external affairs. One of his first actions was to call in Ambassador Bousquet and remind him firmly of the importance of respecting the authority of the federal government, to which he was accredited. That included, he stressed, keeping the federal government informed of his activities with regard to Quebec, and recognizing it as the proper channel of communication in all matters of interest to it. Paul Martin, for his part, sought to reassure English Canadians about the new links with France. They were "in no way...of interest only to French Canadians," he told the House of Commons on May 22, and could cover such areas as investments, immigration, defence production, science and tourism.[4] He referred to Prime Minister Pompidou's assurance in January that France's "renewed interest" was not limited to the Province of Quebec. Shortly afterwards, Martin met with Foreign Minister Couve de Murville at a NATO meeting in Holland; they issued a communiqué saying that the talks held during Prime Minister Pearson's visit to Paris were bearing fruit and that plans for programmes of cooperation between Canada and France were developing in a manner satisfactory to both countries.

The deeper reality surfaced on June 1 when Jules Léger presented his credentials as ambassador to President de Gaulle. In keeping with custom, he prepared a short address to the head of state. Usually, such statements were highly laudatory of the host country and of relations between the two. Indeed, Bousquet's, in 1962, had been a veritable paean of praise of Canada. However, when serving in Paris as Canadian ambassador to NATO from 1958 to 1960, Léger had often found the French representatives exasperatingly difficult as, acting on de Gaulle's instructions, they attempted to increase France's role in that organization. In fact, Léger had suffered a heart attack while in that post and had been transferred to a quieter one as ambassador to Italy. On taking up his new duties in Paris, he felt the need, in which he was strongly supported by Cadieux, to clarify the Franco-Canadian relationship from the outset. After referring briefly to past relations between the two countries, he declared, "Our [Canada's] evolution since 1960 has assumed a pace that resembles that of a revolution. These developments cannot turn against France; our origins and our tradition forbid it. The question is whether they will occur without, or with, France." In the normal course of events, he went on, they could take place without it. Canada could find elsewhere whatever it needed for its economic expansion and its material well-being. But that easy path did not correspond to Canadians' "deeper aspirations." In January, the prime minister had told the president how much importance the Canadian government attached to the development of "a new level of confidence" between Canada and France. He was thinking particularly of Quebec whose ties with France were so deep and rich and which should normally be so intense. But he was thinking also that "the image of France should be present right across Canada, that continent—that old New France—discovered by a handful of men of our blood."[5]

The effect of the blunt statement on de Gaulle was like that of the proverbial red rag to a bull. Setting aside the remarks he had prepared, the president spoke extempore; then, rather than allowing his press attaché to issue the usual bland press communiqué, he wrote out his response and made it public.

> General de Gaulle, who listened to the Canadian Ambassa-
> dor with attention, agrees with him that one of the
> fundamental problems that Canada must face at present is
> its development. He noted that, according to the Ambassa-
> dor, the question was whether that development would
> take place with or without France. The concerns of the
> Ambassador concur with those that the Prime Minister
> himself expressed to General de Gaulle a few months ago.
> In reality, without France, a certain balance would be
> difficult for Canada to maintain in every respect.
>
> The General told the Ambassador that France was
> anxious for that balance to be maintained. To achieve that,
> it seems to him necessary that the practical relationships,
> particularly the economic ones, evolve in very different
> circumstances than the present ones. Be that as it may,
> France is present in Canada, not only through its represen-
> tatives, but also because many Canadians are of French
> blood, language and thought. In short, they are French,
> except for the matter of sovereignty.[6]

On the last point, de Gaulle appeared to leave part of his thought unsaid and that we will deal with in due course. At any rate, he never forgave the incident. Without violating the letter of diplomatic etiquette, which meant continuing to receive Léger on formal occasions as required by protocol, the ambassador was ostracized for his entire mandate.

Notwithstanding suspicions in Ottawa about Bousquet's activities, there was no clear evidence that he was circumventing the federal authority in his dealings with Quebec. Shortly after meeting with Gérin-Lajoie in Dorion, he wrote to Cadieux, putting forward "on an unofficial and personal basis" a number of suggestions for an "intellectual accord" or framework agreement between Canada and France, within which the provinces could make their own arrangements in their areas of jurisdiction. Martin replied that the federal government needed time to consult the provinces and other bodies before taking a decision.[7] In the meantime, and in order not to delay matters, he suggested that a provisional arrangement could be made between the Departments of Education of France and Quebec,* plus any other interested institutions, along the lines of the ASTEF agreement. That meant that the federal government would have to give its approval through an exchange of letters. Simultaneously, it would be possible to negotiate the "intellectual accord" between Paris and Ottawa with the participation of the interested provinces. As Martin envisaged it, such an accord should "enable the latter to establish, directly with your country in the future, the desired exchanges in the intellectual sphere." Martin also wrote to Gérin-Lajoie that the federal government had "no intention to delay or prevent the projects contemplated in that area." On the contrary, it wanted them to increase in number as soon as possible and it considered "completely natural that the province [of Quebec] play a leading role."

One casualty of the increasingly complex nature of Franco-Quebec relations was Charles Lussier. A well-meaning amateur in the field of diplomacy, his situation was made more difficult by the lack of clear policy guidelines and channels of authority. Officially, he continued to report to the Department of Industry and Commerce, but Claude Morin, deputy minister of federal-provincial affairs, was assuming a more direct role in international matters. Gérin-Lajoie was also taking steps to transfer all programmes of international cooperation to the new Department of Education. As for Lapalme, he continued to be a divisive factor. On a trip to Europe in the early summer of 1964, he telephoned Lussier from Bordeaux and asked him to arrange a meeting with Malraux. The French minister proposed lunch in his own

---

* The Quebec Department of Education was created in May 1964; Paul Gérin-Lajoie became the first minister.

home, but did not follow through, and so Lussier invited Malraux, Lapalme and a few others to his own apartment. Lapalme was outraged at the missed opportunity and accused the delegate general of arranging the luncheon to feed his own ego. When he invited Malraux to lunch in a restaurant the next day, he took along the cultural attaché, Robert Elie, but pointedly excluded Lussier. In Quebec for his holidays that summer, Lussier sought an interview with the premier to clarify the situation of the delegation general. By then, Lesage had arrived at the conclusion that he had become part of the problem and could no longer function effectively in Paris; the premier was casting about for a replacement.

As it happened, a few months earlier he had appointed a long-time friend and senior officer of the federal Department of External Affairs, Jean Fournier, as chairman of the Civil Service Commission. Fournier and other French-Canadian diplomats had taken satisfaction in the rise of Marcel Cadieux, one of their own, to the top position in the Department of External Affairs, but they soon realized that it was a mixed blessing. While their English-Canadian superiors, such as Norman Robertson, treated them with consideration, particularly after the government's decision to increase the bilingual character of the diplomatic service, Cadieux casting himself in the role of their putative father, was particularly demanding of them. They resented his attitude, and several, including Fournier, had left the department. One who was still there, but was not happy with his situation, was Jean Chapdelaine. In his twenty-seven-year career, he had served as assistant under secretary for external affairs with responsibility for Europe and later as ambassador to Sweden and then to Brazil. With such a background, he expected a senior post in Ottawa or Europe as his next assignment; instead, in 1963, Cadieux had made him ambassador to Egypt and Sudan, a not unimportant post. Aware of his feelings of disappointment, Jean Fournier suggested his name to Lesage for the Paris post. On leave in Canada at the moment, Chapdelaine was invited to lunch with Lesage and the minister of industry and commerce, Gérard-D. Lévesque. The offer was made and accepted, effective January 1965. Lussier accepted a position in the federal civil service. One of his last achievements in Paris was to negotiate the purchase of a new and larger building on rue Pergolèse, near the Arc de Triomphe, to house the delegation general and enable it to handle the rapidly increasing activity.

On the French side, efforts continued to be made to negotiate substantive cooperative ventures with Quebec. Pierre Lefranc, one of de Gaulle's most faithful followers and at that time director general of the *Société française de Radiodiffusion* (SOFIRAD), made several trips to Quebec at his request. The president recognized the potential of radio and television in increasing cultural links across the Atlantic; he also hoped that the colour television the French had developed, SECAM, would be adopted in Quebec. Lefranc's task proved more difficult than he anticipated. Several French missions were in Montreal and Quebec City at the same time, and he exchanged impressions with them.[8] "Certainly Quebecers wanted their equal rights to be recognized in the Canadian federation and particularly to have Francophones treated as equals with Anglophones," he wrote later, "but for them France was far away, and moreover, it did not have the means to ensure a real presence," particularly compared to the financial resources and the inherent dynamism of the Americans. Although francophone and even francophile, the people he spoke to "especially did not want to put themselves in a position of neo-colonialism that would make them miss their pseudo-freedom." They accepted that they were the sons of France with its prestigious culture, but they saw themselves as "totally emancipated sons." They had suffered from the past indifference of the French and still held it against them. They did not welcome visitors like him with the exclamation, "We were waiting!" but rather, "What has got into you suddenly? A little moderation!" In other words, "they saw us coming and kept their distance." That reticence, together with the limited means at his disposal, convinced Lefranc that France was not a serious alternative to Quebecers' "powerful English or American associates."

Another French mission reached a similarly realistic conclusion. As part of its efforts to cope with the flood of "*pieds noirs*," or Europeans who had left Algeria after independence, the French government conceived a plan to relocate some six thousand farmers in Canada, and preferably in Quebec. In early 1964, a representative of the Ministry of Refugees crossed the ocean to examine the possibilities. While the Lesage government was favourable in principle to the plan, there were serious problems. First, while much was made of the vast extent of Quebec's territory, most of it was on the barren Canadian Shield and ill-suited for agricultural purposes. And the climate, with the long winters and bitter cold, was a brutal contrast to that of Algeria. The "*pieds noirs*" were also accustomed to colonial conditions with abundant cheap native labour that they could exploit at will. Finally, when the matter was raised in the Quebec Cabinet, serious doubts were expressed whether French Canadians would accept them; it was already proving difficult to integrate the trickle of regular immigrants into Quebec society. The French mission recognized these problems and moved on to investigate the possibilities in other provinces. Eventually a few families did move to Canada. Far more, however, opted for Latin America.

The difficulties that the French were experiencing in establishing a new relationship with Canada and Quebec reflected the long years of separation from their former colony and their lack of knowledge and understanding of the North Americans. Perhaps the most balanced assessment of Quebec placed before the French public during 1964 was made by Raymond Aron, university professor and regular contributor to the daily newspaper *Le Figaro*. As one of the French professors invited to lecture at Quebec universities with funds from the Canada Council, he had developed some penetrating insights into the current situation. In an article entitled *"L'Etat du Québec sera-t-il indépendant?"* he sought to clarify it for his readers.[9] French Canadians, he pointed out, had always been nationalists in the sense of "the will to preserve the originality of their culture and to manage their own affairs." However, as long as they remained "a peasant population, tightly organized by the Church, closed off from urban and industrial civilization," their nationalism was defensive in character and the federal system permitted "peaceful co-existence, if not a community of values of the two ethnic groups." With rapid urbanization, they came to resent the lag in their development compared to that of English Canadians. And to the extent that they considered themselves victims of discrimination or in a situation of inferiority, they would respond by demanding independence.

English Canadians, for their part, Aron went on, had done nothing, as victors, to "denationalize" French Canadians. They had left them their religion, laws, customs, language and a large measure of autonomy, and had thus, for the most part, a clear conscience. But they forgot the essential: that which men can least live without, "the feeling of being recognized." They did not feel it necessary to learn French, dismissed the brand spoken in Quebec as a dialect, and considered French Canadians as "folkloric survivors" not worthy of a dialogue between equals. Yet it was precisely that dialogue that was being demanded. As for the future prospects, the French ethnic group was obviously numerous enough and had enough territory to form an independent state. And it was unlikely that English Canadians would forcibly resist an independence movement that had broad popular support. Thus, it was up to them to see themselves as their French-Canadian compatriots saw them. However, there were "few examples in history of such wisdom, or perhaps one should say, of such courage."

Another French observer, *Le Monde* journalist Claude Julien, had developed an interest in Canada. He had visited Quebec before World War Two to attend meetings of the *Jeunesse Chrétienne*, one of the rare organizations to arrange meetings between French and French Canadians at that time. In the 1950s and 1960s, he returned to North America several times and got to know a considerable number of Canadian and Quebec personalities. Julien's principal concern was the

American influence, not on Canada, but on Europe. Following an extensive tour in the fall of 1964, he wrote a series of articles, then published a book, *Le Canada, dernière chance de l'Europe*.[10] He found it "irritating," he wrote, to see English and French Canadians exhausting themselves in a debate that was essentially futile because they did not take into account its international dimensions.[11] It was equally irritating to see that so few Europeans appreciated the impact that Canada could have on their own future. Even if Western Europe were completely united, it would not have the same weight as the United States, especially if the latter should practically absorb Canada as it was in danger of doing. Europe needed every counterweight it could find, and, for that role, Canada was in a privileged position with its extensive natural resources, high level of industrialization and ties with both France and Great Britain. Inversely, only Europe could help Canada to avoid economic assimilation into the United States. Accordingly, it was not against anglophone Canadians that francophones had to defend themselves; both groups had to join in defending the Canadian identity against the United States.

Quebec separatists compared their situation to that of the colonized peoples of Asia and Africa, Julien noted, but Quebec was not a colony either of Ottawa or of Washington. On the other hand, there was no guarantee that political independence would free it of American economic control. The break-up of Canada would merely leave the United States to pick up the scattered pieces. The separatists wanted to avoid that outcome by integrating Quebec into a francophone Commonwealth. But France needed all Canada and all Canadians as allies. What was required, therefore, was to use the crisis to develop a new, stronger and more dynamic Canadian society, able, thanks to its ties with the Commonwealth, to avoid succumbing to American hegemony. That was the thrust of the Lesage government, but in substituting an "inventive" nationalism for the previous conservative kind, it had also encouraged separatist tendencies. Still, its successes were a clear demonstration that the very notion of separatism was "a false solution to a real problem;" the exaltation of nationalist sentiment was no substitute for intellectual laziness or incompetence.[12] Julien called on Canadians to "invent" their country anew on a more just and thus more effective basis.[13] The anglophones, he advised, had to correct the violations they had inflicted on the fundamental principle of equality between the two ethnic groups. Quebec had to speed up the Quiet Revolution undertaken by the Lesage government and catch up to the rest of Canada. In short, strengthening national unity was "the primary condition of Canadian independence from its powerful neighbour." And that independence was "indispensable" to a Europe anxious to avoid falling under the domination of a giant that would control the immense resources of North America right up to the Canadian North.

What was the impact of Aron and Julien's assessments on public opinion in France? It is difficult to estimate, but in view of the general good will towards Canada, and towards French Canadians in particular, they probably struck a responsive chord. On the other hand, it is highly unlikely that they affected de Gaulle's thinking which was evolving in a very different direction; and in any case, the two writers were strong critics of his régime on other issues, and he seldom if ever heeded his adversaries.

On November 9, 1964, Jean Lesage arrived in Paris for his third visit as premier, after a busman's holiday in Greece, Italy and the Middle East. Hugues Lapointe joined him from London, and Jean Chapdelaine from Cairo, for consultations. Since they knew each other well from their years of service in Ottawa, the meeting went smoothly. In the previous months, progress had been made regarding the status of the delegation general in Paris. Following a discussion with Lesage the previous month, Prime Minister Pearson had made another appeal to Prime Minister Pompidou, repeating the suggestion that the British formula be adopted. For his part, Jules Léger spent considerable time throughout the autumn trying to negotiate a settlement with officials in the Quai d'Orsay, but they still proved inflexible. A few days before Lesage arrived in Paris, Pearson sent Pompidou a detailed proposal. Finally, the French prime minister decided to cut the Gordian knot and impose a solution. When he received Lesage, he told him that the delegate general would have the same privileges as other foreign diplomats, but that his name would not appear on the diplomatic list. In other words, faced with a choice between giving more or giving less than was requested, France chose the first alternative.

For Lesage, the important thing was to find a workable arrangement; he concurred. In a statement following his meeting with Pompidou, he thanked both the French and Canadian governments for their cooperation. The situation had been delicate, he commented, since Quebec had asked for "neither diplomatic nor consular status, but a special status...similar to that granted to our Agency General in London." That was "practically achieved" and he was happy about it. In fact, the matter had not been put to rest. The federal government interpreted the arrangements as substantially the equivalent of those in London, while the French and Quebec governments viewed them as substantially diplomatic privileges. The latter interpretation was the more accurate. When Chapdelaine took up his duties, he was given a regular diplomatic card which even bore the title of ambassador: according to French protocol, he was entitled to that rank because he had held it in the Canadian diplomatic service. He also received diplomatic car licence plates and was given direct access, in the course of his activities, to all French government offices including the Presidency. Lapointe's situation in London, while comparable in practical terms, was certainly less elevated in the diplomatic hierarchy.*

Another Franco-Quebec negotiation was at a critical stage. Before leaving for Europe, Lesage had sent Lussier the latest draft text of the proposed Franco-Quebec exchange agreement, by then limited to the field of education. Respectful of existing procedures, the delegate general handed it to Ambassador Léger for transmission to the president. It called for an initial budget of $2,200,000 per year, half from each government. Accompanying it was a statement that Paul Martin was "entirely favorable" to such an "entente" which would make possible direct contact between the French and Quebec educational services "pending an *accord cadre*" between Canada and France. The words had been carefully chosen: the term "accord" was recognized in international law, while "*entente*" was a more ambiguous term that did not necessarily refer to an arrangement between sovereign countries. In his letter accompanying the Franco-Quebec document, Lesage referred to it as an accord and expressed the hope that it would be signed by the French and Quebec ministers of education. In other words, he—or more likely his advisers—was seeking to establish the very precedent that Ottawa was anxious to avoid.

On examining the document, Léger realized that it also contained other objectionable features from the federal government's standpoint. One of the most disturbing was the reference to Quebec as a "country." He referred the matter to the Department of External Affairs and was instructed to delay the presentation until the differences had been resolved. He soon discovered that the document had already been communicated to the Elysée Palace through other channels. Accordingly, he went ahead with the presentation, but added a "reservation" that the Canadian government considered the proposed "accord" to be only "of a technical and provisional nature" and "destined eventually to be replaced by a general cultural "accord" between Canada and France covering all aspects of cultural relations between the two countries as well as all the provinces and regions of Canada wishing to take advantage of it."[14] With the next negotiating session between

---

* Having taken the decision, the French authorities were concerned to avoid establishing a precedent. When the government of Ontario decided to open an office in Paris in the early 1980s, they granted it only the designation of "delegation" and its privileges were far more restricted. And when the North Korean commercial agency was elevated to the rank of delegation general in late 1984, the French government made clear that it did not carry the same privileges as the Quebec delegation general.

French and Quebec officials due to begin in Quebec City on November 20, Jean Basdevant, director general of cultural affairs at the Quai d'Orsay, flew to Ottawa to try to reconcile the differences. He was well qualified for the assignment, having served at the French embassy after World War Two and having a more informed and balanced view than most French officials of the situation in Canada.

Once again, President de Gaulle received Lesage in a private meeting followed by lunch. A small sensation was caused when the Paris edition of the New York *Herald Tribune* revealed that Léger had not been invited to the lunch. Lesage was genuinely upset when he learned of the omission the same morning. He had deeply appreciated the ambassador's assurance of "whole-hearted cooperation," which conformed completely to his own wishes. During his other appointments in Paris, he had deliberately arranged for Léger to accompany him. At his request, a Quebec official rushed over to the Elysée Palace to see if the situation could be corrected. The director general of the Cabinet Office, Georges Galichon, put him off by pointing out that the luncheon was a private affair and that the names would not be made public. However, someone leaked them to the newspaper. In all probability, the "Quebec mafia" had struck again. The person generally suspected was Xavier Deniau who had good connections in the Elysée Palace. Later, Lesage tried to make amends by referring publicly to the ambassador as his "close personal friend."

The private meeting with General de Gaulle went well. The two men approved "in principle" both the proposed status of the delegation general and the draft education agreement; they also discussed in general terms the "difficulties" with Ottawa.[15] As he had done on his previous visit, Lesage inquired about the possibility of the president's visiting Quebec, but once again received a non-committal reply. De Gaulle had just accomplished the considerable *tour de force* of visiting a dozen Latin American countries while still recovering from a prostate operation; he was not ready for another trip. The premier noted that he had developed a greater interest in the prospect of Quebec separatism. In a familiar ploy, de Gaulle declared categorically that "all that" which was happening in Quebec was bound to end in some form of independence. Taken aback for an instant, Lesage responded as firmly as he dared that there was "no question of that."[16] They went on to other subjects.

De Gaulle's attitude did not extend to other parts of the French government. Three French Cabinet ministers, André Malraux, Christian Fouchet and Alain Peyrefitte attended a dinner given by Léger in Lesage's honour. When Xavier Deniau asked Lesage to meet with the France-Quebec Committee of the National Assembly that he had organized, Lesage mentioned the matter to Pompidou, explaining that he did not want to encourage separatist sentiments. The prime minister arranged for him to be received instead—with Léger—by the president of the National Assembly, Jacques Chaban-Delmas. At a press conference, a journalist asked Lesage for his reaction to a speech that Pearson had just made calling for a decentralization of authority in Canada while maintaining a strong central government. He replied that it was the kind of thing he would say himself. There was no doubt, he added, that a new constitution and a new kind of federalism based on cooperation and mutual understanding were "being brought into being."[17] He was also questioned about the separatist demonstrations that had marred the visit of Queen Elizabeth to Quebec City just before his departure; he dismissed the subject as press sensationalism and the actions of "a small gang of extremists" who didn't even dare to present candidates in an election. As for pro-separatist sympathies or activities in France, he had seen " no evidence of that." What about Quebec's right to sign a cultural or educational agreement directly with the French government? "I'm a lawyer," he retorted, "I know my law." The message was clear: he recognized Ottawa's treaty-making power.

In an interview with Claude Julien, Jean Lesage maintained his positive stance towards Canada and Quebec's place within it.[18] During his stay in Paris, he told the *Le Monde* journalist, he had had a meeting with representatives of French and Belgian firms to plan their joint participation in a new steel industry in Quebec. As for the automotive sector, General Motors had decided to build an assembly plant there, and Peugeot and Renault were following suit. The Goodyear Tire Company plant was scheduled to begin production soon, and the French firm Michelin would certainly sign an agreement with the province to set up its own production facilities there. Together with other secondary industries which were anticipated, those projects offered the assurance of a high level of prosperity and employment. In the area of federal-provincial relations, the prospects of reforming the federal system to meet Quebec's needs were "extremely positive." The province had no intention of seceding from Canada; rather it wanted to build a country where bilingualism was "really respected" and one which reflected the presence of "Anglophones, Francophones and other minorities." He was hopeful that his approach would gain acceptance throughout Canada and lead to "happy solutions."

If de Gaulle still had any doubts about where Jean Lesage stood on the future of Canada, a glance at the report of the interview in *Le Monde* should have dissipated them. In Canada, Pearson was delighted. "You have contributed greatly to restoring a better balance to some European views of Canada and our national problems," he wrote to Lesage on November 16; his statements were a service "to all of Canada." While the federalists had undoubtedly scored a point or two, they had no cause to relax. The Quebec premier faced strong pressures within his administration to take a more nationalist stand; and in France, General de Gaulle and the "Quebec mafia" were seeking to tip the scales in the same direction. "I don't know where de Gaulle is heading nor if he reflects the state of mind of France," Jules Léger wrote to a friend in late October. "Less and less I think, but this devil of a man in this devil of a country is creating a devil of a situation. It will take me a while to sort it out."[19]

During the winter of 1964–65, a race developed between officials in Ottawa and Quebec City over whether the Franco-Canadian *accord cadre* (framework agreement) or the Franco-Québécois education agreement would be signed first. As the chief French representative, Jean Basdevant conducted the negotiations with consummate skill, curtailing Ambassador Bousquet's enthusiasm for Quebec and tempering the demands of the hard liners on both sides. One of the knottiest problems concerned the title of the Franco-Quebec document. Claude Morin, strongly seconded by André Patry and Louis Bernard, pressed for the term "accord," or at least, "joint declaration," a term that also implied an inter-governmental agreement. Marcel Cadieux resisted determinedly. In the end, Basdevant persuaded the Quebec negotiators to accept the word "*entente*," less well defined in international legal terminology. The term "*accord cadre*" was confirmed to describe the Franco-Canadian document. Despite the competitive and often conspiratorial atmosphere, some consultation did take place between Ottawa and Quebec City. The Department of External Affairs was shown the draft agreement between France and Quebec, and Cadieux sent the Franco-Canadian one to Morin "unofficially," asking if he thought it would be acceptable to the Government of Quebec. The department's objective, he explained, was "not to restrict or control in any way the different exchange programmes that the Province of Quebec might wish to develop with France" in the areas of culture, science and technology, but to put in place a simplified procedure to "regularize" such activities between Canada and foreign countries. It also wanted to encourage the development of exchanges between France and the rest of Canada; as soon as the federal Cabinet had approved the document, other provinces would be consulted about their possible interest. The Canadian government might also wish to negotiate similar accords with Belgium and one or two other countries.

As part of the federal government's campaign to assert its prerogatives, Paul Martin stopped in Paris in mid-December, on the way back from Cyprus, for a discussion with Maurice Couve de Murville. Again they issued a joint communiqué expressing satisfaction at the increase in bilateral exchanges between the two governments.[20] In addition to the cultural agreement under negotiation, trade was to be increased, a long-dormant Canada-France Joint Committee resuscitated and a Canadian economic mission sent to France. Canada was opening consulates general in Bordeaux and Marseilles. The next day, Martin officially opened the one in Bordeaux in the presence of Jacques Chaban-Delmas, who was also mayor of that city. Robert Choquette, a well known Canadian dramatist and poet, and an eloquent spokesman for a united Canada, became the first consul general. (The post in Marseilles, opened in May 1965, went to another distinguished French Canadian, Eugène Buissière, until then associate director of the Canada Council.)

On January 20, 1965, Premier Lesage presented the heads of Quebec's Paris, London and New York offices to his Cabinet colleagues and led a discussion on their mandate. The priority, even in France, the three representatives were instructed, was the development of economic projects designed to enhance industrial expansion. The status of the delegation general in Paris having been settled satisfactorily, relations between it and the Canadian embassy were expected to be harmonious. Jean Chapdelaine accepted the directives willingly. Considering himself first and foremost a professional diplomat, he had no desire to become involved in games of one-upmanship or intrigue. Besides, in contrast to his relations with Cadieux, he and Léger were good friends. During his visit to Paris in November 1964 to meet with Lesage and Lapointe, Chapdelaine had been welcomed warmly by the Légers and they had been helpful to him in his move. The two men had agreed that they would work closely together in the best tradition of their profession, respecting each other's prerogatives and keeping each other informed as circumstances required.

Quebec won the race of the agreements. The Cabinet approved the text of the *entente* on February 3, 1965, and authorized Paul Gérin-Lajoie and Claude Morin to fly to Paris to sign it. The ceremony took place on February 27, with the French minister of education, Christian Fouchet, and Jean Basdevant as co-signatories. The document set out nine categories of French assistance, including exchanges of university professors, researchers and students, teacher training, the improvement of technical education, and closer alignment of the two educational systems. A *Commission permanente de coopération franco-québécoise* was to be established to carry out the projects and ensure future collaboration. In his public statements, Gérin-Lajoie was discreet. The *entente* was non-political, he commented; there was no thought of "restoring the links which existed before 1763."[21] Nor was it a mother-child relationship; the "new Quebec" was a younger brother, and "more interested in material assistance than moral encouragement." Gérin-Lajoie's stay in Paris coincided with the release of the first volume of the federal Royal Commission on Bilingualism and Biculturalism. In it, the commissioners, in an attempt to shake English Canadians out of their lethargy and indifference concerning the situation of the francophone population, declared that Canada was experiencing "the worst crisis in its history." In Paris, that statement was broadly interpreted as meaning that Quebec nationalism had assumed such proportions that the break-up of the country was likely. The Lesage government opposed that eventuality, Gérin-Lajoie made clear; the report referred to existing "wrongs," but these were being righted. While he hewed closely to official policy in that statement, Gérin-Lajoie was enjoying the challenge of attempting to out-manoeuvre the federal government. In the negotiating process, he told the press, Ottawa's role had been limited to that of "consenting observer."[22] As for the impending *accord cadre*, he sought to minimize its importance.[23]

Following the signing ceremony, the Quebec minister of education was received by Couve de Murville and Etienne Burin des Roziers, secretary general of the presidency staff, and finally, at the end of his stay, by de Gaulle himself. The president expressed his pleasure at the signature of the *entente* and stressed the importance of scientific and technical exchanges in the new relationship. He also inquired about the state of relations between Ottawa and Quebec. What Gérin-Lajoie responded remains unclear. He did pay tribute to the role played by Bousquet, who had just completed his tour of duty in Canada, in developing Franco-Quebec relations and he told the president of the unique tribute that had been paid to Bousquet the previous month when he was received on the floor of the Quebec Legislative Assembly. De Gaulle had noted Gérin-Lajoie's reference the previous day to the *entente* as the possible "cornerstone" of a "great cultural community of French-language countries."[24] He expressed approval of the concept, but noted that some of the "peoples" who would normally be members, for instance, the Walloons in Belgium, the Romansch in Switzerland and the French Canadians, did not control their own destinies. The implication was that until they did, they would not be able to participate fully. France also had to tread carefully, the president remarked, in order to avoid creating "a false impression" of imposing itself on its former colonies. That objection would disappear, Gérin-Lajoie replied, if Quebec took the lead in promoting such an organization. In the immediate future, the province intended to respond to requests from francophone Africans for aid, particularly in the field of education. A beginning had been made by the federal government, but the personnel for aid projects came from Quebec and it intended henceforth to act on its own. Of course, it was anxious to coordinate its activities with those of the French government. Referring to another of his geographical areas of interest, de Gaulle asked about Quebec's relations with Latin America. It was, after all, he noted, the "centre of Latinity" in North America. Gérin-Lajoie's ambitions did not yet extend to such distant horizons, and he responded non-committally.

In order to protect the Canadian government's position, Paul Martin and the chargé d'affaires at the French embassy in Ottawa signed an exchange of letters on the day that the *entente* took effect, by which the Canadian government gave its assent "to an *entente* or understanding between France and Quebec covering a programme of exchanges and of cooperation in the field of education."[25] Although disappointed at not having the *accord cadre* in place in time, Martin put the best possible face on the situation. No precedent had been created, he told the House of Commons: an earlier exchange of letters had taken place between the French ambassador and himself in December 1963 in which the Canadian government gave its assent to programmes of exchanges and cooperation with ASTEF. He did not point out a significant difference: the ASTEF agreement had been signed on the French side by a senior French administrator on behalf of a French administrative unit; the *entente* had been signed by a minister on behalf of the French government. Asked if "any province" was to have the right to make such agreements as "an independent signatory," the secretary of state for external affairs replied, "No." One of the most important, if not *the* most important attributes of Canada's international personality, and one which accrued exclusively to the Canadian government, he pointed out, was "the power to negotiate and conclude agreements or treaties of a binding character in international law on behalf of the whole country or of any part thereof with foreign countries." The procedure that had been followed was in keeping with the Canadian government's status under both international law and Canadian constitutional law. Standing alone, the *entente* would not have been subject to international law. The federal government was prepared to cooperate with any province "in facilitating, in appropriate circumstances, the negotiation and conclusion in a similar manner of agreements between the province and foreign governments in the fields of education and culture."

Within Quebec, very different interpretations of the significance of the *entente* were advanced. While Lesage and Gérin-Lajoie remained discreet, Jean-Marc Léger described the *entente* as an important step towards an international role for Quebec.[26] Jacques-Yvan Morin, for his part, asserted that, Jules Léger having "done everything to block the *entente*" and the Quai d'Orsay having resisted it as well, General de Gaulle had "intervened personally" to ensure that it was signed.[27] One journalist, Jules Leblanc, reported "reliable sources" as saying that Quebec intended to "exercise its international competence in negotiating and signing, freely and without any intermediary, ententes with various countries."[28] André Patry and Claude Morin, both of whom had been directly involved in the negotiations, subsequently presented more mitigated but nonetheless positive assessments. Patry described the *entente* as "an important step in the constitutional evolution of Quebec,"[29] and Morin called it "an event without precedent."[30] Attempts to reduce the impact of the *entente* by drawing a parallel with agreements made by other provinces were misleading, Morin argued, since it was different in nature, containing political and legal elements not found in any other case.

Chapter 9

Tension Rising

A few weeks after his return from Paris, Paul Gérin-Lajoie threw a bombshell into the continuing debate over Quebec's international relations. In a speech to the Consular Corps of Montreal on April 12, he rejected any federal control over the province's actions and informed the foreign representatives based in Quebec that their diplomatic privileges would depend in future on reciprocal treatment for the staff of Quebec's offices abroad. The threat appeared to mark a major escalation in demands for increased autonomy, and, in some eyes, for outright independence. It was taken all the more seriously since Gérin-Lajoie, in addition to being the Quebec minister most directly involved in external relations, had become vice-premier on the resignation of Georges-Emile Lapalme from the Cabinet the previous September. In the circumstances, it was assumed that he was expressing government policy.

In retrospect, the initiative for the dramatic statement appears to have originated with the government's legal advisers. As part of the study of Quebec's external powers prepared for the legislative committee on the constitution, André Patry had contributed a text in which he sought to make the strongest possible legal case for a distinct international role.[1] From the point of view of classic international law, he noted, the central government in a federal state dealt with foreign countries. In some instances, however, member-states had a "restricted but real" *jus tractatuum*—treaty-making power—carried over from earlier confederal arrangements; thus the doctrine was not "completely in conformity with the facts."[2] According to Oppenheim and Lauterpacht in their authoritative text, *International Law,* while the position of some member states was "overshadowed" by the federal state, they were "part sovereign states," and thus "international persons for some purposes."[3] Furthermore, Patry pointed out, the constitution of a federal state could concede to them the exercise of international competence in certain areas, and international law had only to take note of the new situation and accept its consequences. That had been the situation after World War One when the British Dominions and India were admitted to the League of Nations, and after World War Two when the Ukraine and Byelorussia, members of the Union of Soviet Socialist Republics, became members of the United Nations.

While the Canadian provinces had no "international personality" at present, Patry recognized, neither could the federal government carry out treaties in their fields of jurisdiction. That "defective" system was no longer satisfactory to Quebec; it had "the duty to obtain, both as a province and as the national State of French Canadians, constitutional recognition to have direct and unhampered relations with foreign States and international organizations in their fields of jurisdiction in order to resolve their specific problems." It also required that right to deal on the international plane with fields of jurisdiction it shared with the federal state, and with civil rights. In short, from an international viewpoint, Quebec was "legally incompetent," and, as a result, could not develop normally. If it could not acquire within the federal system "the necessary complementary legal powers to enable it to assume its destiny as the national State of French Canadians," then there remained the possibility of leaving the federation and negotiating "a confederal alliance."[4] Whatever the solution, it could no longer "escape its international role nor refrain any longer from playing it directly."[5]

In the same set of studies, Jacques Brossard, a former Canadian diplomat who had become a militant Quebec nationalist, argued along similar lines that it was not the federal state, but "the entire federation," that is, the federal state and the provincial states, "that possessed the external sovereignty." Accordingly, in his view, that sovereignty should be exercised "according to the division of powers between them."[6] Among the prerogatives he suggested for Quebec was the right to demand reciprocity of foreign states, in particular with regard to certain consular privileges. Finally, in a separate text, Jacques-Yvan Morin urged constitutional changes that would enable Quebec to break out of what he described as a straitjacket limiting its international competence.*

Before addressing the Canadian corps, Gérin-Lajoie also received a briefing from Claude Morin, in which the deputy minister outlined what he considered to be the government's options with regard to

---

* See, for instance, Jacques-Yvan Morin, *L'Etat fédéral en droit international* (Paris, Université de Paris, Institut des Hautes Etudes Internationales, 1961–62).

international agreements and participation in international conferences.[7] On the first score, Morin identified nine possibilities. At one
end of the scale, Quebec would leave the government of Canada "to
negotiate and decide everything," regardless of the subject of the
proposed agreements. At the other, the constitution would be amended
to recognize Quebec's "limited international competence in certain
areas." In between were a range of formulae calling for consultations,
framework agreements or simple exchanges of information. For
Morin, the ninth option was "clearly the ideal." With regard to
international conferences, it was desirable, he argued, that the federal
government invite the Government of Quebec, and perhaps the
governments of other provinces, to designate delegates to be part of
Canadian delegations to conferences of specialized agencies of the
United Nations and of some other bodies dealing with matters of
provincial jurisdiction. In some cases, distinct Quebec delegations
should attend, albeit under the umbrella of the Canadian delegation.
They would not have a separate vote. Quebec also wanted to be consulted
in advance on all matters likely to be raised at such conferences.

A further factor underlying the Consular Corps speech was the
attitude of the United States authorities on the subject of diplomatic
privileges. With literally hundreds of foreign offices, ranging from
unofficial representatives to the United Nations to tourist bureaux
and lobbies, operating on their territory, the Americans were extremely parsimonious in granting such recognition. As a result, the
Quebec agency general in New York had fewer privileges than its
counterparts in London and Paris. Without consulting the federal
authorities, Patry had gone to Washington, D.C., and met with
officials of the Department of State to argue that the anomaly be
corrected. The Americans were circumspect, in part because of government policy, but even more because Patry's direct approach aroused
their suspicions about his real motives. They made it clear that any
negotiations would have to take place through the proper channels,
that is, between the two national governments. Patry had that
experience very much in mind when he prepared Gérin-Lajoie's text.*

According to the latest Vienna Convention on the subject, Gérin-
Lajoie told his diplomatic audience, the function of consuls was to
promote the development of commercial, economic, cultural and
scientific relations between their state of origin and their state of
residence. In their own case, the "state of residence" was clearly
Quebec.† Furthermore, they could only carry out their duties insofar

---

* He also used his excellent contacts in the Consular Corps to generate the
invitation.
† A very dubious proposition since the word "state" in that context refers to
countries recognized in international law. (author's note)

as the laws and regulations of the "state of residence" allowed. In 1961, the Quebec government had passed an Order-in-Council granting certain fiscal privileges, such as exemption from income and succession duties, on a reciprocal basis to career consuls operating in Quebec. Now that Quebec had "the embryo of a consular service," which enjoyed in practice the privileges and immunities usually granted to consular officials, the government would be proposing reciprocal arrangements with the countries represented by consuls in Montreal.

The Quiet Revolution, the minister went on, had led to a feeling in Quebec that the province was unduly restricted within the century-old constitutional framework. Since 1960, it had begun to use its legal powers; it was not going beyond them. At the same time, it recognized that there was "something absurd" in the existing arrangements; for instance, a state was authorized to carry out an international agreement but not to negotiate it in the first place! The Canadian constitution, Gérin-Lajoie explained, was silent on the subject of international authority except for Article 132 (pertaining to the implementation of imperial treaties by the federal government) and this article was rendered obsolete by the Statute of Westminster. Nowhere was it stated that international relations were a purely federal matter; only because of "repeated practices over a period of forty years" had the central government assumed "the exclusivity of relations with foreign countries." This was of little consequence in an earlier period, but the situation had very different connotations at a time when relations between states covered all aspects of social life. For that reason, it had become necessary for "member-units" of a federation like Canada to participate "actively and personally in the development of international conventions that interested them directly." Quebec was demanding this "limited *jus tractatuum*" and also the right to take part in the activities of "certain international organizations of a non-political nature." Many of the latter had been established to solve problems of a local rather than general nature. Quebec wished to play such a direct role "in keeping with its personality" in several areas of international importance. In concluding, the minister of education declared that it was "no longer acceptable, either, for the federal State to exercise a sort of surveillance and monitoring of Quebec's international relations."[8]

To the diplomats in attendance, the threat of having their privileges curtailed was serious enough; to become pawns in a federal-provincial power struggle was even more worrisome. A number of them concluded that the Lesage government had become separatist. What they did not know was that Gérin-Lajoie had spoken without the authority of the Cabinet, or even of the premier. At that moment, Jean Lesage was in Florida for a brief holiday after delivering the annual budget in his capacity as minister of finance. The minister of education flew down shortly afterward and, somewhat apprehensively, gave him a copy of the text. His response was enigmatic. After glancing through it, he said, *"C'est bon, Paul, c'est bon."*[9] Did the comment indicate approval of the contents? Or was he saying that it was a good political coup in the constant competition being waged by his senior ministers for publicity? In point of fact, a good headline was frequently referred to as *"un bon coup"* and Lesage was not above playing that game himself. Another even more plausible answer is that, under the Florida sun and interested more in his golf score than in other matters, the premier was not in a mood to become upset over a subject that was not a high priority for him. At any rate, Gérin-Lajoie was sufficiently encouraged to repeat the message on April 22 in Quebec City before a group of university delegates from France, Belgium and Switzerland. According to one newspaper report, he even went further than before, remarking that the France-Quebec *entente* had been concluded "without the cooperation of the federal government," which was only "informed afterward."[10] Although inaccurate, that assertion added fuel to the public debate that had been stirred up by the initial speech. Pro-separatists were delighted; Jean-Marc Léger declared Gérin-Lajoie's arguments "remarkable, lucid, courageous."[11] Federalists expressed alarm that matters were getting completely out of hand. In a major speech in the House of Commons four days earlier, Prime Minister Pearson had called for recognition of the fact that, "in the historic and linguistic and cultural sense," Canada was "composed of two nations that must have equal rights and equal opportunity in our land."[12] For some Canadian nationalists including former Prime Minister Diefenbaker, the concept of two nations was anathema, and they saw Pearson's espousal of it as encouraging separatism. Already under attack for that statement, Pearson tried to moderate the tone of the public debate around Gérin-Lajoie's speeches by remarking at a press conference that he was sure the Quebec minister would agree that it was the Government of Canada that made treaties with other countries, and that, following the appropriate procedure, the latter dealt with Ottawa. His critics were not reassured.

The next day, Paul Martin issued a carefully prepared statement designed to stem the criticism.[13] The constitutional position was clear, he declared; Canada as a whole had "the only international personality in the community of sovereign states" and only the government of Canada had the authority to enter into treaties with other countries. But, as in the case of other federal states, there was a "lack of harmonization" between treaty-making and treaty-implementing powers. None, however, allowed member-states to make treaties "freely and independently of the federal authorities;" if that happened, the result would be "neither a federal union nor a state. It would be an association of sovereign powers." The federal government, Martin stated, had "exclusive responsibility for the conduct of external affairs as a matter of national policy affecting all Canadians." At the same time, it did its utmost to assist the provinces in achieving their particular aspirations and goals. Quebec was "the custodian of special cultural values" and had "a major role" in developing that "unique heritage." Ottawa supported it fully in that regard, as had been demonstrated in the negotiations of the *entente* when "the Quebec and federal authorities cooperated actively in a procedure which enabled the Province of Quebec, within the framework of our constitution and our national policy, to participate in international arrangements in a particular field of interest to the province." Provinces desiring to enter into arrangements with other countries could discuss possible modalities with the competent authorities of such countries, but when a formal arrangement was to be concluded, "the federal powers must necessarily come into operation." With regard to international organizations, the federal government's approach reflected "the same constructive spirit:" Canadian representation was designed to reflect "in a fair and balanced way," provincial and other interests.

Interviewed on television on April 24, Lesage took his distance from Gérin-Lajoie's position, pointing out that the Province of Quebec claimed "the right to make agreements but not treaties with foreign countries."[14] Treaties, he commented, involved "the question of sovereignty and the right to declare war," and these were not subjects within Quebec's competence. On the other hand, he and Gérin-Lajoie held that Quebec should be free to "negotiate and finalize agreements with other countries" in fields of provincial jurisdiction. Whether he meant that the province should do so independently of Ottawa, or within the federal framework, was not clear. The more ardent federalists were far from satisfied. In an editorial entitled "This Far and No Farther," the Toronto *Globe and Mail* supported Martin's position, but declared that there could be no retreat from it.[15] The federal government had to preserve "complete control" of foreign affairs. In the House of Commons, Diefenbaker scoffed at the distinction between agreements and treaties; even the expression "cultural entente" was to him merely a new name for a treaty.[16] He also insisted on knowing whether Gérin-Lajoie was right in saying that the federal government had only been informed after the fact of the signature of the *entente*. Pearson replied that the federal government "was indeed in touch with the Government of France," and that Quebec and French officials had prepared the *entente* "with the knowledge and approval and cooperation of the federal authorities." It had been "worked out" under a "kind of umbrella" agreement in the form of an exchange of notes between France and Canada. Questioned in turn, Martin revealed that he had discussed the procedure to make the *entente* effective in international law with Couve de Murville and that it had been devised through "three-way discussions...among the officials of the Canadian, French and Quebec governments."[17] There was a precedent, he recalled: the negotiation of the sale of Columbia River power in the United States by the province of British Columbia not long before.

In Quebec, Daniel Johnson, leader of the opposition in the Legislative Assembly, also joined the debate. To counter dissatisfaction over his leadership within his own party, the *Union Nationale,* and concerned that the separatist movement was drawing support away from it, he had decided shortly before to adopt a more nationalist stance on current issues. Whatever position the Liberals took, he went further. In response to Lesage's call for "special status" for Quebec within Canada, he demanded "equality or independence." And reacting to Gérin-Lajoie's Consular Corps speech, he declared that Quebec must obtain "complete control of its international fields of competence."[18]

Gérin-Lajoie, driven by his own political ambitions, was not prepared to abandon the issue; he continued to insist that Quebec needed the right to enter into international agreements in its fields of jurisdiction. The federal government could not represent Quebec abroad, he told *Le Devoir* correspondent Gérard Pelletier, since it was "a more anglophone than francophone entity," and, in foreign policy matters, "less respectful of Canadian duality than in its domestic policy, and that is saying something."[19] André Patry has placed the blame elsewhere. In his book, *Le Québec dans le monde,* he accuses "a group of federal officials, mostly of French language," of carrying out a campaign "motivated by their feelings of frustration" against the presence of Quebec on the foreign stage.[20] Undoubtedly, the "hard-liners" in Ottawa included a number of French Canadians, and prominent among them was Marcel Cadieux. That situation reflected the fact that the debate over the future of Quebec was being conducted essentially by French Canadians of opposing views, while English Canadians were often cast in the role of somewhat bemused spectators. As for any sentiments of frustration, it seems more likely, in view of the fact that French-Canadian talent was at a premium in Ottawa at that time, that such feelings were more prevalent on the Quebec side.

The principal result of Gérin-Lajoie's Consular Corps speech within the federal government was to strengthen Cadieux's hand in pursuing his two-fold policy of asserting the authority of the Department of External Affairs over Canadian foreign policy and of giving that policy a more bilingual character. Upset at the claims emanating from Quebec that Ottawa had had no meaningful role in bringing about the *entente*, he and his fellow-jurists, Allan Gotlieb and Max Wershof, were determined to clarify once and for all the respective roles of the federal and provincial governments in international affairs.

Unlike most other Canadian officials, Cadieux was also aware of the importance of cultural exchanges and of information as instruments of foreign policy. Those budgetary items, he reminded his colleagues, accounted for about half of the expenditures of the French Ministry of Foreign Affairs, and suggested that Canada would be well advised to take a leaf out of the French book. Accordingly, while the debate caused by Gérin-Lajoie's speech proceeded in public, Paul Martin submitted a memorandum to Cabinet recommending that the cultural activities of the Department of External Affairs be expanded and that the proposed cultural agreement with France be concluded as soon as possible. These steps were necessary, he argued, to strengthen Canadian diplomacy and also to counter the trend towards direct relations between France and Quebec, which were assuming worrisome dimensions. If no federal initiatives were taken, the minister warned, the position of the Canadian government would be eroded through piecemeal arrangements that could be cited as precedents and lead to further demands on the part of the provinces to act independently. Martin also recommended that the funds allocated for cultural exchanges with France be quadrupled, passing from two hundred and fifty thousand dollars in 1964–65 to one million dollars in 1965–66. Cabinet approved his requests in early May 1965. Authorization was also granted to establish a new division of cultural affairs to administer the programme; a University of Montreal professor of French literature and Sorbonne graduate, René de Chantal, became the first director. Learning that a move was afoot in Quebec City to obtain direct representation at UNESCO headquarters, Cadieux also advised that Canada's participation in the activities of that body should be increased as a matter of national importance; he also proposed a system of liaison with the provinces to consult them on policy matters and have them represented on Canadian delegations.

Another area targeted for greater activity was development aid to francophone countries. The principal obstacle to progress in that regard was that the External Aid Office, while responsible to the secretary of state for external affairs, was independent of the department itself and was staffed almost entirely by English Canadians whose interests were oriented more towards Commonwealth countries, the first recipients of Canadian aid. For that reason, and because of limited diplomatic representation in other potential recipient countries, only $539,000 of the $900,000 allocated during 1961–64 were actually spent. Shortly after taking office, the Pearson government authorized $4,000,000 for aid to French-speaking African countries (out of a total of $200,000,000 in the foreign aid budget) in the following year, but, again, only $1,243,000 were spent. In frustration, External Aid Office officials suggested that arrangements be made to simply integrate Canada's contribution into that of France. While that course would have resolved the problem of French suspicions about Canadian motives in intervening in their preserve, it was rejected as incompatible with Canada's independent role in the world. There was also the matter of Ottawa's competition with Quebec City, which was extending to the African continent.

The Quebec government, or at least, certain elements in and around it, had been trying for some time to launch a separate development aid programme. At the instigation of Jean-Marc Léger, twenty scholarships were granted in 1962 to Gabonese students to study in Montreal. And, following one of Patry's trips to North Africa, a medical dispensary was offered to Morocco. (Ottawa succeeded in blocking that project.) When the Department of Education was created in 1964, a *Service de la coopération avec l'extérieur* was created within it. The first director, Gaston Cholette, got in touch with the External Aid Office to explore the possibilities of coordinating their efforts in the field of education. His main objective was to ensure his department's participation in the selection of teaching personnel for service abroad instead of the existing practice whereby the External Aid Office carried out the recruiting directly without taking the province's own needs and prerogatives into consideration. The Department of External Affairs was favourable in principle, providing that aid, like cultural activities, was recognized as falling within the ambit of Canadian foreign policy, and that it had the right to monitor it from that perspective. External Aid Office officials, however, were reluctant to abandon even part of their mandate and posed a number of conditions: recruitment by the Quebec authorities was to be limited to school teachers and not include university professors; negotiations with developing countries were to be carried out through the federal government's diplomatic channels; the choice of candidates was to be approved by both the EAO and the receiving countries; and the persons selected were to be under the authority of the federal government during their service abroad.

In February 1965, Lesage wrote directly to Pearson, urging a less rigid attitude.[21] Since universities in Quebec fell under the authority of the province, he argued, university professors should also be recruited by the Department of Education. Other Quebec residents serving on aid projects should also sign contracts with it. Aid programmes should be developed jointly by the two federal and provincial agencies. And Quebec should have direct contacts with developing countries in order to make sure that programmes in its areas of expertise were as efficient as possible. It took federal officials two months to devise a reply for the prime minister's signature, and it conceded nothing.[22] Foreign aid, Pearson finally told Lesage, was an important element of Canada's foreign policy, and as such, must reflect its "national characteristics and objectives" as well as its "place in the international community." It must also "correspond closely to our obligations towards both the developed and developing world, as well as to Canada's financial, technical and cultural means." Another essential consideration was that recipient countries had to determine their own priorities and projects; aid programmes must not be used as "an instrument of political penetration." In the past, the prime minister recalled, various methods of provincial participation in aid programmes had been devised to meet different situations. Teaching personnel were sometimes considered to be independent suppliers of services, even though on leave from a department of education. The premier would agree, he was sure, that it was not desirable to oblige everyone to sign a contract with a provincial department. While Quebec had, indeed, a role to play in "the immense task of aiding the developing francophone countries," respect for the ground rules worked out over a long period was essential to the success of the Canadian programme. If "supplementary explanations" were necessary, the prime minister concluded, a meeting of officials could be arranged. In the meantime, he hoped that Lesage would authorize the necessary steps to enable Canadian teachers to begin their foreign service in the autumn.

The reaction in Quebec City to Pearson's letter was strongly negative. By that time, a plan had been formulated to establish the province's own foreign aid programme as an integral part of its international relations in its fields of jurisdiction. In a meeting with Pearson in early May, Lesage asked for an "opting-out" arrangement similar to ones that had been negotiated recently in the social service sector. Under that concept, Quebec would assume full responsibility for administering aid programmes in francophone countries, thus relieving the federal government of the burden; in return, Ottawa would compensate it for the expenses involved. Diametrically opposed to federal policies, the proposal was not discussed seriously. Lesage himself was neither surprised nor disappointed at that outcome; he had put the plan forward largely to appease his more nationalist advisers. Finally, he and Pearson agreed to ask their officials to prepare an *entente* defining the roles of the two governments. In the meantime, negotiations continued at the officials' level on possible "interim arrangements" to send some teachers to Africa that fall. It was eventually agreed that they would be placed under contract by the Department of Education, then seconded to the External Aid Office. Ottawa was to assume most of the costs. As for the proposed *entente*, it never materialized; the gap between the two policies was too great to be bridged.

The Quebec government gave further evidence of its determination to develop its international relations when it established in August 1965 an Inter-Ministerial Committee on External Relations. (The proposal, according to Morin, originated with André Patry.)[23] The temptation to create a full-fledged department had been resisted for fear of upsetting the federal government still further; and it was felt that, for the moment, a committee would serve the same purpose. The premier became the responsible minister, Morin the chairman and André Patry the "technical adviser." The committee's terms of reference, as originally proposed, were "to coordinate the relations that the different ministries already have with foreign States so as to ensure a true Quebec policy in the field of foreign relations," and "to stimulate initiatives...to assert vigorously an ever greater presence of Quebec in the international community."[24] With an eye on Ottawa, Lesage modified the text before submitting it for Cabinet approval; the published version stated the objectives as the coordination of "existing relations abroad" and ensuring "the unity of the government's policy." In communicating the decision to the press, Lesage added that it demonstrated once again the Cabinet's intention to assert Quebec's presence "both within Canada and the international community."

In September, the rector of the University of Montreal, Monseigneur Irenée Lussier, undertook a tour of francophone countries in Africa and Asia in his capacity as president of the *Association d'universités partiellement ou entièrement de langue française*. It was organized on the initiative of Jean-Marc Léger, the association's secretary-general, and was paid for by the Department of Education. It was a perfectly normal, and even highly desirable, undertaking, and Lussier (Charles' brother) was not a man who would allow himself to be used as a political tool. However, the apprehension in Ottawa had reached such a level that Paul Martin felt constrained to remind Gérin-Lajoie yet again that his department must not circumvent the External Aid Office through the establishment of direct contact with developing countries.[25]

A further incident reflected the growing tension and distrust between the two governments. In response to repeated inquiries by Tunisia about the possibilities of development assistance, Canada had signed a cultural and technical cooperation agreement with that country in November 1964. In March 1965, the Tunisian ambassador to the United Nations, Mongo Slim, who was also accredited to Canada, flew up to Ottawa to discuss possible projects. From there, he went on to Quebec City where he was taken in hand by Patry and had a meeting with Gérin-Lajoie. Subsequently, he had an invitation sent to the Quebec minister of education to visit his country. It was channelled through the Department of External Affairs, where it remained for three months, presumably while officials pondered how to deal with it. Martin only learned of it in a conversation with the Tunisian foreign minister, Habib Bourguiba, Jr., at the United Nations in September. He informed Bourguiba that only the federal government could make agreements with foreign countries and was assured that Tunisia had no intention of infringing that rule. Finally, after a letter of protest from Quebec, the letter of invitation reached its destination. Gérin-Lajoie responded by sending Patry to Tunis to see what aid projects could be undertaken immediately. Patry met with the foreign minister and senior officials. As a beginning, a scholarship was granted to a Tunisian student for the current academic year. A plan was also discussed for twenty Quebec teachers to be sent to Tunisia, but when Ambassador Slim raised this with Ottawa, the reaction was so negative that it was dropped.

Gérin-Lajoie did not have the time to act on the invitation to visit Tunisia before the Lesage government was defeated in June 1966. One of the Cabinet's last decisions in that sector was to approve a draft law setting out its development policy. The premier sent the draft to Pearson for comment. One article stipulated that whenever the Department of Education, using its own funds, sent advisers to developing countries or agreed to receive trainees or students, it would "inform" the External Aid Office. Once again, Ottawa reacted adversely. Morin telephoned to assure his federal counterparts that the article was negotiable, but there really was little disposition to compromise. The matter was postponed until after the Quebec elections.

During that period, the federal government was making a belated but serious effort to assume the responsibilities it claimed for itself in the development field. Notwithstanding his difficult situation, Jules Léger spent a great deal of time with officials in the three French ministries most involved in aid cooperation, attempting to establish joint projects; his efforts yielded only meagre results. In a wide ranging letter to de Gaulle in early 1966, designed to maintain the good rapport established between them two years earlier, Pearson expressed his pleasure at the prospect of Franco-Canadian coordination of their aid programmes. The general responded non-committally that he was happy that the African continent was not to be excluded from Canada's programme. The matter remained there.

In a more realistic vein, the federal government decided to make the External Aid Office more effective. A dynamic businessman, Maurice Strong, was appointed president and Henri Gaudefroy, director of the *Ecole Polytechnique* in Montreal, director of francophone programmes. They were promised the latitude and funds to do the job. The appointments marked a much needed fresh start in Canada's role in development cooperation.

One of the items on the agenda of the meetings between Pearson and Lesage in early May, 1965, was a Quebec plan to sign a second agreement with France, this time in the field of cultural affairs. According to Morin, it originated with Cultural Affairs Minister Pierre Laporte and his deputy minister, Guy Frégault, who felt that the previous *entente* placed them in some sort of subservience to the Department of Education.[26] They also hoped to add lustre to their activities by signing an agreement in Paris with the great André Malraux. Lesage was not convinced of the necessity of the step, but went along with the plan. Two weeks earlier, Paul Martin had made a statement, declaring that while the federal government had "exclusive responsibility for the conduct of external affairs as a matter of national policy affecting all Canadians," it was "ready and anxious to use its powers," within that framework, to assist Quebec and the other provinces "in furthering matters of special interest to them."[27] Once it was established that a province's objective in seeking an agreement in its area of jurisdiction fell "within the framework of our constitution and our national policy," it could "discuss detailed arrangements directly" with another country, but when a formal international agreement was to be concluded, "the federal powers relating to the signature of treaties and the conduct of overall foreign policy must necessarily come into operation." In his meeting with Lesage, Pearson raised no objection to a second *entente*, providing it met those conditions, and the province accepted the *accord cadre*, or framework agreement, that was being negotiated with France.

At that head-of-government level, there appeared to be no serious problem with such an arrangement, but at lower levels of the two administrations the situation was very different. In Quebec City, Gérin-Lajoie had endorsed Morin's objective of recognition for Quebec's uninhibited international competence in certain fields. That position had strong support among senior officials, including Frégault. In their view, the new set of negotiations provided an occasion to advance that cause. In Ottawa, the relevant senior officials were equally determined to maintain the federal prerogatives. When Morin discussed the matter with Cadieux, the under secretary told him bluntly that Ottawa would not be "taken in" again, and that any system of cultural exchanges with France would have to be available to all Canada.[28]

The subject was discussed by the Quebec Cabinet between the first meeting with Pearson, and two others held a week later. Gérin-Lajoie asked for Cabinet endorsement of Morin's ninth option, but Lesage was more circumspect; he declared himself satisfied with the traditional arrangements under which the federal government had the right to negotiate and conclude international agreements while the provinces remained free to decide whether to apply them in their fields of jurisdiction. Few of the other ministers were interested in international affairs, or in quarrels with their federal colleagues. A consensus was reached to see what could be achieved by discreet diplomacy, but to avoid public confrontation. When he met again with Pearson, Lesage found the prime minister, always ready to go an extra mile for the sake of harmony, surprisingly open to greater powers for Quebec. On his return to Quebec City, he reported to his Cabinet colleagues that an *"entente de principe"* had been reached concerning "Quebec's extra-territorial relations." He was soon to learn otherwise. In Ottawa, Pearson was told firmly by an alarmed Cadieux and others that Quebec's demands were not only contrary to existing policy, but unconstitutional. In Parliament, the official Opposition, having learned of the meetings, accused the prime minister of making secret deals with Quebec at the expense of Canada. Pearson returned to a firmer posture. On his recommendation, the federal Cabinet decided to proceed with the negotiations in view of a cultural agreement with France and to undertake other agreements with French-language countries so that any provinces wishing to do so could arrange exchanges with them. One million dollars were allocated for such purposes.[29]

Once again, two simultaneous sets of negotiations began with France. In preparing the cultural *entente*, Pierre Laporte was instructed to act independently of the federal authorities. That strategy got off to a bad start. Shortly before he was to leave for Paris, news of his intentions was leaked to the press in Ottawa. He called a press conference in which he acknowledged the accuracy of the report and went on to say that the federal government had not been informed of the planned negotiations. In a headline characteristic of those in a number of newspapers, the Winnipeg *Free Press* declared, "Quebec again Bypassing Ottawa."[30] Reminded of the content of the meetings between Pearson and Lesage, Laporte retreated and told the Legislature that he was having a letter prepared to explain the purpose of his trip to the federal authorities. Personally, he, like Lesage, was less interested in scoring points off Ottawa than in tangible achievements.

On the French side, attitudes varied towards Quebec's new initiatives. In a meeting with Chapdelaine in early May, André Malraux had commented that cultural *ententes* were now *"dépassées"*—outmoded; in his view, specific projects such as art exhibitions and exchanges of artists were more meaningful. A few days later, when he received Chapdelaine for the first time, Prime Minister Pompidou was also sceptical. Following the guidelines he had received from the Quebec Cabinet in January, the delegate general identified Quebec's priorities as the attraction of French capital, techniques and expertise. The presence of French capital, he stated, would have cultural ramifications since it would Francisize the business world, and that, in turn, would stimulate further cultural and other exchanges with France. For the French, Quebec was also "a springboard" for the conquest of the American market. It could play that role all the better since it—in fact, French Canada—had taken its destiny in its own hands and had its own state and government. Pompidou assured Chapdelaine of his warm feelings towards Quebec but expressed doubts about its ability to maintain its distinctiveness from "the American colossus." France had the same concern, he remarked, but was developing counterweights such as the Common Market.

Even within the French Foreign Office, opinions were divided on how to deal with Quebec. As director general of cultural affairs, Jean Basdevant's concern was to bring about both a cultural agreement and an *accord cadre* without showing bias towards either level of government. However, that attitude was being challenged by none less than de Gaulle himself, who railed frequently against the "traditionalists" in the Quai d'Orsay who, he complained, showed more concern for diplomatic propriety than for positive action. One diplomat who was not in that traditional mould was Jean-Daniel Jurgensen. A former member of the National Assembly, he was currently director of American affairs, a post which gave him responsibility, in his words, for everything from the North Pole to the Magellan Strait. When he was at the United Nations in New York in 1950, he recalled later, he and his wife had become nostalgic for a French atmosphere, and had made a quick trip to Quebec.[31] They were very disappointed: they found Montreal to be just another North American city, and worse still, firmly in the hands of the English "masters." The hotel they stayed at functioned uniquely in English. Even in Quebec City, they were refused a room at the Château Frontenac when they asked for one in French; when they returned and repeated the request in English, they received one. Generally, the French Canadians were still "asleep." The French diplomat and his wife flew back to New York in a state of outrage. When Jurgensen arrived in Montreal in April 1965 as part of his first tour of the territory to which he had been assigned, that experience was still vivid in his memory. He got in touch with Pierre-Louis Mallen and asked for a briefing on the changes in the province since the Lesage government had taken office. The RTF correspondent spoke to him for two hours, setting out the arguments that had led him to espouse personally the cause of Quebec independence. They discovered a "common passionate interest in the cause of the French people of America," Mallen wrote later, and laid the basis for close cooperation towards that objective.[32] Subsequently, Jurgensen telephoned often from Paris, and, on his visits to Quebec, Mallen made sure that, in addition to his official contacts, he met actual or potential separatists, including René Lévesque, then a minister in the Lesage Cabinet but widely considered to have separatist leanings.

From his strategic position in the Quai d'Orsay, Jurgensen soon assumed the *de facto* leadership of the "Quebec mafia." The network was growing. Another member, Bernard Dorin, also a diplomat, was attached to the office of the minister of education, Alain Peyrefitte. René de Saint-Légier de la Saussaye, diplomatic counsellor to the president, was, if not a member, at least sympathetic to the cause. Through him, Jurgensen was able to pass material to de Gaulle without going through his minister, Maurice Couve de Murville, or Hervé Alphand, secretary-general of the Ministry of Foreign Affairs, both of whom frowned on their intrigues on behalf of Quebec. According to Anne and Pierre Rouanet, whose book, *Les Trois derniers chagrins du Général de Gaulle*, is generally accepted as accurate, Saint-Légier slipped the material on Quebec collected by Jurgensen into the documentation prepared for the president to read on weekends in Colombey-les-Deux-Eglises.[33] "General de Gaulle saw a large number of pieces written by Rossillon and Dorin on Quebec," they quote Saint-Légier as saying; "They reached him through me." Gilbert Pérol, press attaché at the Elysée Palace, was also considered an ally by the group. As a further source of information available to the general, the Rouanets mention the *Services de documentation, d'enquête et de contre-espionnage* (SDECE), the secret service organization attached to the Presidency.* It was directed by Jacques Foccart, secretary general of francophone affairs, and a long-time collaborator of General de Gaulle. The SDECE had a unit in Quebec, the Rouanets report, and "people like Rossillon often crossed paths in separatist circles with its agents."[34] One of the latter, a "Colonel Flamant," a former parachutist, even proffered practical advice to the separatists on tactical measures. The SDECE reports, "put into more decent form," also reached the president's eyes.†

In Paris, Pierre Laporte obtained a much-prized meeting with

---

* Samy Cohen in his book, *La Monarchie nucléaire* (Paris: Hachette, 1986, pp 71–73), does not substantiate Rouanet's assertion that Foccart directed the SDECE but does confirm his strong influence over its operations and his ability to use the spy service as de Gaulle required.
† Asked in 1980 if it was possible that de Gaulle used the SDECE to inform himself of developments in Quebec, former Prime Minister Michel Debré responded, "It was available to him; he would have been crazy not to use it." (Michel Debré, interview with author, December 26, 1984.)

Malraux, and on leaving his office on May 14, he told journalists that "agreement in principle" had been reached on a second *entente*. The statement was at odds with the impression received by Marcel Cadieux from the Quai d'Orsay during a trip to Paris that another *entente* was not considered necessary since cultural exchanges could take place under the existing one. However, at the first meeting of the *Commission permanente de coopération franco-québécoise* in Quebec City on May 26 and 27, 1965, which was attended by French Minister of Education Christian Fouchet, the new French ambassador to Canada, François Leduc, and Jean Basdevant, the news was confirmed. The French and Quebec delegations each agreed to prepare a draft text and the signing ceremony was scheduled tentatively for Paris in November. The news galvanized the federal officials into action and they resolved to obtain a framework before that deadline. Cadieux explained that decision to Leduc and complained that the French government was still failing to keep Ottawa informed of its dealings with Quebec. The ambassador, who was a much more cautious man than his predecessor, was already becoming uncomfortably aware of the delicate task that he had inherited; he responded evasively. Also ill at ease was Basdevant, who explained to Canadian officials that France was anxious to avoid becoming involved in Canadian internal affairs, and, consequently, did not wish to reveal to one party what negotiations were going on with the other.

Another sensitive matter in the Franco-Canadian relationship reappeared in the same period. In early February 1965, the Pearson Cabinet learned that a private Canadian company, Dennison Mines, had negotiated an agreement to sell three-quarters of a billion dollars worth of uranium to France over a period of twenty years. From Ottawa's perspective, it was an attractive deal both because of its commercial importance and because it would remove a source of irritation between the two countries. France no longer needed Canadian ore urgently since other sources had been discovered at home and in francophone Africa. However, the prospect of a secure source of supply was attractive, and perhaps even more important, the agreement was an adroit move by de Gaulle to circumvent the Anglo-Saxon attempts to restrict sales to countries who committed themselves to use the uranium only for peaceful purposes. The deal was also a challenge to the Canadian government to prove its assertions that it wished to develop close relations with France and to demonstrate its ability to take some distance from Washington.

Casting about for a way of approving the sale without violating its international agreements, the Canadian government explored the possibility of enlisting the cooperation of Euratom, the European Atomic Energy Community created in 1957. It, too, opposed the use of nuclear power for military purposes, but, at France's demand, had never insisted on plant inspections to ensure respect of that policy. If Euratom approved the sale, the Canadians reasoned, Canada might be relieved of the obligation to carry out such verifications. Some Cabinet ministers, anxious for the deal to go through, were prepared to accept a French assurance that the material would only be used for peaceful purposes. Others pointed out that, once the Canadian uranium was handed over, it would no longer be distinguishable from that from other sources, so inspections would be meaningless. De Gaulle was not interested in such stratagems. His purpose remained to develop France's nuclear military capacity to demonstrate its independence, and he had recently approved a new programme to build a hydrogen bomb. As a matter of principle, he was not prepared to accept any impediments whatsoever to France's freedom of action. The news of the projected sale was broken by the Toronto *Globe and Mail* on May 5, and, when questioned in the House of Commons, Pearson expressed the hope that "a mutually acceptable basis" could be found to complete it.[35] At the same time, he gave the assurance that the government intended to respect its international commitments. Spokesmen for the opposition parties insisted that there be no departure from them. Determined to leave no stone unturned, Mitchell Sharp, the Canadian minister of trade and commerce, flew to France in a last-ditch attempt to work out a solution with the French secretary of state for scientific, atomic and space affairs, Yvon Bourges. His instructions were to do everything possible to maintain the current level of production of uranium in Canada, but without violating the international agreements. Bourges, for his part, had no negotiating flexibility at all. Sharp returned home empty-handed.

The relative positions of Chapdelaine and Léger in Paris reflected the general atmosphere of the triangular relationship. The two men continued to have good personal relations, exchanging visits and even taking long walks through Paris together on weekends. While recognizing that they served different masters with increasingly divergent views, they strove to have correct official relations as well, and to respect the agreement they had made to share information as much as possible. In dealing with the French authorities, however, the delegate general was at a distinct advantage. He was received at a diplomatic reception at the Elysée Palace even before the Canadian embassy had notified the Quai d'Orsay officially of his arrival; and taking their lead from the president, French officials showed him every courtesy. In comparison, Léger was treated as something of a pariah. While they could not refuse to deal with him, many officials adopted an attitude of stiff formality and were only minimally cooperative. Fortunately, the ambassador and his wife Gaby had loyal friends and even sympathizers, including at least one Cabinet minister, who helped them through the difficult period.

Jean Chapdelaine was received for the first time by General de Gaulle on July 26, 1965. The president greeted him as *"Monsieur l'Ambassadeur"* and talked with him for forty minutes.[36] He enquired about the progress of Franco-Quebec relations under the *entente* and listened carefully to the delegate general's enumeration of projects underway. He also showed an interest in the projected cultural *entente* to promote, in his words, "the respect, purification and extension of the influence of the French language." Chapdelaine referred to the proposal, dear to Gérin-Lajoie's heart, of a community of French-language peoples. De Gaulle raised again, as he had with Gérin-Lajoie, the analogy between Quebec's situation and that of the Walloons in Belgium and the Romansch in Switzerland. They were "privileged" in comparison, he commented; Quebec was a state and had the territorial and administrative base, as well as the "levers" that a state provided for effective action. The Canadian constitution was also very "elastic." The delegate general assured him that, even in the existing situation, great developments were possible in Quebec; the government of Quebec had "the sinews of peace and war," and was strengthening them every day. They discussed economic cooperation, including the projected steel plant, and the importance of establishing French industries in Quebec as a way of changing the working language from English to French. The rapid development of Quebec was "one of the most significant facts of our period," de Gaulle declared. All the more reason for France to get involved, Chapdelaine rejoined; moreover, Quebec was a springboard for the conquest of markets and minds in North America and of ensuring that the North American continent would never become totally Anglo-Saxon. When Chapdelaine expressed his appreciation for the "very generous status accorded to the Delegation General," de Gaulle asked wryly, "And what does *Monsieur* Martin-ne [pronouncing the name *à l'anglaise*] think of all that?" Chapdelaine answered that the Canadian foreign minister had to protect his rear from the questions and criticisms in Parliament. When the meeting ended, the president assured him that his door was always open if the delegate general had "any request to make." In his report of the meeting to Lesage, Jean Chapdelaine declared enthusiastically that it was a confirmation of the interest de Gaulle took "in Quebec, its development and its self-assertion;" he was "completely devoted to the government's cause." The premier was so delighted that he had copies of the letter distributed to the whole Cabinet.

A parallel letter from Jules Léger to his head of government was a revealing contrast. After a year as ambassador to France, he estimated that the president would "probably continue to be irksome;" however, at seventy-five, time was running out for him. Canada's difficulties with de Gaulle were related in large part to the "defiant atmosphere" of Franco-American relations; while he had been helpful in many respects, his "anti-American bias" was now "playing against us." On the other hand, that sentiment was not deeply rooted in the French population and would not last much longer than he did, "unless the Americans act very foolishly." In retrospect, Léger's diagnosis appears to have been somewhat off-base: de Gaulle had an interest in Quebec quite apart from his relations with the United States. But he was right on one score: Canada's difficulties were directly related to the general's tenure in office.

On September 1, the Quebec Cabinet approved a draft of the cultural *entente*. In communicating the text to Chapdelaine, Morin emphasized that the words "Government of the French Republic" and "Government of Quebec" rather than simply "France" and "Quebec" had been used deliberately to mark a further step towards recognition of the province's right to enter into agreements with foreign countries. He and his colleagues had never considered the proposed *accord cadre* as a "set of shackles" in the sense that future *ententes* "would automatically flow from its existence." The two sets of relations could "co-exist." To make that point plainly, it was important that the *entente* be signed before the *accord cadre*; otherwise Ottawa would claim that it fell within the framework agreement, that they had "got us;" and other countries would believe that Quebec had fallen into line. Accordingly, the signing ceremony was being planned confidentially for November 24, just before the second meeting of the *Commission permanente*. However, Pierre Laporte was prepared to fly over earlier if it became necessary to beat Ottawa to the draw. At the same time, Quebec must not appear publicly to be in a hurry; consequently, it was desirable to see that the signing of the *accord cadre* was delayed until after that date.

Throughout that autumn of 1965, Morin discussed the Quebec draft of the *entente* periodically with Cadieux and other officials in Ottawa.[37] In the end, the under secretary of state for external affairs succeeded in having dropped from the text a certain number of expressions, for instance, "country," "people," "state," and "citizens," that could reinforce the impression of the province as an entity distinct from Canada. As Morin himself concedes, the constitutional situation was preserved. Quebec also lost the signing race. On September 27, Marcel Cadieux led a delegation to Paris to attend a meeting of the Franco-Canadian Economic Committee, and to finalize the details of the framework agreement. Working directly with Basdevant, he achieved a number of his objectives. The director general of cultural affairs shared his view that, rather than being restricted to Quebec, France's activities should be extended throughout Canada; and he reacted positively to the federal government's plan to expand its activities not only within France but also into other francophone countries. The French also consented to the signature of the framework agreement on November 17, one week earlier than the *entente*. In return, the Canadians agreed that the French ambassador to Canada, and not the foreign minister, should sign on behalf of the French government, a change that reduced the symbolic nature, but not the legal implications, of the occasion. Cadieux was unsuccessful in one respect: the French refused to include a reference in the framework agreement to the Canadian constitution which would acknowledge the division of powers between the federal and provincial authorities, and thus recognize the federal government's responsibility for foreign affairs.

On his return to Canada, Cadieux discussed the two draft documents by telephone with Claude Morin and confirmed the date of the signing ceremony. Morin accepted the *fait accompli* and assured him that Quebec would see that the two ceremonies did not give rise to "fanciful interpretations."*[38] On October 28, Cadieux sent Morin a copy of the draft framework agreement and accompanying letters, and informed him that Prime Minister Pearson intended to send final copies to Lesage and the other premiers in advance of the ceremony. He asked if the Quebec government proposed to "place the cultural *entente*...within the framework of the cultural accord, and refer to it on signing the *entente*." If not, a simultaneous exchange of letters would be necessary between the French and Canadian governments, as had taken place the previous February. Cadieux also asked to be sent a final version of the *entente* as soon as possible. Morin responded by sending a copy of the latest French counter-proposals, including a change designed to meet Cadieux's recent objections. On the inter-relationship between the two documents, he told Cadieux as diplomatically as possible that for reasons that he would explain orally, it was "preferable not to place the cultural *entente* within the framework of the France-Canada accord."[39] With regard to the draft accord, Morin expressed concern about the reference it contained to the field of education; he suggested that the reference be deleted or that provincial jurisdiction be made more explicit.

On November 17, 1965, Paul Martin and François Leduc signed the accord, its purpose described as "to develop exchanges between the two countries in the field of culture, science, technology and the arts." To meet Quebec's objections, the reference to education had disappeared and the article dealing with exchanges between universities had been

* In *L'Art de l'impossible*, Morin writes, "Since it was neither really advantageous nor perhaps even possible for us to precede the federal government, it was preferable to take advantage of the fact that we had the last word." p. 52.

modified to specify that they would be "encouraged" rather than actually brought about by the two governments "within their respective competence." The accord was valid for five years and renewable automatically if not renounced six months before its expiration by either party. In the accompanying exchange of letters, Martin informed the ambassador that exchanges in the fields of "education and cultural, scientific, technical and artistic relations" could be concluded with France by the Canadian provinces "within the framework of the said accord." In that case, the French government would "inform" the Canadian government. A further safeguard was added: the legal "capacitation" to conclude such "*ententes*" would result either from the fact that they would refer to the cultural accord and the accompanying exchange of letters, or from the consent of the federal government. In his response, Ambassador Leduc simply "took note of the information;" in other words, France was not committed to respecting that provision.

Seven days later, on November 24, the France-Quebec cultural *entente* was signed in Quebec City by Pierre Laporte and François Leduc. The text revealed that Cadieux's objections had been met on one point: the references to "countries" and "peoples" had been replaced by "France" and "Quebec," or by other expressions such as "the parties." On the other hand, no reference was made to the accord, so a further exchange of letters between Martin and Leduc was released simultaneously. In his letter, the ambassador referred to the "discussions that have taken place between Quebec, French and Canadian authorities concerning the conclusion of an *entente* for cultural cooperation between France and the Province of Quebec." As the minister knew, agreement had been reached between the French and Quebec authorities, and the *entente* had been signed that day. He asked him to "confirm that this *entente*...receives the approval of the Canadian government." Martin replied that it did.

Who won the mini power struggle? Through the accord and the exchange of letters, the federal government asserted what was essential for it—the exercise of Canadian sovereignty. Provisions for exchanges had also been extended to cover not only Quebec but the other provinces; and direct federal action had been sanctioned as well. Quebec, for its part, succeeded in signing a formal agreement that contained no reference to federal competence. As for the respective dates of the two sets of documents, that turned out to be of little consequence; France and Quebec could develop their bilateral relations without any formal obligation to inform Ottawa. Writing later, Morin claimed that the new arrangements represented a "gain" over the previous situation.[40] Without the federal government realizing it, he argued, Quebec "was henceforth in a position not only to plan exchange programmes or even discuss political problems with French representatives, but also to concert with France as if it were nearly sovereign, and, thanks to French support, to be invited one day, on the same basis as other nations of the world, to international conferences." This achievement, he conceded, was "administrative," not constitutional or legal in nature, "Canada having made certain that the signature of those *ententes* did not call into question its international personality." These claims for Quebec were considerably overdrawn. Even before the *entente* was signed, Paul Martin had stated that a province could have direct communication with foreign governments, but, before arrangements could be legally binding, the federal power had to come into play; that did not change. As for Quebec's being "nearly sovereign," the claim recalls the remark that it is difficult to be nearly pregnant; either one possesses the *jus tractatuum* or one does not. Similarly, nothing in the *entente* bears out the claim that Quebec acquired the right to be invited to take part in international conferences "on the same basis as other nations of the world."

From the French point of view, the balance sheet was positive. Mechanisms for direct cooperation with Quebec had been put in place without alienating Ottawa or violating international law; the possibilities of increased cooperation with the federal government and other provinces were also enhanced. But the principal winners were undoubtedly those Canadians, and particularly Quebecers, who stood to benefit from more intensive contacts with France. The competition had not only given added impetus to France-Quebec relations; it had stirred the once-complacent Department of External Affairs into taking a more active interest in relations between the two countries.

The evening following the signature of the cultural *entente*, Pierre Laporte flew to Paris for the second meeting of the *Commission permanente*. Gérin-Lajoie joined him there. They called on Couve de Murville, Alain Peyrefitte, and other ministers, and were given considerable media publicity. Conforming with practice, de Gaulle received them in his office at noon, and then for lunch. Once again, Léger was excluded. In their pre-luncheon conversation, the president expressed his pleasure over the signature of the *entente*, which he interpreted as evidence that France was compensating for its abandonment of New France in 1763 and for two centuries of indifference. While that rectification of history was obviously important to him, he was also interested in the future. There are two versions of what happened next. According to the one sent to Lesage, the president declared, as he had done to the premier, that the events set in motion in Quebec in recent years were certain to lead to independence. Impressed by the pronunciamento, one of the Quebec ministers agreed. Independence was a relative situation, the other commented, and would always be circumscribed by geographical and other conditions that made Quebec necessarily a part of North America. Whatever the future, it would always have special relations with the rest of Canada and the United States. The other version of the conversation is Gérin-Lajoie's.[41] Aware of the general's broad historical perspective on human affairs and the interest he had shown in Quebec's independence, the minister of education took the initiative and asked him where he thought recent events would lead. From then on, the two versions agree: de Gaulle replied that they would result in some form of independence, possibly along the lines of France's current relations with its European neighbours. That viewpoint was clearly at odds with the position of the Quebec government as expressed in an article published over Lesage's signature in *Le Monde* on the occasion of the signing of the *entente*. The development of closer relations with France, it ran, was a logical step in the Quebec people's efforts to occupy the economic sector, develop its cultural identity and continue to bear witness to the French culture in North America. It would "enable the French language and cultural community to become more itself without ceasing to be Canadian."[42] At a press conference before leaving Paris, Laporte expressed similar views, "We in Quebec have a duty to give Canada the best French culture possible, and this is to be found in France. We are not doing Canada a bad turn by seeking it there, but merely serving it to the best of our ability."[43]

The decisions taken at the three-day meeting of the Franco-Quebec *Commission permanente* that was held after the signing ceremony reflected the growing range of activities between France and Quebec. The second *Biennale de la langue française* was to be held in Quebec City in 1967. Quebec would supply books to French libraries to inform the public of life in the province. Long-standing problems with the distribution of French books in Quebec would be studied and the possibility of co-publishing examined. A French documentation centre (to distribute French scientific and technical information) would be established in Quebec, and a Quebec documentation centre in France. Proposals would be examined to create a series of chairs of Quebec literature at French universities. Under the arrangements already in place for the exchange of teachers and professors, twenty-eight young French "*coopérants*"* would arrive shortly in Quebec.

At about the same time, the Department of External Affairs published an even more extensive list of projects that it had negotiated. Among them were a possible chair of Canadian studies in France, increased exchanges of university professors, artists, film and media personnel, and scientific information. A Canadian documentation

* Young men who volunteered for work in developing countries as a substitute for compulsory military service.

centre would be established in Paris. In short, the competition to develop relations with France was intensifying.

The conclusion of the *entente* and the *accord cadre* marked the high point of activity in Franco-Quebec relations during the Lesage government's tenure of office. During the late phase of the negotiations, the premier had been on holiday in Italy, Lebanon and Israel, but had resisted suggestions from his advisers to turn up in Paris to lend his prestige to the Quebec ceremony. With elections due in 1966, the diplomatic manoeuvering interested him much less than domestic issues of more direct relevance to the public. Over lunch, just before Christmas, André Patry urged the premier to approve a series of new initiatives in Africa.[44] Quebec, he argued, should develop direct, continuing links with French-speaking African countries parallel to those of the federal government. It should also insist on recruiting not only teachers but all other professionals from within the province, and Quebec officials should be able to communicate directly with their African counterparts with regard to their activities. In brief, Quebec should not only have a direct role in Africa, but a "*droit de regard*," a say, concerning federal programmes. To assert that policy and to gain experience, Patry recommended, the government should launch "pilot projects" in Tunisia and in Morocco, both of which had shown an interest in dealing with Quebec. Lesage listened sympathetically, but was not prepared for the moment to go beyond the allocation he had already approved in principle of three hundred thousand dollars in the 1966–67 budget for aid projects.

Jean Chapdelaine's year-end report was noticeably sober.[45] Progress in Franco-Quebec relations had been made in the field of education, he wrote to Lesage, but cultural relations were more difficult to assess. In the economic sector, which had the highest priority, the situation was less satisfying. Great efforts were being made, but he had reached the conclusion that France would never make more than a supplementary contribution to Quebec's industrial development, which would depend, first of all, on the efforts of Quebecers themselves, and secondly, on American enterprise.

Chapdelaine's more prudent attitude was justified on other grounds. On December 19, 1965, de Gaulle had been re-elected president for a seven-year term, but only in the second round of voting. That was a serious blow to his prestige and also to him personally, since he had always prided himself on having an intimate relationship with the population over and beyond political parties and other intermediary bodies. Now, in his first electoral contest (in 1958 he had been unopposed), Frenchmen had refused to give him the clear mandate he had asked for. At any rate, he was seventy-five, and it was highly unlikely that he would serve out a full term. The post-de Gaulle era was already beginning, Chapdelaine told Lesage in early 1966.[46] However, Quebec was well established in Paris; that was a reality that could not be called into question. As delegate general, he himself had an excellent "rating" with the president and at all levels of the French administration. Nor was Quebec's "privileged position" likely to be affected by the ups and downs of relations between Ottawa and Paris. In fact, sometimes the federal authorities even asked the delegation general to use its "good offices" to bring Ottawa and Paris closer together on a particular issue. Even if things were not as easy in the post-de Gaulle era, Quebec's position as the largest French-language group outside France, its geographical situation as the doorway to America, its current vitality and its place in the world gave it necessarily a privileged position with any conceivable new French government. It would certainly preserve the substance of its position in France and perhaps also some of its "special entrées."

On the federal side, Paul Martin persisted in his efforts to minimize the damage to Franco-Canadian relations as a result of the competition with Quebec. On Pierre Laporte's return from Paris, he wrote to him to express his appreciation for the public comment that the *entente* would enable Quebec "to serve Canada to the best of our ability."[47] For his part, Martin added, he found it "completely natural" that Quebec should "develop its cultural relations with France in that way." Later when he was in Paris himself for a NATO meeting, he met with Couve de Murville and was assured that the *entente* did not pose a threat to the federal government's authority. Marcel Cadieux, less easily convinced, followed up on the signature of the *accord cadre* with a request to Paris for "clarification" of the text with the objective of establishing that the French government recognized Ottawa's jurisdiction over international affairs. He did not get satisfaction. He also sent Morin a draft of a statement entitled "Federal-Provincial Procedures to Govern the Conclusion of International Agreements in Fields of Provincial Jurisdiction." It proposed that any province wishing to negotiate an agreement in the area of public, as opposed to private, international law should inform the federal government of its intention and of the nature and scope of the project. The federal government would then advise on its compatibility with Canadian foreign policy, and consultations would take place on any aspects that had foreign policy implications. Before signature of such an agreement, the provincial government would communicate the final text to the federal government for concurrence; it would also have to be sanctioned following the signature by an exchange of notes between Canada and the foreign country. On the other hand, with regard to international agreements between the federal government and a foreign country in a field of provincial jurisdiction, Ottawa would merely inform the provincial governments of its intention and of their scope. Predictably, the reaction in Quebec City to the proposed arrangement was negative. Morin and his colleagues decided to delay their response until after the Quebec elections when, it was anticipated, the Liberals would be returned and Premier Lesage would authorize them to pursue their international objectives with greater vigour.

In early 1966, another shadow was cast over Franco-Canadian relations when de Gaulle decided to withdraw France's military forces from NATO and to expel all other NATO forces from the country. In retrospect, the move appears less surprising than at the time. A few weeks before returning to power in 1958, the general had told American journalist Cyrus Sulzberger unequivocally, "I would quit NATO if I were running France."[48] NATO was "no longer an alliance," he commented, it was "a subordination," and after France had "regained" its independence, the country might be linked with the Western countries in a formal alliance, but could not accept that "a superior like the United States be responsible for us." The proposal he had made to President Eisenhower in 1958 for a Franco-British-American triumvirate was in part a probing operation to test the United States' readiness to share its power, and he had concluded that it would not do so. He had repeated the exercise with President Kennedy, suggesting a reorganization of the Atlantic Alliance with a view to "joint actions towards the neutral countries of Africa and Asia."[49] Once again, the Americans had demurred. While de Gaulle liked, or at least was intrigued by, Kennedy, he had developed an aversion for President Johnson at their only meeting during his trip to Washington to attend Kennedy's funeral.[50] That encounter had fuelled his distrust of the United States and strengthened his determination to take his distance from it.

By the beginning of 1966, de Gaulle judged that the time was right to make his move. The first French nuclear bomb tests in the Pacific were scheduled for that year. After receiving Soviet leaders Krushchev and Bulganin in Paris, he was to make a return visit to the Soviet Union in the early summer and needed to establish his credibility as leader of a third force capable of negotiating with the superpowers. At home, Finance Minister Michel Debré was able to report to him that, thanks to its remarkable economic recovery, France had repaid the debt to the United States accumulated after World War Two; in that way too, its freedom of action was further enhanced.

In deciding to separate France militarily from NATO, de Gaulle reflected one of the most enduring traits of his personality, his intense patriotism. During World War Two he had frequently rebelled at French forces having to take orders from Anglo-Saxon commanders;

he found it intolerable that they still had to serve under an American commander-in-chief. And he viewed NATO headquarters in Paris, as well as the presence of foreign troops, exempt in some respects from French law, as an affront to French national sovereignty. He did not want his great-grandchildren to grow up, he commented, with the impression of living in an occupied country.[51] De Gaulle's personal situation was also a factor in his decision. The close electoral race had made him realize that time was running out for him and it increased his sense of urgency to accomplish his goals. As he himself recognized, he was also showing signs of age. "The General has become very impulsive," Couve de Murville remarked with some concern to a close collaborator about that time.[52]

De Gaulle made his announcement at a press conference on February 21, 1966. Most of his ministers, convened as usual for such occasions, were taken completely by surprise. So were France's allies. Canada, like the other NATO members, only received the decision officially in an *aide-mémoire* dated March 10. While France was withdrawing its forces from the integrated defence programme, the document stated, it was remaining a member of the non-military, or consultative, part of the alliance. By April 1, 1967, the Canadian units on French soil had to be withdrawn or transferred to French command. Prime Minister Pearson's immediate reaction reflected the sentiments of many Canadians who followed such matters. He was assailed by "a feeling of deep despair and frustration," he wrote later in his memoirs; a country which had suffered more than any other from the absence of collective action for defence "should have learned for all time...that there is no safety or hope in national sovereignty alone."[53] For Canadians to be told to leave France and, in fact, to move to Germany was "an ironic sequel to the history of Canadian forces crossing the Atlantic in this century." In an uncharacteristically blunt remark, he asked "a senior member of the French Embassy" who expressed his regrets, whether he thought the Canadians "should take our hundred thousand dead with us to German territory."

De Gaulle's move was all the more grating in Ottawa since it ran counter to the Canadian policy of collective security that had been developed since World War Two. First the United Nations, and then, with the advent of the cold war, NATO, had become cornerstones of Canada's foreign policy. For Pearson and other Canadian leaders, NATO was far more than a military alliance; it was the embryo of an Atlantic community, something of which the general was, incidentally, also distrustful. Even on East-West relations, there were marked differences between the two countries. Canada stood for Western solidarity under American leadership as the best means of containing Soviet expansionism and eventually negotiating *détente*. De Gaulle

recognized the value of NATO to Western security and made it clear
that, in a genuine crisis, France would be on the American side, but his
primary objective was a France with "*les mains libres*"–free hands—or
as free as possible in an interdependent world.

In determining the Canadian reaction to de Gaulle's move, one
factor was of primary importance: for domestic political reasons, the
Pearson government genuinely needed good relations with France. On
reflection, the prime minister also recognized that de Gaulle's target
was the United States, and not Canada, and that the general could hardly
have required the Americans to leave and allowed the Canadians to
stay. He was even "right up to a point," Pearson conceded, in feeling
that NATO had lost some of its relevance as the international situation had changed.[54] Had adjustments been made "to give the European
side of the coalition greater influence and power," it might have been
more difficult for France to withdraw; indeed, "de Gaulle might not
have wished to do so." With hindsight, that viewpoint appears to be
unduly optimistic, but it was completely in character for Pearson. He
could even understand de Gaulle's feelings towards the United States:
they were those, he wrote in his memoirs, of a man who had suffered
indignities when he was weak and who had become strong again.

Having dropped his bombshell, de Gaulle, again true to form,
adopted a more conciliatory tone. The necessary adaptation would
take place piecemeal over a period of three years—when the NATO
treaty was due for renewal—he stated in his *aide-mémoire* of March
10, in order to avoid France's allies being "inconvenienced." He was
also prepared to negotiate new bilateral agreements with the United
States and Canada for the use of French facilities in the case of a
conflict involving the alliance. Furthermore, while the headquarters
of SHAPE, the Supreme Headquarters, Allied Powers Europe, would
have to go, he held out the possibility of keeping the NATO Council,
the political wing of the alliance, in Fontainebleau. In Ottawa,
Pearson, Martin and their advisers, attuned to Canada's traditional
foreign policy role as conciliator, began immediately to seek ways to
minimize the negative consequences of the French action. They
quickly developed a variety of compromise arrangements, but the
Americans, seriously aggrieved at what they considered de Gaulle's
ingratitude and national chauvinism, succeeded in rallying the other
NATO partners to a tough stance. On March 18, the NATO Council
declared that no system of bilateral arrangements could substitute for
the current multilateral ones. French access to American nuclear
weapons under a "double key" security plan, that is, one in which an
American and a French key were necessary to use them, was also
cancelled. France reacted by requiring prior notification of NATO
flights over its territory.

Still seeking to have a moderating influence, Pearson sent a lengthy despatch to de Gaulle, recalling their meeting two years earlier and expressing his satisfaction that their decision to intensify relations between the two countries was bearing fruit. On the international scene, he recognized that differences existed in French and Canadian outlooks, but noted with satisfaction that France did not intend to leave the North Atlantic Treaty Alliance completely. The two countries were in agreement on the essential, the quest for peace, he stressed, and in that regard, he was sure they would always be side by side. In NATO discussions of the situation, Paul Martin, for his part, sought to avoid isolating France from the other member countries as much as possible.[55] At the time, the Soviet Union was pressing for a European security conference, from which the United States and Canada would be excluded. The smaller European states feared that de Gaulle, who viewed the proposal with favour, would use the occasion to pursue his goal of French leadership of all the countries west of the Iron Curtain. To avoid that happening, a counter-proposal was developed for a security conference sponsored by NATO and its Communist counterpart, the Warsaw Pact. Martin urged that some formula be devised that de Gaulle could not reject and which would "tie his hands" during the visit he was about to undertake to Moscow. In direct opposition to the Americans, the Canadian minister also urged that a decision on moving the NATO Council's headquarters out of France be postponed at least until de Gaulle's return, at which time the results of his talks with the Soviet leaders could be assessed. Although he achieved little, Couve de Murville expressed his appreciation to Martin for his efforts. As it turned out, de Gaulle's mission was relatively unsuccessful. The new "troika" composed of Brezhnev, Podgorny and Kosygin met him, in Lacouture's words, with "a wall of courteous immobility."[56] In October the decision was taken to move the NATO Council to Brussels.

At the close of the NATO Council meeting at which de Gaulle's decision was considered, Martin and Couve de Murville had issued a joint press release declaring that relations between their two countries were satisfactory and announcing that the French foreign minister was to visit Ottawa in the autumn. The reassuring statement was to set a pattern in which Martin would raise his concerns about issues that were marring the relationship, only to be reassured by Couve de Murville that they were not serious; then the two men would inform the public that all was well. One source of friction, during that period, concerned Governor General Vanier. As Vanier approached the end of his five-year term a plan was conceived in Ottawa to have him visit France and be received as the Canadian head of state. For him and

Madame Vanier, it was a cherished dream that would crown his career in a brilliant manner and symbolize their attachment to both countries. For the Canadian government, two further considerations made the plan attractive. First, it would further the policy of *rapprochement*, and second, it would strengthen the office of governor general. Constitutionally Queen Elizabeth II was the Canadian head of state, but, in her absence—that is, most of the time—the governor general performed the functions of that high office in her name. Since under the constitutional monarchy, both acted on advice from the Canadian government, the result was the same. While Canadians generally accepted the arrangement, foreigners sometimes saw it as an indication that Canada was not completely independent. To counter such thinking, the Canadian government wished to have the governor general received as head of state in foreign capitals, and Vanier's predecessors had been so received in the United States, Portugal and South Africa. In view of his close relations with de Gaulle, and of the fact that he had received him in 1960 as the French head of state, it seemed appropriate that Vanier should make a return visit as the Canadian equivalent.

In February 1966, the Canadian embassy in Paris was instructed to raise the matter informally with the Elysée Palace. The Queen had given her approval, the French were told, but the visit could only take place if the governor general were given head of state treatment, that is, if he were invited to stay at the Elysée Palace or another official residence, if the Canadian flag were flown beside the tricolor throughout Paris, and if other appropriate rules of protocol were respected. Whether because of the current ambivalent state of Franco-Canadian relations or because of the great importance he accorded to the niceties of protocol, General de Gaulle's reaction was negative. He replied that he was touched that Vanier wished to repay the visit that he had made to Canada, and that he prized his friendship highly, so there was no reason that the visit should not take place. However, since the Queen, and not the governor general, was Canadian head of state, Vanier could not be accorded the honours due to that rank. Ottawa responded that, when the Queen travelled outside the Commonwealth, she did so as the British head of state, and so could never return de Gaulle's visit to Canada. Indeed, she had been consulted and felt it quite in order for a Canadian governor general travelling abroad to be received in that manner.

De Gaulle made a counter-proposal. He would receive Vanier at the Elysée Palace for a private discussion and a meal; then they would go to Rambouillet, the presidential country residence, for a day and a half. There were precedents for that course as well, he pointed out, including the visits of Chairman Krushchev of the Soviet Union,

Chancellor Adenauer of West Germany and Prime Minister Macmillan of Great Britain. The Canadian government was still not satisfied. The allegations that Lesage had been accorded head of state treatment in Paris still rankled, and it wanted the difference between the two visits to be crystal clear. At any rate, it pointed out, the three persons cited were not heads of state. De Gaulle refused to budge. In the end, the project was abandoned, leaving Pearson and other ministers in Ottawa highly indignant, but even more concerned that the news of the rebuff should not become public knowledge. The Vaniers were deeply hurt.

Chapter 10
Vive le Québec libre!

When the *Union Nationale* under Daniel Johnson took office in Quebec on June 16, 1966, preparations for Expo '67 were already well under way. Development of the site on two islands in the St. Lawrence River was well advanced and the national pavilions were mushrooming. As Canadian commissioner, Pierre Dupuy was consulting closely with the federal and Quebec governments on a wide range of topics, including their respective roles in receiving foreign dignitaries. The Canadian government was to issue the formal invitations, but Premier Lesage who had fully expected to be still in power had made it clear that he intended to receive personally the heads of state or their representatives and to take the opportunity to make Quebec better known abroad. At the same time, he was determined that the visits should not be marred by domestic quarrels, and gave instructions that federal and provincial officials were to cooperate closely in making the necessary arrangements. Unfortunately from that perspective, one of Premier Johnson's first decisions with regard to Expo '67 was to appoint André Patry as Quebec chief of protocol with special responsibility for receiving foreign visits of the highest level. For those who knew the bright but temperamental law professor and his feelings toward the Department of External Affairs, the appointment was a recipe for trouble. However, Johnson liked Patry personally and enjoyed the game of political upmanship in which he, Morin and others liked to engage with Ottawa.

In France, the news of the change of government had been received by the relatively few Frenchmen interested in the subject with surprise and even consternation. While de Gaulle and Lesage had not developed a close personal rapport, the General had been impressed by Lesage's personality and competence, and that perception had been an important factor in his decision to support the province's modernization. Johnson, on the other hand, was an almost totally unknown factor to de Gaulle, and his position as leader of the *Union Nationale*, with its record of parochialism and corruption, was hardly reassuring. De Gaulle was probably unaware that the new premier's scepticism with regard to Quebec's international ventures had receded in recent times as he had realized that such ventures could be useful in pursuing his domestic goals, notably the decentralization of the federal system. On the other hand, the general most probably knew that Johnson was a stronger Quebec nationalist than Lesage as indicated in his slogan "equality or independence." He did have first-hand information from one member of the Elysée staff. Alain Plantey, a senior member of the secretariat general for African affairs, had visited Quebec in May on his return journey from the French West Indies. In his subsequent report, he noted that an air of tension and even despair pervaded the province. The role of the Catholic Church was being called into question, young people were in a mood of crisis, French-Canadian businessmen felt frustrated, and the federal policy of bilingualism was proving an illusion. "Watch out," he concluded, "the pot is about to boil."[1]

A few days before taking office, Johnson confirmed to Chapdelaine the new government's intention to develop Franco-Quebec relations. In July, Johnson despatched Paul Gros d'Aillon, a native French-man and one of his close political advisers, and Jean Loiselle, a member of his staff, to Paris. The message they bore was, in Gros d'Aillon's words, that the new government did not intend to interrupt the cooperation with France; on the contrary, it wished to "extend and deepen it."[2] Neophytes in such international missions, the two men hesitated to use the facilities of the delegation general which they identified with the Lesage administration. The journalists with whom they got in touch were sceptical, generally taking the attitude: show us. They were better received by members of the "Quebec mafia," who were eager to be assured that their ambitions for Quebec had not received a fatal setback. Xavier Deniau invited them to lunch and introduced them to other members of the National Assembly. Philippe Rossillon, Jean-Daniel Jurgensen, Bernard Dorin and Martial de la Fournière offered their encouragement and support. Gros d'Aillon and Loiselle even had a cordial meeting with two right-wing Gaullist ministers, Jacques Taittinger and Alexandre Sanguinetti. Although they had no specific mandate to do so, the two emissaries raised with Jurgensen the possibility of Johnson's visiting Paris. On their return to Quebec, they persuaded the premier to send a letter directly to de Gaulle, repeating the message they had delivered and intimating that he would like to meet the president in Paris as soon as their respective schedules permitted[3] (Chapdelaine had made the same suggestion).

Three months earlier, on April 20, 1966, Mayor Drapeau, in the course of his visits to a number of capitals to promote Expo '67, had been received at the Elysée Palace by de Gaulle and had asked him if he would accept an invitation to visit the exhibition. The general was pleasant but non-committal. Following protocol, Jules Léger transmitted to him the formal invitation from the mayor a short time later. And on September 6, the ambassador delivered a second one from Governor General Vanier to visit Canada in 1967 on the occasion of the celebration of the centenary of Confederation. "We will be particularly happy to welcome you in the capital of Canada," Vanier told him, and also at the 1967 Universal Exposition at which France would play "an important role." In addition to visiting Ottawa and Montreal, he suggested, de Gaulle might perhaps wish to visit "one or two other Canadian cities." Then on September 13, Jean Chapdelaine took a third invitation to the Elysée Palace, this one from Daniel Johnson. "The government of Quebec has joined with the Canadian government in making possible an international exhibition in Montreal from April 28 to October 31, 1967, in which France has kindly agreed to participate," the letter ran. "On the occasion of this exhibition on our territory, and in the name of the Government and people of Quebec," de Gaulle was invited "to visit Quebec and be our guest in our capital, where the heartiest welcome awaits you."[4] Chapdelaine presented a second from the premier expressing appreciation for de Gaulle's personal interest in Quebec.

"General de Gaulle's first reaction," his diplomatic counsellor, René de Saint-Légier, recalled later, "was purely and simply to refuse."[5] He had been to Canada six years earlier, and Pearson had visited France; thus, the exchange had been completed. "You really don't see me going over just to attend a fair," he remarked scornfully to Saint-Légier and Burin des Roziers.[6] Perhaps the recent difficulty over Vanier's proposed visit was also a deterring factor; how could he be received as head of state by someone he had refused to recognize as having the same rank? The situation in Quebec was also far from clear. "Except in cases of emergency," Bernard Tricot, one of his closest advisers, has explained, "the General refused to commit himself too early to matters that were not yet 'ripe', or to face situations that were not well defined."[7] Furthermore, as part of his international initiatives, he had just returned from a major trip to Phnom Penh, during which he had criticized American policy in Vietnam and had sought to encourage Cambodian nationalism. In short, he had other priorities. The most important consideration, however, was revealed by de Gaulle himself a few months later in the form of a hand-written comment on a despatch from the French embassy in Ottawa, suggesting that congratulations be sent to the federal government in the New Year on the occasion of the centenary of Confederation. "There is no question of my addressing a message to Canada or celebrating its 'centennial'," he wrote.

> We can have good relations with the whole of Canada. We
> must have excellent ones with French Canada. But we
> have not to congratulate either the Canadians or ourselves
> for the creation of a 'State' founded on our defeat in the past,
> and especially for the integration of a part of the French
> people into a British entity. At any rate, that entity has
> become very precarious.[8]

In the circumstances, de Gaulle replied on September 24 in a cordial
but vague tone to both the Canadian and Quebec invitations. "You
cannot doubt," he told the governor general, "that, Canada having
received me so well each time that I have gone there, particularly...in
1960, I would be happy to be able to return." Nevertheless, Vanier
would understand, he was sure, that "in the present circumstances,"
the possibility of another visit "would certainly raise questions that
must be examined at leisure." As for the Universal Exposition in
Montreal, "a very great and special importance" was attached to it in
France, and accordingly, the Republic would not fail to mark it in "as
striking a way as possible." He was replying to Johnson's "friendly
personal letter" in the same vein. For those who knew de Gaulle, the
message was that he had no intention of making the trip. But what
were "the present circumstances" that prevented him from doing so?
With characteristic ambiguity when he still did not want to show his
hand, he left Vanier and his advisers to answer the question for
themselves. To his staff members, Etienne Burin des Roziers and René
de Saint-Légier, he was more precise, "If I go, I am liable to set the
place on fire. For the moment, I have better things to do."[9]

The tone of de Gaulle's letter to Johnson—his first—was much
warmer. "The faith that you express in the deep friendship and active
cooperation between Quebec and France touched me greatly," he told
the premier, "and I want to underline to you that my conviction
corresponds exactly to yours."[10] The opening of the delegation general
and the signature of the "*accords culturels*" were "the first evidence of
our intention to restore life and substance to everything that is
distinctively ours and that neither time nor separation have been able
to wipe out." But that was only a beginning, since France now knew
"what a brilliant future was opening for Quebec and how much
everything calls for us to broaden and consolidate our solidarity."
While he was "not yet able to respond" to the invitation to be the guest
of Quebec, "all France" attached exceptional importance to the exhibition and wished that it should be marked in as striking a manner as
possible. He concluded by assuring Johnson that he would receive him
"with the greatest pleasure" in Paris.

In the next few months, de Gaulle had several opportunities to receive first-hand reports on Quebec. In early September, Christian Fouchet, who in addition to being minister of education was one of his oldest and most faithful associates, visited Quebec City, with a short detour to Ottawa. Paul Martin learned of the projected trip only when the French minister informed him that he would be attending a meeting of francophone ministers of education in Quebec City and holding consultations with the Johnson government. Annoyed at what he considered a breach of a condition he had posed to Couve de Murville, that such ministerial visits should include Ottawa, Martin nevertheless decided, in order "to observe the proper diplomatic civilities," to issue a belated invitation.[11] On his return to Paris, Fouchet made a report to Cabinet on which a subsequent press release was based.[12] The minister had been "struck by the loyalty of the French Canadians" to France, the release stated, and impressed by their accomplishments. Since 1759, they had grown from sixty thousand to six million. Cooperation with France was developing rapidly. Three hundred French teachers were at work in Quebec. The Montreal *métro*, "an achievement of French engineers," would soon be finished, and the future French pavilion at Expo '67 was "a remarkable piece of architecture." Both the federal and Quebec governments had confirmed their invitations to the president to visit the exhibition, but, at the Cabinet meeting, "he did not indicate if he would be able to go to Canada." Following Fouchet's presentation, General de Gaulle had intervened to recall "the special ties between France and Canada." French Canada, he had stated, was in a way "a regeneration" for the French themselves.

On September 29 and 30, Couve de Murville made a quick trip from the United Nations in New York to Ottawa and Quebec City. In Ottawa, Paul Martin asked him to urge de Gaulle to accept the invitation to Expo '67; many other heads of state were attending, he argued, and the event would not be a complete success without him. Normally, Martin would also have accompanied Couve de Murville to Quebec, but, fearing that he would be "embarrassed publicly" by "some injudicious speech," he pleaded urgent Cabinet business and stayed away. That proved to be a wise decision. In an uncharacteristically moving statement in Quebec City, the French foreign minister extolled the new direct relationship between his country and Quebec.[13] Their separation had been "painful and certainly premature," he declared, but they had found and recognized each other again. Nothing must be excluded from the network of exchanges developing between the "two communities." Moreover, behind France lay an emerging reality where their common destiny might be determined: *la francophonie*. For observers of Gaullist France, Couve de Murville's words, always carefully chosen to reflect the president's, were highly significant. They would have been still more impressed if they had known that during his stay in Quebec, discussions had been held on the possibility of establishing an on-going committee of French and Quebec ministers to oversee and direct the relationship.

Then, in October, still another trusted associate of the general, Minister of State Louis Joxe, visited Montreal and Ottawa. Officially, his mission was to open the *métro*, one of Drapeau's imaginative schemes. The mayor had hoped that the achievement would be crowned by the presence of de Gaulle himself at the opening ceremony, but he had declined, in part because the occasion did not merit his presence, but also because of the growing ambiguity of his relations with Ottawa and Quebec City. Joxe spent two days in Ottawa and met with the prime minister and several other ministers. Very conciliatory, he expressed his appreciation of Canada's attempt to be helpful in connection with France's withdrawal from NATO, and listened sympathetically to a range of proposals for cooperation between the two countries. Pearson recalled with enthusiasm his own visit to France in 1964, remarking that he had never been better received anywhere; he asked Joxe to transmit to the president, along with his personal respects and best wishes, his hope that he would visit Canada in 1967. The prime minister also hoped that he would visit not only Montreal, Quebec City and Ottawa, but also some other city, such as Vancouver, in order to see something more of the vast country. Joxe indicated that he was personally favourable to such a visit but explained that everything depended on the outcome of National Assembly elections scheduled for March 1967.

Finally, a fourth high-ranking Gaullist, Michel Debré, made the trip to Ottawa and Quebec City in January 1967. At that moment minister of economics and finance, he was second to none in his loyalty to the general. Debré's official purpose was to receive, along with his father, an honorary doctorate from the new University of Sherbrooke, but, like his colleagues, he was also on an intelligence-gathering mission. Taken together, and even excluding other sources, the four ministers were able to provide the president with valuable insights into the latest developments in the Canadian and Quebec capitals. Perhaps the most interesting information for de Gaulle related to the Johnson administration and particularly its vision of Quebec's relations with the rest of Canada; however, in Ottawa, too, significant developments were taking place. During the federal elections in November 1965, three influential Quebec men, Jean Marchand, a union leader, Gérard Pelletier, newspaper editor, and Pierre Trudeau, law professor, had won seats in Parliament as Liberals. Their main purpose in entering politics was to stem what they considered to be the erosion of the authority of the federal government through continued concessions to Quebec. Marchand, considered the senior of the trio, entered the Cabinet immediately as minister of manpower and immigration, while Trudeau was made parliamentary secretary to the prime minister, a post which gave him privileged access to Pearson and his key advisers.

Relations between de Gaulle and the "three doves," as they were popularly known, got off to a bad start. Soon after taking office, Marchand decided to fly to Paris to convince the French authorities to relax restrictions on the recruiting of immigrants to Canada. The Canadian government was also anxious to make him known in French governmental circles as a prominent member of the generation of the Quiet Revolution. Ambassador Léger was asked to request an audience with the president and other personalities. It was refused on the grounds that de Gaulle had adopted a policy of receiving only heads of state, or government leaders and foreign ministers. Since he had received some ministers of the Quebec government, the reaction in Ottawa was very negative. Martin protested the affront to Couve de Murville at a NATO meeting in Paris, shortly afterward, but the French minister, in Martin's words, "was not prepared to fall foul of his master."[14] During that same period, John Halstead, a senior member of the Department of External Affairs, called at both the Quai d'Orsay and the Elysée Palace to enquire diplomatically whether the constitutional implications of dealing directly with Quebec were perhaps misunderstood. From the cool reception, he concluded that the practice would continue unless some action was taken by Canada to alter de Gaulle's attitude. In Ottawa, Ambassador Leduc, acting on instructions and often very uneasily, continued to bear the brunt of the federal government's displeasure.

During the fall and winter of 1966–67, de Gaulle was in fact weighing the possibilities of a visit to Expo '67. Increasingly intrigued by what was happening in Quebec, he felt an obligation to respond positively to Johnson's invitation, but he had no interest in the federal one. There are several versions of how the problem was resolved. In his book, *Vivre le Québec libre*, Pierre Mallen asserts that the critical solution was devised at his home in Montreal.[15] One of his dinner guests, the director of the Port of Montreal, and incidentally a federal government employee, suggested that if the president were to come, he should arrive in the impressive new passenger liner, *Le France*. The port authorities could mobilize the ships and make the arrival a sensational event. A short time later, Xavier Deniau re-appeared in Quebec and confided to Mallen that de Gaulle wanted to make the trip, but he wanted "to make history, not tourism." For de Gaulle, the important thing was Quebec; he wanted to land in Montreal, make an official visit to the province, and assist Quebecers to extricate themselves from their "subordinate situation." He wished to tell them that France, too, was "awakening," and he wanted to make the French aware of the situation in Quebec, of which they were "totally unconscious." In fact, a major objective of such a trip would be to change French public opinion.

The problem was that the federal government had established a fixed protocol for visiting heads of state that called for them to arrive at the military airport in Ottawa, be received in the federal capital, and only then visit Expo '67 and some other part of Canada. De Gaulle would go to Ottawa, Deniau reported, "since Ottawa exists," but he "absolutely refused" to do so at the outset, and if the impasse on that point was not broken, the trip would not take place. Mallen heard Deniau out, then remarked that the federal government's rule was already being infringed: the emperor of Japan [in fact, the Crown prince—author's note]—would be landing first in Vancouver. And he added, "Why necessarily by airplane?" If de Gaulle arrived by ship, he could land in Quebec and sail up to Montreal; conveniently, it was impossible to continue by water to Ottawa. As the two men discussed the possibility, it occurred to them that he could go first to St. Pierre and Miquelon, the French possession that he had liberated in 1941 but never visited. Since he would not be able to land there in the type of aircraft he would use for a transatlantic crossing, he had a perfect pretext for touching down in Quebec first, then going on to the islands. Excited over their plan, Mallen and Deniau drove to Gros d'Aillon's home in Outremont to present it to him, and through him to Johnson. That evening, Deniau flew back to Paris to communicate it to the Elysée Palace.

Robert Bordaz, who served in Montreal as commissioner general of the French pavilion at Expo '67, has given a different version of the way in which the alternative plan originated.[16] Another fervent Gaullist, and one who had the rare privilege of direct access to the president, he, too, had been won over to the cause of Quebec's independence since his arrival in Montreal a couple of years earlier. For reasons of French prestige, but also to encourage that movement, he was determined that de Gaulle should make the voyage. Bordaz mentioned to Drapeau that the general could arrive by sea and sail up the St. Lawrence at night; the shorelines could be illuminated by huge fires to bid him welcome.* Captivated by the idea, the mayor assured him that the whole population would be massed along the route. With such a prospect, Bordaz was even more concerned to learn that de Gaulle was still hesitating, and asked for an appointment with him. The general received him in mid-January 1967.

For a Gaullist, the commissioner general argued, a negative decision was "inexplicable." Expo '67 was largely a French-Canadian undertaking (sic) and was viewed as an occasion "to reveal the

---

* As when the *La Capricieuse* arrived in 1858.

importance of Quebec to the world." If, through his absence, the president indicated that France was disinterested, Quebecers would be "profoundly disappointed" and would interpret his absence as "a new abandonment following the cruel one in the eighteenth century" which they still resented. Struck on his Achilles' heel, de Gaulle reacted strongly. He was hostile to Confederation, he declared, and felt it was unjust; he did not want to give the impression, in going to Canada, that he approved of it. "I don't want them to attribute to me what I don't think." Bordaz replied, "*Mon Général*, you will say what you want." They spoke of how he might make the trip, discussing the sea route which would make it possible to land first in Quebec. Bordaz mentioned the possibility of sailing up the St. Lawrence by night and repeated Drapeau's assurances that the whole population would turn out. The general's interest was aroused. "Do you think there is enough draught?" he asked. Bordaz reassured him on that point as well. De Gaulle promised to let him know his decision.

One further version of the genesis of de Gaulle's maritime option must be recorded. Jean Chapdelaine has recounted that, unaware that the idea had been raised elsewhere, he commented to René de Saint-Légier that, if the president did not want to arrive first in Ottawa, he had only to travel by sea, since ships could not sail beyond Montreal.[17] Even if the suggestion was not original, his position as representative of the government of Quebec most certainly gave it weight. Whatever the paternity of the plan, it fell on receptive ears. On January 26, Deniau wrote to Mallen, "Your ideas have found their way right to the Elysée."[18] And he added that de Gaulle was thinking of arriving by sea and the ship had already been reserved. On February 13, de Gaulle received Jean Chapdelaine, then confirmed the decision: he would arrive in Quebec City on the *Colbert*, an ultra-modern cruiser launched in 1959 and considered the flagship of the French navy. He would spend a day and a half there, two days in Montreal, then fly to Ottawa for a day before returning to France. He asked the delegate general to keep the decision secret until Ottawa was informed.

In Quebec City, André Patry moved to establish the provincial government's control over visits to Expo '67 by foreign dignitaries. Jean-Paul L'Allier, recently returned from studies in France, was appointed to assist him as coordinator. Mario Beaulieu, the premier's executive assistant, became chairman of a committee to oversee all government activities in that regard. On the federal side, Lionel Chevrier returned from his post as high commissioner in London to become federal commissioner general of state visits; he was to be assisted by Brigadier Robert Moncel as coordinator. According to Patry, three ground rules were quickly established by the federal and provincial representatives.[19] All official visitors would be received first in Ottawa, then would go to Quebec City. No federal ministers would accompany them there, that task to be left to a member of the Quebec Legislature. And Quebec security forces would have full responsibility for their security in Quebec City. Patry also sent a set of guidelines to heads of consulates concerning the visits of ministers of their governments. That particular move precipitated a sharp protest from Cadieux to Morin, warning that, if such invasions of federal prerogatives were repeated, the consulates would have to consider them "*non-avenues*," that is, non-existent.[20] Undeterred, Patry adopted the same attitude with regard to what he considered Cadieux's intervention in Quebec's affairs and went one step further: he sent the consulates an order of precedence for ceremonial occasions that he had had approved by the provincial government, but, of course, not by Ottawa.

In September 1966, half a year before Expo '67 was to open, President Léopold Senghor of Senegal arrived in Canada on a state visit and soon got caught up in the Ottawa-Quebec tug of war. Three months earlier, the heads of the francophone African states had approved his concept of a cultural community. Canada was mentioned as a possible member. Senghor conceived the community as a series of concentric circles with France and the African countries at the centre and having the most intense relations, other former French colonies such as Haiti, Algeria, Morocco, Tunisia and former Indochina next, and a third, more loosely connected, group including Canada, Belgium, Luxembourg and Switzerland on the outside. In short, Canada's prospective role was viewed as relatively peripheral. The perception within both the federal and Quebec governments was very different. In Quebec City, Morin and Patry saw *la Francophonie* as a vital link in the network of foreign contacts that they were striving to put in place. In Ottawa, it was viewed as a counterpart to the Commonwealth and a useful vehicle to provide a better balance in Canadian foreign policy; active Canadian participation in the new body was also considered essential to check the Quebec entrepreneurs.

Senghor began his visit in Ottawa, and, after being briefed by his hosts, made it clear that he was thinking in terms of Canadian, and not just Quebec, representation in the proposed organization. He had no intention of encouraging Quebec independence, he declared, since it was a serious threat to the bilingualism and biculturalism of the whole country, and would lead to eventual absorption by the United States of the other provinces. In Quebec City, Premier Johnson and his colleagues gave a banquet in the African statesman's honour and were deeply impressed by his eloquent French and his passionate commitment to the francophone concept. Their sentiments changed when he said that all of Canada should join the proposed organization, and even more, when he proposed a toast to the Queen. Several ministers remained seated. The next day, Johnson tried to convince Senghor that, without a strong and autonomous Quebec, francophones in the other provinces would be in a very precarious position.[21] After that initiation into Canadian politics, Senghor sought refuge in ambiguity whenever the language issue was raised.

One of the matters carried over from the Lesage administration was the invitation to Gérin-Lajoie to visit Tunisia. Patry persuaded the premier to send Marcel Masse, the new minister of state for education (a junior position to that of the minister), on a discreet mission to Tunis to propose a specific aid project as a first step to developing a direct link with that country. Johnson assigned his executive assistant, Mario Beaulieu, to accompany him, in part to keep a watch on him, since Masse was a former member of the RIN and was considered a radical still, and in part because the premier, a cautious man, did not want Masse to commit the government too deeply. As it turned out, when the two men arrived at their destination, they found that the Canadian ambassador to Tunisia (residing in Switzerland) had preceded them. The Tunisian authorities showed no interest in their offer of aid and direct links. They returned home as discreetly as they had left.

Another project submitted to Johnson during his first months in office called for a meeting, under Quebec's auspices, of ministers of education of francophone countries. When word of the plan reached Ottawa, it was immediately perceived as another plot to establish direct external relations. In response to a question in the House of Commons, Paul Martin acknowledged that he was aware of it and looked forward to hearing from Quebec on the matter.[22] He also recalled that international practice required that the Canadian government sponsor any inter-governmental conference that might be held in Canada. That warning appears to have blocked any further initiatives in Quebec City for the moment.

In early 1967, the Department of External Affairs undertook a thorough review of Canada's relations with France. Its conclusions provide a useful insight into the federal government's perception of the situation a few months before de Gaulle's visit. The French government had indicated its interest in closer ties with Canada, the Cabinet was advised, and General de Gaulle had told Pearson in Paris that he wanted the relationship to remain intact for both sentimental and political reasons. His aims were probably to achieve a healthier balance in which French Canadians would be able to assert themselves within Canada, and Canadians generally within North America. Encouraging progress had been made recently in Franco-Canadian relations, but serious complications and difficulties persisted. As France's colonial power diminished, its international role depended primarily on its cultural position. That situation led it to react positively to Quebec's request for support in developing a new dynamic personality. General de Gaulle's attitude, while intensely personal, was supremely important. He regarded French Canadians as former Frenchmen and he was prepared to do a great deal to help them. How he envisaged the greater assertion of Quebec within Canada was not clear, but he might well have developed the view that the federal system was no longer viable. He probably did not intend to weaken Canada as a country, but his attitude was open to misinterpretation and exploitation. Supporters of Quebec separatism, both in Quebec and France, were determined to use every opportunity to promote their cause. What should be done in the circumstances? Canada's bilateral relations with France and other French-speaking countries should be developed as much as possible, and France should be supported on multilateral issues as much as Canadian national interests permitted. It should be explained to the general and his entourage that Canada was eager to facilitate Franco-Quebec relations, but within the framework of bilateral relations between the two countries. At the same time, it should be made clear that the proper channel of diplomatic communication with any part of Canada was through Ottawa. Finally, clandestine activities of the dozen or so pro-separatist Frenchmen had to be carefully monitored and counter-measures developed. In this contest, a visit by de Gaulle to Canada was of great importance and preparations for it had to be made with the utmost care.

Consulted on the situation by officials in Ottawa, Jules Léger was more philosophical, but also more realistic. Many, although not all, of the difficulties in the relationship were related to the president personally, he remarked. De Gaulle's great sensitivity, his sharp tongue, his unforgiving nature, his double standards in dealing with Quebec and Ottawa, and his overriding interest in French Canada as reflected in his disregard of the domestic and constitutional niceties in Canada, all made matters difficult. While his imprint on many aspects of French policy would persist for many years, he himself would not, and after he left office, tensions in the relationship would ease. In short, time was on Canada's side. In the meantime, while it was necessary to defend the federal position, confrontation should be avoided. Important benefits to Canada had been achieved in the past three years notwithstanding the irritations and dangers inherent in the current situation; however, one word from one man whose reputation for taking revenge when thwarted had not diminished with his years could suddenly reverse that situation.

As a reflection of the seriousness with which the Department of External Affairs was taking the matter, a special unit was established to monitor Quebec's international activities; and Allan Gotlieb was appointed special adviser on federal-provincial matters to deal with the legal aspects of the increasingly delicate situation. A special task force also was set up under Gotlieb's chairmanship with responsibility for the development of cultural agreements with a number of countries, cooperation with the provinces on external aid, state visits to Expo '67 and Franco-Canadian relations generally. Parliamentary Secretary Pierre Trudeau, Marc Lalonde, a prominent figure in the Prime Minister's Office, and senior officials in the Privy Council Office, were to be kept closely informed of developments. Ambassador Leduc was called in once again and informed that "proper channels" had to be respected in communicating with provincial governments, and that de Gaulle's eventual visit had to be discussed in the first instance with the federal authorities. The president, he was told unequivocally, was expected to come to Ottawa before visiting Quebec. Leduc hewed to the official French line that no decision could be reached until after the French legislative elections scheduled for March.

That was the situation when the Canadian government learned that de Gaulle had told Chapdelaine on February 13 that he had a tentative plan to fly from Paris to Newfoundland, then sail on a French warship to Montreal. Deeply upset, Cadieux tried to obtain confirmation from Leduc who, after consulting Paris, recognized that there was some substance to the report, but appeared to have little precise information. On March 17, two days before the second ballot in the French elections, the Montreal newspaper *La Presse* broke the news that de Gaulle would arrive in Quebec City aboard the "most impressive vessel in the French navy." He would be "received triumphantly" by Premier Johnson in Quebec City, where they would sign "several cultural treaties," then the general would go on to Expo '67. In that way, he would show that he considered that the government of Quebec, and not the federal government, represented French Canada. The offices in Ottawa buzzed with concern and indignation. Questioned in the House of Commons on the newspaper report, Martin was evasive. He had had an "informal discussion" with the French ambassador, he conceded, but the details of the president's visit had "not yet been finalized."[23] "If and when" the general decided to visit Canada, it would be "the most natural thing in the world" that he visit Quebec, where the majority of French-language Canadians lived. The minister hoped that he would also find it "desirable" to visit other parts of Canada.

There were other indications of worsening relations. In early March, Governor General Vanier died, and de Gaulle sent a personal representative, Claude Hettier de Boislambert, chancellor of the *Ordre de la Libération* and one of the original Gaullists, to attend the funeral. Some Canadian ministers and officials were annoyed at the stiff formality of the president's message of condolences to Madame Vanier and at the fact that he did not send someone of higher rank to represent him. De Boislambert, for his part, took umbrage at the treatment he received. The American representative, Vice President Hubert Humphrey, was taken to the church in a limousine with a police escort, he complained; he himself had had to walk the short distance unaccompanied. Humphrey was also offered a luncheon; he was not. Finally, he was vexed when Madame Vanier, whom he had known in London and Algeria, had expressed her husband's great disappointment at de Gaulle's refusal to receive him as a head of state. Subsequently, Leduc asked Cadieux if such "second-class treatment" was retaliation for de Gaulle's behaviour towards Léger and Marchand, for his own direct relations with Quebec and for the treatment accorded Quebec ministers in France. In his memoirs, Paul Martin dismisses the charge of inferior treatment as "bunkum."[24] Madame Vanier got in the last word—for the moment: before moving out of Rideau Hall, she sent an unambiguous message to de Gaulle, "1940."

A second unpleasant incident occurred over the celebration on April 9 of the fiftieth anniversary of the battle of Vimy Ridge, the great but costly victory of Canadian troops in World War One. The ceremony was conceived as part of the centennial activities, and the Queen was asked to preside over it. This time, it was de Gaulle who was annoyed on two counts: first, he had not been consulted about the attendance of a foreign head of state; and second, the Queen was not, in his eyes, a Canadian, but rather his opposite number across the Channel. He forbade French representation. Undoubtedly, in view of his well-known sensitivities and the delicacy of current relations, he should have been consulted, even though the ceremony was primarily a Canadian matter. Apparently, the error originated in the office of the Canadian minister of veterans' affairs. In the subsequent flurry of consultations, Prince Philip agreed to stand in for the Queen, but de Gaulle would still not agree to attend or be represented. Since the ceremony could not be cancelled, Prime Minister Pearson sent Léo Cadieux, his associate minister of national defence, a strong-willed man in whom he had great confidence, to see that it went off properly. It was not a happy occasion. In the end, the French were represented by a brigadier-general, a moderate military rank, but, incidentally, the same held by de Gaulle. Prince Philip was in bad humour because he felt he had been made a pawn in the controversy and he muttered that the Canadians should hold their own ceremonies without royal participation. For Léo Cadieux, one of the most touching moments occurred when the French general apologized for the slight to Canada's war dead and commented that the twenty thousand ordinary citizens who lined the route truly represented the honour of France. In the

House of Commons, John Diefenbaker interpreted the incident as a loss of face for Canada.[25] When de Gaulle received Jean Lesage, many guns were fired, the former prime minister complained, but "when Canada as a nation turned up at Vimy, nobody from France was there."

Having decided to visit Expo '67, and determined his strategy, de Gaulle despatched two simultaneous messages on April 15. One was to the new governor general, Roland Michener. He had "reserved his response" to Vanier's invitation of the previous September and was now "happy to confirm" that he could accept "the kind invitation." He planned to make the trip, if that was convenient, in the second half of July. The French ambassador could work out the details with the appropriate Canadian officials. He was also accepting the invitation from the premier of Quebec.[26] In his letter to Johnson, de Gaulle also confirmed the date of May 18, that had been arranged through Chapdelaine, for their first meeting in Paris.[27]

As it happened, Pearson and Johnson were scheduled to meet in Montreal on April 16, also their first private encounter. High on their agenda was international affairs. On February 28, Johnson had introduced a bill in the Quebec Legislative Assembly to change the title of the Department of Federal-Provincial Affairs to that of Inter-Governmental Affairs. In addition to federal-provincial relations, it was to have responsibility for delegations and agencies outside the country. The step was a logical one, particularly since the deputy minister, Claude Morin, was already chairman of the Inter-Ministerial Commission on External Affairs. Johnson had chosen the new title carefully to avoid stirring up another hornets' nest in Ottawa, as would have happened had the terms "external affairs" or "international affairs" been used. The word "inter-governmental" seemed relatively safe since Ontario already had a department of that name. In proposing second reading of the bill on April 13, the premier had been equally circumspect, pointing out that it did not give Quebec any rights it did not already possess, but aimed rather at "exercising more efficiently and fully" those it had.[28] The new department, he explained, would administer the *ententes* with France, undertake negotiations as required when Quebec decided to extend, within its fields of constitutional authority, it relations with other countries, "cooperate" with the External Aid Office in sending Quebec specialists to developing countries, and "take an interest in the participation Quebec might hope for in the work of certain international organizations." Finally, it would examine the numerous international conventions with which Canada could not comply without provincial consent. He hoped that the federal government would also take action to "institutionalize" prior consultation when negotiating treaties in provincial areas of jurisdiction.

On the whole, Johnson's stance was moderate and responsible, in contrast to some of his earlier statements as leader of the opposition. During his nine months in office, he had revealed his true political character, that of a Quebec conservative, always ready, as he once said, to give Confederation a kick in the behind, but not the last one. His general objective can be described as giving French Canadians, as a nation, greater security within Canada, not breaking up the country. His interest in international relations was primarily a function of that domestic goal. Among Johnson's personal qualities, Pearson was to discover at their meeting, were great personal charm and urbanity, and the ability to reassure, if not persuade, others in person-to-person exchanges. The prime minister was pleasantly surprised: Johnson explained his occasional "lapses from common sense and moderation," he wrote later, by the necessity of handling the "wilder men" in his entourage, and he asked for patience and understanding.[29] He also convinced Pearson that he was "quite genuine" in his desire for "a united Canada with a contented Quebec that would not nurture separatists." In fact, the prime minister concluded, somewhat bemused, he was "in some ways...easier to get along with than Jean Lesage."

On the subject of de Gaulle's visit, it soon became evident to Pearson that Johnson was better informed than he was, and that the premier approved of the plan being bruited about for the general to visit Quebec first. With his deep sense of history, Johnson argued, de Gaulle "would never understand why he could not land, in state, at Quebec." He also quoted no less than four other cases of visits to Expo '67 that were not scheduled to begin in Ottawa. Pearson replied somewhat abashed that he and his colleagues were "still waiting to hear whether he was coming at all, and if so, when." (He only received the news of de Gaulle's acceptance after the meeting.) The two men also discussed Johnson's forthcoming visit to Paris in May. Once again, Johnson was reassuring: nothing "unfortunate," he assured Pearson, would happen.[30]

Scheduled to be in Paris on April 23 on other business, Paul Martin raised the matter of de Gaulle's itinerary with Couve de Murville. Canada wished to welcome the general as a world figure, he stressed, and that could only be done properly if he arrived first in the national capital. If de Gaulle had the unity of Canada at heart, he would do so. Whatever his personal reservations, Couve de Murville was firm: de Gaulle intended to visit Ottawa last. Moreover, he saw no reason to identify his visit with the centenary celebrations. Martin was upset but powerless to change the decision. A few days later, Jules Léger, aware that the deterioration of Franco-Canadian relations was a matter of concern to the French foreign minister, tried again. He recognized how difficult it was for France to maintain a balance between Ottawa and Quebec City, the ambassador told Couve de

Murville, but he felt that it was the people in the Elysée Palace, not the Quai d'Orsay or the French government in general, who were aggravating the situation. It was likely to continue to be delicate, particularly during the general's visit; he hoped the Canadian government could count on his help. Léger's intervention was futile: while he tried frequently to reduce their negative effects, Couve de Murville executed loyally his superior's wishes.

In a final effort to ward off a crisis, Léger succeeded in obtaining an appointment with the president himself on the grounds that he wanted to review with him the accomplishments in Franco-Canadian relations since Pearson's visit more than two years earlier. De Gaulle was relaxed and amicable. Progress was satisfactory in the cultural sector, they agreed, but less so in the economic sector. De Gaulle conceded that French businessmen were so accustomed to government protection that they had difficulty in functioning without it. When they turned to the situation inside Canada, he remarked that, while the existing problems were a purely Canadian matter, it was evident to him that the country was at a difficult moment in its history. It was, in fact, two distinct entities, perhaps two states. At the same time, they had certain important elements in common that should be preserved in order to avoid the threat of Americanization. Léger was willing enough to discuss the situation, but was concerned about appearing to acquiesce in anything resembling a direct intervention by France. In classic diplomatic procedure, he asked if he should request instructions from his government on that point. De Gaulle dropped the matter.

In the light of his encouraging meeting with Johnson, Pearson tried to maintain as moderate a public stance as possible concerning relations with Quebec. At the same time, he was under increasing pressure from both inside and outside the government to be firm and unequivocal (something he always found difficult). On April 26, he read a prepared statement in the House of Commons on the Quebec Department of Inter-Governmental Affairs.[31] "A certain ambiguity of wording" had given rise to the interpretation that it would be entrusted with responsibilities for "relations between Quebec and foreign countries and for the negotiation of agreements with foreign governments or bodies." There should be "no ground for such a misunderstanding." The constitution clearly gave the federal government "exclusive responsibility for the conduct of the country's external affairs," and that situation could not be altered by a provincial legislature. The government of Quebec was, "of course," aware of that, and there was no reason to believe that the new department's activities would not be "fully consistent with the constitutional position of Canada." As for provincial agents abroad, they did not have the authority to transact official business affecting Canada or "any part thereof in any field" without prior agreement between the Canadian government and the foreign government concerned "on the matter to be transacted with provincial authorities and the manner in which this is to be done."

Prepared by Marcel Cadieux and his colleagues in the Department of External Affairs, the text was directed particularly at their opposite numbers in the Quebec administration. Among the latter, André Patry was their particular "*bête noire*" at the moment. Negotiations with him concerning de Gaulle's schedule were proving very difficult. As chief of protocol, he was determined that from the moment he set foot in Quebec territory until he left it, the province would be responsible for his programme, and the federal role would be kept to a minimum. Officials in Ottawa were equally determined to assert the federal presence. One question in their minds was whether Patry was acting on his own initiative or under a mandate from Premier Johnson. A confidential source of information within the Department of Inter-Governmental Affairs assured them that he was operating largely on his own and that his attitude reflected his own views and predispositions rather than any policy direction. Many people in Quebec City also found him rigid and abrasive, the same source revealed, and looked forward to his being transferred after Expo '67. In the meantime, he had to be contained as best possible.

Next it was the turn of Ottawa to exacerbate the situation. For some months, negotiations had been proceeding with Belgium with a view to a cultural agreement. Canadian officials proposed an *accord cadre*, or framework agreement, modelled on the one with France; but the Belgians were concerned that it might encourage their own two language groups to emulate Quebec in undertaking direct foreign negotiations. The Canadians were happy to accommodate them, and plans went ahead for a classic type of treaty. Consulted about the possibilities of developing contacts with the Walloon, or French-speaking, population, Quebec officials reacted strongly against that approach and tried to persuade the Belgians to accept an *accord cadre*. On the other hand, when a federal official checked with Premier Johnson, he appeared to have no strong objections. The signing ceremony was set for May 8 when the Belgian king's brother, Prince Albert of Liège, was to be one of the first official visitors to Expo '67 (which was inaugurated on April 27). Five days beforehand, the provinces were consulted, or more accurately, informed, of the event. The reaction from Quebec City was sharp. Johnson was persuaded to send a telegram on May 7, declaring that the proposed signature without prior consultation with Quebec of a cultural accord covering some areas of its constitutional jurisdiction had caused "general astonishment."[32] As a result, the Quebec government would be obliged to "disassociate itself" from the agreement.

Patry went further. In a telegram, addressed to the deputy commissioner of Expo '67, Brigadier Robert Moncel, he declared that the Canadian ambassador to Belgium, Paul Tremblay, who was accompanying the royal couple, was *persona non grata*, that is, not welcome, in Quebec. It was the turn of the federal officials to get upset. Pearson was advised to call Johnson and threaten to call off the prince's visit. The prime minister asked for a complete briefing on the subject, and when he received it, concluded that Quebec had some cause for complaint: it had not been consulted adequately through the whole negotiation, even though it was known in Ottawa that the province, too, was in touch with the Belgians with a view to concluding an agreement. Two issues were at stake, Pearson was told: whether such consultations were obligatory, in which case the provinces would have an effective veto over federal treaty-making; and whether cultural affairs were a matter of exclusive provincial jurisdiction. Pearson finally wrote to Johnson saying that the treaty did not infringe on Quebec's jurisdiction, hence the absence of consultation. He also made the threat to cancel the Belgian visit, but placed the blame on Patry in order to give the premier a way out. That merely placed Johnson, in turn, in a difficult position. He could not repudiate a senior official, yet he did not want to be responsible for a further escalation of the controversy. Marc Lalonde flew to Quebec City with a mandate from Pearson to negotiate a solution. Finally, in a characteristic stance, Johnson gave Patry his full support, placed the blame on the federal officials, then said that, in order to avoid any further embarrassment to the Belgian visitors, he was allowing Tremblay to accompany them to Quebec. The next day, he got in a final lick in the Legislative Assembly, charging that the Belgians had been duped and that the federal and Quebec Liberals were conspiring to wipe out Quebec's autonomy. Pearson decided to leave well enough alone for the moment, and the exchange ended there.

Daniel Johnson made his first and only official visit to Paris on May 17–24, 1967. What were his objectives? First of all, to strengthen Franco-Quebec cooperation in practical ways such as financial investments, joint economic projects, scientific and technical exchanges, and the recruitment of large numbers of French teachers. (Only the last item went beyond those goals pursued by Lesage.) Second, he wanted to convince de Gaulle of the importance of his visit as an integral part of the Quebec government's plan to seek a new relationship with English Canada. According to Anne and Pierre Rouanet, he had two messages for the president: "*Mon Général*, Quebec needs you," and "It's now or never."[33] They were well designed to appeal to de Gaulle's sense of duty as the head, or rather the personification, of France, to his strong feeling of sympathy for French Canadians, and to his awareness that time was running out in his own career. On his arrival at Orly airport, Johnson set the tone of his visit by expressing the hope that it would help to "rid us of the feeling of claustrophobia from which we suffer in Quebec."[34]

While they were in many ways very different personalities, de Gaulle took to Johnson almost immediately when they met on May 18. He even overcame his initial negative reaction to the premier's Anglo-Saxon name and compensated by pronouncing it "*à la française.*" "What an idea to call oneself Johnson," he commented later, "he deserves to be called Lafleur like everyone else."[35] The premier had been forewarned that the general often used provocative statements to test his interlocutors. True to form, de Gaulle started out, "I am very fond of Canada. I have many friends there, including [the late] General Vanier, a great friend of France."[36] Johnson parried: he, too, had great admiration for Vanier's "military virtues," but not at all for his political ideas; he was "a federalist and a British imperialist." "Ah," the general replied, "I always held that against him." The ice was broken. Johnson made a fervent appeal to de Gaulle to use his visit to Quebec to crystallize its new relationship with France, and to lend his prestige to Quebec's efforts to obtain constitutional change. He then produced a list of no less than seventeen requests for French assistance. De Gaulle listened carefully, intervening only occasionally to make remarks such as, "You can count on me, it will be done."[37] When the time allotted for the meeting had expired and Johnson prepared to leave, he was bidden to stay. "My dear President," the general said, "let's get to the bottom of things."[38] The form of address was not particularly surprising; French prime ministers were addressed with their title of president of the Council of Ministers. The core of the sentence was more revealing: for de Gaulle, getting to the bottom of things, an expression he used frequently, meant dealing with them seriously. Unfortunately, there is no reliable information on what transpired next.

Following the meeting, de Gaulle played host at a luncheon for forty persons, this time including Jules Léger whom Johnson had asked to be invited. The general was clearly pleased with the turn matters were taking. In proposing a toast, he referred to Quebecers as "an exemplary and very dear people," "a branch of our own."[39] The cooperation being developed between them was proof that "all Frenchmen, wherever they come from and wherever they are," were now profoundly convinced of their common destiny. Unlike the traditional effusive statements of earlier French leaders on such occasions, it was a genuine aspiration. Two days later, the two men met again and the cordial relationship was developed further. By the time Johnson left for home, the general's reservations about making the transatlantic crossing appear to have vanished. According to the Rouanets, he decided to go because Daniel Johnson had convinced him that Quebecers were "tackling their problem" and merited his support.[40]

The tangible results of Johnson's pilgrimage to the mother country were also significant. A joint communications satellite, *Harmonie*, for direct transmissions to Quebec, was discussed; Johnson agreed to contribute one half of the estimated cost of forty million dollars. Talks were held by Quebec Finance Minister Paul Dozoisand and Economic Adviser Jacques Parizeau with their French counterparts concerning a possible oil refinery in Quebec; and arrangements were made for Quebec scientists to work at the SACLAY nuclear centre, south of Paris. French engineers were to join their colleagues in Quebec in studying the possibilities of increasing the voltage in high tension electrical transmission lines. Still, the profusion of good will was not sufficient to bring about some important projects that both governments desired. A plan by the *Société Péchiney* to construct an aluminum refinery in Quebec, and utilizing the abundant hydroelectric energy coming available, had been abandoned a short time earlier and could not be resuscitated. And the Michelin Tire Company, which the Quebec government had been trying for several years to persuade to build a plant in Quebec, had opted for a site in Nova Scotia, primarily because the labour force was more quiescent there. In neither case was de Gaulle able to reverse the decision.

De Gaulle received another Canadian visitor the following month. Pauline Vanier was returning to France alone to spend the summer and he invited her to a private luncheon with him and Madame de Gaulle. Still hurt over his refusal to grant her husband's wish to be received as Canadian head of state, she felt further aggrieved that Johnson, according to the media, had been accorded that honour. The meal was not a pleasant affair. Madame Vanier was shocked to learn during their conversation that de Gaulle was sympathetic to some form of independence for Quebec and intended to influence events in that direction during his visit.[41] She argued strongly with him, but he refused to be dissuaded. At one point, he recounted that Johnson had told him that the situation of French Canadians was so "impossible" that during World War Two he had refused to serve under "*les Anglais.*" She retorted that, in that case, he could have joined the Free French. She left the Elysée Palace in tears (the second time the general had made her cry) and upset at the thought of how General Vanier would have felt. Feeling she had to do something, she telephoned several French Cabinet ministers she knew, including Alain Peyrefitte, whose daughter was the Vaniers' godchild, and asked for their help. None dared to intervene.

In Quebec City, arrangements were rushed forward for the general's visit. Marcel Masse was appointed minister responsible for the visit, but, still young and inexperienced, he was largely overshadowed by Patry and others. Maurice Custeau, *Union Nationale* member of the Legislature, was placed in charge of the "*Chemin du Roy,*" the two hundred and seventy kilometer route along which the president was to be driven from Quebec City to Montreal. The first long road to be built in the French colony, it was believed to have received its name in anticipation of a French monarch's visit. Arrangements were made for semblances of the Arc de Triomphe to be built over the highway in towns and villages, for French and Quebec flags to be mounted on trees, poles and buildings, and for blue *fleurs de lys* to be painted on the pavement at two meter intervals throughout the entire distance. A public holiday was declared and school buses were mobilized to bring adults and children to the roadside from the surrounding areas. They were to be grouped at various villages to represent the regions of France (regardless of their own region of origin). Over three hundred thousand French and Quebec flags were to be distributed, but no Canadian ones. The separatists made their own preparations. Three to four hundred RIN members were mobilized in Quebec City for the general's arrival; they were supplied with copies of *La Marseillaise* and with French flags and placards bearing, among other inscriptions, "*France libre, Québec libre*" and "*Vive le Québec libre.*" Other RIN members were situated along the route where de Gaulle was to make brief stops; the party's president, Pierre Bourgault, was to wait with the largest group in Montreal.

Increasingly apprehensive, federal officials sought to maintain the Canadian character of the visit, but often felt like unwelcome outsiders. In fact, the plans were worked out in large part by Gros d'Aillon and Loiselle, who made almost weekly trips to Paris, with Jurgensen, Dorin, Rossillon, de Saint-Légier and Pérol. The federal representatives dealt mainly with Ambassador Leduc and Commissioner Bordaz on the French side and Patry on the Quebec side. Even after de Gaulle had accepted the invitations, Martin and his officials continued their efforts to persuade him to begin his tour in Ottawa and to extend it to western Canada. That plan was "not acceptable to the French government,"[42] they were told; the general wished to land at Quebec City, and visit it and Montreal first. Pearson raised the matter in Cabinet, and some ministers expressed the view that de Gaulle's preference should be rejected simply; in the end, it was accepted rather than risk cancellation and the hullabaloo that was certain to ensue. De Gaulle also refused to budge on the matter of the reception to be given on the afternoon of his arrival. In keeping with the format that had been established for head-of-state visits, the federal government planned a reception by Governor General Michener in his Quebec residence at the Citadel. The general insisted instead on hosting his own reception on the *Colbert*. Jules Léger counselled acquiescence once again[43] and Paris was informed that the general's plans would be accepted "with reluctance."

On June 16, Martin, on his way home from other business in Europe, was received by de Gaulle in Paris and they discussed the arrangements. The general was very pleasant, and, according to Martin's report of the interview, said that "while France had an obvious cultural affinity with Quebec, he intended to speak in Ottawa of Canada's confederation and its bicultural character." Then, Martin adds, "convinced that de Gaulle was willing to make amends, I said nothing of our resentment at his diplomatic escapades." Almost desperately anxious to have the visit go smoothly, he appears to have been taken in. It was agreed that the president should arrive at the deep-sea dock at Anse-aux-Foulons just below Quebec City, be greeted there by the governor general who would escort him to the Citadel, then turn him over to Premier Johnson for the rest of the stay in the province.

The haggling over details continued. A few days before de Gaulle's arrival, Johnson telephoned Pearson to say that he could not consider riding with the governor general and the president from the dock to the Citadel. Where would he sit, he wanted to know, in the jump seat? The prime minister joked that perhaps he should drive. However, ready as he always was to walk an extra mile for the sake of peace, Pearson compromised again. The governor general would welcome the general, then get into his own limousine and go straight to the Citadel; meanwhile, de Gaulle and Johnson would lead a cavalcade through the city and then join him there. Relations between the Canadian and Quebec representatives in Quebec City were so strained on the eve of de Gaulle's arrival that each side held separate, concurrent press conferences to brief foreign journalists. Johnson told one group that the president's visit would serve to make English Canada more aware of the "French fact," and to make Quebecers more conscious of their existence as a "distinct group."[44] Asked what Quebec wanted from the rest of Canada, he warned that it would be a dangerous mistake to confuse "nationalism" and "independence." Starting from the *status quo*, he and his fellow nationalists wanted to negotiate their "economic, educational and cultural *épanouissement*,"* whereas the separatists wanted to separate first and negotiate afterward. In 1962, Johnson recalled, the two separatist parties had received only ten per cent of the vote (in fact, eight per cent—author's note); the majority of the population did not want to separate. De Gaulle's visit would

* Approximately, self-realization.

illustrate that Quebecers were not alone in the world, but rather that they shared in a universal culture, and it was through the two cultures that Canada would find "internal peace." French Canadians, for their part, would realize what a blessing their culture was for themselves and for the universe. De Gaulle was not coming to an underdeveloped country which expected him to bring gifts, but to make contact with a country that had a role to play in the *Francophonie*. Quebecers were a little like the successful grown-up son who receives his father and says, "See how well things are going."

While Pearson remained in Ottawa, Paul Martin was at the dockside, still hoping for the best. He and Couve de Murville, who had arrived twenty-four hours in advance, had had dinner the previous evening and had discussed the arrangements a final time. In response to the Canadian minister's continuing concerns, the French minister assured him, in Martin's words, "Of course, he'll behave."[45] After all, the French were "civilized."[46]

Before boarding the *Colbert* in Brest on July 15, de Gaulle had already indicated that he had a very different scenario in mind. "I am going to strike a strong blow," he confided to his son-in-law, General Alain Boissieu. "Things are going to get hot. But it is necessary. It's the last chance to rectify the cowardice of France."[47] He confirmed this intention to the ever-zealous Xavier Deniau, who had come to see him off. "They are going to hear me over there; it will make some waves."[48] As yet, however, he had not formulated a specific plan. "I had decided on a general orientation," he told Jurgensen later, "I was waiting for the event, the crowd, to judge just what I would say, at what place, at what instant. But I knew that I was going to do something."[49]

Since the weather was bad during most of the crossing and, at any rate, the *Colbert* had little open deck space, de Gaulle spent most of his time working on his speeches in the admiral's cabin, which he had pre-empted. With him he had voluminous files, including, according to one source, one from the SDECE, the secret service. The male secretary of the ship's commandant, Admiral Paul Delahousse, typed de Gaulle's hand-written and painstakingly re-worked texts and made copies for distribution. On July 21, the *Colbert* weighed anchor off Saint-Pierre, and de Gaulle spent much of the next day on the islands that he had considered as a possible place of exile during the war. The next evening, two Canadian frigates took the *Colbert* under escort as they entered Canadian waters, and they sailed across the Gulf of St. Lawrence and up the St. Lawrence River. The only inauspicious aspect of those first hours in Canadian waters was that the commander of the escort was a unilingual English Canadian; when de Gaulle invited him aboard for breakfast, Commander Delahousse had to double as interpreter. In his recital of the events, Lacouture intimates that it was a deliberate way of reminding the General that Wolfe, and not Montcalm, had won the battle of the Plains of Abraham.[50] In fact, such thinking was far from the federal officials' minds; it was, rather, a regretable oversight.

The *Colbert* arrived off Anse-aux-Foulons at 7:30 a.m. on the morning of Sunday July 23 and was surrounded by a swarm of power boats with French and Quebec flags. It was reported later that the ship was flying the French, but not the Canadian, flag, but the charge was later denied. It was towed into position at the dock by two tugboats. The governor general, the lieutenant-governor, the premier, Paul Martin and Couve de Murville, Ambassadors Léger and Leduc, and a relatively small crowd were in place, when de Gaulle appeared in his brigadier-general's uniform at 9:30.* The band of a French-Canadian regiment, dressed in the red tunics and tall fur busbies of the British tradition, struck up *God Save the Queen*. The separatists in the crowd jeered and broke into *La Marseillaise*, anticipating the band. The governor general greeted de Gaulle first, then came Premier Johnson. Addressing Michener, de Gaulle declared himself "touched" by the welcome and added, "Between Canada as a whole and France, there is not, never was, nor will ever be other than esteem and friendship." He looked forward to going to Ottawa shortly "to salute you, salute the Canadian government and discuss with it the relations between my country and yours." Then, the demands of protocol satisfied, he turned to Johnson and, in notably more vibrant tones, told him of the "immense joy" he felt to be "*chez vous au Québec*," among the French Canadians. He brought a message of "affection, memory and hope." And he concluded with five vivats, "*Vive le Canada*," "*Vivent les Canadiens francais*," "*Vive le Québec*," "*Vive la Nouvelle-France*," and "*Vive la France*." He and Johnson then got into the lead car of the Quebec cavalcade and moved off to the city, while the federal representatives raced off to the Citadel. On arriving on that small piece of federal territory, de Gaulle laid a wreath on the tomb of General Vanier, then spent about twenty minutes with his hosts before resuming his programme with the premier.

At the Hôtel de Ville, he gave the first indication of the direction of his thinking. "You are the élite," he proclaimed to a crowd of local personalities. He knew that a French-Canadian élite had been formed, he told them, that it was becoming "more active, more efficient, better known every day." That was "the basis of everything," "the essential." All else would follow. The allusion was meaningful: from his experi-

---

* When the *Colbert's* guns signalled its arrival, Léger whispered to his wife, "The hostilities are beginning; the French are firing first." (Madame Gaby Léger, interview with author, May 1, 1982)

ence with the African colonies, de Gaulle had concluded that a people could not manage its own affairs unless it had a corps of qualified persons in the various fields of national life. On his previous visits, he had had the impression that French Canada lacked such a group. Now, in the seven years since the beginning of the Quiet Revolution, he assumed that it was in place. From the Hôtel de Ville, de Gaulle was taken to the religious sanctuary at Sainte-Anne de Beaupré, half an hour's drive down the river, for mass and lunch, then to the impressive new campus of Laval University in Sainte-Foy. Addressing the staff and students there, he referred to the fact that the chancellor, Cardinal Roy, had been in London during the war. The resistance of the Free French had been short, he remarked, compared to that in Quebec. In mid-afternoon, he returned to the *Colbert* where he received some three hundred dignitaries. At one point, he drew Paul Martin aside and asked him if everything was going to his satisfaction. Told it was, he said, "You'll see, all will go well in Ottawa too."[51]

At a banquet tendered by the Quebec government that evening, the general delivered the principal message of his trip. Two hundred and four years after its "inconsolable sovereignty" had been "wrested" from that soil, France was still present: the "French Canadians," with their "determination to survive as an unshakeable and compact collectivity" and after a lengthy "passive resistance," had now developed the ambition "of taking hold of the means of emancipation and development that the modern era offers to a strong and enterprising people that wished to have the right to self-determination and take its destiny in its own hands in every respect." "With all its soul," France welcomed that "advent of a people;" it was in conformity with "the equilibrium of our universe and the spirit of our time." As Quebec emerged and raised itself up, relations would become closer and more numerous between the "French on the shores of the St. Lawrence and those in the valleys of the Seine, the Loire, the Garonne, the Rhône and the Rhine." What the French people had begun with Jacques Cartier had been continued with "extraordinary tenacity" through their "powerful vitality and their miraculous fecundity, will power and fidelity." What the "French fraction of Canada" intended to become on their own, and on their own soil, what the "French here, once they have become their own masters" would have to work out with the other Canadians in order to safeguard "their essential characteristics and their independence in contact with their colossal neighbour," all that could not be other than useful to all men. In that regard, he assured them, through Premier Johnson, of his "ardent confidence and deep affection."

There is an expression in Quebec: never offer your client more than he wants to receive. No doubt that de Gaulle offered his hosts more than they wanted to hear. Afterward, Daniel Johnson was not available for comment; Jean Lesage made his way to Couve de Murville and expressed his concern that the speech had gone too far. On the other hand, René Lévesque, on the point of breaking with the Liberal party to found the movement *Souveraineté-Association*, was delighted. The speech, he declared, was "a masterpiece of inter-Canadian brinkmanship," and he marvelled that a seventy-seven year old man was able, in a few sentences, to express "the whole ambiguity of our situation as Francophones in Canada."[52] Paul Martin and Jean Marchand, the only federal ministers present, refused to make any statement.* In his memoirs, Martin refers to the "rather objectionable tenor [of the speech], ambiguously setting out Quebec's role in Canada."[53] Lacouture maintains that the phlegmatic Anglo-Saxons simply did not understand that de Gaulle was already calling for a "Québec libre."[54] In Martin's case, it was more likely he was so anxious that everything should go well that he refused to understand the message. When the speech was over, he rose, despite his misgivings, and joined in the applause. De Gaulle did say "*Vive le Canada*" along with his other vivats, he consoled himself. In Ottawa, Marcel Cadieux interpreted the statement as a public confirmation of de Gaulle's thinking and policy for some time and as a clearly constituted interference in Canada's domestic affairs, particularly in view of the current constitutional debate. However, given the delicacy of the situation, he advised Pearson not to react publicly as long as the president did not go any further.

The next morning, the lengthy procession set out shortly after nine along the "royal road." In the lead were de Gaulle and Johnson in an open Lincoln Continental convertible. (In the rush of preparations, the advisability of using a French automobile had been overlooked. At the last moment, Custeau also noted that the car had Ontario licence plates; he had them ripped off and they made the trip to Montreal illegally.) Behind them came twenty other limousines bearing digni-taries and officials. Since Martin had decided to go directly to Montreal, Jules Léger represented the Canadian government. Al-though the weather was dull and rain fell sporadically, the crowds were large and a festive mood prevailed. Work crews from the Quebec Department of Public Works rushed to replace the flags that fell to the ground and to repaint the *fleurs de lys* as the rain washed them away. De Gaulle had requested as much contact with the population as possible; he was well served. In the dozen towns and villages they

---

* When Martin and Marchand arrived that evening, they found that no provision had been made for a federal representative at the head table. When Martin protested, he and his wife were squeezed in at either end.

drove through, he was given a warm welcome and responded in kind, developing his theme of the previous evening. At his first stop, Donnaconna, he ignored a sudden shower and disembarked long enough to shake some hands and declare that it was "indispensable" that "a country take its destiny in hand." He could "see" and "sense" that was happening.[55] At Sainte-Anne de la Pérade, he stated that he was able to recognize "the soul of French Canada, the soul of Quebec:" it was that of "a people, part of the French people" that wanted to be itself. "*Eh bien*," he assured them, "you will be what you want to be, that is, your own masters."[56] In Trois-Rivières, the half-way point of the day's journey, he proclaimed the process of self-determination to be irreversible. It was "the genius of our time" that every people, wherever it lived, should be master of its own destiny. He was convinced that precisely that was taking place in Quebec. And France had "a duty" that it was determined to fulfill "to assist French Canada in its development." Conversely, French Canada would contribute to the progress of "the old country."

Running somewhat behind schedule, the procession stopped for lunch in Trois-Rivières and, on the grounds of the seminary, the guests were served buffalo steak, blueberries (from the United States), and other supposedly typical local dishes. De Gaulle was obviously in excellent form and, after only a brief rest, impatient to be on the way again. Johnson was less enthusiastic. "If he continues like that," he confided to someone during the luncheon pause with regard to de Gaulle's escalating language, "by the time we get to Montreal we will have separated."[57] During their conversations in the limousine between stops, de Gaulle and Johnson discussed the goal of constitutional reform, which the premier referred to as "the last chance" for Canada. As a first step in that direction, he mentioned, an inter-provincial conference was scheduled for November, at which he planned to set out Quebec's demands. According to the Rouanets, de Gaulle dismissed the conference as an "*éteignoir*" (a cone-shaped device used in churches to extinguish candles). A deficient régime, he remarked, could not be reformed from within.[58]

At a stop in Louiseville in mid-afternoon, the mayor described de Gaulle affectionately as not only a great man, but as "*un vieux copain*,"—an old chum. The general responded that the Quebec people was already "itself."[59] The "vocation" of the French on both sides of the Atlantic was "to set an example for all men." He ended his brief speech with the challenge, "Forward." There and at other stops, his series of vivats began with the name of the local town and included Quebec, French Canada, New France and, finally, France, but Canada was noticeably absent. Another was also missing. RIN members brandished placards with their slogan, "*France libre, Québec libre*," and "*Vive le*

Québec libre," and when de Gaulle launched into his vivats, they shouted them in response. He appeared to take no notice of them.

As the cavalcade neared Montreal, the weather cleared and the crowds increased. By then de Gaulle was standing most of the time, acknowledging the cheers. The procession was nearly an hour late when it reached the centre of the city. Mayor Drapeau had assembled a select group of dignitaries—what de Gaulle liked to call disparagingly "notables"—on the terrace of the Hôtel de Ville. The media had reported that the general would appear on the balcony on the other side of the building, in Jacques-Cartier Square, a favourite meeting place for young Montrealers: a crowd had begun to assemble there as early as four o'clock. A large number of tourists, fulfilled after a day at Expo '67, and hoping for a glimpse of the great man, swelled the local crowd. Another crowd formed on the opposite side of the building where he was to arrive. Loudspeakers reported on his progress, creating an atmosphere of expectancy and impatience. People chanted, "*On veut de Gaulle!*"—we want de Gaulle. Signs floated above their heads bearing the slogans "*Vive le Général de Gaulle,*" "*Bienvenue au Général de Gaulle,*" and less frequently, "*France libre, Québec libre*" and "*Vive le Québec libre.*"

The cavalcade arrived at seven-thirty p.m. Mayor and Madame Drapeau greeted de Gaulle. All three waved to the crowd as the refrains of *La Marseillaise* and *O Canada* intermingled, and they disappeared into the building. Inside, they took the elevator to the mayor's office, on the same floor as the terrace where the "notables" were waiting. There, the president signed the "*livre d'or,*" the guest book, shook hands with a few special dignitaries, including Cardinal Léger, Jules Léger's brother, and went to the washroom.

In the meantime, on Jacques-Cartier Square, the calls of "*On veut de Gaulle!*" were becoming more insistent and people were looking up at the balcony in anticipation. There is some uncertainty about what happened next. According to the best available information, the official schedule called for him to "salute the crowd [that is, the dignitaries] on the terrace."[60] However, the copy carried by de Gaulle's aide-de-camp, Commandant Flohic, had a typewritten addendum stating that he was to "address the crowd gathered in the square." Someone responsible for the physical arrangements obviously had the same impression, since he had had a microphone installed on the balcony. That was certainly not in the mayor's plans. In fact, while inspecting the arrangements, a short time earlier, Drapeau had seen an electrician setting up the microphone and had told him to disconnect it since it was not required. The worker had done so, but, not wanting to give up his privileged position to take a photograph of the famous statesman, he had remained on the spot.[61] On the way to the terrace to meet the dignitaries, de Gaulle saw the balcony and moved toward it. The French chief of protocol, Bernard Durand, thinking that he was confused because of his short-sightedness, tried to redirect him towards the terrace. De Gaulle was insistent, "I have to speak to those people who are calling for me." "*Mon Général*, there is no microphone," Drapeau interjected. "And what is that?" de Gaulle asked, pointing to the one that had been disconnected. Drapeau protested that it was not working, but the electrician, overhearing the exchange, said that he could hook it up again. And he did.

It is clear that de Gaulle wanted to address the crowd, and it was natural that he should do so. He had done nothing else all day and this crowd was of record size. Besides, contact with masses of people was one of the greatest pleasures in his life. Whether he had a premeditated message to deliver to the Montreal crowd is less certain. When he appeared on the balcony, the crowd roared with delight, and his first reaction apeared to be one of appreciation for their welcome, topping all the others he had received during the day. "An immense emotion fills my heart in seeing before me the French city of Montreal," he began, "In the name of the old country, in the name of France, I greet you with all my heart." Then, employing an old oratorical device, he continued in a conspiratorial tone, "I am going to tell you a secret that you will not repeat." The crowd reacted first with surprise, then, entering into the spirit of things, with pleasure. "This evening, here, and all along my route, I found the same kind of atmosphere as that of the liberation." Without having time to reflect on the analogy, the crowd responded well. "And along my route, besides that," he continued, "I noted what an immense effort of progress, of development, and consequently of emancipation you are accomplishing here. And it is in Montreal that I must say it, because if there is an exemplary city in the world because of its modern successes, it is yours." With that, he clearly established contact with what he saw as the citizenry of Montreal amassed below him. "I say it's yours," he continued, "and I venture to add, it is ours." That oratorical device, flattery by association, also went over well. "If you knew," he continued in the same confidential tone, "what confidence France, itself awakened after such immense ordeals, now has in you! If you knew what affection it is beginning to feel for the French of Canada! And if you knew how much it feels obliged to support your forward march, your progress! That is why it signed some agreements with the government of Quebec, with my friend Johnson, so that the French on either side of the Atlantic might work together in the same French undertaking. And moreover, the support that France is going to give you, increasingly each day, it knows that you will return it because you are building up élites, factories, businesses and laboratories that will astonish everyone and which, I am sure, will enable you to help France one day."

From the ground level in the square, the figure high above with the deep and vibrant voice seemed for an instant like some beneficent oracle come to deliver an inspired message. The crowd roared its approval. "That is what I have come to say to you this evening," he continued, "and I add that I will take away with me an unforgettable memory of this incredible meeting in Montreal. All France knows, sees and hears what goes on here, and I can tell you, it will be the better for it." Then, following his usual pattern, he shouted, "*Vive Montréal! Vive Québec!*" The separatists, brandishing their placards, chanted "*France libre! Québec libre!*" and "*Vive le Québec libre!*" challenging him to include their slogan as well. The crowd cheered them on. He had given them almost all they wanted to hear, they wanted to see if he would go all the way. The moment he had been looking for since before he left France had arrived. Besides, de Gaulle never avoided a challenge. "*Vive le Québec!*" he repeated, then after a pregnant pause, "*libre!*" It was done. The crowd was silent for a moment, unbelieving, then burst into wild applause. "*Vive le Canada français et vive la France!*" he added, almost as a postscript, and turned and disappeared inside the building.

Chapter 11

Outrage or Blunder?

Daniel Johnson, Jean Drapeau, Couve de Murville, François Leduc and Jules Léger were waiting for de Gaulle at the entrance to the terrace. Their faces were sober. The atmosphere on the terrace was suddenly quiet but tense. "I think I may have embarrassed you," de Gaulle remarked to the premier.[1] Clearly taken by surprise and discomfitted, Johnson responded, "You used the slogan of an opposition party, *mon Général*," then recovering his composure, added, "but don't worry, we'll work it out." To Claude Morin, Johnson said in an aside as they moved forward, "We are going to have some problems."[2] Others were equally shocked. Couve de Murville was near to losing his celebrated composure. When Commandant Flohic asked him for his reaction, he answered gravely, "Yes, he was wrong to speak."[3] Later, he was to qualify the incident as "a mistake." Once again, he would be the one who would have to pick up the pieces. François Leduc was dismayed. Even René de Saint-Légier, perhaps the member of the general's staff most sympathetic to the separatists, was, in Chapdelaine's words, "stunned."[4] Still, accustomed to the general's ways, he commented stoically, "what is said is said." Gilbert Pérol, too, who was in charge of de Gaulle's texts and thus knew their content, was also caught off guard. The president certainly did not want to throw his support behind separation, he told Paul Chouinard, one of Johnson's advisers, "*Allons*, he's not crazy, the old guy."[5] René Lévesque left the receiving line to speak to Pierre-Louis Mallen. The events of the day were important, he told the French broadcaster, but he regretted that, on the balcony, the general had gone "a little too far."[6] Mallen, enchanted by the incident, protested that it was necessary to "shake up public opinion and open up lots of people's eyes." Lévesque recognized that what had happened was going to "accelerate lots of things," but still felt that "one word too much" had been said. While he was a

stronger Quebec nationalist than Johnson, he was opposed to intervention from any source in Quebec's affairs.

As for de Gaulle himself, once on the terrace, he resumed his role
as if nothing untoward had happened, shaking hands with the
dignitaries who filed past in the receiving line, then making a brief
and orthodox speech to them. He ended it with a single vivat, "*Vive
Montréal!*" His listeners were polite but subdued. Afterward, Daniel
Johnson accompanied him to Bordaz's residence on the side of Mount
Royal, where he was to stay. They spoke of the incident on the way, but
little is known of the content of their conversation. Robert Bordaz had
rushed ahead to greet them on their arrival. After wishing the general
a restful evening, Johnson left immediately in the limousine; de
Gaulle turned to Bordaz and asked him, as he was wont to do in such
circumstances, what he thought "of all that." The commissioner-
general replied that he had accomplished precisely what he had come
to do; it was just the right thing in the right place.[7] The general
appeared pleasantly surprised after the glum reaction on the terrace.
He then closeted himself with Couve de Murville and Leduc, who had
arrived meanwhile, for a twenty-minute consultation. After they had
left, de Gaulle put the same question to Flohic as he had to Bordaz.[8]
The aide-de-camp replied in the same vein, reminding him of the
wartime experience he had related at Colombey-les-Deux-Eglises
shortly before their departure and which had convinced him of the
hatred of French Canadians for "*les Anglais.*"* For him, de Gaulle's
action, he declared, was a wish fulfilled; indeed, one of his "greatest
hopes." The French-Canadian feeling of inferiority, "carefully maintained" by their English-speaking fellow citizens, had been given a
deadly blow by the whole affair, including the extraordinary French
pavilion, the ultra modern Montreal *métro* and the magnificent
Colbert. By then, de Gaulle appeared to be not only reassured, but
pleased with his accomplishment. Perhaps his instincts had served
him well once again. The "notables" were upset, but that was to be
expected. He had done what he had come to do: provoke a crisis that
would be helpful to French Canadians in determining their future.

Prime Minister Pearson had watched the dramatic event on television in his official residence in Ottawa. "I could hardly believe my ears
when I heard the words he uttered, '*Vive le Québec libre,*'" he wrote
later. "This was the slogan of separatists dedicated to the dismember-
ment of that Canada whose independence de Gaulle had wished to see
assured...when he proposed my health in Paris."[9] He was even more
upset about the "secret" that the general had confided to the crowd that
the day's events reminded him of the liberation of Paris. He interpreted the statement as a comparison between the situation of French

* See Chapter 6, page 88.

Canadians and that of Parisians under the Nazi occupation; that he found "completely unacceptable." He "grabbed a pencil and started to write a reply." Then the telephone started to ring and a flood of telegrams to arrive.

Paul Martin, for his part, heard the speech on the radio. He had travelled to Montreal in the government's private railway car and had had it parked on a siding near the Queen Elizabeth Hotel so that he could use it as his operational headquarters. Thus he was only half a kilometer from the Hôtel de Ville. Martin had spoken to the prime minister by telephone, a short time earlier, and while he conceded that there "wasn't very much about Canada" in the de Gaulle's speeches during the day, he rationalized that the general was, after all, speaking in Quebec.[10] He was still clinging to the assurance he had been given on the *Colbert* that everything would go well. The reference in the speech from the balcony of the Hôtel de Ville to the liberation made him "squirm," but he still refused to believe what he was hearing when the words "*Vive le Québec libre*" were pronounced. The expression, he told the others who were with him in the railway car, was not necessarily sinister. He soon found that was a minority reaction, at least in federal circles. Marcel Cadieux and Jean Marchand, whom he reached by telephone, were much more critical; and when he got through to the prime minister, he was surprised at the emotional depth of his reaction. Pearson told him, in Martin's words, to "hightail it back to Ottawa" for a special Cabinet meeting on the subject the next morning. Jules Léger was out of telephone contact early in the evening, but when the external affairs minister did get in touch with him, he found him to be "dumbfounded" as well. Nevertheless, true to form, the ambassador advised calm and caution.* The best strategy, he recommended, was to do nothing and see what happened on the other side. Martin also tried to reach Couve de Murville at the Queen Elizabeth Hotel, where he was staying, but in vain. Finally, he reached Leduc, who was sharing the same suite, and was told by him that the foreign minister was getting ready for bed and had given instructions that he was not to be disturbed. Martin asked the ambassador to express the Canadian government's concern over General de Gaulle's speech. Leduc merely indicated that he was not surprised at its contents. Not able to pursue the matter further, Martin asked Léger to try to make direct contact with Couve de Murville in the morning, and retired to bed himself.

The lights also burned late and the telephones were in heavy use in

* Notwithstanding all the difficulties they had had to bear in the past three years, the Légers' sense of proportions and humour did not forsake them. Gaby's first reacted on hearing the spectacular vivat, "It's the buffalo—they should not have served him anything so hard to digest for lunch." (Interview with author, May 1, 1982)

Ottawa that night. With Pearson operating out of his study at the prime minister's residence, consultations among politicians and officials continued for several hours. Most of the opinions he received, including several hundred telegrams, corresponded to his own and spurred him to take a strong stand. While he sketched out a statement to submit to Cabinet in the morning, officials of the Privy Council, the Prime Minister's Office and the Department of External Affairs worked on one as well. Martin arrived in the capital at ten o'clock the next morning and went directly to Parliament Hill, where he and Pearson had neighboring office suites. The Cabinet meeting was delayed until noon to enable consultations to continue, and to allow ministers time to reach the capital. The prime minister was primarily concerned about the reaction throughout Canada. A statement would have to be issued "very promptly," he told his colleagues when they assembled; public opinion would "quite rightly slaughter" them if they ignored the incident and received de Gaulle in Ottawa as if nothing had happened. Time was of the essence, as the president was due to arrive the following afternoon. "It's the only time that I saw Mr. Pearson behaving like Jean Marchand," Marchand, himself a firebrand, recounted later. "He was really scandalized."[11]

At the beginning of the Cabinet meeting, most of the English-speaking ministers seemed to be as confused about the situation as they were annoyed. According to Paul Martin, at least one, Arthur Laing from Vancouver, wanted simply to break off diplomatic relations with France.[12] Attention was focused particularly on the ministers from Quebec, who were assumed to be most knowledgeable about the situation and what to do about it. Generally they took a hard line, arguing that the federal government's prestige in Quebec was at stake, and that a firm response was necessary. However, while the responsibility for the crisis had to be laid squarely at de Gaulle's feet, they warned of the danger of identifying him with French Canadians and creating a wave of sympathy for him. Paul Martin, after fluctuating between anger fueled by a feeling of betrayal and a refusal to believe the worst, returned to his characteristic stance of conciliator-cum-strategist. Once again, the exceptional diplomatic talent of Couve de Murville was evident. In a telephone conversation that morning, he had confided to Martin that the incident was a matter of shock and concern to members of de Gaulle's entourage too, and that they were anxious to minimize its negative effects. Grasping at the possibility that the offensive vivat might have been a momentary lapse, Martin urged his Cabinet colleagues to make the most moderate statement compatible with the domestic political reaction. There were indications that Premier Johnson was also unhappy over the incident, he reported, and would be inclined to play it down rather than exploit it. The importance of limiting any damage to relations with France also required a very careful formulation. The external affairs minister's plea had a moderating influence on his colleagues, and before they broke for lunch at one, a consensus was emerging that they should take a position that was firm but which left the door open for de Gaulle to explain himself, or at least left the ball in his court. If they criticized him too sharply, the general might take umbrage and cancel the visit to Ottawa; on the other hand, should he come, special precautions would have to be taken to avoid protest demonstrations against him.

Before the Cabinet assembled again shortly before four o'clock, Pearson, Martin, Marchand and other Quebec ministers worked intensely to find a wording that would meet all those requirements. A draft once agreed upon, it was passed on to the officials who suggested a few further nuances. Opinions within the full Cabinet were still widely divergent when the prime minister presented the proposal, but, a very considerable diplomat as well, he won approval for it. The underlying calculation behind the carefully chosen words was that de Gaulle would probably not come to Ottawa after taking cognizance of the statement, but it was unlikely that he would go so far as to break off diplomatic relations. In case he did come, some precautions were decided upon: the public meeting on Parliament Hill would be replaced by a smaller one on the grounds of Rideau Hall, which only selected guests would attend, and the proposed meeting with the Cabinet would be cancelled to avoid embarrassment.

In the meantime, de Gaulle carried on with his schedule. The federal representative to Expo '67, Lionel Chevrier, called for him at nine a.m. and accompanied him to the Ritz Carlton Hotel to meet members of the local French community. Uncertain how to deal with it, Chevrier was determined to avoid the subject foremost in everyone's mind, and had prepared himself to explain the historic sites along their route. The general was not interested in tourism and tried to engage a conversation about the sensational reaction to his balcony speech and the evident strength of the separatist movement that it reflected. It was a dialogue of the deaf. From the hotel, de Gaulle was taken to the site of Expo '67 where he visited the French, Canadian and Quebec pavilions, and was then received for lunch at the Hélène de Champlain restaurant by Pierre Dupuy. He also went to Dupuy's apartment at the ultra-modern new apartment building, Habitat, on the Expo site, for a short rest. At the restaurant, speculation was rife whether he would refer to the events of the previous evening, and what vivats he would deliver. Like the commissioner-general, he stuck to his prepared—and safe—text and concluded with "*Vive le Canada*" and "*Vive le Québec.*" In the afternoon, he toured the Expo site by automobile, then, after a rest at Bordaz's residence, hosted a dinner in honour of the Quebec government at the French pavilion. There is no record that he even mentioned the controversial subject during the day. Queried by journalists, members of his staff downplayed its significance. The president had never intended to encourage the separatists, they declared, and, at any rate, the words "*Québec libre*" did not mean "liberated" but rather "emancipated" Quebec, a subtle but real difference.[13] Once again, the hand of Couve de Murville was evident in that line of argument.

Johnson's staff also tended to downplay the importance of the incident. The separatists, on the other hand, made the most of it. The leader of the *Ralliement National*, Gilles Grégoire, stated that de Gaulle had been able, in only two days in Quebec, to sense that independence was imminent, and predicted that it would occur in 1970.[14] He summoned the federal authorities to begin the transition at once. After having dismissed de Gaulle earlier as "an old fool," RIN leader Pierre Bourgault also came to his defence. The "Anglo-Saxons," he declared, should "have the decency to keep quiet," rather than preventing de Gaulle from "aiding the poor little Quebec people in its struggle for life and liberty."

At six p.m., Prime Minister Pearson read the federal Cabinet statement at a televised press conference.[15] He was sure, he began, that Canadians in all parts of the country were pleased when the president of France received such a warm welcome in Quebec. However, "certain statements" by him tended to encourage "the small minority" of the population whose aim was to destroy Canada. As such, they were "unacceptable to the Canadian people and its government." "The people of Canada are free," he declared. "Every province is free. Canadians do not need to be liberated." Indeed, many thousands of Canadians had given their lives in two world wars in the liberation of France and other European countries. Canada would remain united and would reject any effort to destroy that unity. It had always had a "special relationship with France, the motherland of so many of her citizens." And Canadians attached "the greatest importance" to their friendship with the French people. "The strong purpose of the Government of Canada" had been and remained "to foster that friendship." He hoped that the discussions later in the week with General de Gaulle would demonstrate that he shared this purpose. The key word in the message was clearly "unacceptable." Its meaning was unambiguous: in diplomatic parlance, to declare someone or something "unacceptable" is a strong rebuke. Less clearly stated but nonetheless evident was a demand that de Gaulle justify his actions in terms of Franco-Canadian relations. The alternative was to interrupt his schedule and return home.

Because Ambassador Leduc was still in Montreal, a member of the French embassy staff was asked to go to the Department of External

Affairs to receive the message officially. He expressed his personal embarrassment at being left in the dark concerning the whole matter and his regrets at its destructive effects. De Gaulle himself was informed of the contents of the text by Couve de Murville while he was dressing for dinner; his immediate reaction was: "We will see about that later."[16] There were many empty places in the dining room of the French pavilion that evening. Paul Martin had cancelled his attendance. The premier of New Brunswick, Louis Robichaud, telegraphed his refusal to attend. Most of the guests had learned of the federal statement and watched the general carefully. He made only an indirect allusion to the whole matter in his speech. "Neither you nor I have lost our time," he said to Johnson, who was seated beside him. "Did something perhaps happen? If, on this occasion, the president of the Republic was able to be useful to the French of Canada, he will be deeply pleased."[17] Otherwise, his text added nothing new to what he had said in Quebec City. Johnson, for his part, made an even more elliptical—and safer—reference to the controversial subject. He noted that France had bequeathed Quebec not only its language and culture, but also "the cult of freedom," individual and collective. "Large or small," he declared, "all nations have the right to live and control their destiny."

After the dinner, de Gaulle returned to his residence where he examined Pearson's statement with Couve de Murville and Leduc. Then he telephoned Pompidou in Paris, waking him up at five a.m. Since Ottawa apparently considered him an undesirable personage, and in any case, his Quebec mission was completed, he informed his prime minister, he was returning to France the next afternoon.[18] The aircraft, already in Ottawa waiting for him, was ordered to Montreal. "From the moment that the Canadian government does not understand what I want to do and takes things in that way," he commented to Flohic before going to bed; "I'm not interested in continuing my trip."[19] Couve de Murville returned to his hotel and informed Jules Léger of the decision; he passed it on to Marcel Cadieux in Ottawa. Cadieux in turn telephoned Pearson's assistant, Mary Macdonald, and suggested that the prime minister be advised at once. She decided that he needed his sleep; he was told early the next morning. Mrs. Martin took the same attitude.

Jules Léger and Couve de Murville had agreed to meet at quarter of nine in the morning, after the ambassador had received instructions from Ottawa. Their meeting was short and unproductive. The French foreign minister said that the general had made up his mind and there was no possibility of changing it. That, he added, was probably the best course in the circumstances. Even a direct communication between him and Martin might complicate matters still further. Time would have to be allowed to repair the damage. The federal Cabinet met in another emergency session shortly after nine o'clock and received Léger's report. External affairs officials counselled a minimal reaction. The advice was accepted. It was also decided that Chevrier, not Martin, would see the general off at Dorval airport. A Cabinet statement was released after lunch; it was brief and restrained. The government had been advised that General de Gaulle had decided not to continue on to Ottawa, but rather to return to Paris as soon as the programme organized for him in Montreal was completed. His decision was "easy to understand in the circumstances." While those circumstances were not due to the government, they nevertheless were "very regrettable."

As usual, de Gaulle was on time for his first appointment of the morning, a tour on the Montreal *métro*. "The General is leaving," Jurgensen confided to his friend Mallen as they followed him into the station. "He is taking the plane back to Paris this afternoon."[20] A Radio-Canada journalist, on his toes, telephoned Dorval airport and discovered that the aircraft had already arrived there. He broke the story in mid-morning. Following the *métro* tour, the general visited the new Place des Arts, then went to the University of Montreal, the heart of nationalist sentiment in Quebec. By then the news of his impending departure was spreading quickly and the atmosphere was electric when he arrived. As University chancellor, Cardinal Léger, whose views were close to those of his brother, introduced him with studied formality to a capacity crowd in the auditorium. The destiny of the "French of Canada" was either progress or decline, de Gaulle told the gathering.[21] They formed part of "that great totality" that he described as France, "that great totality of intelligence, sentiment and reason" which was "indispensable to world equilibrium and progress, ...[and also] to peace." The contribution of the University of Montreal was "decisive proof of what our people is worth and what it wants in that regard." More radical members of the audience, previously inclined to dismiss him as over-aged and increasingly irrelevant, listened to him with new respect.

At noon, Mayor Drapeau took over the role of host. First, he offered the general a reception at the look-out on the top of Mount Royal from which both Jacques Cartier and Samuel de Champlain had gazed down upon the present site of Montreal and the magnificent vista extending south to the Appalachian Mountains. Then they returned to the Hôtel de Ville—the 'site of the crime'—for a luncheon. Since it was the last event in the general's truncated schedule, it suddenly assumed special importance. In the previous hectic days, Drapeau had had his introductory remarks very much in mind, but had had no time to prepare a text.[22] A traditional French-Canadian nationalist, he had taken out of his files a quotation he loved from historian Chanoine

Lionel Groulx and had put it in his pocket. He had a still more important source of inspiration. He considered himself the spokesman for the "little people" of Montreal and asked himself, as he moved about the city, what message they would want him to give to the president of France. His speech was in answer to that question. It was not intended as a rebuttal to the general's balcony cry. The two men had spent most of the morning together, sharing several limousine rides, and neither had mentioned the subject nor the federal government's response. For the mayor, de Gaulle's use of the words "*Vive le Québec libre*" had been the emotional reaction of an old man who had had an exhilarating, but tiring, day. The Canadian government, he felt, had reacted too strongly, if they had let him continue to Ottawa, they would have been able to find out what everyone was asking: what did he really mean? and less damage would have been done.

From the time of his arrival at Anse-aux-Foulons, Drapeau told de Gaulle in his introductory remarks, they had all witnessed "a real explosion" of feeling that remained undefined.[23] What was that feeling? It could not be nostalgia, since the roots of his French-Canadian compatriots were "deeply anchored in the Canadian soil." His own family had been there for fourteen generations. Was it gratitude? "Gratitude to Charles de Gaulle personally, yes. Gratitude to France? To ask the question is to express doubt. For we have learned to survive alone for two centuries." With the exception of one brief visit some years earlier, none of de Gaulle's predecessors as president had ever indicated that he attached as much importance to the existence of French Canada as the general had done. That was not a reproach, it was an observation. Still, Drapeau continued, even if there did not exist a feeling of gratitude towards successive French governments, there was nonetheless "a natural gratitude towards one's mother for having inherited [in this case—author's note] the virtues, the language and the culture of French civilization." French Canadians had maintained those virtues, but as for the language, culture and civilization, "it was necessary to hang all that in the barn at times...while the richer and more cultured people returned to France." Those who remained had continued for five generations to speak and teach French when there were no links with France. Did Frenchmen know that, at one stage, teaching was carried out with the only copy of a French grammar that was left in the colony? It was placed on a lectern, and a nun was the only person authorized to turn the pages.

Since then, times had changed; French texts were published in Montreal and even distributed to other places where they were not available. But French Canadians did not want the hopes stirred by the president's visit to end in disappointment. Thus he expressed a wish: that future presidents resemble de Gaulle and have faith in the existence of French Canada. Why have faith? Because it had now been proven that French Canada could survive. Yet French Canadians were not satisfied with that. They had not forgotten that their ancestors had colonized the country and carried the French language "from one ocean to the other." Even several important American cities owed their foundation, and some regions their beginnings of civilization, to the early French Canadians. He hoped that the new relations that seemed to be developing between modern France and modern French Canada would be marked by that resolve not to make short-term profits, but to open the world to an important civilization. He also hoped that those Frenchmen who came in the future would bring with them the same pioneering spirit in order to assist in "intensifying the renewal of French Canada," so that it would better serve "all of Canada" and, indeed, the whole North American continent. For, the mayor declared, "we are attached to this immense country." He concluded with the quotation from Lionel Groulx: "We belong to that little group of peoples...who share a particular kind of fate—a tragic fate. Their anxiety is not over whether they will be rich or unhappy, great or small, but over whether tomorrow they will see the dawn or disappear." That was the state of mind French Canadians wanted to get rid of, and in so doing, in becoming "masters of their own fate, they were happy to also serve their common ancestral land, France."

In a brief few minutes, the feisty little mayor, playing his self-appointed role as spokesman of the people, had risen above the other actors in that intense drama. Even though the message was in marked contrast to his own, General de Gaulle was clearly impressed. If any one event justified his trip to Quebec, he declared as he began his speech, it was the mayor's "truly eloquent and profound allocution."[24] "For the French, in particular for their President," the words would "go much farther." Still, he was not about to give ground. During his visit, "as a result of a sort of shock that neither you nor I could do anything about,—it was elemental and we were all struck by it—...I believe that I was able, as far as you are concerned, to get to the bottom of things." That was not only the best policy, but "the only worthwhile one in the end," particularly when what was at stake was "the destiny of the French-Canadian people, or a Canadian-French people, whichever you prefer." Each would draw his own conclusions from what had happened and act accordingly, "you [French Canadians] continuing your task in this Canada of which you are the heart, in this America where you have established yourselves," and France which could either "be itself, that is, strong, vigorous and humane, or decline, that is, fall apart and disappear and thus deprive humanity of the brightest prospects it ever had." The allotted "tasks" of both drew on the same inspiration: they were French. That implied that they should draw closer together in every respect. The accords signed between the two governments were a beginning. The rest, "everything that swarms about, schemes and scribbles," was unimportant.* He hoped that when he had left "the presence of General de Gaulle in this Quebec in full expansion, this Quebec starting to move, this Quebec making up its mind, this Quebec becoming master of its own fate," would have contributed to the momentum.

Deflected from his purpose only momentarily by the mayor's heartfelt statement, de Gaulle had delivered his last direct message to what he termed the North American branch of the French people. Inevitably, reaction to the two speeches varied. Once again, Pearson witnessed the scene on television.[25] "I was very proud—as a Canadian," he wrote to Drapeau afterward, "to hear such moving and eloquent words which combined a broad and true Canadianism with love and loyalty to the tradition, culture and language of French Canada. You gave us a lesson yesterday in grace, wisdom and patriotism that will do much to heal the wounds inflicted on our country in the past few days." The mayor had made it easier to carry on with the task of bringing about a better understanding and a greater feeling of unity among all Canadians, so that those who, like him, had been part of the country and its heritage for so long, would be "honoured in Vancouver and Halifax as you are in Quebec, and feel as much at home there as you do in Montreal." Paul Martin telephoned to congratulate Drapeau. "Why didn't you call me yesterday before the federal government's statement was issued?" the mayor challenged him.[26] The unfortunate ending of the president's visit might have been avoided.

Exemplifying the other end of the opinion spectrum, Pierre-Louis Mallen wrote afterward that Drapeau had "made the worst speech in his life;...his sentences were obscure, their syntax incorrect, their linkage arbitrary; the repetitions were numerous."[27] The French journalist had only "derision" for the "concern by a member of the defeated community who had reached the top of the social ladder not to prejudice the conqueror." De Gaulle had "remained unperturbed" during "that painful moment,...feigning not to notice...that he was talking gibberish" and he had responded "by being charming." In his three-volume biography of de Gaulle, Jean Lacouture has accepted Mallen's interpretation of the scene even over that of Jean Drapeau himself, who gave him a personal interview. The mayor's speech, he writes, was "a rather curious hodge-podge of unctuous civilities and peevish reproaches," and quotes Drapeau as saying to the general when he sat down, "*C'était tficil [difficile], mon cher Monsieur*," a demeaning reflection on the mayor's accent.[28]

* A very inadequate rendition by the author in English of a vintage Gaulle-ism, "*Tout ce qui grouille, grenouille, scribouille.*"

Chevrier, Dupuy, Léger, Chapdelaine and a handful of others accompanied the general to the airport and said goodbye to him at the foot of the aircraft ramp. Someone in the modest crowd on the observation deck cried, "It's only an *au revoir*."[29] In fact, it was an *adieu*. In Ottawa, when Mrs. Michener went to the kitchen to break the news to the French chef, Zonda, that the banquet scheduled for that evening was cancelled, he was in the midst of preparing a couple of hundred individual puddings trimmed with French flags made of sugar. He gave vent to his rage by smashing them one after the other with his fists. The extra-length bed that had been built especially for the president was dismantled and placed in storage; it was to serve seventeen years later during the visit of the Senegalese president, Abdou Diouf. The staff of Government House ate well that night. In the banquet hall, the Micheners and Pearsons, long-time friends, ate alone and tried to joke over the situation.

A question that persists in many minds is what would have happened if the Canadian government had not declared de Gaulle's conduct "unacceptable," and if he had gone on to Ottawa as scheduled. Despite the federal government's apprehension and the general's lack of enthusiasm, it seems likely that everyone would have performed his allotted function, albeit somewhat stiffly, and barring unforeseeable events such as public interventions, the schedule would have been completed successfully. Whether it was in fact deliberate or spontaneous, he might well have tried to explain away his controversial vivat. After all, it was one of his common strategies, after he had taken a strong position on an issue, to soften the blow by more conciliatory gestures. Moreover, with his strong sense of protocol and propriety, he would have conducted himself, in the words of one of his close associates, in a "civilized" manner. Certainly, during his drive to the Ritz Carlton Hotel the morning after the balcony scene, he was not at all reluctant to discuss the subject.

As for the public pronouncements that would have been made, Pearson's texts are available.[30] De Gaulle was always for Canadians, the prime minister would have said at the welcoming ceremony, "the man of the eighteenth of June 1940, the man of courage and faith." He was also "*la France*, mother country of millions of Canadians,...source of a European civilization and a world-wide culture,...a modern, dynamic country in full expansion and always concerned to combine progress and human values." Canada, too, was "a country of dynamic progress," and Canadians, "proud of their diverse origins," were "working together to build...a country strong and united." It was a country "as free as any in the world, facing its future with national pride and confidence, while cherishing its historical ties with the two mother countries....Canada, free, strong, and united." Obviously, in the prime minister's case, the wish was father to the thought, but the message was designed both to urge Canadians to make it true and to counter his guest's doubts that it might ever happen.

In his address at the state banquet, Pearson would have told de Gaulle that Canada had "particularly close relations and...special ties of friendship" with three countries, Great Britain, France and the United States. While French Canadians reached out to France with "a deep and strong affection," English Canadians welcomed the fuller recognition of French culture and traditions, and of the French language, as a positive and valuable asset in developing a strong and united country from sea to sea with a distinctive destiny and identity. All Canadians were becoming increasingly conscious that their dualism "must be a partnership." To the dualism was added the diversity derived from Canada's having been "fortified and enriched by the cultures and talents of many peoples of many races." Canadians did not fear that diversity: the various components of it were a "common richness." But the Canadian ideal of unity in diversity was "not only essential in Canadian life," it was also "the pattern for good international relations." Fragmentation, whether national or international, was not the answer to current problems nor were cultural absorption and political centralization. If unity in diversity could not be achieved in Canada, what hope was there for the world? Pearson intended to conclude his speech by quoting de Gaulle's statement in Ottawa in 1960 that Canada was "a state which has found the means to unite two societies...; which exercises independence...; which is forging a national character...alongside a very powerful federation, [and is] a solid and stable state."

What would General de Gaulle have responded? No text has been revealed, but as the *Colbert* prepared to return to France without its precious cargo, the commandant's attention was drawn by his secretary to a stack of copies of the speech that had been prepared for Ottawa. What should be done with them? he asked. Captain Delahousse took one copy and told him to get rid of the others. In 1984, when clearing out his personal files, Delahousse had another glance through it, decided it was of no great significance, and threw it away as well. Questioned a few months later, he recalled that the speech had started out by expressing de Gaulle's pleasure at being in Ottawa, then repeated the assurance given at Anse-aux-Foulons that no problems existed between the Canadian and French governments.[31] The rest of the text was what one would expect of a statesman visiting another country. It made no reference to the themes that de Gaulle had developed at the banquet in Quebec City. Two explanations are possible: either de Gaulle had left open the possibility of adding further material to take into account what happened in Quebec, or he had intended to calm any waters that had been stirred up there. In either case, in the view of Michel Debré, who was so close to the general for so long, he would probably have stuck to generalities in order to finish his visit on the proper note.[32] As part of the Ottawa schedule, two hours had been reserved the next day for a private discussion with Pearson; the two men would have had ample opportunity to discuss their differences.

All that, of course, is academic speculation; the fact remains that de Gaulle's cry of "*Vive le Québec libre*" and the federal government's response disrupted the programme. "I don't see how the rest of it could have been saved," Ambassador Leduc commented later,

> nor what course it would have taken. The General had accomplished what for him was the essential part of the trip when he visited French Canada at the invitation of Mr. Johnson. He had brought him his support in his struggle to maintain its French identity and had received a welcome beyond anything he expected. All the rest was incidental, including the visit to Expo '67 and the visit to the federal government.[33]

As he flew over Quebec on the way home, de Gaulle sent a message to Johnson thanking the Quebec population for its "unforgettable welcome." Then he began to prepare for the next step: explaining his actions at home and abroad. He knew that he was in for a tough fight. Couve de Murville showed him an editorial in the London *Times* of that morning, referring to the visit to Quebec as a sign of his "erratic decline." According to Gilbert Pérol, the general was "very affected" by the assessment.[34] "I recognize that what I said was premature with regard to the French Canadians who are perhaps not ready to face a new situation," he remarked to Roland Nungesser, secretary of state for finance, who was in the official party, "I realize that I went very far. It's going to make a terrific fuss."[35] Nonetheless, he continued, he had been helpful not only to French Canadians but also to the federal government, which had no interest in allowing the "Canadian problem" to deteriorate as the black problem had done in the United States. Drapeau had said to him, we have been waiting for you for two hundred years. At his age, he would not return to the North American continent. When would a French president again visit Canada? And would he dare to "state the problem of the French Canadians?" In the circumstances, he thought that "it was better that de Gaulle do it."

During the seven-hour journey, he summoned one official after the other and asked for their reaction—"confessed them" was the term his staff used in such circumstances—and gave his reasoning. "*Mon*

Général," Jurgensen told him enthusiastically, "you paid the debt left by Louis XV [in abandoning New France]."[36] "I knew I had to do something," de Gaulle responded, "but what, when, where? At the end of that extraordinary day, I had to respond to the people's call....I would not have been de Gaulle if I hadn't done it." He repeated the same message to René de Saint-Légier, then added, "I am going to be dragged in the mud. Look at the foreign press. You'll see the French press. They are going to indulge in some indecent expressions towards me and towards France. I'll take care of it. What I did, I tell you, I had to do."[37]

When he was field officer, de Gaulle's precept, in a tight situation, had always been to attack. Now as he neared his destination, he prepared to put on a bold front. The members of his government had been summoned to Orly airport at four a.m., to demonstrate their support of his action. They too had been taken by surprise by the Montreal declaration; even Prime Minister Pompidou remarked with his characteristic dry wit, "That's one speech he didn't show me," and added as Johnson had done, "We're going to have problems." However, like Couve de Murville, Pompidou was accustomed to pulling the general's chestnuts out of the fire. Olivier Guichard, the minister of industry and a devoted follower of de Gaulle's for twenty years, was "stupefied" by what had happened.[38] Still, he knew that, under the general's model of personal government, ministers had no claim to be consulted with regard to significant political decisions, and, like his colleagues, he turned out to receive the general's explanation and to learn what they should do to handle the embarrassing situation. Only two ministers failed to appear: Minister of Agriculture and former Prime Minister Edgar Faure, a more independent-minded man who was not only "stupefied" but shocked at the general's conduct, and Information Minister Georges Gorse who did not have time to return from southern France where he was on holiday.

Hervé Alphand, then secretary general of the Ministry of Foreign Affairs, has described the airport scene, "Some ministers did not try to conceal their irritation. 'He's nuts', one said. 'This time he has gone too far', said another. Then the great man appeared, tired but smiling, raised his arms to the sky on seeing them...and everyone forgot his concerns."[39] De Gaulle's first words to them, like a tourist returning from holiday, were, "*Ah, messieurs, c'était magnifique, magnifique!*" and he apologized for bringing them out so early. They fell in line to shake his hand and then followed him to a quiet corner where he gave them an initial briefing. When he had finished, they seemed much more relaxed, some even chuckling over his description of the balcony incident. Couve de Murville, ever stoical, told them that there was "no reason to get upset."[40] De Saint-Légier assured them that the president had been right to act as he had done and that everything had been "*très bien.*"[41]

The attack that de Gaulle apprehended had already begun. The Paris daily newspaper *Le Monde*, which he had helped to create in 1945, led off in an editorial on July 26 entitled "Excess in Everything." It accused de Gaulle of having undertaken, from the moment he set foot on Canadian soil, "one of those oratorical escalations" at which he was a past master. In twenty-four hours and over three hundred kilometers, he had progressed "from patriotism to nationalism, then to separatism." In adopting the slogan of the partisans of Quebec independence, he had gone much further than the Liberals' "*Maîtres chez nous*" or his host Johnson's "*Québec d'abord*"—Quebec first. How was it possible, the editorial continued, not to question and be disturbed about "that brutal irruption into the internal affairs of a State?" Was the Gaullist doctrine, "so often and loudly proclaimed," of no interference in the affairs of others "merely a matter of circumstances?" The exaltation of nationalism, the anti-American phobia, the glorification of everything French, "had reached a fever pitch and seemed to constitute a sort of provocation." The general's judgment was also faulty on the basic question at issue. As justly resolved as French Canadians were to correct the imbalance with regard to their anglophone compatriots, and from which they had suffered for three centuries [sic], it could well be asked what would be the fate of an independent Quebec? The material aid that France could offer was limited, even though the current enthusiasm in Montreal was met with the warmest sympathy.

The next most important French daily newspaper, *Le Figaro*, generally favourable to the government, judged that de Gaulle's conduct and tone had "gone far beyond what a Head of State can allow himself in visiting a friendly country." However, the paper was prepared to give him the benefit of the doubt concerning his motives: perhaps he had been carried away a bit by the atmosphere "deliberately created by the most ardent partisans of Quebec autonomy." It was to be hoped that in his next statement he would "remove the doubts, erase the misunderstanding and reinforce Franco-Canadian friendship." *Le Combat* was more severe. France had rallied behind "a few Quebec enthusiasts," but had "alienated a nation, perhaps for a long time." In its "clairvoyant and paroxysmal aspects," the Quebec outburst was disturbing: General de Gaulle was proving "less and less discreet and more and more offhand in his international activities." What he had said to the Canadians suggested that he could say "anything to anyone anywhere. *C'est alarmant.*" *L'Aurore* was even blunter: "This time the question has to be asked squarely: what is going on under General de Gaulle's *képi* [military hat]?" It was "extremely unpleasant" to have a president of the Republic "expose himself to criticism in interfering in others' affairs." Ironically, outside his committed supporters, de Gaulle fared best with the Communists, whom he even refused to consider as proper Frenchmen. *L'Humanité*, for example, recalled that resistance to American expansionism had been one of the causes of Canadian Confederation. Every day that threat was growing. The establishment of a "national State of the French-Canadian people" within a new confederation was "a precondition for joint opposition to Yankee imperialism."

The Western press was even more severe than the French. Among the more moderate, the *Times* was more sorrowful than indignant. The friends and allies of France, whom de Gaulle made into adversaries but who would never be enemies, it commented, turned the other cheek while waiting for better days. Soon, he would be gone; the *entente* would survive him. It must be depressing for "the old soldier fading away slowly in the Elysée, carrying off a few sorties to confound his supposed enemies, but realizing that those whom he sought to wound feel only a friendly regret coupled with continuing admiration for his country, plunged into a state of perplexity." The Washington *Post* adopted a similar position. It was "not the true General de Gaulle, but a caricature of the French President" who had visited Canada. "No responsible statesman could deliberately appeal to French-Canadian separatism as he had done, contrary to all the norms of mutual respect for the internal affairs of another nation." More and more, what de Gaulle did made people "less furious than sad, and perhaps less sad than amused." Even the European press outside France was severe in judging his escapade. By his "mulish oratorical crescendo," commented the Lausanne *Gazette*, the general had "transformed into a diplomatic failure what could have been a great contribution to French prestige." It was hard to believe that he had really calculated the effects of his action, which was necessarily counter-productive since France did not have the means to pursue a policy of confrontation in North America. Following on other failures, that "semi-rupture" of relations with France's ally, Canada, would increase the doubts in French public opinion about Gaullist foreign policy.

Among the French politicians, François Mitterrand, who as the Socialist presidential candidate in the 1965 elections had forced de Gaulle to go to a second ballot, remained discreetly silent, but Gaston Defferre, chairman of the caucus of the *Fédération de la gauche* in the National Assembly, spoke for the non-Communist left.[42] Either General de Gaulle had decided before leaving France to intervene in Canada's internal affairs, he charged, or he had let himself be carried away by the atmosphere he found in Quebec. If the first interpretation were true, he had committed "a grave impropriety;" if the second, he

had "lost his self control." A country like France could not have at the
helm a man who, carried away by passing moods, made improvised
statements, or, even worse, statements that did not reflect a conscious,
deliberate policy. The French had the right to know which was the
case. Valery Giscard d'Estaing, president of the *Fédération des
républicains indépendants*, who had resigned shortly before as minister of finance to prepare his own ascent to the presidency, referred to
the dangers of "the solitary exercise of power" that characterized de
Gaulle's style of government.[43]

Finally, the Breton separatists reacted by producing car stickers
bearing the words "*Québec libre. Bretagne libre.*" Since their movement had been declared illegal, policemen stopped the offending cars
and ripped them off. One section of the movement reacted by blowing
up two radio transmitters. A quick poll of French public opinion
indicated that, for the first time, many Frenchmen were "stupefied and
shaken" on a foreign policy issue.[44] Fifty-six per cent of Parisians were
hostile to and disapproved of de Gaulle's conduct in Canada, twenty-
seven per cent approved of it, and seventeen per cent "didn't know."
Forty-six per cent thought that he was motivated by a desire to counter
the influence of the United States, sixteen per cent thought his action
was directed against Great Britain, sixteen per cent thought he was
preparing to bring about the reunification of France and French
Canada, and twenty-two per cent thought he was merely expressing
sympathy for the French-speaking population of Canada.

These domestic reactions were even worse than de Gaulle anticipated, and the personal attacks hurt him deeply. A few days after his
return, and after yet another disheartening look through the morning
press, he said to Bernard Tricot, the newly-appointed secretary
general of the Elysée, "It will also be part of your function, if you notice
one day any hesitation in the thinking of the Head of State, any
confusion in his remarks, to..." Ill at ease, Tricot interrupted, "You can
count on me, *mon Général*," and switched to another subject.[45] The
exchange reflected what was probably de Gaulle's only fear, that of
losing his mental faculties. Referring to Marshal Pétain, he had once
remarked, "Old age is like a shipwreck." And on resuming power in
1958 he stated, "I won't offer you the spectacle of my degeneration."
His critics were reminding him implicitly of that vow.

In a first attempt to stem the flood of criticism, de Gaulle's faithful
supporters scrambled to reassure the public. On July 27, Robert
Poujade, one of the national secretaries of the UNR-UDI, the Gaullist
parliamentary coalition, issued a statement.[46] The general's visit was
not, and could not be, "a diplomatic voyage," he declared; it was, above
all, a moving visit by "the most illustrious of living Frenchmen" to "the
Frenchmen who had been abandoned, forgotten in former times" but

who still looked to the land of their ancestors "with fidelity, nostalgia and fervour." Rather than speaking to them with "prudent words of well-meaning banality" as his critics would have done, he wanted to "leave the evidence of his passage on the soil of Quebec" and to "confirm solemnly to the French of Canada" that they had the same role to play in the New World as France was playing on the global stage. By asserting their "ethnic, psychological and political originality," they constituted an essential element in the new equilibrium that General de Gaulle was seeking in international relations.

Next, members of the Elysée staff gave an anonymous briefing to a journalist at the popular weekly, *L'Express*, explaining that, for the general, Canada, as currently constituted, was not "a true national entity."[47] If it continued to exist, that would be "at best as a two-headed structure like the former Austro-Hungarian Empire" (which had collapsed from internal divisions and that very structure in 1918), or as an economic unity like the European Common Market. The progress made in the past seven years by French Canadians was so great that, in his view, it should normally end in independence. In that situation, de Gaulle felt that he must support "the struggle of the cousin-people," as President Nasser of Egypt had done in the case of the Algerians when they were fighting against France.

A Toronto *Globe and Mail* journalist, Keith Spicer, was chosen to deliver the general's message to Canadians. In a discreet briefing on July 28, Gilbert Pérol sought to calm the waters without in any way retreating from the position de Gaulle had taken. Everything the president said was intentional, Pérol stated, "He said what he wanted to say;" there was no "slip of the tongue." At the same time, he had not wanted to violate protocol and "regretted profoundly" the way the trip had ended. While he had intended to go to Ottawa "out of courtesy," his main objective was to show France's interest in what was happening in Quebec, that is, "the *épanouissement*—flowering—of a French community taking its destiny in its own hands." He also wanted to challenge Canadians to tackle their problems with "a certain boldness" and he hoped that "the affair" would serve to accelerate the efforts of the two communities to find "a mutually suitable solution." At the same time, he had no political objectives on behalf of France. The destiny of French Canadians was for themselves to decide. That was the sense of his words "*Québec libre*." Ottawa had reacted as if the expression was synonymous with "*Québec indépendant*," that was "an exaggerated interpretation." The general did not want to endorse the RIN slogan; even at home, he was not a party man. At any rate, he had not gone beyond the language of Quebec politics; Johnson himself had referred to "equality or independence." Pérol rejected the charges of deliberate discourtesy to Canada that had been reported in the press.

He denied the story that the *Colbert* had not been flying the Canadian flag as it approached Anse-aux-Foulons. (His denial was confirmed years later by the ship's commandant, a man who did not share de Gaulle's views on Canada and Quebec.) Nor was the general being offensive in appearing in uniform as Diefenbaker and others had charged; he always wore his uniform on trips abroad. Pérol also raised the veil slightly on how de Gaulle would have conducted himself in Ottawa. At the luncheon with Pearson and the provincial premiers, he would have made a "tactful speech" and would have referred to Canada's problem of co-existing with the United States. He would have spoken entirely in French (which would have made it impossible for most of the premiers to follow him—author's note). Ending the interview with Spicer on a personal note, the press attaché conceded that the general's language had been "perhaps too strong." But he was clearly not authorized to concede that point officially. A few hours after the interview, Pérol telephoned Spicer with an addendum, clearly inspired by higher authority. The important thing was "to let things calm down and each side evaluate what happened." There were, "thank God," many positive aspects to the situation, and those were the ones the French wanted to stress. Their ardent desire was for "serenity and friendship."

Sphinx-like in public, de Gaulle himself was still very involved in his recent experience and its repercussions. "If you had seen that enthusiasm," he told Jean d'Escrienne, one of his aides-de-camp who had not made the trip to Quebec, on the way to Colombey-les-Deux-Eglises the first weekend, "those Frenchmen who had been waiting for so long for a sign, a word, some support from France to help them to get out of their inadmissible situation....I had no right to disappoint them."[48] He had, therefore, "triggered the contact." Perhaps it had been "a bit premature," but he was old; it was "then or never." In contrast to the olive branch that Pérol had extended to Canada through Spicer, de Gaulle was in no mood to climb down. In a despatch to Paris on July 26, Ambassador Leduc attempted to pour oil on the troubled waters. He himself was not being badly treated in Ottawa, he reported; Pearson, normally a peaceful man, had had to respond to anglophone pressure. He suggested various ways of "healing the wounds." The general noted in the margin of the telegram, "The point is not to heal Mr. Pearson's wounds. The point is that the French people of Canada should have full control of their own fate."[49]

If de Gaulle was able to dismiss Pearson's feelings, he was anything but indifferent to the reaction in France to what was being referred to as his Montreal *esclandre*, or scene. Quite apart from the criticism of the press, which he simply assumed was against him, he was concerned over what he considered the public's lack of appreciation of his action: most people appeared to think of it as at best a bad joke, and at worst a serious blunder. It was a serious political matter in that his judgment was being called into question. At the Montreal Hôtel de Ville on the day of his departure, he had declared, "All France is watching us here at this moment. It sees you, it hears you, it loves you." Fortunately for him, that was not true. Most Frenchmen were uninformed and—except for a vague positive feeling—uninterested in their North American cousins. And at any rate, it was the holiday season and most of the national economy was about to shut down for the month of August. People had more pleasurable things on their minds. For that reason too, the trip to Quebec had been covered by fewer journalists than any presidential trip abroad since de Gaulle had taken office; many people considered that he was, indeed, merely going to attend a fair. More serious was the reaction within the government. According to Jurgensen, "not one politician out of eight" even within the Gaullist party supported the general's action, and "in the various ministries, among the diplomats and senior officials, there were clear insinuations that the explanation of the incident lay in the field of psychiatry."[50] Most of Jurgensen's colleagues in the Quai d'Orsay were "sick about de Gaulle's infringement of protocol."

At the first Cabinet meeting after his return on July 31, de Gaulle presented his version of events.[51] For a long time he had been under pressure to make another trip to Canada, but he did not want to go to Ottawa. Finally he consented. During his previous trips he had noted "a certain warmth" for France, but "the French-Canadian fact" had not yet crystallized. This time he had been met with a tide of enthusiasm even greater than he had imagined. French Canadians no longer accepted the system into which they were locked. They had "the unanimous conviction" that after a first century of British oppression, a second, under the British North America Act of 1867, had not brought them liberty, equality and fraternity; the broad base of the population wanted no more of such domination. Canadians, generally, however, had not been aware that such a situation even existed. Now, thanks to his intervention, they were.

During his trip, de Gaulle continued, he had developed three broad themes: Quebec was a segment of the French people; it had to take its destiny in hand; France had shown a deplorable lack of interest in French Canada for two hundred years. On the last point, the monarchy had been weak at the time that New France had been abandoned. The élite and administrators had returned to France. Only the "*populo*"— the lowest class—stayed on. Since then they had grown from sixty thousand to six million. And they had remained French. In the name of France, he had "taken note of that obvious passion of French Canadians for France." In his public utterances, he had not said "revolt." The French Canadians had to make some arrangements with their neighbours, the Americans and "the English." Both Canada and France had an interest in bringing that about. The arrangements could be based on the principles of freedom and independence. The prerequisite was a state of Quebec, and that was being created. Of course, the government in Ottawa could not let his statements pass unheeded; but it was something France had to do and he had done it. When the Canadian government declared his remarks "unacceptable," he could no longer go to Ottawa; in any case, he had no great desire to do so. Then, there was "the fury of the Anglo-Saxons," as they were hurt to the quick. That the Anglo-Saxon press was furious because attention was drawn to the French fact in Canada was understandable, but that the French press should follow suit was "unbelievable." It had reached the lowest level of degradation, all the more since he had said nothing "disagreable or insulting" for anybody. Indeed, he was the one who felt a legitimate grievance. "They thought I was off my rocker," he grumbled.[52]

De Gaulle finished his explanation to Cabinet by asking every minister to examine what he could do to follow up on the initiative he had taken and to develop Franco-Quebec relations as rapidly and as completely as possible. "When you make a breakthrough," he had already remarked to Alain Peyrefitte in military terminology, "you have to occupy the terrain."[53] He went around the table asking each one what steps he could take. To most of their responses, he replied shortly, so do it!

Following the Cabinet meeting the minister of information, Georges Gorse, called a press conference and presented a statement, which had been vetted personally by de Gaulle, summing up the briefing.[54] All the ministers had rallied behind the president, it began; the Cabinet was "unanimous." Responding to an "indescribable wave of emotions and determination," the general had "made known unequivocally to French Canadians and their government that France intended to assist them in attaining the objectives of liberation that they had set themselves." A declaration published by the federal government declaring unacceptable "the wish that Quebec should be free" made the visit to Ottawa obviously impossible. It was self-evident that France had no ambitions to control or exercise sovereignty over part of Canada; but having "founded, administered, peopled and developed it for a century and a half," and being aware of "the existence and ardent personality of a French community," France could certainly not disinterest itself from the fate of a population "originating in its own people and admirably faithful to its country of origin;" nor could it consider Canada as a foreign country like any other.

In his own remarks, Gorse adopted a somewhat more moderate tone.

The unpleasant reaction of the "Anglo-Saxon press" to the president's action was understandable, he commented, but the Cabinet had "understood less" certain French commentaries. If there had not been "a real and acute problem" in Canada, the general's statement would not have stirred up such "noise and emotions." That problem had changed in nature and scope in recent years, and it was unthinkable that General de Gaulle, being who he was and what he represented, should not take public note of that fact. The whole matter posed "no problem" for Franco-Canadian relations, except that Ottawa, in dealing with France, had to "take account of the reality of a French Canada wishing to take its own destiny in hand and dissatisfied with the present situation." Did the general know, a journalist asked Gorse, that "*Québec libre*" was the slogan of the separatist parties? The word "*libre*"—free—belonged to no one, the minister of information answered; de Gaulle did not have in mind "this or that fraction of Canadian opinion, or this or that precise solution to the Canadian problem." There were "many ways for a people to assert its personality and bring about the conditions for its freedom." But, the questioner persisted, was the word "*libre*" the equivalent to "*indépendance*" in de Gaulle's mind in reference to Quebec? "Not necessarily;" there were forms of independence that did not imply separation; the general did not mean to prescribe a particular solution or "intervene in others' affairs." But was his action not an interference in the affairs of another state? General de Gaulle was "first of all the guest of Quebec," and despite the inadequacies of its status, it had a government, a prime minister and the beginning of an international personality. It had concluded "*ententes*" with France that had "the import of international accords." It maintained a "special delegation" in Paris. At any rate, Premier Johnson had declared himself "satisfied with General de Gaulle's declarations." Would the incident disturb Franco-Canadian relations for a long time? No one wished that. The incident had been "exaggerated" by those people who refused to "get to the bottom of things." What did that expression mean? The official statement answered that question "perfectly."

De Gaulle's first counter-attack against his detractors in France had little apparent effect. *Le Monde* publisher Hubert Beuve-Méry sharpened his criticism.[55] It had been proven long ago that the president suffered from "a pathological hypertrophy of the ego," he wrote, and that his political instincts, often accurate in the beginning, had become distorted through "a considerable overestimation of the role and potential of France and its leader." A powerful movement for emancipation had indeed developed among French Canadians, and it was important to make Ottawa and London realize that nothing less than an equal partnership within a "bi-national state" would meet the situation. But was it necessary for that purpose "to arrive in uniform on a warship, adopt the slogan of the independentist extremists, recall the jubilant atmosphere in Paris when Hitler's troops left the city?" "The bottom of things" was that, in separating, Anglo and French Canadians would play more than ever into the hands of their colossal neighbour, whereas their union, however uncertain, offered French Canadians the best chance to maintain their originality. There were better ways of supporting them than "that outburst," the real basis of which was "a nationalist form of egocentrism, an exasperated form of egocentrism and the jubilation of an old man expert in triggering the cheers of crowds." It was one more indication that the head of state was "an old leader who had become intolerable." De Gaulle lashed back at his tormentors in a television broadcast on August 10. The fact that France, "breaking with the absurd and outdated conformity of self-effacement," took "a truly French position" on matters such as "the unanimous and indescribable will for freedom that the French of Canada demonstrated in the presence of the President of the French Republic," all that "stupefied and filled the apostles of decline with indignation."[56]

After taking the time to assess the situation, François Mitterrand poured salt into the wound at a press conference on August 16.[57] The president had been "ungrateful" towards his predecessors in charging them with abandoning the French Canadians to their fate; Napoleon III, he recalled, had even sent the warship La Capricieuse up the St. Lawrence River in 1855. Even given the special links between Quebec and France, and the justified demand of French Canadians for equal status in their own country, there was reason to question de Gaulle's actions in "interfering in the internal affairs of Canada" and in offering his personal opinion on the institutions and future of the country receiving him. How would he react, Mitterrand wondered aloud, if a foreign dignitary, in France on his invitation, took the liberty of expressing himself in Strasbourg or Rennes on the structures of the French nation? Even for someone with the authority of General de Gaulle, it was hard to argue that what was true in France was not true outside. The "fantasies and abuses of personal power, combined in this instance with a ludicrousness," were export articles that added nothing to the country's renown. "Getting to the bottom of things" did not mean substituting oneself for French Canadians to decide for them the nature of their struggle for their emancipation. De Gaulle's intervention was likely to prejudice the "happy outcome" of their demands. France had the right to take advantage of the special relations with the French-Canadian community; but it must not fawn over the particular traits of Quebec any more than over the *amour-propre* of the French of France, "subjected over the past nine years to the constant pressures of an unsavoury jingoistic demagogy." Nor must those people being invited to become more autonomous be left unaware that France's capacity to provide financial and economic assistance would meet only a small proportion of their needs. "Getting to the bottom of things" also meant assessing honestly the ramifications of the course of action that was being proposed. Would French Canadians be "better equipped to defend their traditions, their language, their cultural and economic future through the creation of an independent State than by enhancing their influence and their rights within the Canadian State?" But in any case, that was their business.

Another question to be asked, Mitterrand continued, was what was the best way of "neutralizing the power of attraction of the United States of America?" Whether of French or British origin, Canadians were "first of all Americans" and responded to reflexes that drew them closer to the other peoples of America. In the circumstances, the dissolution of the "Canadian federal pact" risked being of "greater benefit to the super-powerful neighbour than to the distant and often forgotten relative across the Atlantic." Finally, "getting to the bottom of things" did not mean "playing at being a delayed action Bolivar" by proposing nineteenth century ideals to subjugated peoples, but rather "to speak up for the masses throughout the world who continue to be exploited by the coalition of political and economic forces that the General never thought of challenging."

In contrast to the language being used in France, the Canadian government's reaction was mild, and even conciliatory. Jules Léger had stayed on in Canada after de Gaulle's departure and, in the discussions on what to do next, had been able to win support for his view that time and the general's advancing years were the government's best allies. The largely negative reaction in France to his "escapade" was also seen as a sign that there was little support for a policy in favour of Quebec independence. Léger was even prepared to give de Gaulle the benefit of the doubt on his real intentions, recalling that at Dorval airport before boarding the plane, de Gaulle had shaken his hand and said, "*Au revoir, Monsieur l'Ambassadeur.*" At least, someone remarked, he had not said *adieu.* Thus, when word was received in Ottawa that a statement by the French Cabinet was to be issued, the main concern was that it should not trigger another wave of indignation in English Canada and, in turn, provoke a counter-reaction in French Canada. To the relief of Pearson, Martin and the other "moderates" in the Cabinet, that statement broke no new ground, and in Gorse's remarks to the press, there were even grounds for reassurance. At a special brief Cabinet meeting, Paul Martin urged a minimal, or even no, reaction. A short statement was approved, declaring that since the government had already made its position clear "on the unacceptability of any outside interference in Canadian affairs," it had "nothing to add." One minister, Pierre Trudeau (appointed to the Justice portfolio a short time earlier), could not resist going a bit further. He commented to the press that he found the French communiqué "*marrant*"—a joke. For the French Cabinet to declare itself in agreement that the British North America Act, 1867, had not ensured Quebecers of liberty, equality and fraternity was "ridiculous." It was as if the Canadian government were to declare that the current French constitution— "the seventeenth in one hundred and seventy years"—was unjust towards the Basque country, Brittany and St. Pierre and Miquelon. What would be the French reaction, Trudeau wondered, if someone visiting France were to shout "Brittany to the Bretons?"

In Quebec, Daniel Johnson, after seeing de Gaulle off, had also turned his attention to minimizing the damage of the vivat. "It's a pity that happened," he confided to a friend, "As early as Trois-Rivières I felt something would happen. I saw the General becoming impassioned and I said to myself: this day won't pass without a fuss."[58] "It was time he took the plane," he confided to Jean-Paul Cardinal, one of his closest advisers.[59] Still, the premier reflected, the name Quebec had made headlines around the world and attention had been drawn to the dissatisfaction he and others felt with the current constitutional arrangements. Even if things had gotten somewhat out of hand, there existed the possibility of using de Gaulle's visit, and relations with France in general, to improve the situation. He also had to come to the defence of a man who had crossed the Atlantic to demonstrate his support and affection for French Canadians, whatever he chose to call them. And on the purely political plane, he could use the incident to establish himself as the pre-eminent Quebec nationalist, undercutting not only the Liberals but the separatists as well.[60]

For three days, Johnson and opposition leader Lesage, who was still more appalled by de Gaulle's intervention, played a waiting game to see what the other would say. Both party caucuses were divided; public opinion in Quebec appeared to be strongly negative with regard to de Gaulle's adoption of the separatist slogan. Lesage broke the silence first. On July 28, he chaired a long and stormy Liberal caucus meeting. Some strong federalists were prepared to condemn the intervention publicly; a few were delighted with it. One new member of the Legislature, François Aquin, first elected the previous year, had already taken a public position in de Gaulle's defence. It was assumed that René Lévesque and Yves Michaud, another newcomer, would follow suit. Lesage had two objectives: to reject de Gaulle's encouragement of separatism and to place the blame for what had happened on his political opponent. Johnson had been at fault in allowing the stage to be set so carefully for such an unfortunate incident, he told the caucus, and in allowing Quebec officials to engage in a guerrilla campaign to minimize the federal role during the general's visit. The president had also been inadequately briefed on local conditions, including the connotations of the words "*Québec libre.*" Lesage's plan was to have the caucus express support for the federal reaction as normal under the circumstances and to endorse the position taken by Mayor Drapeau in his luncheon speech. The Liberal caucus meeting was long and difficult. Always concerned to maintain team unity, Lesage tried hard to persuade Aquin to rally to the majority view. Finally, Bernard Pinard, one of his closest friends, sent him a note saying that the young member had finally revealed his true colours: he was a separatist.

Compromise proved impossible; the opposition leader resigned himself to lopping off the branch for the sake of the tree. The other members approved a text which Lesage sent to the press corps. Its first words were in praise of de Gaulle, whose "unforgettable" visit had "warmed the hearts" of the millions of descendants of the first French settlers. The general would certainly have noted how "deeply rooted in the Canadian soil" they were, and how well they had developed their French heritage, that they had defended alone until recently. They had added to that heritage a series of economic, industrial, social and political accomplishments of which they were proud. As a result, while France was still their mother country, and they were happy about that, their homeland was Canada. Unfortunately, because of the "unbelievable incompetence" of the premier and his thirst for publicity, the general's visit had left a legacy of "serious, probably tragic, problems." What should have been an important step forward for Quebec had been turned into "deep annoyance" on the part of a majority of citizens, "increasing concern" of future investors and "a regrettable anti-Quebec feeling" in the rest of Canada. What would have happened if de Gaulle had arrived while the Liberals were in power? He would have been received with "the same warmth, the same joy, but he would not have been misled concerning the true goals of Quebec, that is, special status within Canada" where French Canadians had the right to fully develop their culture, language and style of life, and realize their economic ambitions. Instead, Johnson and his government not only bore the heavy responsibility of having badly advised the "illustrious visitor," but, following the general's "very controversial declaration," had done nothing to redress the situation. Was or was not the *Union Nationale* separatist? In any case, in its relations with France, as with the rest of Canada, its policies were a failure.

Later in the day, Johnson followed with his own statement. While he did not convene his party caucus, he met with his Cabinet and found several of his ministers very critical of the general's action. The minister of finance, Paul Dozois, had been holidaying in Spain when the incident occurred, and could hardly believe the press reports. The minister of education, Jean-Jacques Bertrand, and the minister of lands and forests, Claude Gosselin, were also upset over the encouragement de Gaulle had given to the separatists. Still, with the government under attack over the matter, they all rallied and approved a characteristically nuanced statement prepared by the premier. "Courageous and lucid," it read. President de Gaulle had indeed "got to the bottom of things." Perceiving, as few before him had done, the true spirit behind the renewal of Quebec, he had spoken of "emancipation, of Quebec taking its destiny in hand, of *Québec libre.*" In his own words, he had expressed ideas that had been put forward many times by recent Quebec governments. He had paid tribute to the growing conviction of the Quebec people that it was "free to choose its own destiny" and that, like all other peoples, it had "the unquestionable right to self-determination."

The publisher of *Le Devoir*, Claude Ryan, whose position and personal prestige made him the Quebec counterpart of Hubert Beuve-Méry, was more critical of Lesage's than of Johnson's statement.[61] The Liberal leader, he declared, had spoken more as a politician than a statesman. Still, he had drawn attention to the "excessive propaganda and reprehensible scenarios" connected with the general's visit. The occasion had also been marred by "certain strong language condemned by basic international good behaviour." Nevertheless, the statements of the two party leaders had significant common traits, for instance, the assertion of the distinctive, original character of Quebec, its right to determine its own future, the necessity for new constitutional arrangements and the desirability of developing further its relations with France. If de Gaulle's visit had made English Canada more conscious of the urgent necessity for constitutional review and political parties more prepared to agree on a common approach to that subject, then a major step would have been taken in the quest for a lasting "Canadian peace." There was only one way to resolve "the uneasiness stirred up, or more exactly, revealed" by de Gaulle's presence in Quebec, and that was to tackle the roots of the problem immediately.

A public opinion poll taken in late July and early August indicated that while sixty per cent of Quebecers deplored de Gaulle's intervention, forty per cent approved of it.[62] Most did not take it very seriously; many even enjoyed the implicit nose-thumbing at the "*Anglais.*" And after so many years of being ignored, the worldwide notoriety was enjoyable. On August 1, François Aquin announced his decision to leave the Liberal party; a few officials, but no other members of the Legislature, followed him. René Lévesque explained that the incident was not sufficient reason to take such an important step.[63] At the same time, he denounced "the hysteria triggered off by the anglophone press," which "leaped on four words like a mad pack" and seized the opportunity to indulge in "a genuine crisis of francophobia accompanied by the basest insults."[64]

When the Quebec Legislature met on August 3, Aquin made his resignation official.[65] Charles de Gaulle, he declared, had understood "the deep aspirations of the Quebec people." He had grasped "the essence of the drama" experienced by French Canadians, of being "poor in a rich country, second-class citizens in their own country, forced to work in the language of their masters, foreigners on their own soil." In response to the cry *"Vive le Québec libre,"* "the soul of a whole oppressed people reverberated spontaneously" and the word "liberty," that some people had not even dared to murmur previously, had been "exorcised." On that day, the president had revealed Quebec to many Quebecers and Quebecers to the world. Aquin ended his eloquent speech by repeating the words *"Vive le Québec libre."*

Speaking next, Premier Johnson declared that the government was happy to have invited the general, who had received "a triumphal, unprecedented and unequivocal welcome." He deplored all the more that, "under extremist pressures," the Canadian government had felt obliged to make a statement forcing him to return to France without passing through Ottawa. The population would never forget that, "in words touching the heart of all Quebecers," the president had "raised the problem of the distinctive identity of Quebec and its immense effort of self-assertion." While some Canadians still found that fact difficult to accept, Quebec had never been "a province like the others;" now the whole world knew it was true. As a result of the "historic moments" they had lived through, two centuries of isolation were ended and the "vital link" with France definitely established. New perspectives were opening up for the people of Quebec. That was the reality that General de Gaulle "saw and expressed eloquently." As for the government, it would pursue its "fundamental objective," the adoption of a new constitution "establishing the legal and political recognition of the French-Canadian nation and conferring on Quebec, within the limits of interdependence that characterized the period, all the constitutional authority necessary for the full development of its identity." It was for that purpose that it had accepted "eagerly," the previous January, an invitation by the premier of Ontario to attend a conference on the theme "Confederation for Tomorrow."

On August 12, the results of a province-wide survey carried out by

CROP, a highly reliable public opinion polling firm, revealed that a majority of the population now approved of both the general's visit and his espousal of the cry "*Vive le Québec libre.*" However, the respondents interpreted the vivat, not as an invitation to separate, but rather to "enhance the measure of freedom that Quebec already possesses within Canada."[66] The federal government's reaction was considered "too harsh;" Johnson's position was approved "moderately," Lesage's was the least popular. Jean Drapeau's luncheon speech was the most popular of all. Seizing the occasion, Johnson rose in the Legislature as soon as the findings were released to propose a motion of thanks to General de Gaulle for visiting Quebec; the motion also blamed the federal government's "intrusion" for his inability to complete the trip.[67] Accepting the political reality, Jean Lesage endorsed the proposal and added an expression of "deep gratitude." "Has he become a separatist?" a *Union Nationale* member interjected from across the floor. The Liberals were "very happy" with the reception the population had given the general, the opposition leader continued; he deserved it for all he had done and said on behalf of Quebec. Quebecers also appreciated his assurances that he would continue to take "a very special interest in French Canada, particularly in Quebec."

In early September, Paul Martin obtained Cabinet approval to send a message to Couve de Murville, addressing him as "dear colleague and friend" and expressing his sincerest regrets that the general's visit had been cut short. The dust having now settled, he suggested that it was time to resume discreetly the exchanges that had been so useful to their two countries in the past. He would be attending the session of the General Assembly of the United Nations in New York later in the month and suggested that they meet. The French foreign minister could be assured that the Canadian government would continue to cooperate in developing Franco-Canadian relations on the basis of friendship and mutual respect. He would welcome information from Couve de Murville on the French government's position.

In the usual August political lull on both sides of the Atlantic, the general's sensational cry gradually faded from public attention except as a subject of cocktail conversation. The most intriguing question remained: what had he really meant by his message from the balcony of the Montreal Hôtel de Ville? True to form, de Gaulle had succeeded in cloaking it in an aura of mystery and uncertainty. Even his Cabinet ministers and others close to him were divided over whether he had intended to throw his support behind the Quebec independence movement or whether he had been carried away by the enthusiastic reception he had received throughout the day.

The analogy with his cry of "*Vive l'Algérie française*" came readily to mind. Shortly after returning to power in 1958, he had visited the strife-torn colony, and faced with a massive crowd composed largely of "*pieds noirs*" and military personnel shouting "*Vive l'Algérie française*," or, in other words, keep Algeria French. He had responded: "*Je vous ai compris*"—I have understood you. Interpreting the words as an indication of his support for the preservation of the colony, his audience broke into frenetic cheers. In fact, with his love for and feeling of communion with the masses, he had merely responded by saying what they wanted to hear, but characteristically, he had used words capable of several interpretations. In his memoirs, he recorded later, "I threw out the words, apparently spontaneously in form but basically well calculated, with the intention of evoking enthusiasm without allowing them to commit me further than I had resolved to go."[68] Two days later, at Mostaganem, he did pronounce the words, "*Vive l'Algérie française*." He was at the end of an exhausting schedule of speeches and meetings during which that slogan, and the arguments behind it, had been drummed continually into his consciousness. What was different at Mostaganem was that it was the Arabs who were chanting the slogan. Obviously tired but moved by the reception he was given everywhere, particularly by the Arabs, he shouted back the words he had been resisting since his arrival. "At the moment of his peroration," recalls Michel Droit, a veteran French correspondent who was following the tour, "when the General cried '*Vive l'Algérie*', his voice remained suspended for a fraction of a second, as if seeking an adjective," then let the word '*française*' escape his lips."[69] Afterward, Droit had the impression, in observing de Gaulle's face from a distance of five or six meters, that he was "hardly satisfied" with his choice of words, that they had "gone beyond his thoughts" and that he was "probably annoyed with himself for having allowed himself to be taken in." Later, de Gaulle himself recounted to journalist J.-R. Tournoux, "I saw a surge of real fraternal feelings....I didn't want to miss any chance. It was superficial."[70] He "always knew and had decided that it would be necessary to give Algeria its independence," he told another journalist, André Passeron.[71] All the rest was strategy. In the case of a less complex person, such an explanation would suffice. However, it does not take into account the affective side of de Gaulle's character and the likelihood that his emotions would assert themselves when he sensed a close rapport with a crowd, particularly if he was tired. The general could not admit such a possibility; to do so would have been tantamount to a confession of weakness or bad judgment. Nevertheless, it remains a feasible explanation.

Among the French ministers, Prime Minister Pompidou appears not to have dwelt on the question whether the Quebec outburst was intended or accidental; for him, it was essentially a further problem on his agenda. For Couve de Murville, it was a mistake, but not premeditated.[72] The general had been profoundly touched by the "indescribable welcome" he had received, the foreign minister recalled later in his memoirs.[73] Quebecers "found and acclaimed themselves through France" as they recalled their common origin. "It was all that which de Gaulle saluted in Montreal with his cry in that emotion-laden and unforgettable day,...caring little if he was using the slogan of the separatists." Once it was done, he had no regrets and commented: "It will probably be useful."[74] One of de Gaulle's oldest and most loyal associates, Roger Frey, then minister of the interior, shared Couve de Murville's view.[75] The vivat was an "instinctive reflex," he commented later, "a cry from the heart." Like many other Frenchmen, the general had strong positive feelings toward French Canadians who had maintained the old French language, and so he appreciated all the more the reception they gave him. To consolidate the new relationship, and as the personification of France, he wanted to cancel out the abandonment of 1763. Another long-time companion-in-arms, Louis Joxe, reached the same conclusion. Beneath the intellectualizing and gruffness, de Gaulle was an affective, even sentimental individual— traits that occasionally led him into inconsistencies with his broader policies.[76] He was quite capable of going too far in order to please a crowd that touched his emotions. He also had a personal need to go beyond the position of others, and even of his own declared policy. In the case of Quebec, he was influenced as well by his experience with decolonization, which led him to feel that independence movements were irreversible and that others had to accommodate to them as best they could.

Other ministers were inclined to feel that the vivat had been carefully calculated and executed. The minister of information, Georges Gorse, accepted that interpretation and prepared the government's public position accordingly.[77] Michel Debré accepted de Gaulle's explanation, given to him in a private conversation a week after the event, that he wanted to challenge French Canadians to carry their thinking and their actions to their logical conclusion, that is, to independence, which he had already decided was desirable.[78] The general felt that they were too hesitant to do so. In that sense, his analogy to the liberation of France in 1944 was intentional and Pearson's interpretation of it was accurate.

Asked later if the general had realized that "*Vive le Québec libre*" was the slogan of the independentists, Debré replied that he should have known, and most likely did. Minister of Defence Pierre Messmer also accepted the view that the vivat was deliberate and well prepared.[79] De Gaulle, he commented, "rarely went beyond his thoughts and intentions." On the other hand, if, in defending his action on his return to France, he indicated that it was premeditated, this did not necessarily mean that in fact it was: "The General never retreated, he advanced." Edgar Faure had a similar reaction. De Gaulle did not allow himself to be carried away, he told Raymond Tournoux.[80] On the other hand, he had probably not foreseen the events of July 25. Faced suddenly with an unexpected situation, he reacted true to form. Afterward, he adopted an intransigent position.

The younger ministers were inclined to accept the president's actions uncritically. The secretary of state for development cooperation, Jean Charbonnel, a "pure" Gaullist and the youngest man in the Cabinet, was taken completely by surprise, but rallied loyally and set to work to help prepare the president's defence.[81] André Bettencourt, secretary of state for foreign affairs in the summer of 1967, was similarly uncritical.[82] Did the general go too far? he was asked. "De Gaulle always wanted to go further [than others] without going too far." A third member of the younger generation, Yves Guëna, asked an old friend, Roger Varus, an official who had accompanied the president, the question on everyone's mind, "Was it intentional?" "Without a doubt," he was told.[83] He needed no further confirmation.

Finally, the views of two of de Gaulle's ministers, who were well aware of his strengths and his foibles, deserve special attention. Maurice Schumann had known de Gaulle since 1940 in London, but his admiration had not obscured his judgment. The vivat in Montreal had reminded him of the one in Mostaganem, he commented; neither was deliberate but was provoked by a sympathetic crowd.[84] Nor were they justified, since they created expectations that could not be fulfilled. In short, they had been mistakes. Olivier Guichard, who had worked closely with de Gaulle since 1946, has written that the vivat "*Vive le Québec libre*" was, on the contrary, "a carefully deliberate provocation."[85] The general had a sense of destiny, he explains, and "it's a sense that gets worse with age." De Gaulle recognized that France could not achieve all the ambitions he had for it, but he felt that he alone could orient it in the right direction. That is what he had tried to do in Quebec.[86] Guichard, too, judged it a mistake.

Opinion was also divided among the French officials on the meaning of de Gaulle's dramatic gesture. For Robert Bordaz, Jean-Daniel Jurgensen and Captain Flohic, all ardent pro-separatists, the decision to launch the cry "*Vive le Québec libre*" may well have been taken on the spot, but in any event it was right, proper, and in keeping with the general's thinking. Bordaz described de Gaulle later as "an extraordinary popular agitator" who used that talent to promote causes in which he believed.[87] In that instance, his cause was the independence of Quebec, not necessarily in the fullest sense of the word—that was not realistic—but within a common market arrangement among completely sovereign entities. The model that de Gaulle had in mind was the "*Europe des patries*," or association of independent homelands, that he prescribed for Europe. Since the general considered Quebec to be "a piece of France," there was no question of impropriety in promoting that goal. As for the term "liberation," he had chosen it to express the desirability of removing the "English yoke" from the necks of "an oppressed people." Accordingly, it was an error to see the United States as his principal target; the English Canadians were the oppressors. At any rate, the Americans would readily accommodate the independence of Quebec.

In general, Jurgensen shared that interpretation.[88] In his view, de Gaulle did not know in advance what he would do to achieve his goal of furthering Quebec independence, nor did he know that the slogan he espoused was that of the RIN. As a rider needs a horse, so the general needed the right situation to produce the effect he desired. Sensing the "temperature" of the crowd in front of Montreal City Hall, he hurled out his message at the right moment, and "a whole people, touched in their deeper instincts, still draw on it for support in fulfilling their desire to be themselves."[89] In that sense, de Gaulle proved to be, at a decisive moment, and just as he had intended, "the catalyst of an evolution, of a revolution." Aide-de-camp Flohic's interpretation was not significantly different. Well before the visit was undertaken, he wished ardently to see the general help French Canadians divest themselves of their inferiority complex "cultivated by the English Canadians" to maintain their dominant situation.[90] The notion of liberation was already implicit in the Quebec City speech. The question was asked frequently whether de Gaulle, whose vision without very strong eyeglasses was very restricted, was able to see the "*Québec libre*" signs along his route from Quebec City to Montreal. He was capable of doing so, Flohic insists. As to the allegation that he was tired when he arrived in Montreal and thus had less self-control, Flohic argues that, although seventy-six, de Gaulle was still a strong man and contact with crowds bolstered his strength rather than sapping it. While there was the usual cultivated ambiguity in the general's historic utterance, there was none in Flohic's mind: de Gaulle threw the support of France behind French Canada's liberation and independence.

Some of de Gaulle's senior staff members have presented a more balanced and credible view. When the general met with Lesage, Gilbert Pérol has explained, he was impressed by his detailed knowledge of the various subjects they had discussed, but he did not find him a man of vision, at least of nationalist vision.[91] Johnson, on the other hand, struck him as a man capable of "taking in hand" the destiny of Quebec. In fact, the general envisaged him playing the same role as he, himself, was playing in the resurrection of France. He also had considerable esteem for Pearson, but he did not see him as a sufficient "motive force" to bring about the changes within Canada that were necessary to meet French Canadians' aspirations. When de Gaulle took the decision to make the trip, he told Pérol that, since he was old, it was his last opportunity; he had to go and leave a "touchstone" for the future. While the expression "*Québec libre*" did not appear in any of the texts he produced aboard the *Colbert*, the idea was subjacent.[92] It was reflected in the speech at the Chateau Frontenac in such expressions as "*affranchissement*"—emancipation—and "*maîtres d'eux-mêmes*"— masters of their own destiny. In short, the formula itself was not premeditated, but its meaning certainly was. As it turned out, the words were presented to the general along the route, but he did not identify them with a particular party. "*Libre*" was a common term in the French political vocabulary, especially in such "revolutionary" situations. When the Montreal crowd shouted the slogan in response to his other vivats, he reflected an instant, then thought "*tant pis*"—so be it—and threw it back. Afterwards, he could not back down. Had it not been for Pearson's statement and the fuss made by the media, he would have tried to minimize the matter as "a passing incident" of no great consequence. However, that reaction, and even more the criticism in France, forced him to defend himself. Did de Gaulle feel later that he had made a mistake? He was by nature a realist, even a pessimist. And he was not a democrat; he made no assumption that the population knew what was best. A leader could only do what he knew was best and take the consequences.

Etienne Burin des Roziers agrees. De Gaulle had reflected carefully before deciding to make the trip, the former secretary general of the Elysée told participants in a colloquium at the Institut Charles de Gaulle in 1980.[93] He realized that it would have historic significance. One problem he faced was to reconcile two principles he believed in: non-intervention by one state in another's internal affairs, and the right, which he had proclaimed solemnly at Solferino, Italy, in 1959, of all peoples to self-determination "providing they have the will and the capability to do so."[94] Another problem was to reconcile his desire, particularly in view of Canada's support of France during the two world wars, not to offend the federal government, and his responsibility to respond to the call for assistance by a branch of the French people. On both counts, de Gaulle concluded that the second consideration had priority. Unlike some French possessions such as Martinique and Guadeloupe, for which independence would be merely fictitious, Quebec did meet the dual criteria he set out at Solferino: it was capable of leading an independent existence, and it had the will, as evidenced by its appeal to France for help in achieving it. As for the principle of non-interference, he reasoned that he could not be accused of initiating the disintegration of Canada; that was already happening. Burin des Roziers confirmed that the words "*Vive le Québec libre*" did not figure in any of the prepared speeches and that the general's use of them at the Montreal Hôtel de Ville was not premeditated. Nor did Burin des Roziers accord much importance to the the use of the word "liberation," which, he pointed out, could well have referred merely to the emotional atmosphere throughout the day and which had touched him deeply.* Certainly, the general saw in the reinvigorated Quebec "the gripping demonstration of the permanence of the French people,...[and] the potency of the sap of the old tree from which the magnificent branch had become detached two centuries earlier."[95] With his life-long preoccupation with the grandeur of France, he sensed, as in 1944, "to the depths of his soul the revenge of [France's] destiny over history." However, having "taken note" in the name of France (through his controversial vivat) of the historic rebirth of Quebecers' national consciousness, he felt that the next step was up to them. His mission thus accomplished, he might not have taken the matter much further, but in the face of domestic criticism, he was stung into taking an even stronger position and, in so doing, strengthened his conviction that he had been right in his actions in Quebec.

Alain Plantey, then another member of the Elysée staff, has a more down-to-earth but not incompatible explanation.[96] De Gaulle was very well informed on the subject of Quebec, and even of the activities of Rossillon and other "Quebec boys." He also recognized that he was far from neutral in the debate over Quebec's future. A sensitive man with a sense of destiny and a taste for action, he was naturally inclined to intervene in some way. In the face of the Canadian government's attempts to circumscribe his visit, he knew he would be taking a "calculated risk" that things would not go well. But, by nature, he reacted negatively to constraints, and particularly to risks. In seeking to understand de Gaulle's conduct, Plantey argues, such considerations are more important than either the spontaneity generated during the two days prior to the balcony speech, or the evident attempts of French Canadians to use him for their own purposes. His primary objective was to "burst the abcess of the Canadian problem" and accelerate a solution in accordance with his own perceptions of it. For Plantey, as well as for Pérol and Burin des Roziers, the words "*Vive le Québec libre*" reflected these perceptions.

As further evidence of his intentions, a few quotations from de

* When he launched the *Rassemblement du Peuple français* in 1947 in a bid to return to power by popular demand, de Gaulle compared the inaugural meeting at Strasbourg to the beginning of the Resistance after 1940. The remark was considered merely oratorical licence.

Gaulle himself are revealing. Bernard Dorin, the only one of the "Quebec boys" to accompany him to Quebec, has recounted a conversation he had with the general in the autumn of 1967.[97] "When I had to take a position," de Gaulle recalled, "I saw in front of me a scale with two dishes. In one there were the diplomats...and...also...the Anglo-Saxons, and anyway, they don't like me. In the other dish there was the destiny of a whole people....Between the [predictable] insignificant agitation and the destiny of a people, there were no grounds for hesitation: the plate on the right was much heavier than the one on the left." The general expressed the hope that, in Dorin's words, "that cry would enable Quebec to save ten years in its emancipation process." René de Saint-Légier has recounted a similar comment during a conversation in the airplane on the return trip from Quebec.[98] What had happened, de Gaulle told him, was "a historical phenomenon that was perhaps foreseeable but it took a form that only the situation itself could determine. Of course, like many others I could have got away with a few polite remarks or diplomatic acrobatics, but when one is General de Gaulle, one does not have recourse to such expedients. What I did, I had to do." There remained, in the event of Quebec's self-determination, the general added, the problem of Canada as a whole. But what kind of Canada? That too was something for Quebecers to determine and then to negotiate with their "English neighbours" in order to preserve "a Canada."

Writing in the inter-war years, de Gaulle had stressed the importance of erecting an aura of mystery around a leader, of cultivating a feeling of uncertainty as to his views and intentions. With regard to his foray in Quebec, he had been true once again to that dictum. Following his dramatic action, there was no consensus. As a result, there was no agreement on the part of friends or foes on how to react to them. Two decades later, what does the evidence suggest? First of all, in making the trip, de Gaulle was responding to what he considered to be a request from French Canadians for support in their quest for self-determination. Highly sensitive to the charge that France had abandoned them in a shameful manner, he felt that he had to correct, or atone for, a historical wrong. He was not certain how far Quebecers wished to go on the path towards independence, but, believing that the process, once started, was irresistible, he was prepared to challenge them to go all the way. While he was not certain that Daniel Johnson was prepared to carry his slogan, "Equality or Independence," to its logical conclusion, de Gaulle felt that he was the first Quebec premier to present the alternatives clearly, and so he was a man with whom one could work. Was de Gaulle also thinking of France's national interests, and particularly of an independent Quebec as a French foothold in North America? Certainly such a prospect fitted into his vision of

France as a resurrected world power, and the leader of a community based on the French language and culture (and, eventually, all Latin-based cultures). That was not, however, his immediate concern. Nor was he motivated particularly by his alleged anti-American sentiments, although his distrust of the Anglo-Saxons was part of his mind-set. When he started out on his voyage, his strategy was, to use one of his favourite expressions, "to throw a stone into the pond" and watch the frogs scatter in every direction; in other words, to create a crisis and see what would happen. If Johnson and other Quebec leaders were serious about wanting a new deal with the rest of Canada, they would take advantage of the situation. He would have given them the opportunity they were calling for, and France would have played its historic role.

What about the cry "*Vive le Québec libre?*" It was not premeditated. Although he himself was highly intelligent and a rigorous thinker, de Gaulle believed that the masses had to be led by emotions and dreams, and he had great confidence in his ability to do that. While he knew the contents of the message he wanted to deliver, he had not identified the words or the occasion before he arrived. But he was certain that they would present themselves to him. They did, in the form of the RIN banners and the shouts from the crowd before Montreal City Hall. He had some doubts whether the situation was completely right, but had to seize the moment or appear to falter, or even worse, to lack courage. He had no choice but to go forward and pronounce the words. Did he know they were the slogan of the separatists? Probably, but he did not consider they had a monopoly on them. Was he carried away by his emotions? Possibly, just as in Mostaganem. After the event, was he satisfied with what he had done? Following an initial hesitation, yes; although he would have handled the rest of his stay in Canada differently if he had had a choice. Just as he had done when he announced France's withdrawal from NATO the previous year, he would have softened the blow to Ottawa by assurances that he did not seek the break-up of Canada, and then would have expressed the hope that French and English Canadians could work out new arrangements to enable their harmonious and fruitful coexistence. He would have offered France's assistance in making that possible. In short, was he favourable to the independence of Quebec? Yes, in some kind of common market or sovereignty-association relationship with the rest of Canada. And that was the objective he crossed the Atlantic to promote.

What was the immediate impact? The Quebec government, that he had come to support and spur on, was embarrassed and drew back from the course he proposed. The Canadian government stiffened its resolve that such an outcome must never occur and found strong public support for that position. The principal beneficiaries were the separatists. A few weeks earlier, Pierre Bourgault and his small band had been very discouraged at the success of the Confederation celebrations and of Expo '67, which was an integral part of them. They had devised the strategy of waving placards and shouting slogans along de Gaulle's route more to signal their own existence than in expectations of winning his support. They had underestimated their own influence. By challenging him to add "*Vive le Québec libre*" to his string of vivats, they had precipitated a political crisis, dampened enthusiasm for the Confederation celebrations, and given their movement a new lease on life. De Gaulle gave the RIN a new slogan, "*Vive le Québec libre. De Gaulle le dit.*"

Chapter 12

Attacks and Counter-Attacks

In France, General de Gaulle's popularity dropped by ten per cent between June and August 1967, a change evidently related to his Quebec adventure. Forty-five per cent of Frenchmen disapproved of his intervention. Obviously he had violated a basic tenet of his political strategy, that of using foreign policy to reinforce domestic unity. Even worse, the bond between him and the masses, the basis of his power, had been weakened. His opponents, increasingly watchful for signs that his régime was beginning to decline, continued to exploit the issue. De Gaulle remained defiant. Shortly after his return, he had ordered Minister of Education Alain Peyrefitte to go to Quebec within the month and to sign some agreements for educational and cultural cooperation.[1] Nothing had been prepared, Peyrefitte objected, and as usual in the month of August, practically everyone in France was on holiday. "*Débrouillez-vous*"—find a way—the president responded vehemently, "the French in Canada" had become aware that something important was happening; there had to be an appropriate follow-up to ensure that the developments behind which he had thrown his support became irreversible. Other ministers received similar instructions.[2]

On August 23, Couve de Murville outlined to Cabinet the state of Franco-Quebec cooperation in education, culture, economic and financial cooperation. De Gaulle declared that the list must be greatly expanded. "Sentimentally and politically," he told the ministers, "the French fact is now on the table both on the spot and in France."[3] The situation was almost unique in the world, he declared, "a country of which part of the people is somewhere else." French Canadians had allowed themselves to be excluded from progress. They now recognized that fact and wanted to advance more rapidly, so they were turning to France. It could not treat them as it did the other countries with which it had programmes of cooperation. A beginning had been made with cultural assistance. They also had to be helped to develop their public service, for instance, by establishing an equivalent of the *Ecole nationale d'administration*. Economically, France had "no real relations" with them; these, too, had to be developed. It would be necessary as well to contribute on a regular basis to their capital financing and to create with them a form of "economic osmosis." Other sectors to be developed were atomic energy, electronics, computers, space flights. Quebecers were anxious to find an alternative to the American-owned Space Agency; they should be brought into France's programmes. Maurice Schumann, minister responsible for scientific research, proposed to examine with them the possibilities of using the telecommunications satellite *Symphonie* still in the planning stage. Edgar Faure made a similar proposal concerning agronomic research. De Gaulle instructed Couve de Murville to present a detailed programme of activities in September, complete with a statement of costs.

There is some uncertainty about whether de Gaulle instructed his ministers specifically to ignore the federal government and to fly directly to Quebec without going to Ottawa first. Later, some did not recall his doing so. Yet, they all acted on that assumption. Peyrefitte arrived first, on September 10, officially to attend the *Seconde Biennale de la langue française* in Quebec City. He was unaware that Daniel Johnson's heart was again performing erratically and that his brother, cardiologist Réginald Johnson, had tried to convince him to enter hospital three days earlier. The premier had refused because of his heavy schedule, but more important, because of his constant concern to keep his illness secret. He did agree to move into a suite at the Hôtel Bonaventure in Montreal, a short drive from the Hôtel-Dieu hospital. It was there that, clad in his dressing gown, he received the French minister. Later in the evening, he dressed and they went to dinner in a nearby restaurant.[4] Peyrefitte handed him a personal letter that de Gaulle had signed in Cracow, Poland, on September 8, during a state visit to that country.[5] "The great national operation you are engaged in seems now to be going well," it read. "The appearance with complete clarity of the French fact in Canada" was henceforth an accomplished fact, and accordingly, "some solutions" were necessary. There could hardly be any doubt that the future developments would lead to "a Quebec enjoying self-determination in every respect." As for relations with France, it was time to "intensify" what had already been started. The French government would be "in a position shortly to make specific proposals in response to yours" in the financial, economic, scientific and technical fields. Peyrefitte would indicate what he was ready to do immediately, and it was "rather considerable," in the fields of education and culture. As for himself, de Gaulle concluded: "Let me repeat that I was touched to the depths of my soul by the welcome Quebec gave me and [also tell you] how much satisfaction I received from our meeting and our conversations on French-Canadian soil following those in Paris."

It was not the kind of message likely to improve Johnson's delicate health. He had succeeded in getting the domestic political scene more or less under control, but the continuing controversy in France was always in danger of igniting it again. In the words of his biographer, Pierre Godin, "the General's zeal was beginning to disturb, if not upset, the Johnsonian strategy whose slow and tortuous evolution bore the marks of his Norman cunning, his precarious health and his desire not to burn his bridges with Ottawa. He was ready to go very far to achieve equality, but in short steps and avoiding, if possible, the break-up of Confederation."[6] For the moment, the premier was placing his bets on the Confederation for Tomorrow conference to be held in Toronto in November, and he needed the goodwill of the other premiers to achieve his goal of constitutional change. For that, he had to convince them of his desire to keep Quebec within Canada. The very mention of de Gaulle could make that task more difficult. The prospect that his letter might become public knowledge was genuinely alarming. At best, Johnson protested, de Gaulle's espousal of Quebec sovereignty was "very premature."[7] He was "moving too fast. It was a time for temporizing, not for adventurism."

When Peyrefitte enumerated the twenty-five proposals that he had brought along, Johnson nodded approvingly until one triggered an alarm button. Meetings of the heads of government every six months? That meant receiving de Gaulle in Quebec every year! In Peyrefitte's words, the thought "terrified" him.[8] Through his visit, de Gaulle had already succeeded in advancing Quebec's interests by twenty years as far as relations with the rest of Canada were concerned, Johnson told the French minister; the next steps had to be carefully considered. They would discuss the whole matter on his next trip to Paris. Beginning to grasp the situation, Peyrefitte did not insist. A subsequent meeting with Jean-Jacques Bertrand, the minister of education, who made no secret of his opposition to separatism, confirmed Peyrefitte's growing impression that the general had gotten ahead of himself. Before leaving Quebec, he returned to the Bonaventure Hotel for another long conversation with Johnson, and to sign a hastily arranged cooperation agreement with him. It called for the creation of a permanent secretariat, a commission to facilitate youth exchanges, to be based alternately in Paris and Quebec City, and periodic consultations between the ministers of education and economic affairs of the two governments.

The French minister left his adviser, Bernard Dorin, who in fact had drawn up the list of twenty-five proposals, in Quebec to flesh out those that had proven acceptable to Johnson and Bertrand. When he in turn left, the Quebec government entrusted him with the response to de Gaulle's letter, which he was to deliver personally. It was prepared for Johnson's signature by André Patry, who, in light of its contents, must have found the assignment galling. Quebec and France were agreed on "a certain reintegration of French Canada into the francophone universe," it stated.[9] However, the premier had to be realistic. "We have very serious economic problems and my first duty is to take a responsible approach." Patry summed up the letter later as follows, "We are not yet rich enough to plunge towards the objective that you seem to be proposing."[10] When Dorin delivered the letter, he was treated to an exposé of the general's views on Quebec. Personally committed to the province's independence, he found himself in full agreement. After Dorin returned to his own apartment, an officer from the president's military staff appeared with a two-star general's hat. While it was never identified, it was in all probability the one de Gaulle had worn in Quebec, and was intended as a gesture of appreciation for his service to their common cause.

Following close on Peyrefitte's heels, the French minister of sports and youth, François Missoffe, arrived in Quebec on September 26 to sign the agreement, called for in the Peyrefitte-Johnson accord, to establish a system of youth exchanges. As a result, the *Office franco-québécois de la jeunesse* came into existence in early 1968. The two ministers' visits were only the *avant-garde* in a steady stream of official visitors that de Gaulle was determined should become a permanent feature of the relationship.

Peyrefitte's visit had marked the development of another relationship between France and French Canada. In Quebec City, a delegation of three Acadians asked to see him in order to make their own appeal for French assistance. They had brought along a letter to de Gaulle, outlining their special needs. While the general's appearance in Quebec had triggered their action, the thoughts behind it were not new. For many generations, successive Acadian leaders had looked to France for support in their struggle for cultural survival. Their efforts had borne little fruit. A *Comité France-Acadie* had been created, and two French writers had published books on the Acadians, but little tangible aid was forthcoming. Judging from his statements in Quebec, de Gaulle did not even seem to be aware of their existence. To add insult to injury, representatives of French minorities in Italy, Belgium and other parts of the world were invited to the *Biennale de la Langue française*, but the Acadians were ignored. Euclide Daigle, publisher of the only Acadian newspaper, *L'Evangéline*, Adélard Savoie, rector of the new University of Moncton, Dr. Léon Richard and Gilbert Finn from the *Société nationale des Acadiens* decided to try to correct what they perceived as merely the latest in a long chronology of historic injustices.

They found a valuable ally in their enterprise. Philippe Rossillon, one of the members of the "Quebec mafia" in Paris, had not been included, to his great chagrin, in the delegation accompanying the general to Quebec. Nor had he been chosen to accompany Peyrefitte to the *Biennale*; a choice which might have been expected in view of his position with the *Haut Commissariat de la Langue française*. Prime Minister Pompidou, under whose authority he fell, he commented later, probably had him excluded because of his "independentist background."[11] Rossillon, in his own words, had been involved in the preparation of the general's visit and had been partly responsible for making it "more sensational than some people wished;" hence the feeling that he should be kept away from Quebec for a while. A man of private means, Rossillon decided to attend the *Biennale* at his own expense and on the way to visit the Acadians, in whom he had become interested as early as 1956. There are two versions of what happened next. According to Rossillon, whose penchant for hyperbole invites caution, he, himself, "motivated by attachment to Acadia certainly, but also by basic feelings of annoyance and frustration,...provoked that little Gaullist episode." On arrival in Moncton, he introduced himself as the "special and personal envoy of General de Gaulle" and told the Acadian leaders "confidentially" that the president of the French Republic desired to conclude a Franco-Acadian accord. After obtaining their agreement, and drawing up with them a list of Acadian needs, he drafted a letter for their signature. They accepted it and made it their own. The Acadians' version is somewhat different: Euclide Daigle prepared the first draft of the letter to de Gaulle; Rossillon made some stylistic changes to conform to French protocol. Whatever the case, the final product, signed by Dr. Léon Richard, president of the *Société*, was well conceived to touch de Gaulle's sensitive chords. "Descendants of the first French settlers in America," it stated, "we have had a tragic history." Still, "thanks to our own sacrifices and our French obstinacy, thanks also to occasional support from France, our mother country, and Quebec, bastion of French civilization in America," Acadians could envisage a better life. However, they still did not enjoy "all the rights to which a people with a long history have a claim." Accordingly, they were submitting to him a list of "requests and suggestions" for assistance. Among them were proposals for support for the University of Moncton in the form of teaching personnel, scholarships, books and equipment; technical and financial support for the newspaper *L'Evangéline*; help in establishing a delegation general in Paris; a French private school; a *cinébus*; and increased cultural exchanges. "We are placing all our hopes in you," the letter concluded, and assured the general of Acadians' "unfailing attachment to their original home-land."

The Acadian leaders flew to Quebec City, where Rossillon was able to arrange a meeting with Peyrefitte through his friend and ally, Bernard Dorin. They presented their letter to him, and after chatting with them for an hour, he agreed to transmit it to the president. Rossillon was still not prepared to leave matters to chance, or even to a minister's good intentions. When he found, a few days after his return to Paris, that the letter had still not reached the Elysée, he gave a copy to Saint-Légier, who put it on the president's desk. De Gaulle reacted positively; not only should the Acadians be invited to France and have their requests considered seriously, he declared, but he, himself, would host a lunch for them.[12] To complete the cycle, Rossillon—again in his own version of events—was the principal author of the general's reply to the letter. "I know what terrible ordeals the French of Acadia have gone through in the course of their history and how they have overcome them," de Gaulle told his petitioners.[13] With exemplary courage and perseverance, they had "remained faithful to our language, our culture, and consequently, to our destiny." For France, that was "a profound reason for admiration and pride." Clearly, "the reciprocal feelings between the French of Acadia and the French of France" had to be reflected in active cooperation; accordingly, he was in "complete agreement" with the wishes they had expressed. They would be receiving an official invitation to visit France, and he, himself, would be happy to discuss with them "our joint actions...in the present and future."

The "Quebec mafia" were delighted with the achievement. By establishing direct communication between the Acadians and the president, they had succeeded in getting a commitment that more cautious French officials such as Jean Basdevant and Ambassador Leduc could not gainsay. Even the Acadians' list of requests had been referred to specifically in the general's letter. Rossillon took particular pleasure in having attracted the ire of Pierre Trudeau during his latest venture. The federal minister of justice denounced his intrusion into Canadian affairs. One might ask how such a controversial person could continue to operate so freely within the French administration? The explanation was revealed a short time later when de Gaulle recognized Rossillon at a reception. "They say a lot of bad things about you abroad," he told him in front of a crowd of dignitaries, "Me, I think a lot of good of it."[14]

Meanwhile in Quebec, Daniel Johnson approved a "protocol" specifying the projects (now twenty-eight in number) negotiated with Peyrefitte, and then left discreetly for a rest in Hawaii. On September 18, Jean-Jacques Bertrand signed the document as acting premier.

Included were provisions for regular meetings at the "highest level" of government—apparently Johnson's reticence had been overcome—,a permanent joint secretariat, and a sharp increase in funds by both sides. Coincidentally, on the same day, René Lévesque announced his new political movement for sovereignty-association.

By mid-September, the federal government, for its part, had completed its assessment of the triangular relationship and determined its policy. Notwithstanding de Gaulle's deliberate ambiguity, External Affairs officials advised the Cabinet, the theme of the inevitability of Quebec independence was implicit in his statements, as was the view that the Quebec government was the government of French Canadians and should have direct French support. Because of the common origin of French and French Canadians, he evidently felt that the rule of non-intervention in the affairs of other countries did not apply. While the general's popularity was declining at home and his intervention was largely disapproved there, he had struck a responsive chord in Quebec. He had also revealed, and even accentuated, the divergent attitudes between English and French Canadians over the current state of the country. English Canadians, preoccupied with national unity, had reacted with resentment; French Canadians, to the degree that they were dissatisfied with the *status quo*, had reacted positively. In one sense, de Gaulle had acted as a catalyst and produced some measure of consensus on two points: the need for Canadians to resolve their inter-ethnic problems; and the importance to all Canada of closer relations with France. In view of de Gaulle's personal views, the prospects of bringing about the latter were hardly encouraging. There was even a question whether he would continue to allow Franco-Canadian cooperation, which had developed substantially since Pearson's visit to Paris in 1964. Another question was whether French-speaking African states would follow de Gaulle's lead in by-passing Ottawa. The Johnson government evidently preferred to revert to the pragmatic and cautious course it had followed before de Gaulle's visit. In the circumstances, the federal government was well advised also to adopt a low-key attitude, acting officially as if nothing particularly untoward had happened, and in Couve de Murville's words, allowing time to heal the wounds. No initiatives should be taken for a while that would require the involvement of the general himself, but contacts should be maintained at lower levels of the French government. At the same time, the development of relations with French-speaking Africa should be vigorously pursued. At home, constitutional reform was urgent, so that the feeling that had been aroused could be defused, and Quebec's cooperation in foreign relations ensured. On the whole, the approach recommended by the Department of External Affairs was insightful and well reasoned. It became official policy. Ironically, it not only gave credence to de Gaulle's objective of "lancing the abcess" of French-English relations in Canada, but it also endorsed Johnson's goal of changing the constitution to improve French Canada's situation.

Back at his post in Paris after a brief holiday, Jules Léger's first task was to assess the impact of de Gaulle's trip on day-to-day relations between the two countries, and to determine to what extent it was still possible to deal normally with the French government, at least at levels below the Elysée Palace. While he found considerable sympathy and understanding among some officials in private conversations, most of them were suddenly much more distant and formalistic, as if waiting to see whether de Gaulle's action marked a genuine change of policy or a short-term aberration. Even Edgar Faure, the minister of agriculture, found it necessary to be discreet. When the Légers returned to their Paris residence, they found a large bouquet of flowers and a warm message of welcome from him. But when a few days later the ambassador raised with him the subject of a trip Faure was planning to Quebec as part of de Gaulle's offensive and suggested that he visit Ottawa as well, the minister replied that, if the general heard of such a possibility, he would cancel the mission. In consultation with Léger, Pearson and Martin decided to insist that at least some of the French ministers, depending on the nature of their missions, should visit the capital, that the federal government should be at least notified in advance of all visits, and that information on their purpose should be provided. The Peyrefitte-Johnson agreement, and particularly the items calling for regular "highest level" meetings and a permanent secretariat, further increased their concern. The report of a joint Franco-Quebec satellite communications project seemed positively sinister to them. To break the pattern of accumulating precedents, Léger was instructed to present the new policy on visits in Paris, while Cadieux was to communicate it to Leduc. Since the French ambassador was considered by Martin and his officials to be an active supporter of de Gaulle's policy rather than a simple executant—the latter was in fact more the case—his conciliatory attitude came as something of a pleasant surprise. However, Leduc held out little hope of a change of policy for the moment.

On September 25, Paul Martin met Couve de Murville for dinner in New York at the residence of the French permanent representative to the United Nations. The Canadian minister was still not only upset over the whole sequence of events of recent weeks; he also felt personally aggrieved and even betrayed, particularly in view of the reassurances he had received from the president himself as recently as in Quebec City that he had nothing to worry about. His own credibility with his Cabinet colleagues had been cast in doubt. In his

autobiography, he reflects his mood at that juncture, "I told Pearson...
that we had to stop all the shenanigans. If Couve de Murville could not
satisfy me,...I would recommend tougher measures."[15] Once again,
the French foreign minister sought to pour oil on troubled waters,
stressing his desire to maintain their friendship, on which Martin
placed such high value. While he defended de Gaulle's actions loyally,
he insisted that the Montreal cry had not meant support for separatism; what the general had in mind was rather a new arrangement of
two cultural communities within a sovereign federal polity. Not yet
assuaged, the Canadian minister replied that, while de Gaulle had
perhaps not meant what he said, his subsequent statements in France,
and a report made by Couve de Murville himself to a committee of the
French National Assembly just a few days earlier, strengthened the
Canadian government's interpretation of his words. None of them, he
was assured, warranted Canadian apprehension. Martin insisted that
the French actions constituted an intervention in Canadian affairs
and, as such, could not be condoned; they could well cause lasting
damage to relations between the two countries. Moreover, the recent
practice of having ministers visit Canada without even getting in
touch with the embassy in Paris beforehand bore the hallmarks of a
deliberate attempt to embarrass the Canadian government. There was
no desire to harm their relations, Couve de Murville insisted, and time,
he hoped, would solve the current difficulties. Perhaps the number of
ministerial visits could be limited in the coming year. Reversing the
roles of aggriever and aggrieved, he said that de Gaulle had reacted
badly to the Canadian government's statement declaring his speech
"unacceptable." The first priority, he suggested, should be to heal the
wounds on both sides. As a step in that direction, he agreed that
whenever French ministers visited a province to deal with foreign
policy matters, Ottawa should be advised in advance through the
French ambassador, and they should normally call at. Ottawa. When
Martin suggested that he himself set an example by visiting Ottawa in
1968, he responded that such a step was quite possible.

   In the improved atmosphere, Couve de Murville volunteered the
information that Peyrefitte, in his visit to Quebec two weeks earlier,
had been struck by the fact that French Canadians were more
American than French. Martin agreed emphatically: Frenchmen had
not realized that they were first and foremost Canadians and deeply
rooted in the North American way of life. Peyrefitte had also been very
impressed by his talk with Bertrand, the French minister went on, and
found him a staunch Canadian. Paul Martin grasped at the straws. If
that message were getting through to Paris, he commented later, the
visit may have done more good than harm. He returned to Ottawa, still
uneasy but more hopeful.

The Franco-Canadian relationship seemed to be settling into a tolerable *modus vivendi* when, on November 27, de Gaulle threw another rock into the pond. In a televised press conference, he returned to the subject of Quebec. As usual, he put on a virtuoso performance. Thoroughly prepared, and with journalists primed with appropriate questions, he spoke without notes, drawing solely on his remarkable memory to reproduce the striking phrases he had so carefully sculpted. Once again, he presented his version of Canadian history.[16] Having "discovered, peopled and administered" Canada for two hundred and four years, the French had "seen fit to leave the place." Subsequently, the sixty thousand Frenchmen who remained received only "infinitesimal new elements" from home, while "millions and millions" of Britons arrived, plus "Slavs, Mediterraneans, Scandinavians, Jews and Asiatics that the Canadian government in Ottawa decided to anglicize." Moreover, the British "applied great tactics of coercion and seduction to induce the French Canadians to renounce their identities." At the same time, "the United States was threatening to swallow up the economy, the character and the language of the country." While all this was going on, France "took no interest in its abandoned children." Yet, "by...a miracle of vitality, energy and fidelity," "a French nation—part of our people"— was now asserting itself in Canada and claiming the right "to be recognized and treated as such." Those sixty thousand Frenchmen had become six million and were "more French than ever." With their motto "*Je me souviens*," they had maintained their language, traditions, religion and "French solidarity." At present, they were moving beyond "passive resistance" and aspired, "like any other people, to becoming masters of their own destiny." "The Anglo-Saxons," together with the "inevitably partial" federal government, had come, however, to dominate the economy, placing the French in an increasingly inferior situation and endangering increasingly "their language, their substance, their character."

Engaged in this "emancipation movement," the "French people across the Atlantic" had naturally turned for support to France which they considered "their mother country, not only as a very precious souvenir, but as a nation with the same blood, heart and mind." They, in turn, could be a "considerable support" to France. For instance, the outcome of the battle for the French language in Canada would "weigh heavily in the struggle to preserve it from one side of the world to the other." That was why the French government had received Premiers Lesage and Johnson "with great joy and interest" and signed with them the first "accords for joint action." But those "rediscoveries" had to be "taken note of and celebrated solemnly on the spot." That was why Daniel Johnson had invited him to Quebec and why he had accepted. Over there, his presence had stirred an "immense wave of

French faith and hope; millions of men, women and children gathered to shout passionately *Vive la France!* and wave hundreds of millions of Tricolour and Quebec flags to the nearly total exclusion of all other emblems." He had been greeted with "unanimous enthusiasm" whenever he had expressed "three obvious truths": "You are French," "As such you must be your own masters" and "You want the modern development of Quebec to be your own affair." Afterward, "everyone sang *La Marseillaise* with an indescribable passion." In Montreal, the second French city in the world and the final stop in his schedule, "the surge of liberation passion" was such that France, incarnated by him, had "the sacred duty to respond forthrightly and solemnly." That is what he had done when he had declared to "the multitude gathered around the Hôtel de Ville" that the mother country had not forgotten its Canadian children, that it loved them, that it intended to support them in their efforts for emancipation and progress, and that it expected them to aid it in return. Then he had summed it all up by shouting "*Vive le Québec libre*" "which fanned to a white heat the flame of determination."

"That Quebec should be free," de Gaulle continued, "that is, indeed, what it is all about." At the point matters had reached in the "irreversible situation," a solution had to be found. To that end, there were two conditions. The first was "a complete change in the current Canadian structure," which was the result of an act granted by the Queen of England a century earlier. Such a change would lead necessarily, in his view, to "the advent of Quebec to the rank of a sovereign State, master of its national life, like so many other peoples throughout the world, some of them not as viable nor even as large as it." Of course, "that State of Quebec would have to resolve freely and on an equal basis with the rest of Canada the modalities of their cooperation in order to control and develop a very difficult environment of immense size, and to face up to the United States invasion." If that were done, and it was difficult to see any other outcome, France was "completely prepared to have the best possible relations with a Canadian entity of this nature." The second condition was that "the solidarity of the French community living on both sides of the Atlantic should be organized." In that respect, things were "going well." The next Franco-Quebec meeting in Paris would give "a still stronger impulse to that great French undertaking." And arrangements had to be made for "all the French in Canada but not living in Quebec," including the two hundred and fifty thousand Acadians who had also maintained "a very moving fidelity to France, its language and its soul," to participate in the common endeavour. "*Allons, allons,*" de Gaulle exhorted his audience in conclusion, "for them too, especially for them, France must be France!"

The press conference over, the ministers, led by Prime Minister Pompidou, trooped out, inscrutable smiles on their faces. The thousand journalists in attendance rushed to file their reports. The only Canadian official present, E. P. Black, who had arrived in Paris only a few days earlier, returned to the embassy still in a state of disbelief, and did the same.

Daniel Johnson received the news in Toronto where he was attending the Confederation for Tomorrow conference. While in Hawaii, he had thought long and hard about Quebec's relations with the rest of Canada and had moved still further away from the independence option. Among his visitors there were Paul Desmarais, a self-made man who had become one of the richest financiers in Quebec, and Marcel Faribault, a conservative nationalist, constitutional expert and president of a leading trust company. They told him that the financial community was very concerned over his links with de Gaulle, particularly since the *"Vive le Québec libre"* incident, and pointed out that the lack of investor confidence manifested in recent months was having very adverse effects on the Quebec economy compared to that of other provinces.[17] (In fact, the decline was partly due to the slowdown in economic activity after a boom associated with Expo '67.) In Quebec City, Finance Minister Paul Dozois confirmed the bad news. Overriding his more nationalist advisers, Johnson agreed to make a statement that would reassure the financial community. In the 1966 elections, he stated in a press interview in early October, the *Union Nationale* had not received a mandate "to build a Chinese wall around Quebec."[18] Nor was that its intention. It had merely promised to use Quebec's existing legal rights to obtain a new constitution "that would enable all Canadians, whether French- or English-speaking, and whatever their ethnic origins, to feel at home anywhere in Canada." And on November 9, three weeks after his return to Quebec, he made a special trip to New York to deliver a similar message of reassurance to the world's largest financial community.

How can one explain this firm commitment on the part of a man who usually preferred to keep his options open? (Actually, he did temper it within Quebec by occasional references to independence as a possibility in the event that equality within Canada was not achieved.) Were financial pressures the sole consideration? Another plausible factor was that his declining health forced him to moderate his personal ambitions and to be more realistic. Equally likely, de Gaulle's open espousal of Quebec independence and the resulting publicity, triggered his essentially conservative instincts and caused him to veer back towards the more traditional position of his party. A final possible explanation exists: with his fine feeling for public opinion, he realized that Quebecers generally were not ready to take the risks implicit in the independence option.

Whatever the explanations, when Johnson arrived in Toronto, he was brandishing an olive branch, not a sword. Greeted by Ontario Premier John Robarts, he declared, "We are all Canadians."[19] In his opening address to the conference, he repeated the demands he had set out at a federal-provincial conference the previous year. Then, he assured the other delegations that the Quebecers had come "with open minds and receptive hearts," and confident that the deliberations would lead to "a new Canada" and a stronger Canadian identity based on "cooperation [and] mutual enrichment" between the two linguistic and cultural groups.[20] His message was greeted with enthusiastic applause. Johnson had hardly finished when the first report of de Gaulle's press conference arrived. Johnson first reacted, "the old guy is screwing me up." Four months earlier, he had been able to control the situation by casting a cloak of ambiguity over the meaning of the general's words; this time, his words were less open to interpretation, and more clearly at odds with his own course of action.

The entire luncheon break was taken up with a strategy session in the premier's suite. The delegation was deeply divided on how to react. Marcel Faribault, who by then had become his constitutional and economic adviser, demanded that the government dissociate itself categorically from de Gaulle's statement of support for Quebec independence and send him a telegram, "*Monsieur le Président*, your declaration has stirred the ire of Quebec."[21] The two most nationalist ministers, Marcel Masse and Jean-Noël Tremblay, threatened to resign if that were done. Masse insisted that the general's long shadow could still be very useful in forcing constitutional change on Ottawa and the other provinces. Johnson said little, and in the end, issued no statement at all. Throughout the conference deliberations, he maintained his optimistic and conciliatory stance, but balanced it with a comment at the end to a journalist that the slogan "Equality or Independence" was more relevant than ever. And with a level of obfuscation that de Gaulle would surely have admired in other circumstances, he remarked on returning to Quebec, "I have taken a sort of bet on a new Canada."[22]

De Gaulle's latest eruption onto the Canadian political scene caused a sensation in Ottawa. Since Pearson was absent in Britain, Paul Martin was acting prime minister. Although Martin wrote later that he was beside himself with rage, he parried questions on the subject in the House of Commons the same day by saying that two considerations had to be kept in mind in judging the statement: Canada's "traditional and steadfast friendship for France," and the obligation "to allow no interference in our domestic affairs."[23] When Pearson returned the next day, the Cabinet met in emergency session. This time there appeared to be no uncertainty about what the general meant. A range of options were considered; among them, a formal break in diplomatic relations, or visa controls to force French politicians and officials to ask for permission and state their purpose when planning a trip to Canada. From Paris, Jules Léger stressed that, in responding, a distinction had to be made between relations with de Gaulle and with France. The French would not understand if relations with France were broken off, but they would understand a strong response to the president. They were now making that distinction themselves. In the end, after having vented their indignation once again, the ministers fell back on the view that de Gaulle was really acting on his own and with little domestic support; and in Martin's words, he "could not last forever."[24] It was agreed that the prime minister would made a firm statement, and Martin would discuss the situation once more with Couve de Murville.

In the House of Commons that afternoon, Pearson appealed to Canadians to be restrained in their response to the general's latest outburst "so as not to serve the purposes of those who would disunite and divide our country."[25] The statement not only "distorted some Canadian history, misrepresented certain contemporary developments and wrongly predicted the future;" it constituted "an intervention in Canadian policy matters," and as such was also "unacceptable." Indeed, it was "intolerable" that a head of a foreign country "should recommend a course of political or constitutional action which would destroy the Canadian confederation and the unity of the Canadian state." The future of Canada would be decided "in Canada and by Canadians...through their own democratic processes." In that regard, Pearson continued, further constitutional changes would be required to ensure that French-speaking Canadians' rights would be "accepted and respected in Canada." The federal government should also "encourage and promote special and close relations between French-speaking Canadians and France and other French-speaking countries." At any rate, Canada was a free country and Canadians in Quebec and elsewhere had the right to exercise fully their political rights in federal and provincial elections. Self-determination was "no new discovery" for them and they did not need to have it offered to them. Pearson ended his statement by repeating de Gaulle's description of Canada during his visit in 1960: Canada was a state that united two societies, that exercised independence, was forging a national character, and was "a solid and stable state."

The prime minister's task was made easier in dealing with the sensitive matter by a recent change in the Canadian political scene. John Diefenbaker had been replaced as leader of the opposition by a much more moderate man, Robert Stanfield. When he responded to Pearson's statement, he commented that there might be no way of stopping the sort of interference that had occurred, but he hoped that Canadians were "mature enough not to allow such an attempt by somebody outside of Canada to affect the relationship among Canadians inside Canada."[26] The leader of the New Democratic Party, T. C. Douglas, was also restrained. Canadians, he advised, should not be provoked into "hysterical and provocative replies."[27] At the same time, they should make it clear that they were quite capable of resolving their own problems. He thought French Canadians would resent the reference to them as "abandoned children" and would not be "enticed by any nostalgic appeal for a new form of imperialism." Finally, the spokesman for the Social Credit group, Réal Caouette, whose remarks were doubly significant because he, more than anyone else in Parliament, represented grass-roots thinking in Quebec, was more blunt. Quebec, he declared, had "more sovereignty within the Canadian confederation than any country connected with France has ever obtained since France exists."[28] De Gaulle said to Quebecers, "Liberate yourselves!" But the Algerians fought France for seven and a half years for independence and, afterward, they were poorer than before. French Canadians could get along without his advice or that of any other head of state, "whether from Great Britain or any other country in the world."

In the Canadian media, de Gaulle's latest charge made headlines, but public opinion appeared to be less impressed, perhaps because of his remoteness, perhaps because his words had an aura of "*déjà vu.*" In Quebec, Liberal leader Jean Lesage, like Johnson, succeeded in avoiding making any statement. One of the rare persons who came to de Gaulle's defence was *Le Devoir* editorialist Paul Sauriol, a traditional nationalist.[29] (Jean-Marc Léger had lost his right to sign editorials following his partisan support of de Gaulle in July.) Sauriol denounced Pearson's statement as "both excessive and maladroit." Why attribute the worst intentions to the president? he asked. Sauriol, himself, saw the general's statement, not as an "intolerable" recommendation that would destroy Canada, but as "the wish for a reform of Canadian federalism that would enable Quebec to remain within it." Few if any other observers accepted that interpretation.

In France, there was no indication that de Gaulle's statement had won more public support for his Quebec policy as a result of the press conference. Gaullists generally rallied once again to his support, but many Frenchmen remained puzzled by his action and by the intensity of his feelings on the subject. Beuve-Méry was notably more restrained than in the previous July. The Canadian government could very well be surprised, he wrote in *Le Monde*, "that France should evoke its new power to call on the French people across the Atlantic to assume their total independence." However, cool-headed Canadians who refused to give in to "the current demagogy" were able to judge how dangerous it would be to be carried away by "the white heat of determination." They, too, were proud of the miracle of French-Canadian survival and were "determined to strengthen their rights by obtaining, if necessary by wresting away, substantial changes in the federal constitution." At the same time, "they were concerned that total independence [of Quebec] might lead in fact to a still more complete control by the United States, or, on the other hand, by a degree of isolation that would inevitably create the most serious economic difficulties and lead to some form of dictatorship." In *Le Figaro*, Raymond Aron wrote that the French had no advice to give French Canadians, whatever assistance they might, and should, provide to them.[30] Nevertheless, he set out his preference to resolve the situation: creative change within Canada.

Among Quebec visitors to Paris in late 1967 were the two separatist party leaders, Pierre Bourgault and Gilles Grégoire, both anxious to follow up on de Gaulle's initiative and to promote their cause in France. Grégoire, the only separatist ever to sit in the Canadian House of Commons—having been elected as a Social Credit member and subsequently leaving that party—told a group of Canadian students that, during World War Two, de Gaulle's *Croix de Lorraine* association raised money in Quebec for the French resistance; now the roles were being reversed.[31] In a few days he would announce the creation of a fund-raising committee in France to bring about independence. Shortly afterward, a Parisian lawyer, Maurice Jacquinot, announced the establishment of an "Action Committee for the Independence of Quebec." Its objectives were to enlist support in French political circles and, as a beginning, to collect one hundred thousand dollars to be sent to Quebec.[32] Jacquinot became secretary general and counsel of the committee; Arthur Simard, a Quebec student, was appointed liaison officer. A Frenchman living in Montreal was also deeply involved in the project. A publication, *Plein Pouvoir*, was founded to proselytize the French population. Over the next months, a range of Quebecers, including René Lévesque, Jean-Marc Léger, Jean-Paul Cardinal and Jacques-Yvan Morin, were in touch with the organization, but most were wary of becoming identified with it. The general attitude among members of the "Quebec mafia" was one of caution.

Paul Martin met with Couve de Murville again during a NATO meeting in Brussels on December 12. He was thoroughly prepared, and armed with a list of bilateral issues to be resolved. He found the French minister less at ease in dealing with de Gaulle's actions than he had been at New York in September, but still gamely loyal to him. De Gaulle had not talked of independence but of sovereignty for Quebec, he argued, and provincial sovereignty was already provided for in the Canadian constitution. The general did not want to encourage Quebec independence. Martin pointed out that the text of the November 27 press conference belied that assertion. They went on to other subjects on the Canadian minister's list. Couve de Murville once again sought to be reassuring. He saw no difficulty in informing Ottawa about visits of French ministers to Quebec and about their purposes, or about arrangements made between France and Quebec within the ambit of the Franco-Canadian accord. He also had no problem with the Canadian requirement that there should be consultation on any proposed arrangement going beyond the terms of the accord, but he gave the impression that would not be necessary. Once again, Martin's personal liking for Couve de Murville, and his sympathetic under-standing of the difficult situation in which the French minister found himself, caused him to avoid pressing him hard. He concluded that, rather than taking a hard line, the best the federal government could do was to continue to press its case and take what steps it could to minimize the effects of any further tremors set off by de Gaulle.

As 1968 began, Jules Léger braced for further problems. The general was showing further signs of age, he confided to a friend, and his ideas were more and more out of date. Worse still, he listened to no one but himself. In that difficult and even unpleasant situation, it was more important than ever for Canadians to remain serene and level-headed. Despite all that had happened, there were still encouraging signs that the Franco-Canadian relationship was still strong. By and large, embassy personnel were still working satisfactorily with their oppo-site numbers in the French administration, and social relations remained congenial. In the previous October, Canada had succeeded in convening a meeting of the long-dormant Joint Committee on Com-mercial and Economic Relations, and the subsequent communiqué had declared that discussions had been held in "a very cordial atmos-phere."[33] Then, in November, a Canadian delegation had attended the first meeting of the organizing committee of the *Association interna-tionale des parlementaires de langue française*. Since the principal moving force behind that initiative was Xavier Deniau, the fact that the delegation had attended at all was a noteworthy accomplishment. Léger might have added persistence and pragmatism to his list of necessary qualities.

At the beginning of 1968, de Gaulle intervened in the selection of a new French consul general in Quebec City and insisted on giving him his instructions personally. His choice was an experienced diplomat, Pierre de Menthon. De Menthon was to communicate directly with Paris rather than through the French embassy in Ottawa. His mission was to develop Franco-Quebec cooperation rapidly, and no budgetary limits would be imposed on him.[34] The Quebec situation would end in "some form or other of independence," de Gaulle stated; it was in France's interest that it become truly independent.[35] He noted that a split existed between "the little people" of Quebec who had understood him well and wished for "one form or another of independence," and "the cadres, the superstructure."[36] The latter were much more prudent and many were in bed with the federal government. Some, for instance, Lesage and Drapeau, were already *dépassés*—outdated. Johnson ran the same risk if he continued to hedge; he was a politician, not a statesman, and lacked the audacity for the position he occupied. De Gaulle also mentioned René Lévesque, but only in passing, as an unknown quantity. Pierre de Menthon left the Elysée Palace convinced that the "*Vive le Québec libre*" had been a deliberate ploy as part of a carefully planned strategy to assist Quebec to independence. He accepted his mission as part of that policy. His enthusiasm was somewhat moderated when Couve de Murville briefed him in turn and gave him what he later termed "counsels of moderation," telling him "not to rush things."[37]

On January 7, 1968, the four Acadian "musketeers," as they were becoming known, Euclide Daigle, Gilbert Finn, Léon Richard and Adélard Savoie arrived at Orly airport thanks to first class Air France tickets provided by the French government.[38] They were met by a reception committee of ministers and officials, and escorted in limousines to the Crillon Hotel on the Place de la Concorde, where, in Rossillon's words, "visiting heads of states and ministers" were usually lodged.[39] Each visitor was assigned his own suite. André Bettencourt, the junior minister of foreign affairs, was responsible for their visit. Rossillon hovered about to make certain that everything went off satisfactorily. For the next two weeks, the Acadians were put through a programme of tourism and official visits that left them so exhausted that at times they took turns going out while the others stayed in the hotel and rested. They soon became aware of the hostility of French officials such as Rossillon against Anglo-Saxons in general and against English Canadians in particular, and determined to avoid being used by them in a propaganda operation against Ottawa. They were touched but somewhat uneasy when Bernard Dorin appeared on television (which was closely monitored by de Gaulle) to explain their visit. In emotional terms, he described the hardships their ancestors had suffered at the hands of the British, even being reduced to eating the leather of their boots to survive. With de Gaulle's personal support, their wishes were taken as virtual commands by French officials. At a meeting at the Quai d'Orsay, one official told them with evident satisfaction that he had succeeded in obtaining the equivalent of one hundred and fifty thousand dollars worth of credits for them. They pointed out that their estimate of the requests that they had submitted was closer to one million dollars. Jurgensen, who was chairing the meeting, took the Acadians' list and slid it across the table to the official with the comment, "You know where my orders are from." He instructed the embarrassed individual to start over again. The only request they made that met any resistance was to meet with officials of the Canadian embassy. The Acadians persisted, and were received by Jules Léger and members of his staff. They assured Léger that they were "good Canadians," and he, in turn, proved so helpful that they dubbed him their "*bon père protecteur.*"

Included in the Acadians' schedule were several trips outside of Paris. On the first weekend, they were flown in de Gaulle's personal aircraft to Nice, then given a tour of the Côte d'Azur that ended in Aix-en-Provence. During the second week, they were flown first to Toulouse to visit the Sud Aviation aircraft plants, and then taken by train to Caen, in Normandy. The apogee of their stay came on the final Saturday. In the morning, they were driven to the Arc de Triomphe to place a wreath on the Tomb of the Unknown Soldier—just as visiting statesmen did, they were told—and then to the Elysée Palace for lunch with the president. When they were shown into de Gaulle's office, he came out from behind his desk to greet them and asked, "*Eh bien*, have you been well received?" Reassured on that point, he sat down among them and began to go over their requests, displaying an impressive familiarity with the details. As they covered the various items, he took notes, then asked, "Anything else?" One request that had not yet been met, they ventured, was for autographed photos of him; they had been told that he did not give autographs. He broke that rule for them. In another personal gesture, the general authorized that twenty-five thousand dollars be taken from the president's discretionary fund to support *L'Evangéline.*

The luncheon, attended mostly by officials, including Rossillon, who had been involved in the visit, was equally cordial and even relaxed. As they moved to the dining room, de Gaulle pointed out a carpet bearing *fleurs de lys* designs and explained that when it was woven, their ancestors were still in France.[40] It was an emotional moment. His after-luncheon toast was equally moving.[41] "*Eh bien, voilà*," he began familiarly. "After more than two and a half centuries of separation, we find ourselves together again, Acadians and French of France. *Ah, Messieurs*, what hardships we have endured during those years! The Acadians, persecuted for so long in that territory of New France where Champlain founded...the first French settlement in Canada; the Acadians who were subsequently chased out, but who returned with courage and tenacity; the Acadians who, thanks to the miraculous fecundity and the admirable courage of their French mamas, now totalled three hundred and fifty thousand rather than two thousand as at the beginning, while the fantastic fidelity of their fathers resulted in their remaining, through their language, intellect, religion and character, as French as ever." As for France, it had gone through many wars, invasions and revolutions, all marked by "brilliant victories and immense misfortunes." As a result, "many acts of forgetfulness and negligence" had been committed with regard to the Canadian French, especially the Acadians. But now, they were "standing erect, very much alive and full of hope." And through the visit of their delegation, they were re-establishing the relations of "Frenchmen to Frenchmen." Contemporary France no longer ignored what Acadians had done, and could do, for the French community as a whole. Dr. Richard replied on behalf of the Acadians. De Gaulle had succeeded in making them feel so much at ease (in contrast to Pearson four years earlier), he recalled later, that he had no difficulty in performing that task.

What was the balance sheet of the Acadians' visit? In the short term, a cultural service was added to the French consulate general in Moncton. Fifty-six scholarships (compared to one in 1967–68) were made available for study in France, and their worth doubled. Nineteen thousand books were rushed to the University of Moncton and other educational institutions. Thirty-one *coopérants* were assigned to New Brunswick, mostly as teachers. Half a million dollars were made available to *L'Evangéline*, not counting personnel and materials.[42] The *cinébus* also arrived. The Canadian government reacted almost complacently. While "some surprise" was expressed that Paris had "seen fit to deal directly with Canadian citizens without using federal and provincial channels," Ambassador Leduc reported, this concern was more than offset by satisfaction that French interests were extending beyond Quebec.[43] Pearson and others had long urged the French to take a greater interest in all French Canadians.

Chapter 13

Power Struggles in Africa

As 1967 drew to a close and 1968 began, the scene of the triangular confrontation spread to Africa. Relations with the French-speaking countries there were not a priority for either Daniel Johnson or Education Minister Jean-Jacques Bertrand, but some officials like Jean-Marc Léger and André Patry, the "*francs-tireurs*" as the premier called them, were still pressing for direct links with them. They found allies in Marcel Masse in the Quebec Cabinet and in members of the "Quebec mafia" in Paris, notably Rossillon, Deniau and Dorin, who saw the whole francophone world as their field of operation and had considerable influence there. In Ottawa, the activities of the two groups were followed as closely as possible, and evidently with deep distrust.

In October 1966, Marcel Cadieux had learned that an invitation had been sent by the minister of justice of Togo, and the president of the newly founded *Institut International de Droit des Pays francophones*, to attend a meeting in Lomé, the capital, the following January. A check of the files in the Department of External Affairs revealed that an invitation from the *institut*, addressed to the minister of justice of the "Republic of Canada," had been received and declined. It was decided to reactivate it, and Pierre Trudeau, a former law professor and at that moment parliamentary secretary to the prime minister, was persuaded to go. In addition to ensuring a federal presence at the meeting, he was to visit some of the African political leaders, assure them of Canada's desire to extend its aid programmes to French-speaking Africa, and make sure that they understood the constitutional situation with regard to foreign affairs. He was also to ascertain their views concerning the *Francophonie* and to express Ottawa's interest in it.

Trudeau's message, to be heard many times in succeeding years, was concise: Canada, as a whole, was a French-language country, and the federal government spoke for all French-speaking citizens; Quebec did not. Following the conference, he called on the presidents of Cameroun, Senegal and Tunisia, and ended his tour with discussions with French officials in Paris. On his return to Ottawa, he reported that the African leaders understood the constitutional situation and the reasons why communications with provincial governments should at least pass through Ottawa. In the circumstances, he was not inclined to take Quebec's unilateral initiatives seriously, providing of course that the federal government occupied the terrain itself by developing an adequate aid programme. With regard to the *Francophonie*, he gathered the impression that it was a rather abstract concept, described by President Bourguiba as a *"communauté de l'esprit,"* and was not intended as a French version of the Commonwealth, which had a whole range of aid programmes. He did learn that President Senghor had written to Premier Johnson, informing him that President Hamani Diori of Niger would be inviting Quebec to a conference of ministers of education. Senghor hoped that it would become, in fact, the founding meeting of the *Francophonie*. The Senegalese president assured him that the federal government would also be invited, and expressed the hope that Ottawa and Quebec City would work out between themselves the choice of representatives, presumably within a single Canadian delegation.

Pearson and his colleagues were pleased with Trudeau's report, and particularly his firm recommendation to develop relations with the francophone countries. The decision was taken to create a new division within the Department of External Affairs for that purpose, and the associate director of the External Aid Office, Henri Gaudefroy, recently recruited in Quebec, was instructed to expand assistance to the former French colonies so that the foreign aid programmes would better reflect the bilingual and bicultural character of the country.

Meanwhile, in Quebec City, the *"francs-tireurs"* had found a possible avenue for direct contacts with Africa. During Alain Peyrefitte's visit, Marcel Masse had learned that in early 1968 a meeting was to be held in Libreville, the capital of Gabon, of a continuing committee of francophone ministers of education (the forerunner of the conference Senghor mentioned to Johnson). The new Quebec minister of education, Jean-Guy Cardinal, a stronger nationalist than Bertrand, agreed that Quebec should try to get an invitation to attend. Johnson endorsed the suggestion, but warned Claude Morin that he did not want any *"histoires inutiles."*[1] At the same time, he took the position that, since education was a provincial matter, the province should be invited directly and not through Ottawa. This set of conditions was a considerable challenge even for the dexterous deputy minister.

Inevitably, the federal government learned of the meeting planned for Libreville, and Cadieux suggested to Morin that they adopt a common approach, which meant essentially a single delegation. Since Quebec had not yet received the invitation it was seeking, Morin played for time. Pearson wrote to Johnson on December 1, also urging a coordinated effort. The premier stalled as well. Shortly before Christmas, Morin went to see François Leduc to appeal for France's intervention. The ambassador told him that, since France "inspired" Gabon's conduct in such matters, the invitation would be forthcoming shortly. He also assured him more generally, in Morin's words, that "France was prepared to do everything we wanted in France-Quebec relations, that is, new formal *ententes*, whether Canada agreed or not."[2] In Paris, Jean Chapdelaine followed up on the matter with Jean-Daniel Jurgensen, who assured him that the plan was progressing well. However, as time passed and no firm invitation arrived, Morin and his colleagues became increasingly apprehensive about possible countermoves on the part of Ottawa. He had good cause: the federal authorities were determined not to allow the precedent of a direct invitation to be created. On January 4, 1968, Jules Léger wrote to the ambassadors of several francophone countries in Paris, informing them that only the federal government was empowered to receive invitations to meetings such as that planned to be held in Libreville and that "any wrongly addressed invitation" would be viewed as "interference in the affairs of our country."[3] He delivered the same message to the French secretary of state for external affairs.

As Leduc had indicated to Morin, the choice of Libreville as the conference site gave Quebec a decided advantage in the contest with Ottawa. The Gabonese president, Léon M'ba, was very close to France. The story is told of a British fleet sailing down the African coast and asking permission to pay a courtesy call on him. He refused. When his French friends expressed surprise, he answered, "You may have forgotten the battle of Trafalgar, but I haven't." Since it was one of the richest of the former French colonies in terms of natural resources (including uranium ore), France kept it under *de facto*, but willing, tutelage. French advisers controlled most of the government offices, including the Presidency. The French ambassador to Gabon, Maurice Delaunay, a former colonial governor, carried the additional title of *haut représentant diplomatique*. As such, he reported directly to Jacques Foccart, secretary general for francophone affairs in the Elysée Palace. He was probably the most powerful man in the country. On the other hand, Canada was only represented in Gabon by the Canadian ambassador resident in Yaoundé, capital of the Cameroun, and he appeared seldom.

President M'ba died in late 1967 and was succeeded by his youthful private secretary, Albert Bongo. At that particular moment, one Canadian ambassador had completed his term of duty and his successor, Joseph Thibault, had not yet come over from Cameroun to present his credentials. Thibault attended the funeral, but had no opportunity to obtain formal accreditation. President Bongo visited France in early January 1968 and met with de Gaulle. Godin writes that they agreed on direct Quebec participation in the Libreville conference.[4] On January 17, a letter from the Gabonese minister of coordination arrived in Quebec City, addressed to the "Ministry of Foreign Affairs of Quebec," inviting it to represent "French Canada." According to some sources, Bernard Dorin composed the letter; André Patry states that it was "inspired largely by France."[5] Claude Morin states that, in bringing about the invitation, France "evoked the province's exclusive competence in matters of education."[6] Whatever the circumstances, Jean-Guy Cardinal accepted immediately.

In order to keep Ottawa in the dark as long as possible, Morin issued instructions that no public reference be made of Cardinal's plans, and, if necessary, knowledge of them be denied. Despite precautions, the news spread, and the Department of External Affairs instructed Ambassador Thibault to fly to Libreville (on the weekly air service) to explain that invitations to international meetings must be addressed to the federal government. Quebec would be represented, he was to assure the Gabonese authorities, but within a Canadian delegation. In Bongo's absence, Thibault met with a Cabinet minister who told him that no invitation had been sent to Quebec. Reassured, he returned to Yaoundé and filed a report to that effect. Ottawa replied that there were serious reasons to believe that was not the case, and sent him back with instructions to emphasize the seriousness of the situation. By then the conference was only days away. In Libreville, again, Thibault found himself being ostracized. His situation was made still more difficult by the fact that he still had not been accredited to the Gabonese government. Finally, he practically forced his way into the office of the vice-president and explained the situation to him. Apparently not aware of the game being played, he declared heatedly that the government had not, and would not, violate proper practices as Ottawa was intimating. He did agree to have a check made of the files and telephoned Thibault later at his hotel to say that they contained nothing on the subject. The ambassador flew back to Yaoundé and wired that information to Ottawa.

In the meantime, the Department of External Affairs had learned that the Quebec government had authorized Cardinal to attend the conference. Thibault was sent back to Libreville for the third time. Perplexed as to how to proceed, he consulted the Gabonese ambassador in Yaoundé, who, trying to be helpful, agreed to telegraph his government and ask that he be received by the minister of foreign affairs. The response came back that Thibault's proposed visit was inopportune and should be postponed. Again he reported to Ottawa. This time a message arrived, appointing him chargé d'affaires in Libreville, a step that did not require formal accreditation and would oblige the Gabonese authorities to receive him. Thus armed, he took the airplane once more. The stratagem was unsuccessful; not only was his request to be received refused, but he was berated by an official for his insistence. As he prepared to leave empty-handed, once again, he saw the Quebec flag flying above the conference center, along with those of the other participating delegations that were to arrive shortly.* He could do nothing more, he informed Ottawa.

Martin, Cadieux and the other Canadian officials involved in the diplomatic chess game refused to concede defeat. Since the Gabonese ambassador to the United States was also accredited to Canada, the Canadian ambassador to the United States was instructed to warn him formally that, if the situation were not corrected, Thibault would not present his credentials and that, for all practical purposes, diplomatic relations would be suspended. A protest was also sent from Ottawa to the Quai d'Orsay, and the Canadian minister of energy, mines and resources, Jean-Luc Pépin, who was visiting Paris on other business, was asked to try to obtain an invitation. He was given a cool reception and failed in turn. According to Patry, the Gabonese government refused to budge, referring to Quebec's constitutional responsibility for educational and cultural matters, and asserting that the invitation that had been issued to Cardinal was "strictly personal."[7]

Jean-Guy Cardinal, an eager neophyte in international affairs, left Quebec with instructions from Johnson to "take a strong line."[8] The premier approved the strategy of creating a precedent that would strengthen the province's demand for control of its international relations in its areas of jurisdiction. At the same time, he was concerned lest the situation get out of hand. A telephone call from Paul Martin, telling him that he was in the process of breaking up the country, increased his uneasiness.[9] Patry sought to reassure him.

The conference took place under the close attention of the media, which concentrated on the "war of the flags" and the treatment accorded the Quebec minister. They were provided with abundant material. Cardinal, alone with Peyrefitte, was lodged in the presidential building and given a seat on stage during the inaugural ceremonies; it was also announced that he would be granted the highest

* "Certain French friends and some of our officials," writes Morin, "provided the flags and had them replace the Canadian flags that the Gabonese had hoisted." (C. Morin, *L'Art de l'impossible, op. cit.*, 125)

Gabonese distinction. In Paris, on his return journey, he was received by de Gaulle, who was curious to meet the new recruit to the Quebec Cabinet and to explore how far Johnson was prepared to go in asserting Quebec's right to an international role. Cardinal assured him that the premier was determined to push ahead on that course and to have Quebec represented at the next education conference which, it had been decided in Libreville, should be held in April in Paris. Johnson, himself, Cardinal reminded de Gaulle, planned to visit Paris the same month. The only point of difference between them appears to have been with regard to the United States. De Gaulle, probably again being provocative, noted that French Canadians seemed better disposed towards the Americans than he was. Cardinal pleaded for understanding; Quebec lived next to a giant and could not ignore that reality.[10] The general responded with a gesture of impatience that the Americans were realists and would continue to invest in Quebec if that was in their interest.

The publicity surrounding Cardinal's visit, and particularly his reception by de Gaulle, rankled deeply in Ottawa and strengthened the federal government's determination to assert itself. As part of the policy of developing relations with the francophone countries, it had decided a few weeks earlier to send a mission to the area with very exceptional terms of reference: it had authority to agree on the spot to forty million dollars worth of development projects suggested by the African governments. Lionel Chevrier, having completed his assignment at Expo '67, was chosen to lead the mission; Henri Gaudefroy of the External Aid Office, and Jacques Dupuis, responsible for francophone affairs at the Canadian embassy in Paris, made up the rest of the team. They began their tour in Paris, where Chevrier emphasized to the French authorities that the mission's task had neither constitutional nor political overtones, and that the Canadian aid programme would not in any way conflict with the French one. The assurance was well received by more traditional officials such as Basdevant, but with suspicion by more pro-Quebec ones such as Jurgensen. The majority, however, were puzzled over the sudden Canadian interest in their privileged area of operations.

The offer of Canadian munificence was useful in determining where the various African régimes stood with regard to the Ottawa-Quebec City (plus Paris) quarrel. The Maghreb countries, Morocco, Algeria and Tunisia, were more interested in receiving aid than in taking sides. The black African countries were generally very cordial to the Chevrier mission (it did not visit Gabon), but evidently not as free from French pressures. Some wished to maintain the prospect of direct Quebec aid as well. The Canadians had no difficulty in committing the funds they had been allotted. On their return to Canada, they recommended that aid to francophone countries be increased to one hundred million dollars per year, and that the number of Canadian embassies in the area be increased. To minimize friction and reduce French distrust, they also advised that the French and Canadian programmes be coordinated as much as possible, even though that might imply collusion with France's policy of maintaining its predominant influence over its former colonies. Since Quebec did not have the means to become a major player in the area, the mission suggested that the differences with it be defused by implicating it in Canadian projects. On resuming his duties in Paris, Jacques Dupuis made a factual report to Jurgensen, who was somewhat taken aback by the scope of the Canadian initiative.

That first phase of the confrontation in Africa occurred during a change of political leadership in Ottawa. Shortly before Christmas, Pearson announced his intention to resign as Liberal leader, and thus as prime minister; a party convention was called for April 6, 1968, to choose a successor. Favoured by the Liberal practice of alternating French- and English-speaking leaders, Pierre Trudeau, though still relatively unknown outside Quebec, emerged as a likely candidate. His chances received a major fillip during a federal-provincial constitutional conference convened by Pearson in early February. The purpose of the meeting was to deal with Quebec's demands for increased autonomy within the federation; the hidden agenda for the federal government was to regain the initiative from the provinces following the Confederation for Tomorrow conference (at which it had had only observer status). Seated beside the prime minister in his capacity as minister of justice, and in full view of the Canadian public since the proceedings were being broadcast live on television, Trudeau challenged Johnson's proposals as incompatible with the federal system. The two men had a lively altercation which dominated the news, and Trudeau became an instant celebrity in English Canada as the French Canadian who had stood up to Quebec.

Following the conference, Paul Martin released a government white paper entitled *Federalism and International Relations*, outlining the federal position on that subject.[11] Only the government of Canada, it stated, was empowered to act on behalf of the country, or parts thereof, with regard "to the negotiation and conclusion of treaties and other international agreements, to membership in international organizations, and to the right to accredit and receive diplomatic representatives."[12] Any sharing of that power with the provinces would render Canadian foreign policy ineffective. At the same time, the provinces were "legitimately concerned with the conduct of foreign relations." The challenge was to develop ways of harmonizing those fundamental considerations, and that could best be achieved through procedures for cooperation and consultation. With regard to international conferences, provincial participation in Canadian delegations was the most promising approach, and guidelines were being developed for that purpose. Similar arrangements were being worked out in the field of development aid. In short, the federal government insisted, "Canada must act as one country in its dealings with other states," but, within that framework, it was prepared to be flexible.

On March 4, the Department of External Affairs sent a protest note to the Gabonese government, expressing "serious concern" over its actions "relative to the Canadian representation at the Libreville meeting."[13] It drew attention to the obviously fictitious claim that Cardinal had been invited in a "strictly personal" capacity, and to the violation of the assurance that no province would be invited. It also protested that a "certain interpretation" had been made of the Canadian constitution. Those actions were "not in conformity with the rules of international law and the maintenance of close and amicable relations between Canada and Gabon." In the circumstances, and while hoping that the Gabonese government would change its attitude, the Canadian government considered it inappropriate for Ambassador Thibault to present his credentials. In other words, relations were, not broken off, but suspended. The reaction from Libreville was prompt and sharp, and took the form of a public communiqué. The Canadian action, it stated, was "one of the rare occasions when a civilized and developed country had taken such an action against a Third World country."[14] The reason for such a "regrettable act" had to be found elsewhere than in the presence of Quebec at a francophone meeting, or the personal invitation to Cardinal, particularly since Ottawa's jurisdiction "never included matters of culture and education, both exclusive attributions of the provinces." The most feasible explanation: that Canada had not been able to fulfill its promises of assistance to Gabon, and Prime Minister Pearson, in political difficulty at home, was trying to turn attention away from "the reality of the Quebec problem." Accordingly, while waiting for Ottawa to adopt "a better attitude," the Gabonese government was postponing the presentation of its ambassador's credentials to the Canadian government. If, as a consequence of the prime minister's "fit of temper," Ottawa wanted to withdraw the two Canadian teachers in Gabon, or the two scholarships granted to Gabonese students—the only aid it was providing at the moment—the Gabonese government would accept that decision.

The Quebec government added fuel to the fire by declaring the federal government's reactions "premature and inopportune," and by asserting that, since the province had authority over "the international extension of its internal jurisdiction," it was "normal" that foreign governments communicate directly with it in its fields of jurisdiction.[15] That, of course, was precisely the point that Quebec was seeking to establish in creating the incident.* However, the federal government was not about to concede it. Entering his last month as prime minister, Pearson tried again to reach an amicable solution. Even though Johnson had not answered his first letter on the subject, he wrote to the Quebec premier on March 8, he wished to put forward in further detail an approach he hoped "would be satisfactory to all concerned and would avoid misunderstandings and differences."[16] At meetings of ministers of education within the context of the *Francophonie*, he proposed, the minister of education of Quebec would, as a general practice, represent all Canada as chairman of the Canadian delegation. Ministers or officials from other provinces with large French-speaking populations should also be members, and one of those ministers might appropriately act as chairman on occasion. If federal advisers were present, "they would, of course, not involve themselves with questions of education but rather with aspects of those conferences which relate to the federal responsibility for international relations." The Canadian Council of (Provincial) Ministers of Education might be asked to recommend the composition of each delegation. If, in the future, conferences of a general nature were called within the framework of the *Francophonie*, a federal minister or official would normally head the Canadian delegation, which would include Quebec representatives and perhaps some from other provinces, and a Quebec minister or official would serve as vice-chairman. In that way, Quebec would be able to play "a full and active role" without weakening Canada either at home or abroad.

While he maintained a firm stance in public, Johnson was becoming uneasy that the dispute over international prerogatives was becoming counter-productive in terms of his real goal to wrest concessions from the federal government in the constitutional negotiations. He saw a real danger of alienating other provincial premiers whose views were closer to Ottawa's with regard to foreign relations. "I am not trying to worsen the crisis," he is quoted by Godin as saying, "on the contrary, my only wish is to get along with Ottawa."[17] He also realized that, if Trudeau succeeded Pearson, as seemed increasingly likely, the federal position would become much more rigid. In his leadership campaign that was under way, Trudeau accused France publicly of manipulating Gabon and intimated that, if Quebec were invited to the Paris conference, diplomatic relations would be broken off with it as well. In some quarters, the threat was taken seriously. Christopher Malone

---

* At a conference in Wingspread, Wisconsin, in October 1969, Jacques Parizeau stated, "We created the incident."

has written, on the basis of an interview with Cardinal, that a French official, possibly Rossillon, assured the Quebec government that "in the event of a severance of relations between Ottawa and Paris, France would immediately recognize Quebec diplomatically as a sovereign State" and would see that "ten or so" African states did the same; "as a result Quebec would find itself independent."[18]

Speaking in the Quebec Legislature on March 12, Premier Johnson ignored Pearson's letters and accused the federal government of "taking out the bludgeon" instead of an umbrella (agreement), and of "barricading itself" behind an anachronistic notion of external relations.[19] Without mentioning him by name, he denounced Trudeau's threat against France if Quebec "dared to attend a conference in France where education, an exclusively provincial field, would be discussed." He insisted that it was quite possible for Quebec to exercise its constitutional rights in international matters "along lines still to be worked out" and which would avoid such childish threats.

Once again Johnson declined to respond to the prime minister's appeal for compromise. To do so would only interrupt the process that had been started, he told Morin; he would wait and see what happened next.[20] The day before the Liberal convention, Pearson made a final try.[21] It was one of the last times he would be writing as prime minister of Canada, he told Johnson; he was doing so because it was his "greatest wish to avoid finding ourselves in a situation which would force the Canadian government to react in a way which would cause a controversy which could do nobody any good." Knowing of the premier's strong positive feelings for Canada, he had the "profound conviction that with good will we could find a solution which would be compatible with the interests and the responsibilities of our two governments." Still, he could not hide his "extreme anxiety" in seeing a *de facto* situation taking shape that was hard to reconcile with the survival of Canada as an independent entity. With regard to the impending meeting in Paris, he suggested that they try out the formula of the Quebec minister of education heading a delegation, which would also include representatives of other provinces.

In his assessment of that letter, Claude Morin does not cast doubt on Pearson's sincerity or good intentions—he describes him as without arrogance or malevolence—but reads into it that, under such an arrangement, the federal government would "necessarily" be able to give instructions to the delegation "even in matters of education."[22] He also implies that Ottawa's motive in proposing the participation of other provinces was to reduce Quebec's importance. Worse still, any "retreat" by Quebec would be interpreted as recognition by it, at least in international matters, of "a certain federal authority in the field of education." In the light of the constitutional negotiations, Morin explains, Johnson therefore decided that "such softening of Quebec's position seemed clearly contra-indicated," and the province should be represented at the meeting in France, as in Gabon, in order to "confirm...the special character it had conquered unofficially in Libreville." On April 9, three days after Pierre Trudeau won the Liberal leadership and eleven days before he was sworn in as prime minister, Johnson replied at last to Pearson's correspondence. The meeting in Paris was merely the second part of the one begun in Africa, he pointed out, and it was only natural that Quebec attend it as well.[23] In any case, education was the only subject on the agenda. The federal government evoked one of its fields of exclusive jurisdiction, foreign affairs, to override the province's exclusive rights in the field of education. The practical suggestions it had put forward were not adequate to resolve that difference; Quebec would be putting forward "more appropriate" ones during the constitutional negotiations.

Overworked and in precarious health, Johnson again postponed his trip to France from April to May, and then until July. He authorized Cardinal to lead the Quebec delegation to the meeting in Paris, but worried whether the minister of education, who was rapidly becoming the darling of the nationalists, would not create still more problems for him. Cardinal's name was even being mentioned as a future premier, and Johnson was feeling the need to keep him under a tighter rein. In a heated discussion before his departure, Cardinal recounted later, the premier accused him of being a "separatist."

Five days after Trudeau became Liberal leader, the Department of External Affairs sent a formal request for Canada to be invited to the Paris conference. The French ambassador also sent a message to Paris suggesting that with the change of prime ministers the moment was opportune to de-escalate the tension between the two countries.[24] The prime minister-designate had his faults, Leduc commented, but he was "a pragmatist and an intelligent realist," with whom it was possible to have "a very forthright and friendly discussion even on such a delicate subject." By dealing with him directly, it would be possible to circumvent "the implacable hostility of the senior civil servants in the Department of External Affairs." Trudeau would recognize that it was not possible for France to change a course of action "well launched and decided upon," but some gesture might be made to him such as reducing the visibility of the Quebec delegation at the conference. Leduc asked for instructions. They came in the form of a succinct handwritten comment by de Gaulle in the margin of the despatch, "We have no concessions and no friendly gestures to make to *Monsieur* Trudeau who is the opponent of the French fact in Canada."[25] The French government refused Ottawa's request and confirmed the arrangements for Quebec's attendance. Jules Léger was recalled to

Canada "for consultations." Like the word "unacceptable," that act was intended to signal the federal government's strong objection while avoiding an outright break in diplomatic relations, or at least placing the onus on Paris if one occurred. In Ottawa, Léger had a moderating influence on the hard-liners. Time and French public opinion, he reminded them, were on Ottawa's side.

Pierre Trudeau was sworn in as prime minister on April 20, two days before the Paris conference was to begin. Mitchell Sharp, who had served as minister of trade and commerce and then of finance under Pearson, became secretary of state for external affairs. With a strong tide of popularity running in his favour as Canada's answer to Jack Kennedy, Trudeau dissolved Parliament and asked for a fresh mandate. The latest conflict with France was dealt with through a relatively muted letter of protest delivered to the Quai d'Orsay by Léger on his return to Paris in early May. In it, the Canadian government "deeply regretted" that France had not responded favourably to its request for an invitation to attend the conference, and expressed surprise that Quebec had been welcomed there.[26] By these actions, France had commited an act that was contrary to international practice and the Canadian constitution. That was all the more regrettable since the Canadian government attached "exceptional importance" to the friendly ties between the two countries. The message ended on a conciliatory note: it wished "to continue the dialogue."

Considering the sensationalist coverage given to the Paris conference, Cardinal's second meeting with de Gaulle, and the Quebec minister's announcement that the province would be present at the next francophone education conference in the Congo (Kinshasa) in 1969, the issue played a relatively small role in the election campaign. The federal government released a document, *Federalism and International Conferences on Education*, a supplement to *Federalism and International Relations*.[27] It reviewed the history of provincial representation at international meetings and outlined the suggestions already made for resolving the dispute in a way compatible with federal and provincial powers. It also suggested that the subject be referred to the constitutional meetings. Drawing on the document, Trudeau explained the federal position in a speech to the *Chambre de Commerce de Montréal* and declared that, in international society, there could be large and small but not "half countries."[28] On an official visit to Canada, President Bourguiba of Tunisia declared, after a meeting with Trudeau, that "until the contrary was proven," he considered that Quebec was part of Canada.[29]

Concerned about the consequences of a Trudeau victory, Johnson tried to repeat a strategy that his predecessor, Maurice Duplessis, had deployed sucessfully in 1958: defeating the Liberals by throwing the

resources of the *Union Nationale* discreetly behind Conservative
candidates. Brian Mulroney, then a young Montreal lawyer, was one of
the persons chosen to execute the plan. Marcel Faribault doubled as
adviser to both Johnson and to federal Conservative leader Stanfield,
and succeeded in having the "two nations" concept of Canada written
into the party programme. The strategists faced an impossible task.
"Trudeaumania" swept the country and millions of young people
discovered politics through him for the first time. On the weekend
before the balloting, Trudeau and Johnson attended an open-air
ceremony in Montreal to celebrate St. Jean-Baptiste Day, the feast of
French Canada's patron saint. Separatist militants attacked the
grandstand to protest both the traditional ceremony and the prime
minister's presence. Most of the dignitaries, including Johnson, fled,
but Trudeau refused to leave and stood in his place scornfully as
bottles and other missiles flew about him. Several policemen were
injured before order was restored and a large number of demonstrators
were taken away. The scene was reported live on television, and
Trudeau's popularity soared. On June 25, the Liberals won an even
greater victory in Quebec than in the rest of the country. Earlier in the
year, Johnson had contemplated calling a provincial election and to
ask for a mandate to negotiate a new and more decentralized
constitution. Trudeau had acted first and could now claim a mandate
for the opposite purpose.

In early July, the Quebec premier suffered another heart attack.His
visit to Paris had been rescheduled to coincide with the Bastille Day
celebrations in Paris, and, at de Gaulle's specific instructions, an
ostentatious reception had been planned. He was to be lodged at the
Trianon, where only Queen Elizabeth II had stayed since its renovation. And he was to be beside de Gaulle on the reviewing stand during
the Bastille Day ceremonies. The Quebec *fleur de lys* was to be flown
alongside the Tricolour. There was no longer to be any question
whether the political leader of Quebec was receiving head of state
treatment. Once again, Johnson's illness was kept secret at home. De
Gaulle was assured that it, and not any lack of enthusiasm, was the
reason for yet another postponement. By then the general was
becoming less enthusiastic himself. He was determined to arrange for
a spectacular reception, if and when his "friend," as he referred to
Johnson, appeared, but the postponements disturbed him, and he was
becoming more aware that, in both their tactics and their ultimate
aims, he and Johnson were not as one. While the premier left to
convalesce, first at La Malbaie on the Lower St. Lawrence and then in
Bermuda, Patry was sent to Paris to reassure the French of the
premier's continued enthusiasm for the Franco-Quebec relationship.
He delivered his message to Saint-Légier in the Elysée Palace, and

also to Michel Debré, André Malraux and André Bettencourt. Sensing some continuing scepticism, the Quebec government also despatched Cardinal, whose rating was highest in pro-Quebec circles in Paris, to confirm that Johnson's illness was not merely of a diplomatic nature.

Much more important, de Gaulle had serious problems of his own. In April, students at the new University of Paris campus at Nanterre, on the outskirts of Paris, started an anarchistic revolt, rejecting the authority of professors and administrators, and proclaiming the need to replace the entire existing form of society with an undefined new one. In May, the movement reached the Sorbonne and then spread to other universities throughout the country. Good-natured at the outset, it became destructive as students took over the Sorbonne, resisted the attempts of the forces of order to disperse them, erected barricades and burned cars in the Latin Quarter. Anxious not to lose its leadership role among the anti-government forces, the Communist-dominated labour union, the *Confédération générale du travail*, entered the scene as well. General de Gaulle was scheduled to visit Rumania from May 14 to 18; not easily diverted from his plans by others' doings, he decided to go ahead. When he returned, he found the capital in chaos. He tried to assert his authority through a television appeal on May 24, but with no effect. One of his greatest talents, his ability to communicate with the masses, seemed to have forsaken him. In response to his stern warning, "Reform, yes; chaos, no," the students chanted, "He's the chaos," and told him to "go back to the museum." For one of the rare times in his life, de Gaulle appeared to lose his decisiveness, even his nerve. The situation, he complained, was *"insaisissable"*—too uncertain for him to grasp. On May 26, when Madame de Gaulle went out to shop, people shouted insults and shook their fists at her limousine. He was shaken. The CGT was planning a demonstration through the city the next day, and it was possible that the crowd could change direction and march on the Elysée Palace. Shades of 1789!

On the morning of the 27th, he called in his son-in-law, General de Boissieu, and told him that, since the French were compromising their future with the "student pranks," and that "certain government leaders" were trembling at the thought of a real test of strength, France no longer needed de Gaulle at the helm. He would do better to go home and write his memoirs.[30] De Boissieu assured him that he could count on the army. Apparently reassured, he said he would go to see if General Jacques Massu, the commander of the French forces in Germany, was of the same mind, then he would speak to the country "from Colombey, Strasbourg, or elsewhere." Telling Prime Minister Pompidou that he felt a need "to take some distance" in order to get a "broad view" of the situation, he left Paris the next morning by helicopter, presumably for Colombey-les-Deux-Eglises. However, he continued on to Baden-Baden, Massu's headquarters. En route he picked up other members of his family. Pompidou and the other members of the government were left completely in the dark concerning his whereabouts. "*Tout est foutu!*"—de Gaulle told General Massu on his arrival. "They don't want anything more to do with me."[31] He asked that the German government be informed of his arrival; the implication was clear that he might demand asylum. Massu spent the next two hours restoring his morale, telling him that he had the full support of the armed forces and that he could not end his brilliant career in such a débâcle. Perhaps that was the reassurance he had been seeking; at any rate, he pulled himself together and decided to return to France.

In the meantime, the mass demonstration in Paris went off peacefully; it seemed that another French revolution might be avoided after all. After spending the night in Colombey-les-Deux-Eglises, de Gaulle arrived in Paris the next morning, appearing much more resolved to fulfil his role as leader of the French people. Eschewing television for radio, the medium that had bought him such success during World War Two, he appealed for support to restore order. Ironically, his words were directed not so much to the "masses" whom he liked to consider his natural allies, but to the bourgeoisie that he so often treated with disdain. Alarmed by the revolutionary atmosphere, they needed him, and this time, he needed them. At his request, they turned out in millions to march down the Champs-Elysées, recreating in a less joyful mood his victory march of August 25, 1944. In a few days, the political balance wheel swung back again.He called parliamentary elections for June 30. The Gaullists won a crushing majority. Georges Pompidou was replaced as prime minister by Maurice Couve de Murville; Michel Debré became minister of foreign affairs. The crisis was over, but de Gaulle had been severely shaken. He recognized that he should retire as soon as an appropriate moment arrived.

On the operative level, the relations between France and Quebec continued to intensify during those politically turbulent months of early 1968. Members of the *Commission des finances et du plan*, a committee of the French National Assembly, led by former Finance Minister Valéry Giscard d'Estaing, spent four days in Quebec in March. In April, a new *Comité économique France-Québec* met for the first time in Paris. The *Commission permanente de coopération franco-québécoise* met in Quebec City the same month. In April, too, the Quebec government created the position of commissioner general of cooperation. Guy Frégault, formerly deputy minister of cultural affairs, was the first appointee. One of his earliest decisions was to refuse an offer from Ottawa to become a member of the Canadian delegation to a UNESCO conference in Paris; his goal was direct

Quebec participation in meetings of the United Nations agency. Still, the new French consul general in Quebec City, Pierre de Menthon, did not find his role as pleasant as he had anticipated. First, Ambassador Leduc did not accept that he could communicate directly with Paris.[32] Second, de Menthon found what he termed "the ballet of the three-member household" complex and delicate.[33]. When, following de Gaulle's instructions, he pushed the direct relationship with too much zeal, he found the Quebecers drawing back. At the same time, he found that they needed to be assured that France's support was both vigorous and efficient. His principal contact, Claude Morin, he wrote later, excelled at the delicate game of weighing the different elements, including those within the Quebec government itself. The attitudes of both Frenchmen and Quebecers as a whole also caused him problems.

> On the French side, indifference was the rule, and readily marked by self-importance. On the Quebec side,...such distrust!...Anglo-Saxon conformity, after such a long period of domination, had rubbed off on the élite. Their sensitivities were so acute, their complexes so numerous: feelings of superiority on the part of those modern Americans who were happy to draw attention to our lack of creature comforts, our backwardness, our old-fashionedness. Feelings of inferiority too, resulting from a sometimes deficient language and the poor quality of a culture not yet firmly established.

General de Gaulle referred to Canada and Quebec again, almost in passing, at a press conference on September 8. Some time earlier, he had thrown France's support—and military material—behind Biafra, a member-state of the Nigerian federation which had unilaterally declared its independence. That move, too, had become highly controversial. He was not sure, he commented in an almost detached manner, at the press conference, that federal systems that replaced colonial régimes, for instance, in Canada, Rhodesia, Malaysia, Cyprus and Nigeria, were always "very good and very practical."[34] In the end, one ethnic group always imposed its authority on the others.

Pierre Trudeau was not long in taking the lead in the disagreement with France. In late August, Philippe Rossillon had appeared in Manitoba without, of course, informing Ottawa of his presence. Learning of his newest foray, the Department of External Affairs assigned an official to follow him. Trudeau referred to the unwelcome visitor in a press conference on September 10 as "more or less a French secret agent."[35] The media described Rossillon as a member of Prime Minister Couve de Murville's staff. That was the first problem that had to be handled by the new French ambassador to Canada, Pierre Siraud. As chief of protocol, Siraud had followed the whole subject of the Paris-Ottawa-Quebec triangle closely since Lésage's first visit to Paris in 1961. His natural inclination was to calm the troubled waters. He issued a press release on September 12 stating that Rossillon's official position was secretary general of the *Comité pour la défense et l'expansion de la langue française*, "one of the numerous bodies" that reported to the Hôtel Matignon (the prime minister's executive offices). He was in Manitoba on a private visit at the invitation of "Francophone representatives" who had been in Paris the previous July, and was the guest of *La Société culturelle de Rivière Rouge*. Foreign Minister Michel Debré also issued a statement denying the spying charge or any impropriety. Questioned on the subject by reporters, Trudeau retreated and substituted the term "non-secret agent."[36] De Gaulle was not prepared to pass over the matter so lightly. In the margin of a despatch from Siraud reporting on his first meeting with Marcel Cadieux and referring to the Rossillon visit, he noted on September 13, "It is time to make *Monsieur* Trudeau aware that his francophobe attitude is in danger of seriously jeopardizing the whole relationship between Ottawa and Paris."[37] Did the remark imply that he himself was ready to reduce the tension? Once again, he remained ambiguous. The incident did have one practical result; less tolerant than Pompidou of Rossillon's adventures, Couve de Murville curbed his travels: it was to be Rossillon's last trip to Canada for five years.[38] He turned his attention towards other parts of the world: according to Mallen, he left soon afterwards for Niger to persuade President Diori to invite Quebec to the next education conference.

Daniel Johnson returned to Quebec on September 19, declaring himself "dangerously well."[39] However, following a medical examination, his doctor told him otherwise. He was determined to carry on to the end. "I'm going to die in action this week," he confided to a friend.[40] At a press conference on September 25, he appeared relaxed and even subdued. Questioned about Trudeau's denunciation of Rossillon, he said he regretted that the prime minister had "lost his cool" over the matter.[41] If he felt that Quebec's relations with France were that harmful to Canada, he continued, he would "consider it his duty not to pursue them." Johnson refused to comment on de Gaulle's reference to Canada as a federal system that was not working. "The General can have his opinions on the Canadian federation," he continued, "we have ours. The problem will not be solved in France. The constitutional problem is in Canada. It will be solved in Canada." Then did he consider, one journalist persisted, that the general was intervening in Canada's internal affairs? That was Ottawa's opinion, he replied. It would have taken many years for Quebecers to become known "across the universe;" with a single phrase, the general had "compensated for the omissions of Ottawa and its foreign service which had never, over the past two hundred years [sic], presented Canada as a country with two cultures." What about the Gabonese incident? The matter had been "badly handled." He had told the prime minister "not to worry, that the matter would be negotiated and a formula found to safeguard the general policy of Canada through the surveillance of someone from the federal government." However, Quebecers "would never give up with regard to relations in the field of education and, especially with the *Francophonie*," they did not want to let Ottawa control "the French oxygen" they needed to live. He hoped that, in the future, Ottawa and Quebec's activities in that area would "add up instead of cancelling each other out." "All the better" if Ottawa spent one hundred million dollars a year in francophone Africa for "tractors, etc.;" however, by coordinating Quebec's efforts with Ottawa's, it would be possible to contribute "expertise and know-how" to francophone Africa, and that was needed more than "tractors for which there are no spare parts." On the whole, Johnson's position on Quebec's role in international relations was clearly sufficiently close to that of the federal government as outlined in the two white papers to make the negotiation of a working relationship possible.

In the light of these declarations, one can well ask what was the message that the premier intended to deliver to de Gaulle in Paris which he was now planning to visit the following month? While going along with the ostentatious public programme, much of it re-scheduled from May, he would certainly have applied his very considerable charm and persuasiveness in private to convince de Gaulle that, in Marcel Masse's words, he had gone too far.[42] Johnson might have found that the general's own enthusiasm for Quebec independence had also been tempered over recent months. But all that must remain speculation: the following day, September 26, Daniel Johnson died of a heart attack. Jean-Jacques Bertrand; a staunch federalist, became premier of Quebec.

Shaken by the news, de Gaulle apparently seriously considered the possibility of attending the funeral ceremonies. His staff at the Elysée enquired about the travel facilities to Saint-Pie de Bagot, Johnson's native village, where he was to be buried. Pierre de Menthon indicated that the general would come "if Quebec expressed the desire."[43] Patry, still chief of protocol, and his colleagues were hesitant, in part because of the "delicate problems" his presence would pose, but, more important, because "politically that presence was not desirable." As acting premier during Johnson's absence, Bertrand had issued clear instructions, "no squabbling with Ottawa." Finally, de Gaulle decided to send Couve de Murville in his place; Jean de Lipkowski, the new

secretary of state for foreign affairs and a strong Gaullist, was chosen
to accompany him. In a letter of condolences to Bertrand, the president
declared that, "for all Frenchmen—those in France and in Canada,"
Johnson's death was "a great loss and deeply felt."[44] No one would ever
forget what he had done "for their cause" in helping to strengthen the
fraternal ties that had become "distended" but were at last being
renewed.

As so often happens in Quebec, the funeral provided an opportunity
for important discussions concerning the new political situation.
Couve de Murville met with Bertrand and also with Pierre Trudeau.
The Canadian prime minister took a conciliatory, almost diffident,
approach. He and Couve de Murville began by discussing several
international questions, then Trudeau mentioned that the name of
Paul Beaulieu, a career diplomat, was being put forward to replace
Jules Léger as ambassador to France. Finally, Couve de Murville
asked if he had any questions to raise concerning relations between
France and Quebec. Anxious to avoid a discussion of specific points of
controversy such as the Rossillon visit, Trudeau suggested that they
examine the general logic of the French policy and the consequences
that appeared to flow from it. He accepted that France wished to
support the French fact in Canada and he had no objection to its
increasing greatly, he said, but he was concerned that some of France's
methods had the effect of weakening the French-Canadian presence in
Ottawa and in the provinces other than Quebec. Couve de Murville
argued that it was natural for France to grant more assistance to
Quebec, since it was the heartland of French Canada and had a special
role in such areas as education. Trudeau pointed out that, constitutionally, all the provinces were on the same footing, and argued that there
was no reason to exclude the others either from assistance programmes or international meetings. While declaring that France
should not pronounce on the Canadian constitutional situation or get
involved in differences between Ottawa and Quebec city, the French
prime minister insisted that Quebec's situation was different. That
assertion was tantamount to taking a position on the nature of
Canadian federalism, Trudeau responded, and, carried to its logical
conclusion, could lead to support for separatism. Couve de Murville
declared categorically that France did not believe in separatism, that
it would be madness, and that France had no interest in Canada's
breaking up; Quebecers, he said, would end up like the Franco-
Americans of New England. Trudeau pointed out that any form of
special or associate status for Quebec within Confederation would
constitute a move in that direction. He also questioned the French
prime minister on his attitude towards eventual requests for assistance from other provinces such as Ontario, and was told that the door

was open as in the case of New Brunswick. Then, Trudeau wanted to know, what was the role of the federal government in such a situation? Couve de Murville was less precise on that point; he was also ambiguous on the French attitude towards federal and provincial representation at francophone conferences. At the end of their meeting, the two heads of government agreed to state publicly that France wanted to assist all French Canadians as much as possible and that it did not want to become involved in Canada's constitutional matters.

While Couve de Murville had once again sought to deal with the real problems by acting as if they did not exist, Trudeau received the impression that he genuinely wished to avoid a diplomatic break with Canada. Like Jules Léger, he was coming to the view that the best strategy was to avoid serious crises and let time do the rest. Presumably, the obvious fact that de Gaulle was nearing the end of his career entered into that calculation. None of that thinking came to light when they met the press. "There is no conflict nor opposition between France and Canada," Couve de Murville declared categorically. Trudeau was not more forthcoming.

Beaulieu presented his credentials to de Gaulle on December 14. Understandably apprehensive after Léger's experience, he was hardly reassured when Lipkowski, a personal friend, told him, "I pity you; the General has the memory of an elephant."[45] A mild-mannered man, steeped in French culture, Beaulieu kept his own statement as inoffensive as possible. De Gaulle was not in a conciliatory frame of mind. He referred pointedly to the fact that the document the ambassador presented was signed by "your gracious sovereign, who is also that of the United Kingdom and Northern Ireland."[46] He was willing to have discussions with Ottawa, he stated, but not on any subjects concerning Quebec. Canada had been formed by two nations. France, which had founded it, certainly did not want to see "grievances, quarrels," developing between them. On the contrary, it wished that they "get on together" and that "Canada find its equilibrium one day under new conditions in the form of cooperation between equal peoples." For that, their two personalities had to be "respected, and not merged." Having said that, de Gaulle assured the ambassador that he would receive "the necessary facilities" to accomplish his mission, since there were "many reasons, whether political or practical," to maintain relations between Canada and France.

While the general conceded nothing on the level of principles, he was evidently prepared to be more flexible in practice. That shift in attitude was also apparent within the administration; French officials were becoming notably more cooperative in dealing with representatives of the federal government. One reason was undoubtedly the change in Quebec premiers. While Bertrand had declared that he intended no change in policy toward France or the *Francophonie*, it was well understood that he would be less inclined to engage in a confrontation with Ottawa to assert Quebec's presence abroad. Another factor was the increased likelihood that the Liberals would win the next Quebec elections. In December, Pierre Laporte, Liberal leader in the National Assembly, visited Paris with an unequivocal message from Jean Lesage that they were opposed to the way Franco-Quebec relations had been conducted under Johnson.[47] France would have to recognize that the Liberals saw Quebec's future as within Canada, he told Lipkowski, and that future would be decided "without the intervention of any other nation, however close to us sentimentally." Laporte even urged that a meeting be arranged between de Gaulle and Trudeau "to clarify certain matters." Lipkowski responded in an accommodating manner. He, himself, didn't think that the general wanted to intervene in Canadian political matters, he told Laporte. In fact, when de Gaulle had given Lipkowski, as secretary of state for foreign affairs, responsibility for relations with Canada and Quebec, he had put the quesion to him and the general had replied, "Not at all. I just want to repair the mistake made by Louis XV." Laporte and Lipkowski agreed that Quebec's future lay within Canada and that the priority in Franco-Quebec relations was economic and financial, rather than cultural and educational, cooperation. Pierre Laporte also met with Jean-Daniel Jurgensen and found him equally pleasant. From those exchanges, he concluded that the French government did not want to pursue its "provocation" of the federal government. Was he taken in? It was at the least a premature assessment, as events were soon to illustrate.

After becoming premier, Jean-Jacques Bertrand was invited to Paris and the date of January 20 was agreed upon for his arrival. He made it clear that he had no intention of allowing the occasion to be used as part of the anti-Ottawa campaign. His first call, he told Ambassador Beaulieu, would be at the Canadian embassy.[48] Quebec's relations with France had been out of hand ever since de Gaulle's "*Vive le Québec libre*," he commented to his staff; they had to be brought under control again. One Quebec civil servant put it more succinctly, "We control our relations with France. What we can't control is General de Gaulle." In late 1968, Bertrand promoted André Patry to the new post of deputy minister of immigration, thus removing him from direct involvement in francophone affairs; Morin and the other strong nationalists stayed on, but tempered their enthusiasm for new adventures.

The burning issue in France-Quebec-Canada relations that fall and winter was who should attend the next meeting of francophone ministers of education in Kinshasa, capital of the Congo (Kinshasa), scheduled for January 13–20, 1969.* "We knew that the situation had become more favourable to Ottawa," Morin has written, "but we could not do much about it."[49] He even accepted the possibility of losing some of the gains made in Libreville in terms of independent representation. The Congo was a former Belgian colony, and, as such, not under direct French influence. The Canadian government had a consulate there even before independence in 1960, and Patrice Lumumba had visited Canada soon after becoming the country's first prime minister. During that visit, ambitious plans were made for Canadian aid. For a time, something of a special relationship developed between the two countries.

In late November 1968, Paul Martin, by then government leader in the Canadian Senate, was asked to represent the Canadian government at a ceremony to mark the fifth anniversary of the University of Rwanda, another former Belgian colony. Not only had Canada contributed to the development of the university, but the first rector was Father Georges-Henri Lévesque, founding dean of social sciences at Laval University (and a strong federalist).† Martin was asked to extend his tour by visiting several African leaders to explain the federal government's consitutional position with regard to the education conferences, and to try to ensure that it would not again be left out. In view of the upcoming meeting, the Congolese president, Joseph Mobuto, was, of course, the key figure. When Martin was received by him, he drew attention to the analogy between the secessionist movement in Quebec and the one in the Congolese province of Katanga, which having received strong outside support, had only been repressed after heavy fighting.[50] He used the two cases to illustrate the necessity of having a strong central government capable of speaking for the whole country in international affairs. His argument was received sympathetically. Martin also put the federal argument to Presidents Senghor, Houphouët-Boigny, and Diori.

In Quebec City, the proponents of an active role within the *Francophonie*, did their best to repeat their exploit at Libreville. Premier Bertrand was persuaded to sign a letter to President Mobuto, assuring him that there had been no change in Quebec's policy since Johnson's death, and that it wished to "strengthen its natural links with the other French-language states" by every means at its disposal.[51] To avoid any question of transmitting the letter through the Department of External Affairs, Claude Morin arranged for the

* The Congo (Kinshasa) became Zaïre in 1971.
† During his visit to Expo '67, the president of Rwanda had been persuaded to accept formally a grant of fifty thousand dollars from Quebec to launch the University; Ottawa increased the ante to one million, and that offer had been accepted instead of the Quebec one.

information officer at the delegation general in Paris, who was to attend the ceremonies in Rwanda as well, to deliver the message personally. The "Quebec mafia" in Paris was mobilized once again to obtain an invitation for Quebec to attend the education conference. Shortly before Christmas, the federal government received an invitation from President Mobuto. Marc Lalonde, of the Prime Minister's Office, immediately got in touch with Claude Morin to arrange for Quebec representation within the Canadian delegation. He proposed Premier Louis Robchaud of New Brunswick—another firm federalist —as chairman of the delegation and held out the possibility of a Quebec minister as co-chairman. At that juncture, Bertrand, too, suffered a heart attack and was taken to hospital. With him absent and the Quebec Cabinet increasingly divided between the more separatist wing, led by Cardinal, and the traditional nationalists, of whom the strongest spokesman was Finance Minister Dozois, the government's position became weaker and more confused.

Trying to make the best of a difficult situation, Morin embarked on the negotiations. Cardinal insisted that he would not attend the conference except as head of a separate Quebec delegation. No agreement had yet been reached when, six days before it was to begin, Quebec received an invitation from the permanent secretariat of the education conferences, which was financed and run by the French. Cardinal accepted and replied that his junior minister, Jean-Marie Morin, would lead the Quebec delegation. Suddenly the worst possible scenario from the Canadian viewpoint seemed imminent: two separate delegations. After a flurry of diplomatic telegrams between the capitals, another message reached Quebec City from the secretariat: following instructions from the Congolese government, Canada would have only one delegation, and Quebec was requested to join the federal one.[52] By that time, the Quebec delegation was already on the way; it had instructions to work out some form of cooperation with the federal delegation in Kinshasa to avoid an open clash. Finally, Morin and Lalonde succeeded in making a deal, and Morin sent new instructions via Jean Chapdelaine in Paris: Jean-Marie Morin was to be co-chairman of the Canadian delegation, but to continue as head of the Quebec delegation and to identify himself as such. The Canadian flag would have precedence over the provincial one, but both flags were to be flown on all official occasions.

A few Quebec officials were still not prepared to accept the arrangement. Without Claude Morin's knowledge, they got in touch with members of the "Quebec mafia" in Paris in a final attempt to have only a Quebec delegation recognized. The French ambassador in Kinshasa tried to convince the Congolese government to send an invitation to Quebec, and when he was unsuccessful, he announced that he would have the conference secretariat send one. He was told by the Congolese authorities that it would be held responsible for any such action. Leaving nothing to chance, Marc Lalonde had himself appointed a member of the Canadian delegation, and rushed to Africa to see that his agreement with Claude Morin was respected. While most of the Africans particularly were bemused by the spectacle of the different flags and sub-identities within the oversized Canadian contingent, no untoward incidents occurred and the work of the conference was not impeded.

Unable to travel, Bertrand appointed Cardinal, who also held the pro-forma title of deputy prime minister, to make the trip to Paris in his stead. However, he took the precaution of asking Jean-Paul Beaudry, his minister of industry and commerce, and a more pragmatic person, to accompany the minister of education. And he instructed them to visit London as well. Paul Dozois was appointed acting premier; he insisted that they enter into no new arrangements with France without consulting the government.[53] Despite the delays in bringing about a return visit by a head of the Quebec government, de Gaulle was determined to mark the occasion with *éclat*. The two ministers were received by an impressive list of ministers and officials and were offered a state dinner in the Elysée Palace. The Canadian government requested that Ambassador Beaulieu be present at the meetings, but the French refused; nor was he invited to the dinner.[54] The Canadian media made headlines of the snub. Asked for his comments, Trudeau remarked that the ambassador knew of other places where he could get a good meal.[55] Clearly, neither head of government was yet prepared to let bygones be bygones. That being said, de Gaulle's rhetoric at the dinner was more moderate and even more detached than in Quebec or in his subsequent press conference.[56] "The French living on either side of the Atlantic" had never forgotten each other, he declared in proposing the toast to Cardinal, and "the painful wound" caused by their two-century separation was beginning to heal. They were now joined together in "the same struggle," that of safeguarding and asserting their "French substance." Once that was accomplished, they would be in a position to cooperate with others as well. He predicted that Quebec, "closely linked to France," would "ensure its French effort through its national efforts."

De Gaulle's less combative tone reflected the difficult year and a half he had been through since his trip to Quebec. He had been deeply hurt by the personal attacks during that time, and even more by the evident weakening of the bond between him and the common people. Like Samson when Delila cut off his hair, his source of strength was being sapped, and with it, his confidence in the grandeur of France. In his seventy-ninth year, his declining physical strength was also discouraging to him. Pierre de Menthon, who accompanied Cardinal and Beaudry to Paris, found the general "tired and disillusioned."[57] He no longer believed in "the early transformation of Quebec," but he was convinced that the seed that he had planted "would finally germinate." De Menthon also found that, while French policy towards Quebec had not changed, it had lost some of its "bite." Officials even spoke confidentially of "depoliticization" of relations with Ottawa. The word was passed "not to make waves," but at the same time, "not to repudiate anything pertaining to Gaullism." In effect, the transition to the post-Gaullist period had begun.

Notwithstanding Dozois' admonition that no new joint projects should be entered into without specific government approval, Cardinal did sign a number of them with Foreign Minister Debré. One committed the province of Quebec to sharing the costs of developing the satellite *Symphonie* as a vehicle for educational, cultural and scientific cooperation. Quebec engineers and technicians were to participate in the project. A Franco-Quebec committee to facilitate industrial cooperation was also agreed upon. And seventy French professors were to be sent to help staff the new University of Quebec, due to open its doors in the autumn. Dozois was furious when he learned through the media of the commitments that Cardinal had made and declared flatly, on the assumption that the minister of education had no authority to do so, that no agreements had been signed. Cardinal reacted sharply in turn at being repudiated, and, according to Dozois, threatened to set up a "parallel government."[58] The rest of the Cabinet was in no mood to add to the list of problems they faced and insisted that the matter be resolved peacefully. The agreements were confirmed.

In Africa, meanwhile, another and still more important meeting was pending. As the current chairman of the *Organisation commune africaine et malgache*, President Hamani Diori of Niger called a meeting for February 17–20, 1969, in Niamey to establish a franco-phone development agency. Once again, the question arose whether Canada or Quebec should be invited, and, consequently, become a member of the new body. According to Morin, "the French interceded with the President of Niger and advised him to invite Quebec [alone]."[59] Mallen writes that Rossillon was despatched to Niamey to see that was done.[60] The federal government took steps to attain its own objective of an invitation for Canada as a whole, with provincial representation within a single delegation. One of its most important assets in pursuing that goal was the Canadian ambassador in Niamey, Paul Malone, a strong and competent diplomat. Diori had been invited to Canada in 1966, and the Chevrier and Martin missions had both visited him in his own capital. More tangibly, Ottawa had agreed to support some major development projects in Niger, including a highway right across the country. In return for a ten million dollar Canadian contribution, it was to be called *La Route de l'Unité nationale et de l'Amitié canadienne.* The French made a counter offer of ten million francs, or about two million dollars, to compensate Niger for any loss of Canadian aid as a result of inviting Quebec. Both sides were to discover that, in Diori, they had an interlocutor of superior calibre, who was not likely to be dissuaded from putting his country's interests first. In November 1968, he sent one of his advisers, Jacques Baulin, to Ottawa to explain the difficult situation in which he found himself. Although a French citizen, Baulin appears to have carried out his mission even-handedly. In meetings with Trudeau and Lalonde, he recounted that France was threatening to boycott the conference if the federal government alone was invited.[61] Diori had answered that he would send invitations to both, with a copy of the one to Quebec for Ottawa. And so he did. In his letters, he expressed the hope that the two governments would work out arrangements among themselves for appropriate representation; in other words, he placed the responsibility where it belonged: on the Canadian and Quebec governments. All this occurred before the Kinshasa formula was developed. It became the basis of an *ad hoc* arrangement for Niamey. The essential difference—and a major concession by Ottawa—was that if the Canadian delegation was not unanimous on a particular matter to be decided, then it would abstain from voting.

Gérard Pelletier, Canadian secretary of state and a close friend of Trudeau's, led the Canadian contingent to Niamey; he was seconded by Jean-Pierre Goyer, parliamentary secretary to the secretary of state for external affairs. Marcel Masse, then minister of inter-governmental affairs in the Bertrand administration, led the Quebec contingent. Ontario and New Brunswick were also represented. Matters did not go as smoothly as Diori had urged. Masse declared before leaving North America that the Quebec delegation was completely autonomous and had no instructions to receive from any other government. When he arrived, he found that no distinction had been made in the list of participants between Quebec and other Canadian delegates; he had the list redone. On the other hand, the federal delegates had the size of the Quebec flag reduced because it was larger than the Canadian one; they also arranged for the Ontario and New Brunswick flags to be flown alongside the Quebec one to reduce its relative importance. While Pelletier was addressing the conference, Pauline Julien, Quebec *chansonnière* and fervent separatist, who had been invited by Diori along with other well-known artists, interrupted with the slogan "*Vive le Québec libre.*" Pelletier passed over the incident with the comment that he had heard her in better voice.

Nonetheless, the spectacle of washing the Canadian linen at an international meeting annoyed not only President Diori, but many other delegates. During the negotiations to set up the development agency, the two French ministers present met privately with Pelletier and Goyer, and made a determined effort to obtain a distinctive place for Quebec in the proposed development agency. After several anxious telephone conversations with Trudeau, Pelletier agreed that it should be recognized as a "member government," but not a "member state." That settled, the creation of the agency was approved, and Jean-Marc Léger, secretary general of AUPELF, was appointed provisional executive secretary; he was to submit a proposed constitution to Diori within six months.

Before leaving for the Niamey conference, Claude Morin had submitted a working paper on Quebec's international relations to a federal-provincial committee that was studying external dimensions of the constitutional review. Since Premier Bertrand had not yet resumed his full duties, the document did not receive Cabinet approval, but probably represented a broad current of thinking in Quebec City. It was becoming increasingly difficult for the provinces to carry out their constitutional obligations without developing external relations, it argued. In the case of Quebec, those relations developed in recent years had been an important element in enabling the province to break out of two centuries of isolation and to receive the same type of support from France that other provinces received from Great Britain. The way in which the exchanges with France were decided precluded an intermediary role for the federal government. Even if Ottawa had the sole right to conclude international treaties, as it claimed and Quebec denied, a new constitution should recognize the right of member states (i.e. provinces) to make binding commitments towards other countries in the areas of their domestic jurisdiction. Quebec also wished to participate directly in international conferences in its fields of jurisdiction and, with regard to development aid, to have its own programmes and send its own missions overseas. The challenge was to develop the necessary mechanisms and procedures to avoid clashes between the two levels of government. In the working paper, Morin put forward a number of practical suggestions for achieving that goal, including a standing liaison committee to resolve disagreements. However, he offered no significant concessions on the fundamental issues dividing Ottawa and Quebec City. Without the premier's seal of approval, the document received scant consideration at the federal-provincial negotiating table. A short time later, Marcel Cadieux presented the federal perspective on Quebec's demands for a direct role in international affairs.[62] The fundamental question was, he stated in a speech at the University of Montreal, "Is a Quebecer also a

Canadian?" If it was held that he was not, there was no possible accommodation between the federal and Quebec positions. If, on the other hand, it was agreed that he was, then Quebec's foreign policy should be integrated with the Canadian one. Everyone agreed that the survival of French Canada required that Quebec participate in the activities of the worldwide francophone community, the under secretary pointed out, and particularly, that it should have close relations with France. However, if Quebec acted alone, it alone would benefit; other French Canadians as well as anglophones would not. On the other hand, if the Canadian government spoke for the whole country, it would have more international impact and Quebec's interests would be more effectively represented both inside and outside Canada. In that way, French-Canadian influence could also be extended outside the *Francophonie.*

Chapter 14
Conclusion

In the spring of 1969, de Gaulle found a way out of his increasingly intolerable situation as a leader in decline. As part of the resolution of the crisis of May 1968, he had promised new forms of participation by the population in public affairs. To meet that commitment, he called a referendum for April 27, asking for approval to reform the Senate and to decentralize the administration by creating new regional authorities. What few people knew, but de Gaulle had been warned, was that the vote would probably be lost. His answer: either he would receive a clear endorsement to carry on, or he would retire. To make certain that the stakes were clearly understood, he told the population in a broadcast three days before the voting that, if the referendum did not carry, he would step down immediately. It was almost an invitation to let him go. The vote was fifty-three per cent opposed. Shortly after midnight, Couve de Murville announced de Gaulle's resignation.

After an interim period under Senate President Alain Poher, Georges Pompidou was elected president in mid-June. Conscious that he owed his victory to the Gaullists and would be held accountable by them for maintaining the general's policies, he appointed Jacques Chaban-Delmas prime minister and Maurice Schumann foreign minister. In fact, in de Gaulle's last two years or so in office, Pompidou had found himself increasingly in disagreement with him over a range of policy issues, and those differences had led to his being removed from the prime ministership in 1968. He viewed the general's attitude towards Quebec as more of a personal fixation than the result of rational policy decisions. "Even more than the substance," Pompidou's biographer has written, "the form [of his actions in Quebec] certainly left him perplexed."[1] In addition to considering the "*Vive le Québec libre*" an error in judgment, he shared the Canadian government's view that France should take an interest in all French Canadians, in all parts of the country, and he was profoundly doubtful of the advantages for them of an independent Quebec. However, since a number of Gaullists were still hewing faithfully to de Gaulle's policy, he had to move carefully. He entrusted Schumann with the delicate task of discreetly improving relations with the Canadian government, without appearing to do so.[2] A charming person with a delightful sense of humour that often belied his realism and competence, the new foreign minister soon found an opportunity to advise Ambassador Beaulieu that both sides should avoid public confrontations as much as possible and allow time to heal old wounds. Pompidou himself sent a veiled message to Ottawa during an interview he gave to Harold King, correspondent for the Toronto *Telegram*, less than a month after taking office: Jacques Cartier and Montcalm were dead, he remarked, and France had no intention of annexing Quebec.[3] At the same time, it would necessarily have close relations with Quebec; the Canadian government would have to consider carefully whether they were prejudicial to good relations with it as well. In other words, Ottawa must not be too sensitive if a balance was to be worked out.

The reaction in Ottawa and Quebec City to the new French government was generally positive. While it was not prepared to lower its guard, or even to modify its policy of asserting its interests and prerogatives, the Trudeau administration was prepared to give Pompidou time to assert his own approach. Premier Bertrand was also more at ease with the new French approach. In June, he, too, had won a political victory: apparently recovered from his heart ailment, and under attack from the most nationalist wing of the *Union Nationale* led by Cardinal, he had asked for a leadership convention to obtain a clear mandate for his leadership and policies. He suggested that any separatists leave the party and join Lévesque's *Parti Québécois*. Cardinal, on the other hand, assured them that there was a place for them under his leadership. On June 21, the premier won the convention by 1325 votes to 938. Shortly afterward, he sent Claude Morin to Paris with a message for Pompidou, assuring him that he gave great importance to relations with France, but in a manner compatible with Canada's integrity. He also asked the president to lift the embargo on visits to Ottawa by French ministers. "I don't see what advantage Quebec would derive from tense relations between France and Canada," he commented in an interview in August.[4]

Occasional incidents still occurred to disturb the three-way relationship. Jean de Lipkowski, whom Pompidou had kept on as secretary of state for foreign affairs, made a visit to Quebec in October 1969. Learning of it in advance, the Department of External Affairs asked that he pay a call on Ottawa. If the request had remained confidential, it might have been granted, but Trudeau mentioned it in public, and to Pompidou's annoyance, it suddenly became another incident. Consulted by Lipkowski, the president decided that he had to stick to de Gaulle's policy concerning visits, and the federal request was ignored.[5] The French minister added fuel to the fire at a press conference in Quebec City by remarking that, as he understood the Canadian constitution, such visits to Quebec were quite in order and there was no need to travel via Ottawa. The press corps besieged Trudeau as he left his office and asked for his reaction. Lipkowski was at Dorval airport in Montreal waiting to board his aircraft when he saw the prime minister on television describing him as a *"petit aristo"* not important enough to be concerned about. The French minister, Trudeau added, had, however, been at the least impolite and had no business interpreting the Canadian constitution to Canadians.

Out of the public view, the Canadian government's reaction was still stronger. Cadieux met with Ambassador Siraud to protest Lipkowski's refusal to visit the Canadian capital, and his subsequent remarks. An *aide-mémoire* was also despatched to Paris for submission to the French government. Beaulieu, who had to present it, was unhappy over the importance given to the matter, but did his duty. Back in Paris, Lipkowski was adamant in defending his conduct. It was Maurice Schumann who succeeded in defusing the situation. When he received Beaulieu in November in Lipkowski's presence, he commented with a mischievous laugh: "Here's the principal accused!"[6] He also announced that France would notify the federal government of future ministerial visits to Quebec, leaving it to decide whether or not to give its assent. What would happen if Ottawa withheld its assent was not clear.

In early December, Schumann and the Canadian minister of external affairs, Mitchell Sharp, met at the United Nations. Both cool-headed men with long experience of government, they got on very well. Schumann insisted that practical circumstances sometimes did not permit a fixed rule that all his colleagues pass automatically through Ottawa on visits to Quebec. Sharp responded that Canada was not asking for that, but pointed out that it would have been normal for Lipkowski, given his responsibilities for international affairs, to do so. He also mentioned his own plan to go to Paris to inaugurate a new wing of the *maison canadienne*, the students' residence at the *Cité Universitaire*, which Ottawa had financed; he asked for Schumann's reaction. Why not, the latter replied; after all, he was the minister of external affairs of a friendly allied nation. He would invite him to lunch. Schumann also assured Sharp that he had no desire to get involved in quarrels over the Canadian constitution, and would confine himself, in dealing with Quebec, to the terms of the Franco-Quebec *ententes* of 1965. Sharp warned that if the *ententes* were interpreted as giving the province the right to negotiate directly with a foreign government, they would have to be re-examined. Schumann said that he did not want to get involved in any such interpretations.

The attitude of the Pompidou and Bertrand governments affected other aspects of the triangular relationship as well. In Paris, Beaulieu and Chapdelaine, friends and former colleagues, found it easier to work together. Both had ready access to ministers and officials, and less attention was paid to political considerations. In December 1969, the francophone ministers of education met again in Paris, and the French let it be known beforehand that they would respect any arrangements made by Ottawa and Quebec City regarding their representation. For Bertrand the priority was not to score points against the federal government with a view to eventually establishing Quebec's distinctive presence on the international scene, but rather to ensure that it participated effectively in international meetings in its fields of jurisdiction. For some Quebec officials, beginning with Claude Morin, that position was disappointing, but it did prove fruitful. The Quebec minister of state for education became head of the Canadian delegation at the Paris meeting. It was also agreed that if the different members of the delegation disagreed on a particular matter, the delegation as a whole would abstain from voting. The more harmonious atmosphere even extended to Gabon. In August 1969, a few weeks before Ambassador Thibault completed his tour of duty in Cameroun, he received instructions from Ottawa to fly to Libreville to discuss an important matter. There he was received effusively by the minister of foreign affairs and the minister of education, and fêted with champagne, which they drank to the health of their respective heads of state. The ministers dismissed the earlier treatment Thibault had received as a "misunderstanding," and commented that Canada was too great a country not to comprehend the situation. The reconciliation was sealed shortly afterwards when Thibault's successor presented his credentials. The hiatus had lasted just under two years. Canadian aid to Gabon was soon resumed and greatly expanded.

In March 1970, Schumann remarked to a French journalist that "the development of friendly relations with the Government of Quebec did not exclude a policy of friendship and alliance with the federal government of Canada."[7] However, like his predecessor Couve de Murville, he was not always able to impose that policy on his colleagues and on pro-Quebec elements in the French government. As a result, the second Niamey conference on March 16–20, 1970, convened to establish the *Agence de coopération culturelle et technique*, was again marred by conflict over the respective roles of the federal government and Quebec. This time, the proponents of a distinctive international role for Quebec found themselves on the defensive.[8] The African heads of state were agreed that only sovereign states should become members of the new body. In the charter he proposed, Jean-Marc Léger, to the surprise of many who knew him as a convinced Quebec separatist, confirmed that principle. As a result, Quebec seemed to be effectively excluded from membership. However, the "Quebec mafia" again mounted a campaign on its behalf. Since only sovereign states were to be eligible to join the new organization, Diori planned to invite only the Canadian government. He came under strong pressure, first from the French ambassador to Niger, then, at a meeting in Tchad, from Jacques Foccart who was still secretary general for African affairs in the Elysée, and Yvon Bourges, a junior French minister, to issue an invitation to Quebec as well.

Once again Diori sent his French adviser, Jacques Baulin, to Ottawa with a suggestion that invitations be sent not only to the Canadian government, but also to the four provinces with significant francophone populations, and that they should agree on a single delegation. Marc Lalonde, who dealt with Baulin, was adamant that Ottawa's prerogatives be respected. As the date of the meeting drew near, the tempo of negotiations and the tension increased once more. Lipkowski sent a personal message to Diori, insisting that Quebec be invited directly; the federal government sent an emissary to Niger with a proposal that Quebec be invited "through Ottawa." Finally, after checking with Ottawa, Baulin agreed that the province could be "notified" of the conference. In the course of the haggling, both French and Quebec officials made veiled threats to boycott the conference if Quebec was not given satisfactory recognition. President Pompidou's attitude on the whole matter is unclear, but it seems that he was more preoccupied with the possible political fall-out in France, so allowed Lipkowski and the others a relatively free hand. As for Bertrand, he was engaged at that moment in an election campaign against the new Liberal leader, Robert Bourassa, and his main concern was to avoid any acrimonious public debate on the matter.

In the end, Quebec did not receive a special invitation, directly or indirectly, but Diori wrote to Bertrand, setting out his understanding that the Quebec government would participate in the conference and the future organization as part of the Canadian delegation. The premier appointed one of his most trusted officials, Julien Chouinard, secretary general of the government, as head of the Quebec delegates, with clear instructions to avoid political controversy. Claude Morin was left at home, because, in his own words, he had become "a sort of caricatural symbol of categorical political obstinacy," and was seen as the person responsible for Quebec's exaggerated international ambitions.[9] The Canadian delegation was again led by Gérard Pelletier. In Niamey, the matter of Quebec's place in the agency proved the principal stumbling block to agreement on the founding of the new agency and even delayed the signing ceremony. The French lobbied hard for the best possible formula for Quebec. In the end, the province was admitted, not as a member-state, but as a "participating government." Léger became the first secretary general. France, it was decided, was to contribute forty-five per cent of the budget, Canada thirty-three per cent, Belgium ten per cent, and the others ten per cent.

In April, the Liberals were returned to power in Quebec. For the new premier, Robert Bourassa, international relations were of secondary importance, far behind employment and economic growth. As with Pompidou, his main concern was not to allow them to become a domestic political problem. Having won a battle of principle—some would say a symbolic victory—the federal government pushed forward vigorously with its programme of developing relations with francophone Africa to a level comparable to those with Commonwealth Africa. The External Aid Office was transformed into the much larger and better-financed Canadian International Development Agency (CIDA) and made more bilingual.

Charles de Gaulle died on November 9, 1970, thirteen days before his eightieth birthday. External Affairs Minister Sharp attended the funeral service; two members of the Bourassa cabinet represented Quebec. In one of his rare miscalculations, the general had not left himself enough time to complete his memoirs, so his version of his relations with Quebec remains untold. He did refer briefly to his visit to Canada in 1960 and recalled wondering if the country's future did not lie in "establishing a State of French stock, beside another of British stock, cooperating freely in every respect and, preferably, working together as two independent units in order to safeguard them."[10] His model for Canada was still the same as for Europe, a group of independent countries collaborating in specific areas in their common interest, but each maintaining its freedom of action. Whether by chance or collusion, that prescription was also an accurate description of the formula of sovereignty-association advocated by the *Parti Québécois*. De Gaulle tried to move Canada in that direction by strengthening Quebec, encouraging the Quebec leadership to think and act in that sense, and weakening the central authority. As a realist, and even a pessimist by nature, he was well aware that the independence of Quebec was not, as separatists proclaimed, an inevitable development. Throughout his life he had held before his fellow citizens the vision of French grandeur, not so much as a goal to be reached in a determinate time, but as a beacon to strive towards. In similar vein, he had told francophone Quebecers in 1967 that they could become independent if they so chose, but he knew that it depended, as he had said at Solferino in 1959, on their will and capacity. And just as he ended his career in disappointment with the refusal of Frenchmen to rise to the challenge he threw down to them, so he was disappointed with the French Canadians, and particularly with their leaders, including Daniel Johnson. In one of his last recorded references to his Quebec experience, he expressed bitterness, but rather towards his critics at home than towards those across the Atlantic. The "Quebec affair," he protested to journalist Claude Mauriac, was "the best proof" of the insidiousness of

> the bourgeois who want to wipe out France at all costs....
> How could anyone imagine that de Gaulle would remain indifferent in front of the French Canadians who were shouting *Vive la France* and singing *La Marseillaise* while the music was playing *God Save the Queen*? And that after so many years of ingratitude on our part?"[11]

Following de Gaulle's death, the process of normalization, or more accurately, of progress towards a less conflictual set of relationships within the France-Canada-Quebec triangle, was accelerated. French ministers resumed the practice of visiting Ottawa when on Canadian territory. Marking the transition, Schumann flew up from the United Nations in September 1971 for a series of meetings with Trudeau, Sharp and others. Afterward, he told the press that all discord between Canada and France was "henceforth smoothed out and transcended."[12] Approval by the Canadian Parliament a short time earlier of a law recognizing the bilingual and bicultural character of the country, he said, had been an important factor in bringing about the new situation. Cultural and financial exchanges were also developing satisfactorily, but a serious effort was still required in the trade sector. In response to a journalist's question, Schumann said that France would be pleased to receive Prime Minister Trudeau; it was just a matter of fitting a visit into his and President Pompidou's schedules. The rosy picture of the relationship painted by the French foreign minister was exaggerated. Pompidou depicted it more accurately in a coincidental statement in Paris: the links between France and Quebec were so strong that nothing could impair them; accordingly, French policy was to have "special relations with Quebec and good relations with Canada."[13] Schumann recognized the delicacy of that balancing act when he returned to New York from Ottawa, then made a separate trip to Quebec City in October, thus disappointing Ottawa slightly in order to avoid offending Quebec and its sympathizers in France.

While Quebec came to miss de Gaulle's unequivocal support, and the encouragement he gave to the "Quebec mafia," Franco-Quebec relations did continue to develop on a sounder basis. The Acadians were less fortunate. Following their dazzling reception in January 1968, the

Acadian leaders continued for some time to visit Paris regularly at French expense and to negotiate various forms of aid. However, some of the original requests proved unrealistic. Rector Savoie became concerned about the installation of a French *maison de culture* on the University of Moncton campus; as French government property, he learned, it would be outside his jurisdiction. Worse still, the first *coopérants*, or teaching personnel, arrived in Moncton in the fall of 1968 fresh from the student uprisings of May, and sought to re-enact the scenario there. Savoie imagined with dread the situation if they operated out of the *maison de culture*. The project remained a dead letter. As for the *cinébus*, it arrived, painted and equipped for service in Africa, not North America. It was to tour New Brunswick schools, but the school authorities, annoyed at not having been consulted, objected to the intrusion into their field of authority. The vehicle saw little service. The most disappointing development occurred just two days after de Gaulle's resignation. In Paris on one of his missions, Euclide Daigle was told by an official that, since the Canadian government had offered to pay for his tickets, he no longer needed to get them from France. He went to the Elysée to complain, but was turned away empty-handed. Some support was maintained, but the Acadians were once again left largely to their own resources in their difficult struggle for survival.

Another casualty of the new triangular relations was the Paris-based *Comité pour l'indépendance du Québec*. French officialdom had been distrustful of it from the outset. In conformity with the law, Maurice Jacquinot applied to the Ministry of the Interior for permission for it to operate on French territory. In August 1969, three months after de Gaulle's retirement, he was informed that all references to political objectives, including the word "independence," had to be deleted from the title and terms of reference.[14] The organization was renamed the *Comité d'étude et d'information sur les problèmes du Québec*. One of the principal projects, to establish a government-in-exile, was dropped. Most serious of all, the fund-raising campaign was a failure. The *Comité* launched a publication, *Plein Pouvoir*, but, with limited financial resources, it collapsed after twenty issues. Finally, in a desperate bid for help, Jacquinot wrote directly to President Pompidou in December 1970. He was referred by the Elysée staff to Rossillon.[15] The irrepressible proponent of francophone causes suggested the possibility of using the organization as an information-gathering network. Unwilling to become involved in what sounded to him like clandestine activities, Jacquinot did not pursue the matter. By then, the members of the *Comité* were also becoming divided into factions along ideological and tactical lines; some were even violently anti-semitic. By 1975, the *Comité* was moribund.

During Robert Bourassa's first period as premier, from 1970 to 1976, the triangular relationship remained relatively stable. Quebec ministers served as heads of Canadian delegations to meetings of the *Agence de coopération culturelle et technique*. Jean-Marc Léger was scrupulously fair in dealing with all parties. The Canadian constitutional negotiations led to the Victoria agreement of 1971, but Bourassa recoiled from placing it before the National Assembly for fear of separatist demonstrations. Frustrated in their attempts to move the province towards independence, Claude Morin and Jacques Parizeau left the government service and joined the *Parti Québécois*. In Paris, Frenchmen who still supported the separatist cause transferred their hopes to that party.

Lévesque himself was hardly an enthusiast of Franco-Quebec relations. He had served in the American forces during World War Two and commented frequently that he felt more at home in the United States than anywhere else outside Quebec. Accordingly, de Gaulle's anti-Americanism had no appeal for him. On the other hand, French support was a potential card that he could not ignore. In May 1969, he gave a letter to Doctor Marc Lavallée, a close collaborator in establishing the *Parti Québécois*, entrusting him with a mandate to promote "the sovereignty of Quebec and better permanent links between France and French Quebec" during his frequent visits to France.[16] Lavallée recounts that Lévesque also asked him "to explore ...with the French ministers and officials" the possibility of a financial contribution to the party. Accordingly, he met with Rossillon and Jurgensen, mentioning to the latter the figure of three hundred thousand dollars. Jurgensen, he states, volunteered the information that France had contributed financially to the *Union Nationale*, and Lavallée received the impression that the request would be granted. He even writes that Jacques Parizeau was to follow up on the matter. Parizeau has denied any involvement. Nothing more is known on the subject.

Pierre Trudeau's official visit to Paris did not materialize during Pompidou's tenure; the president did not appreciate certain of his acerbic remarks, and, in any case, he had other priorities. Trudeau's relations with Valéry Giscard d'Estaing, who became president in 1974, were much easier. He knew Quebec better than most French politicians, having spent several months in Montreal as a part-time teacher in the early 1950s; he had also led French missions to Quebec as minister of finance. More important, he did not share de Gaulle's almost mystical belief in the uniqueness of the French people nor his deep commitment to the grandeur of France. On the contrary, he was very much a man of the second half of the twentieth century, expert in economics and public finance and fascinated with technological and scientific development. Giscard d'Estaing's first prime minister, Jacques Chirac, was a man of a very different stripe. A strong Gaullist, he accepted the general's position on Quebec as part of the heritage that he was bound to defend and perpetuate, although not necessarily to pursue vigorously. Giscard d'Estaing received Trudeau six months after taking office. They had a positive meeting and the president revealed his own particular formula for dealing with the triangle: non-interference in Canadian affairs, and non-indifference towards Quebec.

The election of the *Parti Québécois* in Quebec in November 1976 stirred a new interest in Quebec separatism. The "Quebec mafia" took on a new lease on life. De Gaulle's prophetic vision was extolled. Gaullist party Secretary General Yves Guëna paid tribute to his "clear-mindedness" that had "contributed to the progress of history." When Claude Morin visited France as minister of inter-governmental affairs in April 1977, Jacques Chirac, at that moment mayor of Paris, wished him "complete success...in the process begun by the Government of Quebec towards independence...within the framework of an economic association." The Giscard d'Estaing administration, on the other hand, stuck to its policy of maintaining a balance in its relations between the Quebec and Canadian governments. Prime Minister Raymond Barre sent congratulations to René Lévesque on his election, but made no reference to his principal political objective. However, when Lévesque visited France in November 1977, Giscard d'Estaing gave him a sumptuous welcome and made him a *Grand Officier de la Légion d'Honneur*. They agreed to annual meetings of prime ministers alternately in Paris and Quebec City, a proposal resurrected from Peyrefitte's list of projects in September 1967, but modified so as not to involve the president. During the course of the visit, Giscard d'Estaing modified his policy towards Quebec to take account of the possibility that separatism might indeed occur. The central question in Quebec, he commented, was "how to ensure the safeguard and affirmation of a Quebec personality...equally attached to the sources of its tradition and to opening up to the currents of modern civilization, equally concerned with its French identity and its American dimension." The debate over that subject did not leave France indifferent, but it was not up to France to intervene; the matter would be decided by Quebecers alone. What they could expect from France was "its comprehension, its confidence and its support," along whatever road they would decide to take.

In keeping with the new arrangements, Prime Minister Barre made a visit to Quebec in February 1979, but preceded it with one to Ottawa. His stay was marked by friction between Ottawa and Quebec City over points of protocol reminiscent of de Gaulle's visit in 1967. Under pressure from both sides to make favourable statements, Barre gave them a lesson in political dexterity and also in proper conduct.

The Socialist victory in France in 1981 raised new questions about France's attitude. Although the new president, François Mitterrand, had strongly criticized de Gaulle's intervention in 1967 and expressed doubts whether independence was in the best interests of Quebec, *Parti Québécois* militants who considered themselves social democrats felt that their chances of French support would be enhanced. They were soon to be disabused. Mitterrand did not share de Gaulle's views on nationalism, nor his vision of the grandeur of France; even his commitment to socialism was open to question. Other prominent members of the Socialist party, including Michel Rocard, did sympathize with the *Parti Québécois*, but their feeling of solidarity fell far short of de Gaulle's commitment to Quebec. In the end, Mitterrand's view prevailed and the government produced yet another version of the triangular relationship: normal relations with Canada, special relations with Quebec. That position was made easier by the fact that, by the time the Socialists were elected, the *Parti Québécois* had lost the referendum on sovereignty-association.

President Mitterrand visited Ottawa in 1981 to attend a Summit conference of Western economic powers. He took care not to appear to intervene in domestic matters, receiving Premier Lévesque discreetly at the French embassy. Later, Trudeau remarked, *"Monsieur* Mitterrand told me that he intended to respect the Canadian constitution. We are asking for nothing more. That established, if the French government wants to have special relations with Quebec, I am the first, being a Quebecer myself, to be delighted."[17] In May 1987, Mitterrand made an official state visit to Canada, speaking to both the Canadian Parliament and the Quebec National Assembly, and making an appearance in every region of the country. Even the controversy over fishing rights in the waters around St. Pierre and Miquelon was not allowed to mar the harmony of the occasion. Canadian biculturalism brought joy to the heart of every Frenchman, the president declared; France and Canada shared the conviction that pluralism was the way of the future.[18] The rhetoric had come full circle.

What was General de Gaulle's longer-term impact on the evolution of Canada and Quebec, and their relations with France? First, it must be recalled that the initiative that led to his involvement did not come from him but from the Lesage government, which appealed for French support to maintain the French fact in North America. His general attitude was that he welcomed the renewal of ties between France and French Canadians, and was happy to try to meet the latter's requests, but that the initiative had to come from them. However, because of a variety of circumstances, he transgressed that principle in 1967 and took the initiative himself. His growing interest in Quebec was motivated by several factors: sensitivity to French-Canadian resentment at being abandoned by France in 1763, a sense of obligation to improve what he considered to be the intolerable situation of a branch of the French people, a concept of France as a world power capable of intervening in any part of the world, and a distrust or even dislike of the Anglo-Saxons, France's historic adversaries. As a leader with a broad historical and spatial vision of human events, he saw his role as that of conceiving and initiating changes, and of stirring others to execute them in their own interest. His objective in visiting Quebec in 1967 was, through some spectacular gesture, to shake up or even destabilize the Canadian political system and to create a situation favorable to Quebec in the impending constitutional negotiations. He also wanted to challenge French Canadians to pursue the logic of their nationalist rhetoric to its conclusion. His preferred outcome was the transformation of Canada into two independent states, one francophone, the other anglophone, which would maintain certain links, common institutions and policies in their mutual interest, but also the freedom to go their separate ways if they found themselves in fundamental disagreement. In promoting that formula, he was conscious that he was violating the principle in which he believed of non-intervention in the affairs of other countries, but he justified doing so on the grounds that French Canadians were an integral part of the French people, and Quebec their nation-state.

That having been said, the cry *"Vive le Québec libre"* was not planned in advance. It was rather, in military terms, a tactical move decided on the spot, but it was in keeping with a preconceived strategy. In Quebec City the previous evening, de Gaulle had delivered a carefully prepared message to the French-Canadian élite: you can be independent if you want to. In Montreal, he repeated it to the masses in different terms and in a different key. In part, the vivat was an impulsive and even emotional response to the reception given him during the day; it was also in part a reaction to a challenge from the separatists to repeat their slogan. That, too, was part of de Gaulle's style; in dealing with the masses, he communicated through emotions as much as through reason. It was a dangerous game if one was not in absolute control of one's emotions, and that was probably the case that day. At the same time, he did not go farther in speaking to the crowd in front of the Montreal Hôtel de Ville than in the Quebec banquet hall.

Both the Quebec City speech and the vivat were a mistake in judgment. He embarrassed his host, Premier Johnson, whom he set out to help, and he did not give voice to widespread popular aspirations as he thought. He alienated Prime Minister Pearson and a great many other Canadians from both language groups who were committed to improving the lot of French Canadians within Confederation. And he stiffened the resistance of many English Canadians to such reforms. Ironically, he stirred Canadian nationalist sentiments, never intense but stronger than he and many Canadians realized. In the longer term, he did not help Johnson or his successors to attain more constitutional powers for Quebec, let alone some form of independence. On the other hand, he did spur the federal government to greater efforts to meet French Canadians' grievances, and thus to strengthen the Canadian polity. Within France, "*Vive le Québec libre*" also proved to be a mistake. De Gaulle's own ministers and supporters were taken by surprise; the media reaction was generally negative, and the population uncomprehending. Generally, it was seen as a monumental blunder, and an indication that he and his régime were in decline. His subsequent attempts to justify his action were unsuccessful. If, as the preeminent French statesman, he had worked closely with both the Canadian and Quebec governments, encouraging and supporting them in their efforts on behalf of French Canadians, he would have had greater success both in Canada and at home. But such was not his nature.

Was then de Gaulle's intervention in Canadian affairs merely, in the words of Quebec historian Pierre Savard, "*un accident de parcours*"—a chance mishap—in the continuing process of building a new set of relationships "on the basis of realities more durable than incendiary speeches?"[19] The balance sheet is more positive. He went very far towards "paying the debt of Louis XV," that is, of countering French Canadians' resentment at being abandoned in 1763. He also helped greatly to develop new links, both tangible and intangible, between France and French Canada, and between French Canada and other parts of the *Francophonie*. Not less significant, though that was not his intention, he goaded the federal government into overcoming its neglect of relations with France and other French-speaking countries. The former French colonies were obvious beneficiaries of that change of policy, but so were both France and Canada. Above all, de Gaulle's place in history is assured as the great French leader who, whether right or wrong in his perspective and tactics, reached out to French Canada in a gesture of solidarity and affection.

Notes

Chapter 1

1 J. Lacouture, *Le Rebelle* (Paris: Editions du Seuil, 1984); *Le Politique* (Paris: Editions du Seuil, 1985); *Le Souverain* (Paris: Editions du Seuil, 1986).
2 C. de Gaulle, *Lettres, notes et carnets* (Paris: Plon, 1980–1987).
3 C. de Gaulle, *Mémoires de guerre. vol. I. L'Appel 1940–1942* (Paris: Plon, 1954), 1.
4 C. de Gaulle, *Lettres, notes et carnets (1905–1918)*, 23.
5 Quoted in J.-P. Guichard, *De Gaulle et les mass media* (Paris: Editions France-Empire, 1985), 316.
6 Quoted in A. Crowley, *De Gaulle* (N.Y.: Bobbs, Merrill, 1959), 44.
7 C. de Gaulle, *La Discorde chez l'ennemi* (Paris: Editions Berger-Levrault, 1924).
8 Quoted in J. Lacouture, *op. cit.*, vol. I, 121.
9 Quoted in J.-R. Tournoux, *Pétain et de Gaulle* (Paris: Plon, 1964), 97.
10 J. Lacouture, *op. cit.*, vol. I, 122.
11 C. de Gaulle, *Le Fil de l'épée* (Paris: Editions Berger-Levrault, 1944), 20.
12 *Ibid.*, 74–76.
13 *Ibid.*, 9.
14 *Ibid.*, 77.
15 (Paris: Berger-Levrault, 1934).
16 C. de Gaulle, *Mémoires de guerre*, vol. I, 13.
17 Quoted in J. Lacouture, *op. cit.*,. vol. I, 266.
18 C. de Gaulle, *La France et son armée* (Paris: Plon, 1938).
19 C. de Gaulle, *Lettres, notes et carnets, 1919–Juin 1940*, 474–76.
20 C. de Gaulle, *Vers l'Armée de métier*, 139.
21 C. de Gaulle, *Lettres, notes, carnets. 1919–Juin 1940*, 478.
22 *Ibid.*, 492.
23 F. Kersaudy, *Churchill and de Gaulle* (London: Collins, 1981). Many citations refer to the French edition: *De Gaulle et Churchill* (Paris: Plon, 1982).
24 Chips, *Diaries of Sir H. Channon* (London: Weiderfeld, 1967), 381.
25 W. Churchill, *The Second World War*, vol. II (London: Cassell, 1949), 128.
26 Quoted in F. Kersaudy, *Churchill and de Gaulle* (London: Collins, 1981), 77.

27 C. de Gaulle, _Mémoires de guerre, vol. II L'Unité 1942–1944_ (Paris: Plon, 1956), 90.
28 E. Spears, _Assignment to Catastrophe_ (London: Heinemann, 1954), 146.
29 Quoted in O. Guichard, _Mon Général_ (Paris: Grasset, 1980), 83.
30 Quoted in Chicago _Daily News_, Aug. 27, 1941.
31 J. Lacouture, _op. cit._, vol. I, 554.
32 Quoted in F. Kersaudy, _op. cit._, 184.
33 Quoted in J. Lacouture, _op. cit._, vol. I, 609.
34 Quoted in J. Lacouture, _op. cit._, vol. I, 555.
35 Quoted in C. de Gaulle, _Mémoires de guerre_, vol. II, 125.
36 Quoted in F. Kersaudy, _op. cit._, 304.
37 Quoted in J. Lacouture, _op. cit._, vol. II, 78.
38 Quoted by J. Chaban-Delmas, in _Espoir_, no. 51, June 1985, 3.
39 C. de Gaulle, _Mémoires de guerre_, vol. II, 378.
40 Quoted in P. Bignard, _Joliot-Curie et l'énergie atomique_ (Paris: Seghers, 1961), 95.
41 L. Barzini, _The Europeans_ (London: Penguin, 1983), 137.
42 C. de Gaulle, _Mémoires de guerre_, vol. I, 5.
43 J. Lacouture, _op. cit._, vol. II, 360.
44 O. Guichard, _op. cit._, 328.
45 Quoted in _Espoir_, vol. 43, June 1983, 23.
46 O. Guichard, _op. cit._, 363.
47 Quoted in C. Ney, _Le Noir et le Rouge._ (Paris: Grasset, 1984), 118.
48 P. G. Cerny, _The Politics of Grandeur. Ideological Aspects of de Gaulle's Foreign Policy_ (Cambridge: Cambridge University Press, 1980), 131.
49 Quoted in J.-R. Tournoux, _Jamais dit_ (Paris: Plon, 1971), 212.
50 O. Guichard, interview with author, January 15, 1985.
51 J.-R. Tournoux, _La Tragédie du Général_ (Paris: Plon, 1967), 485.
52 "I am convinced that the monarchy is the regime best suited to our country," he remarked later. "...but how to bring it about?" (Quoted by O. Guichard _op. cit._, 403).
53 Quoted in J. Lacouture, _op. cit._, vol. II, 238.
54 Quoted in _Ibid._, 285.
55 Quoted in O. Guichard, _op. cit._, 94.
56 Quoted in _Ibid._, 281.
57 June 20, 1953. C. de Gaulle, _Lettres, notes et carnets, June 1951–May 1958_, 130.
58 March 6, 1955. _Ibid._, 237.
59 Quoted in J. Lacouture, _op. cit._, vol. II, 429.
60 Quoted in J. Lacouture, _op. cit._, vol. II, 468.
61 Quoted in J.-R. Tournoux, _Le Tourment et la fatalité_ (Paris: Plon, 1974), 22.
62 Quoted in J. Lacouture, _op. cit._, vol. II, 518.
63 E. Jouhaud, _Serons-nous enfin compris?_ (Paris: Albin Michel, 1984), 53.
64 J. Lacouture, _op. cit._, vol. III, 530.

Chapter 2

1 Quoted in A. Patry, _Le Québec dans le monde_ (Montreal: Leméac, 1980), 49.
2 C. Black, _Duplessis_ (Toronto: McClelland & Stewart, 1977), 490.
3 Quoted in R. Chaloult, _Mémoires politiques_ (Montreal: Editions du Jour, 1969), 42–43.

4 Vincent Auriol, *Journal du Septennat 1947–54*, tome I, 1951. (Paris: Colin, 1975), 175.
5 C. Black, *op. cit.*, 493.
6 *Ibid.*, 493.
7 Quoted in *Ibid.*, 493.
8 *Ibid.*, 493.
9 *Action Catholique*, September 19, 1968.
10 C. Black, *op. cit.*, 495.
11 Statement by Daniel Johnson, Quebec Legislative Assembly, *Debates*, April 13, 1967, 216ff.
12 Quoted in C. Black, *op. cit.*, 485.

Chapter 3

1 A. and P. Rouanet, *Les Trois derniers chagrins du Général de Gaulle* (Paris: Grasset, 1980), 37.
2 Pauline Vanier, interview with author, November 17, 1984.
3 *Globe & Mail*, June 26, 1940.
4 *Le Devoir*, June 29, 1940.
5 Public Archives of Canada, Mackenzie King Diaries, June 23, 1940.
6 House of Commons, *Debates*, July 5, 1940, 1359.
7 Published in R. Lescop, *Le Pari québécois du Général de Gaulle* (Montreal: Boréal Express, 1981), 4.
8 Letter from E. Lapointe to J. L. Ralston, Sept. 30, 1940. In Lapointe Papers, vol. XXIV, file 82.
9 Quoted in Documents of external affairs, vol. XXIV, 1941–43, Part II, 592.
10 *Ibid.*, 592.
11 Secretary of state for external affairs to high commissioner in Great Britain, Aug. 28, 1940. In *Ibid.*, 560.
12 Elisabeth de Miribel, *La Liberté souffre violence* (Paris: Plon, 1981), 48ff.
13 Report of M. May in Archives Diplomatiques, Ministère des Affaires Étrangères, Paris. File CNF, Décembre 1940–Juillet 1942.
14 J. W. Pickersgill, *The Mackenzie Record*, vol. I, 1939–44 (Toronto: University of Toronto Press, 1960), 147.
15 Cabinet War Committee Records, Sept. 26, 1940.
16 Record of a conversation between the (British) secretary of state and Mr. Rougier, Oct. 24, 1940. In Department of External Affairs Documents, RG.25, D1, vol. 777, File 370.
17 Quoted in D. C. Anglin, *The St. Pierre and Miquelon Affair of 1941*. (Toronto, University of Toronto Press, 1966), 48–9.
18 Text in Documents of External Affairs, 1939–41, vol. VII, Tome 2, 1939–41, 642.
19 J. Lacouture, *op. cit.*, vol. I, 456.
20 *Ibid.*, 456.
21 Chargé d'affaires in France, Belgium and The Netherlands to prime minister, January 15, 1941. In Documents for External Affairs, 1939–41, vol. VIII, Part II, 651–53.
22 Text of message to Marshall Pétain, January 8, 1941. In Documents on External Affairs, 1941–43, vol. VIII, Part II, 648–49.
23 Chargé d'affaires in France, Belgium and the Netherlands to secretary of state for external affairs, March 14, 1941. In *Ibid.*, 657–58.
24 *Ibid.*, April 3, 1941, 659–60.

25 Chargé d'affaires in France, Belgium, The Netherlands to prime minister, May 9, 1941. In *Ibid.*, 660.
26 High commissioner in Great Britain to secretary of state for external affairs, September 27, 1941. In *Ibid.*, 662–65.
27 Quoted in R. T. Thomas, *Britain and Vichy: The Dilemma of Anglo-French Relations, 1940–42* (London, Macmillan, 1979), 87.
28 Quoted in D. Dilks, ed., *The Diaries of Sir Alexander Cadogam, 1938–45* (London: Cassell, 1971), 351.
29 Memo from D. Morton to Churchill, June 2, 1941. In Foreign Office Records, FO 371/28235.
30 V. Massey, *What's Past Is Prologue. Memoirs of the Right Honourable Vincent Massey* (Toronto: University of Toronto Press, 1963), 337.
31 Telegram from high commission in Great Britain to secretary of state for external affairs, February 18, 1941. In Documents for External Affairs, vol. VIII, Part II, 1941–43, 605.
32 J. F. Hilliker, "The Canadian Government and the Free French. Perceptions and Constraints. 1940–44." In *International History Review.* vol. II, no. 1, January 1980, 94.
33 Elisabeth de Miribel, interview with author, Paris, November 21, 1984.
34 See G. Arnold, *One Woman's War* (Toronto: Lorimer, 1987).
35 Telegram from d'Argenlieu to de Gaulle, May 14, 1941. Archives diplomatiques, Ministère des Affaires Étrangères, Paris.
36 Memorandum from under secretary of state to prime minister, Sept. 25, 1941. In Documents of External Affairs, *op. cit.*, 617.

Chapter 4

1 Vice-amiral E.-H. Muselier, *De Gaulle contre le Gaullisme* (Paris: Editions du Chêne, 1946), 71.
2 Sept. 17, 1940. Text in C. de Gaulle, *Lettres, notes et carnets. Juin 1940–Juillet 1941*, 115–16.
3 Quoted in D. G. Anglin, *op. cit.*, 134.
4 High commissioner for Great Britain to under secretary of state for external affairs, Sept. 23, 1940. In Documents of External Affairs, vol. VIII, Part II, 1939–41, 771–72.
5 Under secretary of state for external affairs to high commissioner for Great Britain, Oct. 11, 1940. In *Ibid.*, 777–78.
6 L. McCarthy to secretary of state for external affairs, Mar. 15, 1941. In *Ibid.*, 803–04.
7 Quoted in C. de Gaulle, *Lettres, notes et carnets. Juin 1940–Juillet 1941.* 150–51.
8 Minister of national defence for naval services to under secretary of state for external affairs, June 28, 1941. In Documents on External Affairs, 1939–41, vol. VIII, Part II, 826–27.
9 D. G. Anglin, *op. cit.*, 58ff.
10 Telegram from Dominions secretary to secretary of state for external affairs, May 29, 1941. In Documents on External Affairs, 1941–43, vol. VIII, Part II, 815.
11 High commissioner for Great Britain to under secretary of state for external affairs, July 9, 1941. In *Ibid.*, 828.
12 Memorandum from under secretary of state for external affairs to prime minister, July 15, 1941. In *Ibid.*, 829.

13 Memorandum from under secretary of state for external affairs to prime minister, Aug. 15, 1941. In *Ibid.*, 839–40.
14 Acting consul in St. Pierre and Miquelon to secretary of state for external affairs. Oct. 2, 1941. In *Ibid.*, 840–44.
15 High commissioner for Great Britain to under secretary of state for external affairs, Oct. 21, 1941. In *Ibid.*, 844–45.
16 Secretary of state for external affairs to minister in United States. October 30, 1941. In *Ibid.*, 848.
17 Quoted in J. W. Pickersgill, *op. cit.*, vol. I, 319.
18 Dominions secretary to secretary of state for external affairs, December 15, 1941. In Documents on External Affairs, vol. IX, 1942–43, 1634.
19 Quoted in Chicago *Daily News*, August 27, 1941.
20 Quoted in D. G. Anglin, *op. cit.*, 66.
21 C. de Gaulle, *Mémoires de guerre.* vol. I, 231.
22 Quoted in Héron de Villefosse, *Les Iles de la liberté* (Paris: Editions Albin Michel, 1972), 122.
23 Vice-amiral E. Muselier, *op. cit.*, 255.
24 Quoted in P. Billotte, *Le Temps des armes* (Paris: Plon, 1972), 187.
25 D. G. Anglin, *op. cit.*, 75.
26 Quoted in F. Kersaudy, *op. cit.*, 144–145.
27 Quoted in *Ibid.*, 144–145.
28 Dominions secretary to secretary of state of external affairs, December 15, 1941. In Documents on External Relations, vol. IX 1942–43, 1635.
29 Quoted in F. Kersaudy, *op. cit.*, 145.
30 Quoted in *Ibid.*, 145.
31 Quoted in *Ibid.*, 145.
32 Text in Vice-amiral E. Muselier, *op. cit.*, 257.
33 H. de Villefosse, *op. cit.*, 127.
34 Quoted in Vice-amiral E. Muselier, *op. cit.*, 261.
35 Text in Vice-amiral E. Muselier, *op. cit.*, 261–62.
36 Quoted in *Ibid.*, 263.
37 Quoted in Documents of Canadian External Relations, vol. IX 1942–43, 1639.
38 Quoted in *Ibid.*, 1642.
39 Quoted in *Ibid.*, 1644.
40 Quoted in Vice-amiral E. Muselier, *op. cit.* 262.
41 Quoted in *Ibid.*, 264.
42 C. de Gaulle, *Mémoires de guerre.* vol. I, 233.
43 B. Ledwidge, *De Gaulle* (London: Weidenfeld and Nicolson, 1982), 113.
44 C. de Gaulle, *Mémoires de guerre*, vol. I, 232.
45 Quoted in Vice-amiral E. Muselier, *op. cit.*, 264.
46 Quoted in H. de Villefosse, *op. cit.*, 129.
47 *Ibid.*, 131.
48 Telegram quoted in Vice-amiral E. Muselier, *op. cit.*, 265.
49 D. G. Anglin, *op. cit.*, 83.
50 H. de Villefosse, *op. cit.*, 137.
51 Acting consul in St. Pierre and Miquelon to secretary of state for external affairs, 9 a.m., December 24, 1941. In Documents on Canadian External Affairs, vol. IX, 1942–43, 1648.
52 Dec. 26, 1941.
53 Quoted in D. G. Anglin, *op. cit.*, 99.
54 Quoted in J. W. Pickersgill, *op. cit.*, vol. I, 319.

55 Secretary of state for external affairs to high commission in Great Britain. In Documents on Canadian External Affairs, vol. IX, 1942–3, 1649.
56 Quoted in F. Kersaudy, *op. cit.*, 147.
57 Memorandum by acting under secretary of state for external affairs, December 24, 1941. In Documents on Canadian External Affairs, vol. IX, 1942–43, 1655.
58 Memorandum by acting under secretary of state for external affairs, December 26, 1941. In *Ibid.*, 1655–57.
59 Memorandum from assistant under secretary for external affairs to acting prime minister, December 26, 1941. In *Ibid.*, 1657–58.
60 Legation of France to Department of External Affairs, December 25, 1941. In *Ibid.*, 1650–51.
61 High commission of Great Britain to acting under secretary of state for external affairs, December 26, 1941. In *Ibid.*, 1652.
62 Memorandum by acting under secretary of state for external affairs, December 26, 1941. In *Ibid.*, 1655–57.
63 J. W. Pickersgill, *op. cit.*, vol. I. 320.
64 Quoted in Vice-amiral E. Muselier, *op. cit.*, 281.
65 Quoted in *Ibid.*, 282.
66 Quoted in *Ibid.*, 282.
67 Quoted in *Ibid.*, 283.
68 Quoted in H. de Villefosse, *op. cit.*, 140.
69 Quoted in Vice-amiral E. Muselier, *op. cit.*, 299.
70 Quoted in *Ibid.*, 299.
71 Report on interview in air officer commanding eastern air command to chief of air staff, December 28, 1941. In Documents on Canadian External Affairs, vol. IX, 1942–43, 1664–66.
72 Text in Vice-amiral E. Muselier, *op. cit.*, 300.
73 Memorandum by minister-counsellor, legation in United States, December 27, 1941. In Documents on Canadian External Affairs, vol. IX, 1942–43, 1660–62.
74 Quoted in J. W. Pickersgill, *op. cit.*, vol. I., 322.
75 Memorandum by minister-counsellor, legation in United States, December 27, 1941. In Documents on Canadian External Affairs, vol. IX, 1942–43, 1660–62.
76 Memorandum by minister-counsellor, legation in United States, December 29, 1941. In *Ibid.*, 1666–67.
77 W. Churchill, *Complete Speeches*, vol. VI, 6543.
78 Quoted in F. Kersaudy, *op. cit.*, 148.
79 *Ibid.*, 149.
80 Quoted in F. Kersaudy, *op. cit.*, 149.
81 Included in despatch from minister in United States to secretary of state for external affairs, January 12, 1942. In Documents on Canadian External Affairs, vol. IX, 1942–43, 1685.
82 Memorandum from minister-counsellor, legation in United States to minister in United States, January 14, 1942. In *Ibid.*, 1690.
83 Quoted in Vice-amiral E. Muselier, *op. cit.*, 304.
84 C. de Gaulle, *Mémoires de guerre*, vol. I, 234.
85 F. Kersaudy, *op. cit.*, 177.
86 Quoted in H. de Villefosse, *op. cit.*, 158.
87 Minister-counsellor, legation in United States to under secretary of state for external affairs January 27, 1942. In Documents on Canadian External Affairs, vol. IX, 1942–43, 1694.

88 In Vice-amiral E. Muselier, *op. cit.*, 311–12.
89 In F. Kersaudy, *op. cit.*, 151–52.
90 H. de Villefosse, *op. cit.*, 160.
91 Quoted in D. G. Anglin, *op. cit.*, 125.
92 *Ibid.*, 125.
93 Telegram to Savary, May 25, 1942. In C. de Gaulle, *Lettres, notes et carnets–Juillet 1941–Mai 1943*, 275.
94 C. de Gaulle, *Mémoires de guerre*, vol. I, 232.

Chapter 5

1 *Quebec and the Present War. A Study of Public Opinion.* Ottawa, July 1942.
2 Telegram from Churchill to Mackenzie King, April 21, 1942. In Documents on External Relations, vol. IX, 1942–43, 13–14.
3 Quoted in R. Speaight, *Vanier. Soldier, Diplomat and Governor General* (Toronto: Collins, 1970), 227–28.
4 For a detailed treatment of the subject, see R. Atkin, *Dieppe 1942* (London: Macmillan, 1980).
5 Quoted in *Ibid.*, 261.
6 Quoted in *Ibid.*, 253.
7 Alain Boissieu, interview with author, Paris, December 11, 1984.
8 External Affairs Records, H. Wrong to N. A. Robertson, September 24, 1942.
9 Quoted in Winnipeg *Free Press*, Nov. 9, 1942.
10 Quoted in J. W. Pickersgill, *op. cit.*, vol. I, 426.
11 Quoted in *Ibid.*, 428.
12 Memorandum from under secretary of state for external affairs to prime minister, November 11, 1942. In Documents on Canadian External Affairs, vol. IX, 1942–43, 22.
13 Secretary of state for external affairs to high commission in Great Britain. In *Ibid.*, 25.
14 High commissioner in Great Britain to secretary of state for external affairs, November 30, 1942. In *Ibid.*, 26.
15 Quoted in R. Speaight, *op. cit.*, 256.
16 High commissioner in Great Britain to secretary of state for external affairs, November 30, 1942. In Documents on External Affairs, vol. IX, 1942–43, 26.
17 Quoted in J. Lacouture, *op. cit.*, vol. 618.
18 Quoted in *Ibid.*, 628.
19 Memorandum from under secretary of state for external affairs to prime minister, December 12, 1942. In Documents on Canadian External Affairs, vol. IX, 1942–43, 1706.
20 Memorandum from under secretary of state for external affairs to prime minister. In *Ibid.*, 1706.
21 High commissioner in Great Britain to secretary of state for external affairs, December 24, 1942. In *Ibid.*, 1708.
22 Quoted in J. Lacouture, *op. cit.*, vol. I 629.
23 Quoted in P. Murphy, *Diplomat Among Warriors* (New York, Doubleday, 1964), 165–70.
24 High commission in Great Britain to secretary of state for external affairs, June 9, 1943. In Documents on Canadian External Affairs, vol. IX, 1942–43, 28.
25 Chargé d'affaires of United States to prime minister, May 29, 1943. In Documents, *Ibid.*, vol. IX, 1942–43, 1724–25.

Notes to pages 69–79

26 Quoted in memorandum by first secretary, legation to the Allied governments, London, July 28, 1943. In *Ibid.*, 1744.
27 J. W. Pickersgill, *op. cit.*, vol. I, 535.
28 J. H. Hilliker, "The Canadian Government and the Free French. Perspectives and Constraints" 1940–44. *International History Review II*, January 1, 1980, 101.
29 Minister in United States to secretary of state for external affairs, July 22, 1942. In Documents on Canadian External Affairs, vol. IX, 1942–43, 1740.
30 Quoted in W. F. Kimball, ed., *Churchill and Roosevelt. The Complete Correspondence* (Princeton: Princeton University Press, 1984, 379.
31 Extracts from Minutes of Joint Meeting of War Cabinet of Great Britain and Cabinet War Committee, August 11, 1943. In Documents on Canadian External Affairs, vol. IX, 1942–43, 1751.
32 F. Kersaudy, *De Gaulle et Churchill* (Paris: Plon, 1982), 294–95.
33 Under secretary of state for External Affairs to acting under secretary of state for External Affairs, August 24, 1943. In Documents on Canadian External Affairs, vol. IX, 1942–43, 1756–57.
34 Quoted in J. Lacouture, *op. cit.*, vol. I, 737.
35 E. de Miribel, *op. cit.*, 131.
36 Quoted in H. L. Stimson, *On Active Service* (New York: Harper, 1948), 546.
37 C. de Gaulle, *Mémoires de guerre. L'Unité 1942–1944.* (Paris: Plon, 1956), 241–43.
38 Quoted in R. Lescop, *op. cit.*, 100.
39 Quoted in J. W. Pickersgill, *op. cit.*, vol. I, 48.
40 Quoted in *Ibid.*, 49.
41 Quoted in Public Archives of Canada, Mackenzie King Diaries, July 11, 1944, 653.
42 Quoted in D. C. Thomson, *Louis St. Laurent: Canadian* (Toronto: Macmillan of Canada, 1967), 135–36.
43 See B. Goldschmidt, *The Atomic Complex. A Worldwide Political History of Nuclear Energy* (La Grange Park, Illinois: American Nuclear Society, 1980).
44 *Ibid.*, 61.
45 C. de Gaulle, *Mémoires de guerre*, vol. II, 241–43.
46 Quoted in *Le Canada*, July 13, 1944.
47 C. de Gaulle, *Mémoires de guerre*, vol. II, 241–43.
48 Quoted in *Le Devoir*, July 13, 1944.
49 Secretary of state for external affairs to dominions secretary, July 8, 1944. Quoted in J. H. Hilliker, *op. cit.*, 166.
50 Dominions secretary to secretary of state for external affairs, July 27, 1944. In *Ibid.*, 107.
51 Mackenzie King Diary, vol. II, July 28, 1944. Quoted in J. H. Hilliker, *op. cit.*, 107.
52 J. H. Hilliker, *op. cit.*, 107.
53 J. W. Pickersgill, *op. cit.*, vol. II, 67.
54 Vanier to secretary of state for external affairs, September 14, 1944.
55 R. Speaight, *op. cit.*, 307.
56 J. W. Pickersgill, *op. cit.*, vol. II, 468.
57 *Ibid.*, 468.
58 C. de Gaulle, *Mémoires de guerre. III. Le Salut 1944–1946* (Paris: 1959), 253.
59 Quoted in *Le Droit*, August 29, 1945.
60 Vanier to prime minister, November 24, 1945.

61 Quoted in J. Lacouture, *op. cit.*, vol. II, 259.
62 Quoted in Don Cook, *Charles de Gaulle. A Biography* (New York: Putnam, 1988), 294.
63 C. de Gaulle, *Mémoires d'espoir. Le Renouveau* (Paris: Plon, 1970), 251.

Chapter 6

1 B. Ledwidge, *De Gaulle et les Américains. Conversations avec Dulles, Eisenhower, Kennedy, Rusk. 1958–64* (Paris: Flammarion, 1984), 24–26.
2 Quoted in R. Lescop, *op. cit.*, 121.
3 Basil Robinson, telephone interview with author, Ottawa, August 21, 1986.
4 Quoted in *Le Monde*, November 7, 1958.
5 Honourable Howard Green, interview with author, Vancouver, British Columbia, February 16, 1982.
6 Quoted in R. Lescop, *op. cit.*, 22.
7 Quoted in *Ibid.*, 124.
8 Quoted in *Ibid.*, 125–26.
9 Address by Honourable A. Barrette, April 20, 1960 (English version).
10 Quoted in R. Lescop, *op. cit.*, 126.
11 C. de Gaulle, *Mémoires d'espoir.* vol. I, 251–55.
12 F. Flohic, *Souvenirs d'outre-Gaulle* (Paris: Plon, 1979), 82.
13 Francois Flohic, interview with author, Paris, October 26, 1984.
14 C. Girard, *Canada in World Affairs*, vol. XIII (Toronto: Institute of International Affairs, 1984), 161. H. Green and D. Fleming, interviews with the author, February 16, 1982.
15 M. Couve de Murville, *Une Politique étrangère* (Paris: Plon, 1971), 454ff.
16 Maurice Couve de Murville, interview with author, Paris, April 18, 1981.

Chapter 7

1 Quoted in G.-E. Lapalme, *Mémoires. Le Vent de l'oubli* (Montreal: Leméac, 1970). 45–47.
2 Letter of M. Riel to G.-E. Lapalme, January 15, 1972.
3 Charles Lussier, interview with author, November 19, 1980.
4 *Ibid.*
5 Letter from C. Lussier to J. Lesage, July 18, 1961.
6 Text in R. Lescop, *op. cit.*, 129–30.
7 C. de Gaulle, *Mémoires d'espoir.* vol. I. 281–2.
8 *Le Devoir*, October 5, 1961.
9 Press release, October 23, 1961.
10 Charles Lussier, interview with author, November 19, 1980.
11 Allocution de l'Ambassadeur de France à Son Excellence Monsieur le Gouverneur général du canada, May 19, 1962.
12 Rapport d'information par MM. Bosson and Thorailler. Annexe au procès-verbal, Assemblée Nationale, February 15, 1963.
13 Address to the Canadian Society of New York, February 9, 1962.
14 Address to Canadian Chamber of Commerce, London, England, May 9, 1963.
15 Marcel Chaput, *Pourquoi je suis séparatiste* (Montreal: Editions du Jour, 1961).
16 *Le Devoir*, July 24–26, 1963.

17 Memorandum from C. Lussier to G.-D. Lévesque, October 8, 1963.
18 Quoted in *La Presse*, October 8, 1963.
19 Quoted in CIIA Monthly Report on Canadian External Affairs II, October 1963.
20 Quoted in *Le Devoir*, October 14, 1963.
21 Quoted in G.-E. Lapalme, *op. cit.*, vol. III, 243.
22 *Ibid.*, 245.
23 J. Lesage to de Gaulle, October 8, 1963.
24 De Gaulle to J. Lesage, November 7, 1963.
25 Letter from C. Lussier to René Arthur, May 31, 1963.
26 Letter from P. Martin to J. Lesage, June 26, 1963.
27 November 1962.
28 *Le Devoir*, July 25, 1963.
29 Paul Martin, *A Very Public Life. vol. II. So Many Worlds* (Ottawa: Deneau, 1985), 576.
30 Quoted in *Quotidien de Paris*, November 2, 1977.
31 L.B. Pearson, *Mike. The Memoirs of the Rt. Hon. Lester B. Pearson.* (Toronto: University of Toronto Press, 1975), vol. III, 166.
32 Press Conference, January 14, 1963. Quoted in C. de Gaulle, *Discours et messages. IV. Pour l'effort (août 1962-décembre 1965)* (Paris: Plon, 1970), 69.
33 Memorandum to Jean Lesage, January 8, 1964.
34 L.B. Pearson, *op. cit.*, 260.
35 Montreal *Star*, January 16, 1964.
36 L.B. Pearson, *op. cit.*, 260.
37 L.B. Pearson, *op. cit.*, 260–61.
38 Statement by Pearson in House of Commons, *Debates*, March 13, 1964, 869.
39 L.B. Pearson, *op. cit.*, 161.
40 Text in R. Lescop, *op. cit.*, 135–6.
41 L.B. Pearson, *Words and Occasions* (Toronto: University of Toronto Press, 1970), 221–22.
42 Montreal *Star*, January 16, 1964.
43 L.B. Pearson, *Mike, op. cit.*, vol. III, 262.
44 *Ibid.* 262.
45 *Allocution à l'Association de la Presse Diplomatique*, January 12, 1964.
46 J. Léger to J. Lesage, February 19, 1964.

Chapter 8

1 Memorandum from L. Bernard to C. Morin, July 30, 1964.
2 J. Brossard, A. Patry, and E. Weiser. *Les Pouvoirs extérieurs du Québec* (Montreal: Les Presses de l'Université de Montréal, 1967).
3 *Le Devoir*, September 30, 1963.
4 House of Commons, *Debates*, May 22, 1964, 3482.
5 Quoted in C. Girard, *op. cit.*, 189.
6 Quoted in R. Lescop, *op. cit.*, 137.
7 Letter from P. Martin to R. Bousquet, July 9, 1964.
8 Pierre Lefranc, *Avec qui vous savez: Vinqt-cinq ans aux côtés de de Gaulle* (Paris: Plon. 1979), 248.
9 *Le Figaro*, April 24, 1964.
10 Paris, Grasset, 1965.

11 *Ibid.*, 12.
12 *Ibid.*, 173.
13 *Ibid.*, 284–85.
14 Letter from J. Lesage to P. Gérin-Lajoie, Paris, November 9, 1964.
15 Jean Lesage, interview with author, August 13, 1980.
16 *Ibid.*
17 Quoted in the Montreal *Star*, November 11, 1964.
18 *Le Monde*, November 13, 1964.
19 J. Léger to C. Ritchie, October 23, 1964.
20 Published in External Affairs XVII, January 1965.
21 Quoted in the Montreal *Star*, March 3, 1965.
22 Quoted in *Ibid.*
23 Interview with author, May 15, 1982.
24 Quoted in *Combat*, Paris, March 1, 1965.
25 Statement by Paul Martin in House of Commons, March 1, 1965, 11818.
26 *Le Devoir.* March 18, 1965.
27 Quoted in *Le Devoir*, March 6, 1965.
28 *Le Devoir*, February 27, 1965.
29 A. Patry, *Le Québec dans le monde* (Montreal: Leméac, 1980), 63.
30 C. Morin, *Le Pouvoir québécois en négociation* (Quebec: Les Editions du Boréal Express, 1972), 69.

Chapter 9

1 A. Patry, "*La Capacité internationale des états fédérés*" in J. Brossard, et al., *op. cit.*, 18–98.
2 *Ibid.*, 35.
3 L. Oppenheim, and H. Lauterpacht, *International Law* I, 8th edition, (London: Longmans Green), 177.
4 A. Patry, *op. cit.*, 94.
5 *Ibid.*, 98.
6 J. Brossard, *op. cit.*, 438.
7 Memorandum to P. Gérin-Lajoie, April 1965.
8 A. Patry, *le Québec dans le monde* (Montreal: Leméac, 1980), 82.
9 P. Gérin-Lajoie, interview with author, May 15, 1982.
10 Quoted in C. Girard, *op. cit.*, 209.
11 *Le Devoir*, April 13, 1965.
12 House of Commons, *Debates*, April 8, 1965, 44.
13 Quoted in Ottawa *Journal*, April 26, 1965.
14 *Globe and Mail*, April 25, 1965.
15 April 26, 1965.
16 House of Commons *Débates*, April 26, 1965, 395.
17 *Ibid.*, April 27, 1965, 629.
18 *La Presse*, April 27, 1965.
19 Quoted in *Le Devoir*, May 1, 1965.
20 *Ibid.*, 77.
21 Letter from J. Lesage to L.B. Pearson, February 19, 1965.
22 Letter from L.B. Pearson to J. Lesage, April 21, 1965.
23 C. Morin, *L'Art de l'impossible: la diplomatie québécoise depuis 1960* (Montreal: Boréal Express, 1987), 43.
24 Memorandum from C. Morin to J. Lesage, August 23, 1965.
25 A. Patry, *Le Québec dans le monde, op cit.*, 74.

26 C. Morin, *L'Art de l'impossible, op. cit.*, 42.
27 Quoted in the *Canadian Yearbook of International Law 1966*, 265–66.
28 C. Morin, *L'Art de l'impossible, op. cit.*, 44.
29 *Ibid.*, 48–49.
30 May 14, 1965.
31 Jean-Daniel Jurgensen, interview with author, November 16, 1984.
32 Pierre-Louis Mallen, *Vivre le Québec libre* (Paris: Plon, 1978), 92.
33 (Paris: Editions Grasset, 1980), 78–9.
34 *Ibid.*, 78.
35 House of Commons,*Debates*, May 5, 1965, 957.
36 Letter from J. Chapdelaine to J. Lesage, July 27, 1965.
37 C. Morin, *L'Art de l'impossible, op. cit.*, 54ff.
38 Letter from C. Morin to M. Cadieux, October 22, 1965.
39 C. Morin to M. Cadieux, November 4, 1965.
40 C. Morin, *Le Pouvoir Québécois...en négociation, op. cit.*, 75.
41 P. Gérin-Lajoie, interview with author, May 15, 1982.
42 *Le Monde*, November 28, 1965.
43 Quoted in *Time Magazine*, December 10, 1965, 14.
44 Letter from A. Patry to J. Lesage, December 26, 1965.
45 Letter from J. Chapdelaine to J. Lesage, December 28, 1965.
46 Letter from J. Chapdelaine to J. Lesage, March 6, 1966.
47 Letter from P. Martin to P. Laporte, December 1, 1965.
48 Quoted in C.L. Sulzberger, *The Last of the Giants* (New York: Macmillan, 1970), 861.
49 Quoted in J. Lacouture, *op. cit.*, vol. III, 363.
50 *Ibid.*, 370.
51 Roger Frey, interview with author, October 30, 1984.
52 Quoted in J. Lacouture, *op. cit.*, vol. III, 377.
53 L.B. Pearson, *op. cit.*, vol. III, 264–5.
54 *Ibid.*, 265.
55 P. Martin,*A Very Public Life*, vol. II, (Toronto: Deneau Publishers, 1985), 474ff.
56 J. Lacouture, *op. cit.*, vol. III, 402.

Chapter 10

1 Alain Plantey, interview with author, May 1980.
2 Paul Gros d'Aillon, *Daniel Johnson L'Egalité avant l'indépendance* (Montréal; Stanké, 1979), 129.
3 Quoted in P. Godin, *Daniel Johnson* vol. II (Montreal: Editions de l'Homme, 1980), 188.
4 Quoted in *Ibid.*, 188.
5 In *Espoir*, no. 20, October 1977, 11.
6 *Ibid.*
7 B. Tricot, *De Gaulle et le service de l'Etat* (Paris: Plon, 1977), 144.
8 Quoted by M. Fichet, in *Etudes Gaulliennes*, vol. IX, no. 33, April 1981, 53–60.
9 Quoted in A. and P. Rouanet, *op cit.*, 50.
10 Quoted in P., Godin, *op. cit.*, vol. II, 188–190.
11 P. Martin, *op. cit.*, 587.
12 Text in *Politique étrangère de la France*, no. 3.384–3.387, 276–77.
13 Quoted in P. Gros d'Aillon *op.cit.*, 133.
14 P. Martin, *op. cit.*, 588.

15 P.-L. Mallen, *op. cit.*, 92ff.
16 "De Gaulle au Québec," in *Espoir*, no. 31, 1980, 42ff.
17 Jean Chapdelaine, interview with author, July 22, 1982.
18 P.-L. Mallen, *op. cit.*, 99.
19 A. Patry, *op. cit.*, 93.
20 *Ibid.*, 86.
21 A. Patry, *op. cit.*, 89.
22 House of Commons, *Debates*, October 25, 1966, 2200–23.
23 House of Commons, *Debates*, March 22, 1967, 14336.
24 P. Martin, *op. cit.*, 591.
25 House of Commons, *Debates.*, April 11, 1967, 14782.
26 Quoted in P. Godin, *op. cit.*, 196.
27 Text in A. and P. Rouanet, *op. cit.*, 195.
28 Assemblée Legislative, *Debates*, April 13, 1967, 2167ff.
29 L.B. Pearson, *op. cit.*, 413.
30 P. Godin, *op. cit.*, 200.
31 House of Commons, *Debates*, April 26, 1967, 15366.
32 Quoted in C. Morin, *L'Art de l'impossible, op. cit.*, 97.
33 A. and P. Rouanet, *op. cit.*, 61.
34 Quoted in P. Godin, *p. cit.*, vol. II, 202.
35 Quoted in A. and P. Rouanet, *op. cit.*, 61.
36 *Ibid.*, 60–61.
37 Quoted in P., Gros d'Aillon, *op. cit.*, 151.
38 *Ibid.*, 151.
39 Quoted in *La Politique étrangère de la France*, September 1, 1967.
40 A. and P. Rouanet, *op. cit.*, 66.
41 Pauline Vanier, interview with author, November 18, 1984.
42 L.B. Pearson, *op. cit.*, 266.
43 P. Martin, *op. cit.*, 593.
44 Quoted in *La Presse*, July 24, 1967.
45 Paul Martin, interview with author, October 16, 1981.
46 *Ibid.*
47 Quoted in A. and P. Rouanet, *op. cit.*, 82. Confirmed in interview of General Boissieu with author, November 18, 1984.
48 Quoted in *Ibid.*, 82. Confirmed in interview of Xavier Deniau with author, April 23, 1981.
49 Quoted in *Ibid.*, 80.
50 J. Lacouture, *op. cit.*, vol. III, 516.
51 Paul Martin, interview with author, May 3, 1982.
52 Quoted in *Le Devoir*, July 25, 1967.
53 P. Martin, *op. cit.*, 594.
54 J. Lacouture, *op. cit.*, vol. III, 518.
55 Quoted in R. Lescop, *op. cit.*, 160.
56 Quoted in *Ibid.*, 161.
57 Quoted in P. Godin, *op. cit.*, 223.
58 A. and P. Rouanet, *op. cit.*, 155.
59 Quoted in R. Lescop, *op. cit.*, 163.
60 A. and P. Rouanet, *op. cit.*, 122.
61 Jean Drapeau, interview with author, August 2, 1983.

Chapter 11

1 Quoted in P. Godin, *op. cit.*, vol. II, 227.

2 Quoted in J. Lacouture, *op. cit.*, vol. III, 522.
3 Quoted in F. Flohic, *Souvenirs d'outre-Gaulle* (Paris: Plon, 1979), 91.
4 Quoted in P. Godin, *op. cit.*, vol. II, 228–29.
5 Quoted in *Ibid.*, 229.
6 P.-L. Mallen, *op. cit.*, 172.
7 Robert Bordaz, interview with author, April 29, 1981.
8 F. Flohic, *op. cit.*, 91.
9 L.B. Pearson, *op. cit.*, 267.
10 P. Martin, *op. cit.*, vol. III, 595.
11 P. Stursberg, *Lester Pearson and the Dream of Canadian Unity* (New York: Doubleday, 1978), 392.
12 P. Martin, *op. cit.*, 596.
13 Quoted in P. Godin, *op. cit.*, vol. II, 229.
14 Quoted in *Le Soleil*, July 26, 1967.
15 Quoted in L.B. Pearson, *Words and Occasions* (Toronto: University of Toronto Press, 1970), 277.
16 Quoted in A. and P. Rouanet, *op. cit.*, 140.
17 Quoted in *Le Devoir*, July 27, 1967.
18 J. Lacouture, *op. cit.*, vol. III, 526–527.
19 Quoted in F. Flohic, *op. cit.*, 93.
20 Quoted in P.-L. Mallen, *op. cit.*, 202.
21 Quoted in R. Lescop, *op. cit.*, 169.
22 Jean Drapeau, interview with author, August 2, 1983.
23 Text in *De Gaulle au Québec* (Montreal: Editions du Jour, 1967), 84–91.
24 Text in R. Lescop, *op. cit.*, 170–71.
25 Quoted in L.B. Pearson, *op. cit.*, vol. III, 268–69.
26 Quoted in P. Stursberg, *op. cit.*, 394–95.
27 P.-L. Mallen, *op. cit.*, 215–231.
28 J. Lacouture, *op. cit.*, vol. III, 528.
29 Quoted in P.-L, Mallen, *op. cit.*, 237.
30 Printed in L.B. Pearson, *Words and Occasions. op. cit.*, 277–80.
31 P. Delahousse, interview with author, November 19, 1984.
32 F. Leduc, interview with author, December 26, 1984.
33 Letter to author, September 23, 1981.
34 Gilbert Pérol, interview with author, April 27, 1981.
35 Quoted in R. Tournoux, *Le Feu et la cendre* (Paris: Plon, 1979), 334.
36 Quoted in P.-L. Mallen, *op. cit.*, 238.
37 Quoted in A. and P. Rouanet, *op. cit.*, 155.
38 Olivier Guichard, interview with author, January 15, 1985. See his excellent portrait of Charles de Gaulle: *Mon Général* (Paris: Grasset, 1980).
39 H. Alphand, *L'Etonnement d'être* (Paris: Fayard, 1977), 493.
40 Bernard Tricot, interview with author, April 22, 1981.
41 *Ibid.*
42 *Le Monde*, July 25, 1967.
43 Quoted in R. Tournoux, *La Tragédie du Général* (Paris: Plon, 1967), 336.
44 SOFRES poll reported in *L'Express*, July 31–August 6, 1967.
45 Quoted in A. and P. Rouanet, *op. cit.*, 199.
46 *Le Monde*, July 28, 1967.
47 Quoted in *L'Express*, July 28–August 5, 1967.
48 Quoted in J. d'Escrienne, *Le Général m'a dit. 1966–70* (Paris: Plon, 1973), 108.

49 Quoted in P.-L. Mallen, *op. cit.*, 243.
50 Quoted in A. and P. Rouanet, *op. cit.* 159.
51 R. Tournoux, *Le Feu et la cendre* (Paris: Plon, 1979), 334ff.
52 Remark to Alain Peyrefitte quoted in *Ibid.*, 336.
53 Quoted by Alain Peyrefitte in interview with author, October 29, 1984.
54 Texts of statement and press conference in R. Lescop, *op. cit.*, 174–78.
55 Article reproduced in *Le Devoir*, August 5, 1967.
56 Quoted in R. Lescop, *op. cit.*, 179–80.
57 *Le Monde*, August 18, 1967.
58 Quoted in P., Godin, *op. cit.*, 241.
59 Quoted in *Ibid.*, 241–42.
60 P. Godin, *op. cit.*, 244.
61 Le Devoir, July 31, 1967.
62 Poll conducted by R. Quirion for Liberal Party.
63 *La Presse*, July 31, 1967.
64 In his column *"Point de Mire"* in *Dimanche-Matin*, July 30, 1967.
65 Assemblée Législative, *Débats*, August 3, 1967, 4995ff.
66 *Le Devoir*, August 12, 1967.
67 *Ibid.*, August 14, 1967.
68 C. de Gaulle, *Mémoires d'Espoir, op. cit.*, vol. I, 51.
69 Michel Droit, *Les Feux du crépuscule* (Paris: Plon, 1977), 209.
70 J.-R. Tournoux, *La Tragédie du Général, op. cit.*, 290.
71 A. Passeron, *op. cit.*, 314.
72 M. Couve de Murville, interview with author, April 18, 1981.
73 M. Couve de Murville, *Une Politique étrangère*. 1958–69. (Paris: Plon, 1971), 455.
74 M. Couve de Murville, interview with author, April 18, 1981.
75 Roger Frey, interview with author, October 3, 1984.
76 Louis Joxe, interview with author, October 17, 1984.
77 Georges Gorse, interview with author, April 28, 1981.
78 Michel Debré, interview with author, December 26, 1984.
79 Pierre Messmer, interview with author, October 24, 1984.
80 J.-R. Tournoux, *Le Tourment et la fatalité* (Paris: Plon, 1974), 220.
81 Jean Charbonnel, interview with author, October 11, 1984.
82 André Bettencourt, interview with author, October 22, 1984.
83 Quoted in Y. Guëna, *Le Temps des certitudes 1940–69* (Paris: Flammarion, 1982), 179–85.
84 Maurice Shumann, interview with author, December 17, 1984.
85 O. Guichard, *op. cit.*, 419.
86 Olivier Guichard, interview with author, January 15, 1985.
87 Robert Bordaz, interview with author, April 29, 1981.
88 Jean-Daniel Jurgensen, interview with author, November 18, 1984.
89 Jean-Daniel Jurgensen, interview with author, November 16, 1984.
90 F. Flohic, interview with author, October 26, 1984.
91 Gilbert Pérol, interview with author, April 27, 1981.
92 Presentation by G. Pérol at colloquium at Institut Charles de Gaulle in Paris 1977. Text in *Espoir*, no. 20, 15.
93 Text in *Espoir*, no. 34, March 1981.
94 Text in C. de Gaulle, *Discours et messages: Avec le renouveau* (Paris: Plon, 1970), 102.
95 Presentation at colloquium in Quebec City, September 1979. Text in *Etudes Gaulliennes*, vol. VII, no. 27 and 28, September–December 1979.

96 Alain Plantey, interview with author, April 30, 1981.
97 *Espoir*, no. 20, October 1977, 20–30.
98 *Ibid.*, 23.

Chapter 12

1 Alain Peyrefitte, interview with author, October 31, 1984.
2 e.g. François Missoffe. M. Couve de Murville, interview with author, October 19, 1984.
3 Quoted in Y. Guëna, *op. cit.*, 183.
4 Alain Peyrefitte, interview with author, October 31, 1984.
5 P. Godin, *op. cit.*, 255.
7 *Ibid.*, 255.
8 Alain Peyrefitte, interview with author, October 31, 1984.
9 Quoted in P. Godin, *op. cit.*, vol. II, 259.
10 Quoted in A. and P. Rouanet, *op. cit.* 185.
11 Philippe Rossillon, interview with author, April 25, 1981. See also his account in *Etudes Gaulliennes, op. cit.*, 137ff.
12 Alain Peyrefitte, interview with author, October 31, 1984.
13 Letter dated October 28, 1967. Quoted in *Etudes Gaulliennes*, vol. VII, 1979, 141.
14 Quoted in P.-L. Mallen, *op. cit.*, 331.
15 P. Martin, *op. cit.*, vol. II, 598.
16 Text in R. Lescop, *op. cit.*, 185–89.
17 P. Godin, *op. cit.*, vol. II, 267–70.
18 *Ibid.*, 270.
19 Quoted in *Ibid.*, 310.
20 D. Johnson, Opening Address at Confederation of Tomorrow Conference, Nov. 27–30, 1967.
21 Quoted in P. Gros d'Aillon, *op. cit.*, 195.
22 Quoted in *Le Devoir*, December 2, 1967.
23 House of Commons, *Debates*, November 27, 1967, 4710.
24 P. Martin *op. cit.*, vol. III, 601.
25 House of Commons, *Debates*, November 28, 1967, 4774.
26 *Ibid.*, November 28, 1967, 4774.
27 *Ibid.*, November 28, 1967, 4774.
28 *Ibid.*, November 28, 1967, 4776.
29 *Le Devoir*, November 29, 1967.
30 *Le Figaro*, October 13, 1967.
31 Quoted in the Toronto *Globe and Mail*, October 30, 1967.
32 Maurice Jacquinot, interview with author, January 1968.
33 Quoted in R. Lescop, *op. cit.*, 183.
34 P. de Menthon, *Je temoigne: Québec 1967, Chili 1973* (Paris: Plon, 1979), 15.
35 *Etudes Gaulliennes*, vol. VII, 1979, 89.
36 P. de Menthon, *op. cit.*, 16–17. Notes taken by de Menthon after the interview.
37 P. de Menthon, "Les Activités du Consulat général de France à Québec 1967–1972." In *Etudes Gaulliennes. op. cit.*, 90.
38 Most of the following details were obtained from an interview with the four Acadians on June 7, 1986.
39 *Etudes Gaulliennes, op. cit.*, 142.

40 Alain Peyrefitte, interview with author, October 31, 1984.
41 Text in *Etudes Gaulliennes, op. cit.*, 142.
42 The figures are taken from P. Rossillon, *op. cit.*, 145, and are to be treated with some caution.
43 Quoted by P., Rossillon, from despatch of January 26, 1968, in *Etudes Gaulliennes, op. cit.*, 144.

Chapter 13

1   Quoted in C. Morin, *L'Art de l'impossible, op. cit.*, 115.
2   *Ibid.*, 118.
3   Quoted in *Ibid.*, 119.
4   P. Godin, *op. cit.*, vol. II, 316.
5   A. Patry, *op. cit.*, 124.
6   C. Morin, *L'Art de l'impossible, op. cit.*, 121.
7   A. Patry, *op. cit.*, 124.
8   Quoted in P. Godin, *op. cit.*, vol. II, 316.
9   Quoted in *Ibid.*, 317.
10 *Ibid.*, 319
11 (Ottawa: Queen's Printer, 1968).
12 *Ibid.*, 47.
13 Quoted in C. Morin, *L'Art de l'impossible, op. cit.*, 131.
14 Quoted in *Ibid.*, 132.
15 Quoted in *Ibid.*, 133.
16 Letter reproduced as annex to M. Sharp, *Federalism and International Conference on Education. A supplement to Federalism and International Relations.* April 1968, 66–68.
17 P. Godin, *op. cit.*, vol. II, 329.
18 C. Malone, *la Politique québécoise en matière de relations internationales: changement et continuité. 1960–72.* (M.A. Thesis, University of Ottawa, 1973), 185.
19 Assemblée Législative *Débats*, March 12, 1968, 975ff.
20 C. Morin, *L'Art de l'impossible. op. cit.*, 136.
21 Letter dated April 5, 1968. Printed as annex to M. Sharp, *op. cit.*, 70–72.
22 C. Morin, *L'Art de l'impossible, op. cit.*, 138.
23 Quoted in P. Godin, *op. cit.*, vol. II, 332.
24 On April 10, 1968. Quoted in P.-L. Mallen, *op. cit.*, 320–22.
25 *Ibid.*, 322.
26 Quoted in C. Morin, *L'Art de l'impossible, op. cit.*, 142.
27 (Ottawa: Queen's Printer, 1968).
28 Quoted in P. Godin, *op. cit.*, vol. II, 337.
29 Quoted in *Ibid.*, 338.
30 A. de Boissieu, in *Espoir*, June 1983, 7.
31 General J. Massu, *Baden '68: Souvenirs d'une fidélité gaulliste* (Paris: Plon, 1983), 79.
32 F. Leduc, interview with author, April 15, 1981.
33 P. de Menthon, *op. cit.*, 18ff.
34 Quoted in R. Lescop, *op. cit.* 196.
35 Quoted in P. Godin, *op. cit.*, vol. II, 363.
36 Quoted in P.-L. Mallen, *op. cit.*, 329.
37 Quoted in *Ibid.*, *op. cit.*, 327.
38 P. Rossillon, in *Etudes Gaulliennes, op. cit.*, 145.

39 Quoted in P. Godin, *op. cit.*, vol. II, 360.
40 Quoted in *Ibid.*, 365.
41 Quoted in P. Gros d'Aillon, *op. cit.*, 225 ff.
42 Marcel Masse, interview with author, June 14, 1982.
43 A. Patry, *op. cit.*, 107.
44 Quoted in R. Lescop, *op. cit.*, 197.
45 P. Beaulieu, interview with author, April 13, 1984.
46 Quoted in R. Lescop, *op. cit.*, 197.
47 Memorandum from P. Laporte to J. Lesage (undated).
48 P. Beaulieu, interview with author, December 13, 1980.
49 C. Morin, *L'Art de l'impossible, op. cit.*, 143.
50 P. Martin, *op. cit.*, vol. II, 664.
51 Quoted in C. Morin, *L'Art de l'impossible, op. cit.*, 146.
52 C. Morin, *L'Art de l'impossible, op. cit.*, 131.
53 Paul Dozois, interview with author, May 28, 1982.
54 Paul Beaulieu, interview with author, December 13, 1980.
55 Quoted in the Toronto *Globe and Mail*, January 24, 1969.
56 Text in R. Lescop, *op. cit.*, 201.
57 P. de Menthon, *op. cit.*, 18ff.
58 Paul Dozois, interview with author, May 28, 1982.
59 C. Morin, *L'Art de l'impossible, op. cit.*, 183.
60 P.-L. Mallen, *op. cit.*, 331.
61 J. Baulin, *Conseiller du Président Diori* (Eurofor Press, 1986), 75.
62 M. Cadieux, "*Le Québec dans le monde, mythe ou réalité*" Published in *CRI, Mythes et Réalities* (Paris: Editions Pedone, 1972), 129ff.

Chapter 14

1 E. Roussel, *Georges Pompidou* (Paris: Editions J. C. Lattès, 1984), 229.
2 Maurice Schumann, interview with author, December 17, 1984.
3 Toronto *Telegram*, July 10, 1969.
4 Quoted in *Le Devoir*, August 19, 1969.
5 Jean de Lipkowski, interview with author, July 18, 1985.
6 Paul Beaulieu, interview with author, December 13, 1980.
7 Quoted in undated publication of the Ministère des Affaires Etrangères, listing quotes of members of the French government.
8 See C. Morin, *L'Art de l'impossible, op. cit.*, 197ff for details.
9 *Ibid.*, 219.
10 C. de Gaulle, *Memoires d'Espoir, op. cit.*, 250–55.
11 Quoted in J. Maurice, *Mort du Général de Gaulle* (Paris: Grasset, 1972), 125.
12 Quoted in *Le Devoir*, September 24, 1971.
13 Quoted in *Montreal-Matin*, September 24, 1971.
14 Letter from Claude Bussière, Prefet de Police, Paris, to M. Jacquinot, August 29, 1969.
15 Maurice Jacquinot, interview with author, May 1981.
16 Quoted in M. Lavallée, *Adieu la France, Salut l'Amérique* (Montreal, Stanké, 1982), 112.
17 Quoted in *Le Devoir*, November 10, 1982.
18 House of Commons, *Debates*, May 26, 1987, 6430.
19 P. Savard, "*Les Canadiens français et la France de la cession à la Révolution tranquille*" in *Le Canada et le Québec sur la scène internationale, op. cit.*, 495.

Index